"This is an important 'breakthrough' book. understanding of the new religious movem draw heavily on the insights of recent missi ualization and cross-cultural understanding. T approach is exactly what we need for an effective presentation of the gospel to folks who have been seduced by the false promises of non-Christian worldviews."

—Richard J. Mouw
President and Professor of Christian Philosophy
Fuller Theological Seminary

"A thoughtful and needed reassessment of evangelical outreach to new and emerging religious expression in North America.... This resource is not merely a valuable compilation of strategic thinkers in the fields of Christian apologetics and missiology; it synthesizes the two disciplines and offers practical strategies for evangelism in a new day! I commend highly this book to anyone who senses the urgency of proclaiming the gospel with sensitivity and relevancy."

—Rudy Gonzalez
Director, North American Mission Board
Southern Baptist Convention

"This is an important collection of essays which breaks new ground by applying the tools of missiology to the study of new religious movements in the West, and in so doing enables us first to understand these movements adequately and then to respond to them in a contextually appropriate and theologically sound manner."

—Harold Netland
Professor of Philosophy of Religion and Intercultural Studies
Trinity Evangelical Divinity School

"Not only is Western society becoming increasingly pluralistic in attitude, and not only are major Eastern religions such as Buddhism and Hinduism becoming increasingly visible, there is also a growing proliferation of so-called 'new religions' in West and East alike. How will evangelical Christians respond? The contributors to this book unite to plead that Christians need to move beyond a simplistic attitude that simply seeks to refute or exterminate 'cults' and adopt a mature missions strategy.... This book is both theoretically sound and practically helpful. A solid, cohesive work!"

—Winfried Corduan
Professor of Philosophy and Religion
Taylor University

"Sometimes revolutions are caused by the simple recognition of the obvious. The thinking in this book has an excellent chance to start a revolution in the way we evangelicals deal with 'cults' and new religious movements simply because the contributors are taking hold of the obvious: devotees of NRMs are complex human beings who need to be dealt with in multifaceted ways. I am grateful to these scholars who have brought the well-known and successful methods of the missiologists to bear on the project of bringing the saving gospel of Christ to those lost in the NRMs."

—Craig J. Hazen
Associate Professor of Comparative Religion and Apologetics
Biola University

"At last, apologetics and missiology meet! This book breaks new ground in ministry to adherents of New Religious Movements. Proactive in intent and positive in tone, it moves beyond the refutation of heresy by charting a new way forward. It proposes the utilization of proven missiological principles to win actual and potential followers of NRMs to evangelical faith in Christ."

—Ken Mulholland
Former Professor of Missions, Columbia International University
Past President, Evangelical Missiological Society

"This is the best book on the subject of evangelical witnessing to members of the New Religious Faiths in many years and is certainly what the Church needs at this moment in history. . . . It supersedes what has often been an overly confrontational and argumentative approach to youthful believers in favor of one that is both informed by contemporary scholarship and current evangelical thinking on missiology. . . . A useful tool for any and all who seek to share the gospel message with people of different faiths, and especially useful to pastors and churches who have a burden to reach out to the new faith communities as they appear in their neighborhood."

—J. Gordon Melton
Director, Institute for the Study of American Religion
Santa Barbara, California

ENCOUNTERING NEW RELIGIOUS MOVEMENTS

A Holistic Evangelical Approach

IRVING HEXHAM, STEPHEN ROST,
& JOHN W. MOREHEAD II

General Editors

Kregel
Academic & Professional

Encountering New Religious Movements: A Holistic Evangelical Approach

© 2004 by Irving Hexham, Stephen Rost, and John Morehead II

Published by Kregel Publications, a division of Kregel, Inc., P.O. Box 2607, Grand Rapids, MI 49501.

Unless otherwise noted, Scripture quotations are from the *Holy Bible, New International Version*®. © 1973, 1978, 1984 by International Bible Society. Used by permission of Zondervan Publishing House. All rights reserved.

Scripture quotations marked KJV are from the *King James Version* of the Holy Bible.

Scripture quotations marked NASB are from the *New American Standard Bible.* © The Lockman Foundation 1960, 1962, 1963, 1968, 1971, 1972, 1973, 1975, 1977.

Scripture quotations marked NKJV are from *The New King James Version.* © 1979, 1980, 1982, Thomas Nelson, Inc., Publishers.

Cover design: John M. Lucas

Library of Congress Cataloging-in-Publication Data
   Encountering new religious movements: a holistic evangelical approach / by Irving Hexham, Stephen Rost & John Morehead II, general editors.
      p. cm.
Includes biographical references and indexes.
   1. Evangelical work. 2. Evangelistic work—Biblical teaching. I. Hexham, Irving. II. Rost, Stephen. III. Morehead, John.
BV3795.E53 2004
266—dc22   2003022350

ISBN 0-8254-2893-9

Printed in the United States of America

04 05 06 07 08 / 5 4 3 2 1

CONTENTS

Part 3: Practical Application

Contributors

Rev. Dr. Ross Clifford is the principal of Morling Theological College, Sydney, Australia. He has written a number of books, including *Leading Lawyers' Case for the Resurrection; Riding the Rollercoaster: How the Risen Christ Empowers Life* (with Philip Johnson), *Jesus and the Gods of the New Age* (with Philip Johnson), and *Beyond Prediction* (with John Drane and Philip Johnson). Dr. Clifford is the host of the radio program *Sunday Night Live* in Sydney. He is a former president of the New South Wales Council of Churches and has served as a Baptist minister in several Sydney churches.

Dr. David J. Hesselgrave is a former professor of mission and evangelism at Trinity Evangelical Divinity School in Deerfield, Illinois. A missionary in Japan for twelve years, he is past president of the Association of Evangelical Professors of Missions and cofounder and first executive director of the Evangelical Missiological Society. He is a prolific author, coauthor, and editor, with twelve books to his credit, including *Dynamic Religious Movements, Communicating Christ Cross-Culturally, Planting Churches Cross-Culturally, Counseling Cross-Culturally, Scripture and Strategy,* and *Contextualization: Meanings, Methods, and Models* (with Edward Rommen).

Dr. Irving Hexham is professor of religious studies at the University of Calgary in Calgary, Alberta, Canada, and a noted authority on world religions. Dr. Hexham is the author of seven books, including *Understanding Cults and New Religions* (with his wife Karla Poewe) and *The Pocket Dictionary of Cults and New Religions.* He has also edited twelve books and authored numerous articles for journals and books.

Philip Johnson is lecturer in cults, world religions, and philosophy at the Presbyterian Theological Centre, Sydney, Australia, and an adjunct lecturer in Old Testament at Morling College. He holds a B.A. and B.D. from the University of Sydney and is completing an M.Th. thesis on Evangelical Responses to New Religious Movements. He is founder and CEO of Global Apologetics and Mission, a ministry that specializes in contextualized apologetics/missions to new religious movements and world religions. He has written more than 120 articles in various Australian Christian periodicals and has cowritten *Sacred Quest, Riding the Rollercoaster, Jesus and the Gods of the New Age,* and *Beyond Prediction.* He also wrote *The Areopagus Factor* (forthcoming). He is married to Ruth Pollard.

John W. Morehead II is associate director of Watchman Fellowship in Sacramento, California. Mr. Morehead is the cofounder and coeditor of *Sacred Tribes: Journal of Christian Missions to New Religious Movements,* an e-journal that focuses on missiological issues related to reaching adherents of new religions. He also served as guest editor for an issue of the *International Journal of Frontier Missions* that focused on missions to new religious movements. He is adjunct instructor in new religious movements, world religions, missions, and apologetics at Capital Bible College in Sacramento. He served on the board of directors for Evangelical Ministries to New Religions and has provided expertise to the Lausanne Committee for World Evangelization.

Dr. Terry C. Muck is professor of missions and world religions at the E. Stanley Jones School of World Mission and Evangelism of Asbury Theological Seminary, Wilmore, Kentucky. Dr. Muck is the author of eight books, including *The Mysterious Beyond: A Guide to Studying Religion* and *Those Other Religions in Your Neighborhood.* He is the general editor of the forty-three-volume *niv Application Commentary* and the *World Vision Study Bible* (forthcoming).

Kenneth Mulholland is founding president of Salt Lake Theological Seminary, where he has served for the past nineteen years. He holds a Th.M. from Regent College in Vancouver, British Columbia, an M.Div. from Reformed Theological Seminary, and is a Ph.D. candidate in history at the University of Utah. He has lived in Utah for the past twenty-seven years. He is the executive producer of *Bridges: Helping Mormons Discover God's Grace,* a training series that advocates a missiological approach to evangelizing Latter-day Saints.

Dr. Mikel Neumann is associate professor of intercultural studies at Western Seminary, Portland, Oregon, where he supervises the intercultural internship program and teaches in doctoral- and master's-level intercultural programs. He served as a church-planting missionary for twenty-five years in Madagascar under the auspices of CBInternational. Dr. Neumann was the missionary scholar-in-residence at the Billy Graham Center at Wheaton College, Illinois (1995–1996), where he researched the intercultural dimension of small group ministries. His research took him to Chicago, Caracas, Bombay, Accra, and Moscow. His book *Home Groups for Urban Cultures* was copublished by William Carey and the Billy Graham Center in 1999. He has degrees from Western Seminary and Fuller Theological Seminary (M.A. and D.Miss.). He is an international resource consultant with CBInternational, and this ministry has taken him to thirty-five nations to teach, encourage, and help local people.

Dr. Karla Poewe is professor of anthropology at the University of Calgary, Alberta, Canada. Dr. Poewe's professional interests include the history of anthropology, history of Christian missions, new religions, anthropology of Southern Africa, and anthropology of religion. She is currently working on a project on the relationship between new religions and National Socialism in Germany. She has written numerous articles and is the author of eight books, including *Charismatic Christianity as a Global Culture, Understanding Cults and New Religions* (with her husband, Irving Hexham), and *New Religions as Global Cultures* (also with Dr. Hexham).

Ruth Pollard, LLB, University of Sydney, is employed as a lawyer in a state government department in Sydney, Australia. She is married to Philip Johnson and has been involved in evangelistic outreach at the Mind-Body-Spirit Festival. She has undertaken courses at the University of Sydney, studying esotericism in addition to certificate-level courses in theology at Moore Theological College. She combines her legal training with her understanding of alternative spiritualities in ministering to people in all walks of life. She served as secretary of the Sydney University Law Society and was a convener of the Sir Philip Street Lecture Series. Ruth is active in environmental issues, animal rights, and welfare.

Rev. Stephen Rost is pastor of Grace Fellowship of Dixon in Dixon, California. Rev. Rost holds an M.Div. from Talbot School of Theology and an M.A.

from Dallas Theological Seminary. He has been published in *Christian History* magazine, and he is an abstracter for *Religious and Theological Abstracts.* Rev. Rost has served as president of the Society for the Study of Alternative Religions study group in the Evangelical Theological Society and served on the board of directors for Evangelical Ministries to New Religions.

Rev. John Smulo is a Jewish-American Baptist minister serving in Australia, and is also the director of the School of Apologetics at Morling College. Rev. Smulo grew up in California, and, as an adult convert to Christianity, served for a time with YWAM. He holds a B.Min. (Honors) from Morling College and is pursuing postgraduate study at the University of Queensland in Religious Studies. He has completed an honors thesis on developing apologetics to Satanists, published articles in *Sacred Tribes Journal, Lutheran Theological Journal,* and has forthcoming articles appearing in the *Baker Dictionary of Cults* and *The Encyclopedic Sourcebook of Satanism* (edited by James R. Lewis). In addition, he has a fruitful ministry to Satanists, Wiccans, and Neo-Pagans. He serves on the board of directors for Global Apologetics and Mission.

Rev. Harold Taylor is emeritus vice-principal of the Bible College of Victoria, Australia. He holds a B.A. from Melbourne University, a B.D. and Th.M. degrees from the Melbourne College of Divinity, and a Th.D. from the Australian College of Theology. Rev. Taylor served as a missionary for sixteen years in Papua New Guinea and the Solomon Islands, and for twenty years as lecturer in missiology and pastoral care at the Bible College of Victoria. He is the author of *Sent to Heal.* He is an ordained minister in the Uniting Church in Australia and serves on the board of directors for Global Apologetics and Mission.

FOREWORD

To the making of religion there is no end. As the world continues to internationalize and individualize, cultural forms and meanings have mixed to create new religious movements. The diversity of religious options allows individuals to pick and choose their own forms and beliefs. They can systemize these forms in new ways.

I met Julie on an airplane. Her books about power points and flows of energy enthralled me. She told me about the altar in her house. Numerous crystals line the circumference. Within the circle, three pyramids form a triangle. Statues of Buddha, Krishna, and Jesus (representing Buddhism, Hinduism, and Christianity), stand between the pyramids. In the background is a large cross. A Bible, an English interpretation of the Qu'ran, and Sutras are placed among the images. Julie's religion integrates beliefs and forms from different world religions. She believes that the life energy radiating from these elements gives her peace and power.

If numerous people accept Julie's mixing of ideas and forms and develop narratives and rituals to affirm them as plausible, a new religious movement will be born. Otherwise, Julie's religion will merely remain as a distinctive DIY ("Do-It-Yourself") spirituality. Satan contorts shifting cultural influences and the amazing propensity of humans to create their own religions to form new religious movements.

As new religious movements proliferate and increasingly attract adherents throughout the world, new approaches to communicating Christ must be considered. Traditional models generally have been confrontational, aggressive, and countercultural. This book, however, proposes a significant paradigm shift in the theology, theory, and practice of ministry. Although the approaches of the authors vary, this book generally proposes a missiological change from ridicule to empathy, from confrontation to incarnation, from strict apologetics to evangelism, and from proposition to narrative. This book effectively presents a new incarnational model drawn from a variety of disciplines, particularly missiology.

A foundational principle of the text is *incarnation,* a model of ministry imitating Christ, who "became flesh and made his dwelling among us" (John 1:14a). Christ entered into human life so he could communicate with and suffer for humanity. Likewise, to communicate God's ultimate sovereignty to new religionists, ministers must empathetically enter into their lives. New religionists, who experience ministers who understand them and their culture and who share with gentleness and respect, frequently are very receptive to the message of the kingdom of God.

This book is not an armchair analysis of Christian ministry. It presents practical theologies and methodologies for communicating Christ to new religionists. The authors propose that contextually communicating the gospel begins with establishing *common ground.* For example, Satanists believe that people should not "follow the herd" as Christians do, but instead to insatiably enjoy all of life as individualists. Within this context, authentic Christians might be described as "left-handed Christian philosophers." The message of the tarot can be an archetype for sharing the gospel. The story line of the Bible can be communicated within the framework of the Wiccan "Wheel of the Year" myth. The "thin place," where boundaries separating the physical and spiritual worlds are not far apart, becomes an arena for the contextual communication of the gospel. A theology of anointing forms the basis of creative outreach to aromatherapists.

Hesselgrave's pivotal chapter, however, cautions against the overuse of *common ground*:

> Both philosophically and theologically, a method of communication that is over dependent on the discovery and utilization of similarities is open to question. In the long run, the *dissimilarities* between beliefs and practices may be more important and utilitarian. . . . If one's objective is to convert and disciple, the number and importance of these differences will far outweigh the number and importance of supposed similarities. (see pp. 147, 149)

Incorporating oils into Christian practice, for instance, does not Christianize an aromatherapist. Readers are, therefore, encouraged to consider points
of contact and areas of contrast. When communicating Christ in these areas
of contrast, many of the writers advocate using contextual apologetics or appropriate presentation of the biblical narrative.

Encountering New Religious Movements fills a lacuna in missiological literature. It informs the novice of the prevalence of new spiritualities and gives
new terms and categories for understanding them. Contemporary evangelists
will glean incarnational perspectives and models from case studies. The book
is an ideal reader for university courses on contextualized ministry, evangelism, and courses dealing with what have traditionally been called "the cults."

Dr. Gailyn Van Rheenen
Professor of Missions,
Abilene Christian University, Abilene, Texas

The authors welcome discussion about the contents of this book. They may be contacted by e-mail at jmorehead@kregel.com.

NEW RELIGIOUS MOVEMENTS AND CONTEXTUAL MISSION

The end of the twentieth and beginning of the twenty-first centuries witnessed the continued growth and development of a variety of new religious movements. These groups are often called "cults" in popular evangelical discourse, but throughout this book we will use the term "new religious movements."[1] This choice of terminology is a carefully calculated one. There are a variety of differing definitions of "cult" in evangelical literature,[2] but more importantly, there are serious problems with the use of the term. It can be argued that to speak of "the cults" is to engage in an overgeneralization that ignores the great complexity and diversity found in a variety of groups and movements. Perhaps more importantly, adherents within new religions consider the term pejorative. It is the desire of the editors and contributors not to add unnecessary stumbling blocks to the offense of the gospel, and this necessitates sensitivity in our choice of terminology. We also wish to move

---

1. See Christopher H. Partridge and Douglas Groothuis, eds., "New Religious Movements (Definitions)," in *Dictionary of Contemporary Religion in the Western World* (Leicester, England, and Downers Grove, Ill.: InterVarsity, 2002), 286–90. Another helpful discussion on definitions of "cult" and "new religious movements" is found in Irving Hexham and Karla Poewe, *New Religions as Global Cultures* (Boulder, Colo.: Westview, 1997), 27–37.
2. Cf. Walter Martin, *Kingdom of the Cults,* 2d ed. (Minneapolis: Bethany, 1997), 17; Harold Busséll, *Unholy Devotion: Why Cults Lure Christians* (Grand Rapids: Zondervan, 1983), 12; Ronald Enroth, *The Lure of the Cults and New Religions* (Downers Grove, Ill.: InterVarsity, 1987), 20–22; Ronald Enroth, ed., *Evangelizing the Cults* (Ann Arbor, Mich.: Vine Books, 1990), 11; Paul Martin, *Cult Proofing Your Kids* (Grand Rapids: Zondervan, 1993), 21–23; and Richard Abanes, *Cults, New Religious Movements, and Your Family* (Wheaton, Ill. Crossway, 1998), 10–11.

beyond the often confrontational and aggressive tone adopted by many evangelicals in formulating responses to new religions. Thus the terminology and tone in the chapters that follow reflect a more academically informed and missiological approach to the topic of new religious movements.

Another motivating factor is the recognition that Christianity is incarnational, unlike other world religions. This means that God became man in the person of Jesus Christ. Thus, Christianity teaches that God came down into our world and lived among humans as a human. Put another way, the creator of the universe came to earth and got his hands dirty. We believe that the incarnation teaches all Christians that they are to mix with ordinary people, share their experiences, and attempt to understand their beliefs. Yet few Christians take seriously the reality of the incarnation and its implications for missions and evangelism. It is not enough for Christians to preach the gospel *at* people; we must share the gospel *with* people. If we are to reach those who are attracted to new religions, we must understand not only what they believe, but also sympathetically understand why they do the things they do. We need an incarnational approach to evangelism and apologetics that takes us into the world to proclaim the gospel in ways that are heard and understood, not ways that are rejected because they are not heard clearly and are therefore misunderstood.

DEFINITIONS

New religious movements have been defined as "primary religious groups [or] movements that operate apart from the dominant religious culture (in our case the Christian West) in which they are located and, in addition, seek adherents from their new host culture."[3] As evangelicals committed to the importance of doctrine and sound teaching, we will add to this important sociological definition an element that involves belief systems and doctrine. This broader definition would encompass various alternative religions that "accept the basic dominant religious consensus while adopting a significant theological divergence or act in a different manner from the majority."[4]

---

3. J. Gordon Melton, "Emerging Religious Movements in North America: Some Missiological Reflections," *Missiology* 28, no. 1 (January 2000): 87. On the difficulties of defining "new religious movements" see George D. Chryssides, "New Religious Movements: Some Problems of Definition," *Diskus* 2, no. 2 (1997): web ed.; retrieved 6 January 2003, from www.uni-marburg.de/religionswissenschaft/journal/diskus/chryssides.html.
4. J. Gordon Melton, "The Rise of the Study of New Religions" (paper presented at a meeting of the Center for Studies on New Religions, Bryn Athyn, Penn., 1999); retrieved 9 January 2003, from www.cesnur.org/testi/bryn/br_melton.htm.

Of course, in many countries today there is no longer a clear religious majority. Therefore, instead of referring to a majority, we prefer to use the phrase "the mainstream historic traditions of Western culture." With this aspect of our definition in mind, the *historic tradition* or the standard by which doctrines are measured is reflected in biblical revelation and the historic ecumenical creeds of classic Christianity. Thus, evangelicals have focused a great deal of their time on responses to certain new religions that claim in some sense to be Christian, or even a "restoration" of primitive Christianity, yet which have adopted a "significant theological divergence" that puts them at odds with not only Protestant orthodoxy, but Roman Catholicism and Eastern Orthodoxy as well.

Estimates vary as to the number of new religions in North America. A conservative estimate would be somewhere between seven hundred and one thousand, depending upon how the term "new religions" is defined.[5] Although new religions have a long history in the United States, far beyond their common association with a "cult explosion" in the 1960s, various factors have contributed to their growth and spread in the United States and around the world.[6] Scholars debate whether the growth of new religions has been historically stable or whether there has been significant growth in times of social upheaval,[7] but sociological and historical studies seem to indicate that new religions are more likely to form and spread in reaction to times of great cultural change.[8] The continuing forces of modernization, secularization, and globalization may provide the social context necessary for the continued growth and spread of new religions around the globe.

Regardless of the continuing debate among scholars as to the definition, number, and growth of new religious movements, it is the perspective of the contributors to this volume that they represent global, cultural, and spiritual phenomena worthy of serious consideration by evangelical scholars and missiologists.[9]

---

5. Ibid.

6. Philip Jenkins, *Mystics and Messiahs: Cults and New Religions in American History* (New York: Oxford University Press, 2000), 4–5.

7. J. Gordon Melton, "The Changing Scene of New Religious Movements: Observations from a Generation of Research," *Social Compass* 42, no. 2 (1995): 265–76; Rodney Stark and Roger Finke, "A Rational Approach to the History of American Cults and Sects," in D. G. Bromley and J. K. Hadden, eds., *Religion and the Social Order*, vol. 3, *The Handbook on Cults and Sects in America, Part A* (Greenwich, Conn.: JAI Press, 1993), 109–25.

8. Lorne L. Dawson, *Comprehending Cults: The Sociology of New Religious Movements* (Toronto: Oxford University Press Canada, 1998), 42–62.

9. As an observer in the UK has eloquently stated: "Far more notice needs to be taken of the culture of re-enchantment which is beginning to shape the Western mind. In particular,

WHY THIS BOOK?

Toward the end of the twentieth century, a new climate of opinion concerning new religions began to be expressed by Christian authors writing from different reference points in the United States, Canada, Great Britain, and Australia. Through various books, journals, and periodicals, they began to question the evangelical understanding of many new religious groups and movements, and the effectiveness of the dominant apologetic methodology in reaching their adherents. Many argued that the apologetic refutation of "cultic" teachings had not translated into effective communication of the gospel to new religionists in understandable terms. They indicated that this impasse might be overcome through an interdisciplinary methodology that would include the integration of contextualized mission principles into the apologist's task.

A few apologists in both North America and Australia have pioneered some practical ways in which the twin disciplines of apologetics and missiology can be complementary practices in the effective proclamation of the gospel to adherents of alternative spiritual pathways. What these practitioners have discovered in the field is that methodology does not have to become an either-or polarization; instead, it can blend apologetics with contextual mission principles that are rooted soundly in the Bible.

PURPOSE AND FORMAT

The overall purpose of this multiauthor book is to bridge the gap between the disciplines of apologetics and contextual missiology. Because the phenomena of new religions constitutes a global missiological challenge, this book draws together the combined insights of theoreticians and field practitioners from the United States, Canada, and Australia who are on the cutting edge. In line with current secular scholarship in the discipline of new religions, this book casts a net that includes, but is not confined to, the United States. As Danish scholar

new religious and alternative spiritualities should not be dismissed as superficial froth or the dying embers of religion in the West, but are rather the sparks of a new and increasingly influential way of being religious, a way of being religious which is shaping and being shaped by popular culture." Christopher Partridge, "The Disenchantment and Reenchantment of the West: The Religio-Cultural Context of Contemporary Western Christianity." *The Evangelical Quarterly* 74, no. 3 (2002): 250.

Johannes Aagaard has noted, the central shift in the global paradigm has moved from the Atlantic to encompass the nations of the Pacific. This book, therefore, presents innovative trans-Pacific evangelical perspectives on the challenge of new religions, including insights derived from missions, religious studies, church history, and apologetics, all framed for specific application to the topic of new religions. Through this unique approach, this volume will present evangelical scholars and students with academic insights, as well as field-tested models, that will assist in both the understanding of new religions and also the evangelization of their adherents. This will be achieved by a threefold structure: Part 1 looks at biblical and historical perspectives; part 2 addresses methodological issues; and part 3 provides practical application.

In part 1, two chapters are presented that provide the necessary biblical and historical perspective for understanding mission to new religions. In chapter 1, the reader will find the necessary groundwork put forward through an overview of incarnational ministry reflected in the life and ministry of Christ. In chapter 2, we will see examples of contextualized mission in the history of the church and how this might be applied to new religions.

In part 2, four chapters are devoted to various aspects of methodology. Chapter 3 looks at the twin methodologies of the history of religion and missiology and argues that these varying perspectives can be brought to bear on the study of new religions. In chapter 4, a thesis is presented that conceptualizes new religions as global cultures. Chapter 5 discusses the apologetic and contextualized mission model of the apostle Paul in his message at the Areopagus in Acts 17 and its applicability to new religions. Chapter 6 discusses important issues of missionary communication of the Christian faith in both traditional and new religions.

Part 3 moves from issues of biblical, historical, and methodological perspectives to practical application. In the seven chapters of this section, the practical application of cross-cultural missions principles are demonstrated through tested field models applied to a variety of religious movements. The development of cross-cultural missions methodologies represents a new frontier for evangelicals. The models profiled in this section are the only ones we know of that have been developed and tested on the field.

Some movements included for study have substantial numbers of adherents. Others, though smaller in size, have forged significant niches in the religious landscape. We acknowledge that there are other new religious movements that need to be approached missiologically. Unfortunately, as yet there are no known evangelicals with the desire, field experience, and missiological competence to compose essays on other significant groups. We hope this book will inspire and stimulate others to transfer these concepts and applications to the many new religions that simply cannot be covered in this volume.

The book concludes with a chapter that summarizes evangelical responses to new religions and provides suggestions for the creation of a holistic model that might provide a more promising way forward beyond traditional approaches.

To facilitate the learning process and make this book more useful to missiologists, missionaries, apologists, and clergy, as well as to theological and university students, we have included brief discussion questions at the end of each chapter. These can be used in tutorials, seminars, or private study. It is our desire and prayer that this volume would inspire the opening of new doors of opportunity for evangelicals as we seek to grapple with the challenges and opportunities presented by new religious movements.

Part 1

BIBLICAL AND HISTORICAL PERSPECTIVES

CHAPTER 1

THE INCARNATIONAL MINISTRY OF JESUS

An Alternative to Traditional Apologetic Approaches

MIKEL NEUMANN

INTRODUCTION TO INCARNATIONAL MINISTRY

Traditional apologetics, as defined by Christian scholars from Augustine to Bernard Ramm,[1] is certainly a necessary discipline for the informed Christian. The spirit of these definitions, however, has caused many Christians to develop a primarily rational approach toward new religious movements. That spirit, in turn, often breeds an argumentative and defensive posture among Christian apologists. Though we need to understand biblical teaching, in contrast with heresy, it is seldom the first step in approaching people whose views we perceive as errant.

It is the purpose of this chapter to make a case for incarnational ministry in dealing with new religionists. By "incarnational" I refer to the traditional Christian understanding that Jesus Christ, the second Person of the triune God, became human and lived among us for redemptive purposes.[2] The word

---

1. Bernard Ramm defines Christian apologetics as "the strategy of setting forth the truthfulness of the Christian faith and its right to the claim of the knowledge of God." Bernard Ramm, *Varieties of Christian Apologetic* (Grand Rapids: Baker, 1961), 13. The definition in the *Baker Encyclopedia of Christian Apologetics* varies little: "Apologetics is the discipline that deals with a rational defense of Christian faith." Norman L. Geisler, ed., *Baker Encyclopedia of Christian Apologetics* (Grand Rapids: Baker, 1999), 37.
2. This understanding flows from the church fathers such as Athanasius in his *Incarnation of the Word*. From Justin Martyr, *Dialog with Trypho the Jew* (second century): "He existed formerly as Son of the Maker of all things, being God, and was born a man by the Virgin. . . .

incarnation is not used in the Scriptures, and others who have written on the subject tend to describe the concept rather than define it, although Wayne Grudem has given a specific definition and an explanation.[3]

Understanding the incarnation allows us to develop the concept of "incarnational ministry." Hiebert and Hiebert define incarnational ministry as "first and foremost the work of God,"[4] but this description is inadequate for our purposes here. I prefer a definition that flows from both a biblical and missiological[5] foundation:

> Incarnational ministry is an approach to Christian service based on principles derived from the life of Jesus in his relationships, both with those who followed him and those who rejected him.

Before we can use the approach of traditional apologetics, which is driven by knowledge and argument in presenting and defending scriptural truth, we must understand the world of the people we seek to reach. Unfortunately, as Hexham and Poewe rightly state, "Christians are often unwilling to explore the worldviews of other people. Many Christians have developed a tunnel vision, refusing to look at the world except through Christian eyes."[6] In their treatment of new religions, Hexham and Poewe provide insight that encourages Christians to understand and relate to those we seek to reach. By explor-

---

This man is the Christ of God. . . . He pre-existed, and submitted to be born a man of like passions with us, having a body, according to the Father's will" (48). And again, Justin Martyr, *Second Apology* (second century): "For next to God, we worship and love the Word who is from the Unbegotten and Ineffable God, since also He became man for our sakes, that, becoming a partaker of our sufferings, He might also bring us healing" (13).

3. "Although the word [*incarnation*] does not explicitly occur in the Scriptures, the church has used the term to refer to the fact that Jesus was God in human flesh. The *incarnation* was the act of God the Son whereby he took to himself a human nature." [Footnote to the quote: "The Latin word *incarnare* means 'to make flesh,' and is derived from the prefix *in-* (which has a causative sense, 'to cause something to be something') and the stem *caro, carnis-,* 'flesh.'"] Wayne Grudem, *Systematic Theology: An Introduction to Biblical Doctrine* (Grand Rapids: Zondervan, 1994), 543.

4. Paul G. Hiebert and Eloise Hiebert Neneses, *Incarnational Ministry* (Grand Rapids: Baker, 1995), 373.

5. Alan Neely, "missiology," in *Evangelical Dictionary of World Missions,* ed. A. Scott Moreau, Harold Netland, and Charles Van Engen (Grand Rapids: Baker, 2000), 633. According to Neely, missiology is "the conscious, intentional, ongoing reflection on the doing of mission."

6. Irving Hexham and Karla Poewe, *Understanding Cults and New Religions* (Vancouver, B.C.: Regent College Press, 1997), 13.

ing other worldviews, we begin to emulate the incarnational model established by Jesus.

Figure 1. Incarnational Ministry Framework

Incarnational Ministry as Modeled by Jesus	Incarnational Ministry as Exemplified in the Book of Acts	Incarnational Ministry: An Approach to New Religionists
1. Relationship as foundational in Jesus' ministry 2. Levels of Jesus' cultural involvement 3. Practical demonstration by Jesus	1. Activities of the Holy Spirit 2. Ministry of the apostle Paul	1. Incarnation: the necessary perquisite to the approach 2. Application of incarnational principles: • Cultural interaction • Relationship building • Personal involvement • Long-term commitment

INCARNATIONAL MINISTRY AS MODELED BY JESUS

A better understanding of the model Jesus established will require us to have a more relational ministry to new religionists. Does this mean we should never use apologetics in our evangelism? How can we effectively witness to people caught in a web of deception, error, and heresy? We will examine these questions in the light of Jesus' ministry.

First, we must dispense with a couple of misconceptions. The first is this: If we "get it right," people will respond positively. That is not at all true. We can "get it right" and still have people reject our message. For our purposes here, "getting it right" simply means that people have truly heard the life-changing message of the gospel in terms they understand.

The second misconception is that we should not witness unless we have a complete understanding of both our message and the people with whom we desire to share it. Certainly, the better we know our audience the more effective we will be, but we are continually thrown into situations that are less than perfect where we are called upon to share Christ.

Relationship as Foundational in Jesus' Ministry

We can see the theological importance of incarnation from the above references to Christian scholars. More important, Jesus' life demonstrates the importance of the Incarnation. Jesus became human in order that people might have a relationship with God. Verses such as "In the beginning was the Word, and the Word was with God, and the Word was God" (John 1:1), and "In the past God spoke to our forefathers through the prophets at many times and in various ways, but in these last days he has spoken to us by his Son" (Hebrews 1:1–2) give credence to the fact that relationship with human beings was foundational for Jesus' ministry. He took the time and effort to leave heaven and become human. Christ submitted to all that it means to be human, including birth, growing up in a family (moreover, a poor, first-century, Palestinian Jewish family), and acquiring a trade. He experienced the entire range of human experience, yet without sin (Hebrews 4:15).

Levels of Jesus' Cultural Interaction

Jesus' presence on earth is first of all seen at the behavioral or observable level. He was a human and lived among us as a man. He grew up with parents and younger siblings. He presumably apprenticed with Joseph as a carpenter. He lived life in relative obscurity for thirty years. Except for accounts of the events surrounding his birth, the Scriptures are mostly silent about his first three decades of life. However, during that time he developed as a person. He took time to grow up to manhood and did it as all men do. He did not come swooping in as a full-grown superhero. He was born in Bethlehem, in the nation of Israel, of the tribe of Judah, of the lineage of David, and grew up in the household of Joseph and Mary.

At a second, deeper level, Jesus also demonstrated his involvement with people. He grew up under the authority of parents, who obeyed the laws concerning his birth. He was consecrated as the firstborn at birth, with offerings required by the Mosaic Law, and was circumcised. Although many miraculous events surrounded Christ's birth, let us not forget that it was through his humanity that God chose to communicate with us. Jesus grew up under both the Mosaic Law and the Roman law. His injunction, "Give to Caesar what is Caesar's and to God what is God's" (Matthew 22:21), indicates his balance and understanding as a human living under two authorities. Even in his death, with all the inconsistencies at his trials, he submitted to the authorities. Although we understand the greater implication of these events from a theological perspective, it in no way prevents our understanding of his involvement with humans at the authority level.

As a person, he experienced the range of human emotions and privations. His life, from birth to death, was full of human experiences. The New Testament gives us glimpses of his humanity with statements about his joy, sorrow, anger, fatigue, hunger, and thirst, to name a few. He lived life as a person, even though his experience had its uniqueness, and as such could identify with all humanity. He had a personality forged by his human birth and upbringing.

The implications of the Incarnation also include considerations of worldview. Ken McElhanon quotes Ronald Nash in defining worldview as "a conceptual scheme by which we consciously or unconsciously place or fit everything we believe and by which we interpret and judge reality."[7] Jesus was both God and human. In that respect he is unlike every other person. However, looking at his behavior, authority, and experience of cultural involvement with humans, we can see that his core values are certainly understandable in human terms. Broad cultural constructs that would govern other Israelites of his day would have also been true of Jesus. Honoring people of age and position, group orientation, and Near Eastern hospitality were certainly values reflected in Jesus' life. He also confronted aspects of culture that were contrary to God's plan. One example is his expulsion of the moneychangers from the temple. He infuriated the religious and political establishment because he understood their worldview so well he could confront it, leaving no room for misunderstanding his message.

Practical Demonstration by Jesus

Jesus drew people to himself. He said, "Come to me, all you who are weary and burdened, and I will give you rest. Take my yoke upon you and learn from

---

7. Ken A. McElhanon, "worldview," in *Evangelical Dictionary of World Missions*, ed. A. Scott Moreau, Harold Netland, and Charles Van Engen (Grand Rapids: Baker, 2000), 1032.

me, for I am gentle and humble in heart, and you will find rest for your souls. For my yoke is easy and my burden is light" (Matthew 11:28–30). This passage presents Jesus as one who desired that all people would come to him and find life. Frequently, he corrected error and distortion and spoke harshly to those who had abused their power, especially those who refused to repent in spite of the miracles done in their midst (Matthew 11:20–24). An important purpose of Jesus' life on earth was to bring the world to an understanding that he was, in the words of John the Baptist, "The Lamb of God, who takes away the sin of the world" (John 1:29). Jesus' task was to communicate the truth about himself so that people understood the message whether they accepted or rejected it.

Many people followed Jesus for reasons that seem self-serving. Some wanted the necessities of life: food, clothing, and shelter; others sought healing; still others wanted positions in the kingdom. There seems to have been a part of every crowd that was there just to watch and see what might happen. Perhaps they were looking for entertainment. In spite of these onlookers and hangers-on, Jesus did not turn people away. Some people followed him at considerable cost to themselves. Zacchaeus is such a person. As a chief tax collector he would have accumulated wealth through other tax collectors at the expense of the taxpayers. His commitment to follow Jesus, which he proved by giving back his ill-gotten gain, resulted in less wealth for himself (Luke 19:1–9). Jesus drew people who came honestly and forthrightly to follow him. Jesus' involvement with people was such that he drew them to himself because he touched them at their point of need. These needs included physical healing, physical provision, and spiritual freedom. The fact that his personal involvement was the key here cannot be overestimated. His participation in the lives of people was not the sum total of his ministry, but in terms of bringing his truth to people, it played a key role. Though he obviously understood divine and eternal truth, he took the time to be profoundly involved with his audience. His incarnation touched every level of human culture in order to make his message clear. For some people, understanding led to new life; for others, it was a stumbling block.

Christ's teaching was indeed different from what the people had been hearing in the synagogues, and consequently they flocked to hear him. When he spoke, he did so in ways they understood. Many followed, but some rejected him. Those in authority sought to kill him, and eventually succeeded. He had harsh words for those in authority, especially the teachers who led people astray.

In seeking to pursue an incarnational ministry, however, the pattern to follow here is not primarily the harsh words but Jesus' *involvement with people, including his enemies.* His understanding of human need and his response at a deeper level defined his incarnational earthly ministry. Although this approach overshadowed his apologetic ministry, both in terms of time spent and of drawing people to himself, it also undergirded his apologetic ministry when he used it.

INCARNATIONAL MINISTRY AS EXEMPLIFIED IN THE BOOK OF ACTS

These same principles and approaches—understanding people *and* the Scriptures—can be found in the New Testament book of Acts. We see repeatedly how being involved with people and understanding their needs opens the door to their hearts. Throughout Acts, God's people demonstrate an incarnational approach to ministry. Figures 2 and 3 show the relationship between the traditional apologetic approach and incarnational ministry in Acts.

Figure 2. A Model of the Traditional Apologetic Approach.

Problem	Solution
1 ─────────────→ 1a	

In the traditional apologetic approach shown in figure 2, a problem, such as an errant view, is recognized (see step 1). The problem is confronted with truth that deals primarily with the *speaker's perception* of the problem and the solution. The proposed solution is offered only at the cognitive level of the speaker (see step 1a). Deeper levels of culture and personality are not explicitly considered.

Figure 3. A Model of Incarnational Ministry

Process / Level	Problem	Solution	
Surface	Behavior	Positive	Negative
	(1)	(4) Understanding	
Deep	Spiritually: Unregenerate (2) Cognitively: No apprehension of truth Affectively: No appreciation for truth or love for God	(3) Culturally involved Personal relationship Long-term commitment	

⟶ Shows directional development of incarnational ministry.

Figure 3 shows that *behavior* (step 1) is a surface level phenomenon with deep-level spiritual, emotional, and cognitive implications (step 2). Observed heresy or failures in orthopraxy should be examined at the deeper or cultural assumption level that led to the problem. Cultural involvement, personal relationship, and long-term commitment are necessary to identify the deep-level solutions (step 3) that emerge from cultural involvement, personal relationship, and long-term commitment. However, even after understanding has been established, people may still respond positively or negatively, either accepting or rejecting the truth (step 4). But at least now their response is based on a deeper understanding instead of the superficial encounter shown in figure 2. This process can be illustrated from the activities of the Holy Spirit and the ministry of the apostle Paul in the book of Acts.

Activities of the Holy Spirit

In Acts 2, many peoples were gathered in Jerusalem. The Holy Spirit descended from heaven with the sound of a "violent wind." As they were filled with the Spirit, believers spoke in the hearers' own languages. The surface problem was the hearers' inability to comprehend the phenomenon (figure 3, step 1). Simply put, the deep-level problem (step 2) is that this experience was outside the hearers' experience and core values; therefore, they did not know how to react. Some marveled and others mocked. The deep-level solution (step 3) was to understand God's action in terms of the Scriptures. The apostle Peter explained what God was doing and how this fulfilled the Old Testament. The ultimate solution resulted in a behavior change (step 4): About three thousand people were added to the church that day; those who believed and repented were baptized and received the Holy Spirit. The surface level (observable) behavioral change (step 4) was that they were baptized.

An incarnational approach will use the observable data to gain understanding at a deeper level. Understanding discovered there helps build deeper-level connections that will result in appropriate behavior at the surface level. This process requires us to know in some depth the people to whom we are speaking as well as scriptural truth and apologetic evidences. The danger inherent in the apologetic approach of figure 2 is that, although the Scriptures may well be mastered and defended, our audience may hear a different message than the one intended. Greater familiarity with the people we seek to reach might indicate that they do not share our apologetic or biblical frame of reference or concerns, the missing steps 2, 3, and 4 of figure 3.

Acts 6 offers another illustration of the above approach. The Hellenists complained because their widows were being neglected while the Hebrew widows were receiving daily help. If we ask the following questions of the text, according to figure 3, we see the above process unfolding: What is the observable problem (step 1)? What is the deep-level problem (step 2)? What is the deep solution (step 3)? How is understanding created, thereby leading to an observable solution (step 4)?

Much of Acts, as well as other historical portions of the New Testament, can be examined in this way. Applying this method to ministry requires time and effort. Working from observable behavior to understand the deeper problem calls for involvement with people. As communicators of the message of truth, we must be incarnational in our involvement with those we desire to reach. Once we understand the deeper-level problems, we can begin to see how the Scriptures might apply to that situation. This extra step requires thorough Bible knowledge. Being able to move from the deeper-level solution to apply biblical truth resulting in proper behavioral change requires comprehensive ability to apply that truth.

Were it not for the Spirit of God directing us as we seek him in prayer, however, we could not effectively do any of what I have proposed above, because it is the Spirit who gives us the endurance to learn the "why" behind the "what" of people's actions. Only as we study the Scriptures under the guidance of the Holy Spirit can we find those deeper-level solutions and then apply them to effect behavioral change. My plea here is not that we understand the Scriptures less, but that we take the time and effort to understand people more, as Jesus and others did. The process is all part of obeying Jesus' command to "make disciples of all nations" (Matthew 28:19). We cannot make disciples of people we do not know, and we cannot teach them "to obey everything I have commanded you" (Matthew 28:20), if we do not know the Scriptures. Both traditional apologetics and incarnational ministry are necessary.

Ministry of the Apostle Paul

Most of what we know about the apostle Paul occurred after his conversion and after he spent a year in Antioch with Barnabas. A large portion of Acts reports his itinerate ministry.[8] From the beginning (Acts 9:20–30), Paul was a powerful witness for the Lord. Notice that he engaged the Jews immediately after his conversion (verse 20). Shortly after his conversion in Damascus, he "increased all the more in strength and confounded the Jews" there (Acts 9:22 NKJV). Later, in Jerusalem, he spoke "boldly" and "disputed against the Hellenists" (Acts 9:29 NKJV). In both Damascus and Jerusalem, he angered people who wanted to kill him. In both cases, other Christians stepped in to rescue him. Finally, he was sent off to Tarsus (verse 30), after which "the church . . . enjoyed a time of peace" (Acts 9:31). Although Paul's conversion and cessation of persecution was primary in bringing about that peace, it is still worth noting that it was not until after Paul went to Tarsus that the church enjoyed peace. At this early stage in Paul's service for the Lord, his combative nature carried over into his preaching. He was an effective apologist but not yet a peacemaker. He seems to have had few converts at this stage.

Between the events of Acts 9 and his commissioning to mission service in Acts 13, some ten to thirteen years had passed. He spent one year working with Barnabas in Antioch (Acts 11). Though it seems Paul never lost his fire (note his response to Barjesus in Acts 13:6 and the unrepentant Jews in Acts 13:51 on his first journey), he seems to have become increasingly relational as his ministry turned to the Gentiles.

---

8. Dr. Steve Sweatman, CEO and director of Mission Training International, in a presentation at the National Missionary Training Forum in Richmond, Virginia, 9 January 2003, introduced the concept of Paul's development here. The explanation and application are my own.

While Paul spoke boldly, he spoke the message of grace (Acts 14:3). Throughout his journeys, he continued to preach, heal, and cast out demons as a result of the message of grace. The Judaizers followed and harassed him along the way. More than once he was left for dead as he was stoned or beaten (Acts 14:9; 16:22).

Space limitations preclude an in-depth examination of Paul's life. However, highlights from his ministry suffice to show an incarnational approach. Paul grew up in the Jewish community and trained in the tradition of the Pharisees. He had knowledge of those who hassled and persecuted him, yet he engaged in all four levels of culture discussed above. When he spoke boldly in front of Jewish audiences, he did so with considerable insider knowledge of that audience. He had knowledge of Gentile audiences as well. His encounter with the Greeks in Athens (Acts 17:16–34) provides us with a glimpse into both his heart and his method.[9] He was greatly distressed by the ubiquitous idols present in Athens. His heart was stirred and he wanted to present Christ. His method, as revealed by his public addresses includes familiarity with Hellenistic culture and literature, contextual communication, and Scriptural fidelity. He incarnated the message of Christ by understanding the people and their sociocultural background.

We often admire Paul for his great knowledge of the Holy Scriptures; we can also admire him for his knowledge of the people among whom he ministered. His knowledge of the Scriptures and of the audience's cultures enabled him to communicate scriptural truth with cultural understanding and relevance in his incarnational ministry.

INCARNATIONAL MINISTRY:
A PROPOSED APPROACH TO NEW RELIGIONISTS

Most people find it difficult to accept something they perceive as an attack. When we seek to show new religionists that Christianity is the only complete truth, they will understandably become defensive, in spite of our good intentions. Without the benefits of incarnational ministry, we are often perceived as egotistical and arrogant. When our approach is only apologetic and not incarnational, resentment and resistance will often be the consequence.

---

9. See chapter 5 for Stephen Rost's extended discussion of this important example of incarnational ministry.

Incarnation: The Necessary Prerequisite to a Relational Approach

Communication, rightly accomplished, is incarnational. Donald K. Smith states that communication is involvement.[10] If we are to communicate with effectiveness, we must be involved with those to whom we desire to communicate. Personal and cultural involvement requires time, effort, and energy to continually gain understanding of those around us. In-depth relationship is the first step in developing an incarnational ministry.

If we were called to minister to a people whose language we did not know, what would we do? The first thing would be to learn the language, preferably from native speakers. We would introduce ourselves to people in that group, and we would build relationships with them. We would learn about all aspects of their lives. In order to do that, we would make friends and spend time with them. We would visit in their homes, in the marketplace, and in the coffee shops (or the equivalent). We would find those places where people gather and spend time there. We would participate in their celebratory events, both national and familial. Celebrations and other national observances would help us gain a broad understanding of their culture, whereas family traditions, birthdays, naming days, and other significant events would give us knowledge and insights into personal values and knowledge.

If we're willing to invest substantial time and effort, without reservation, to communicate the gospel across cultural and linguistic barriers, why would we not make a similar commitment of time and effort to reach the adherents of new religious movements in our own society? We already speak the same language and have many cultural elements in common. We may even use similar vocabulary, at least at a surface level. However, without understanding the deeper levels of meaning, values, mind-sets, or inner-selves, our presentation of intellectual truth about Christianity may only push people further from Jesus as the embodiment of truth. Without personal relationships, compassionate concern, and genuine love, we often become barriers to the gospel, even as we seek to proclaim the gospel. Our evangelism may take on an argumentative tone without the redeeming voice of sincere friendship. Let us take the time necessary to be involved with people, to understand and relate to them so that we become a bridge for the gospel, not a barrier.

---

10. Donald K. Smith, *Creating Understanding: A Handbook for Christian Communication Across Cultural Landscapes* (Grand Rapids: Zondervan, 1992), 23–40, defines communication as involvement. If there is no involvement, then communication has not taken place.

Application of Incarnational Principles

Figure 4 describes four levels of culture showing the importance of involvement and the application of incarnational principles.

**Figure 4. Relationship Between Cultural Level and
Incarnational Application**

Cultural Level	Incarnational Application
1. Behavioral Level: Easily observable	1. Cultural interaction
2. Social Authority Level: Observable with some careful research	2. Relationship building
3. Experience Level: Can be discovered over time	3. Personal involvement
4. Core Level: Worldview discovery; extremely difficult to ascertain	4. Long-term commitment

Cultural Interaction

The first and easiest level to observe and understand is the *behavioral* level. Here we see how people act, dress, speak, and react to the world around them. It is all quite visible. However, even though at this level of involvement we can observe *what* people do, we do not always understand *why* they do what they do. Edward T. Hall, among others, has written extensively about how human behavior differs across cultures.[11] Cultural interaction is the beginning of discovery and the beginning of the incarnational process. It is the necessary first step in beginning to understand those to whom we wish to communicate.

Relationship Building

A second level of involvement, the *social authority* level, reveals the nature of authority that a group or society respects or honors. Authorities to which

---

11. Edward T. Hall, *The Silent Language* (Garden City, N.Y.: Doubleday, 1959), and idem, *Beyond Culture* (New York: Anchor, 1989).

people will submit may include people, holy books, and governments. As evangelical Christians, we submit to the Bible as our ultimate God-given authority. We also submit to the authority of civil government. Americans, in general, submit to the rule of law. Everyone gives allegiance to someone or something, whether it's a person or an institution. That does not mean we always obey or submit totally to the authorities in our lives, but it does mean they have a high value to us and we look to them for guidance and order—and when we violate the standards of our authorities we typically feel at least a twinge of conscience.

This second level of involvement, the social authority level, gives us a deeper understanding of the people we seek to reach. As communicators of truth, as we understand the authority structure of the people with whom we desire to communicate, we are able to build deeper relationships and communicate more clearly and effectively. Paul understood the authority levels of his day, both Roman and Jewish. When he was about to be flogged by Roman authorities (Acts 22), he knew his rights as a Roman citizen to a hearing before he was punished. He referred to his training at the feet of Gamaliel. His understanding of the social authority level gave him a hearing with each group.

Personal Involvement

The next level of involvement with people is the *experiential* level. Whereas groups and societies will tend to be homogeneous across the first two levels of involvement (exhibiting remarkably similar behaviors and submitting to common authorities), involvement at the experiential level may be somewhat different for each person within the group, because each person's experience will be different from everyone else's. Two people living in a society where the rule of law is a high cultural value may receive the same number of traffic tickets— let's say three. However, the way that each responds may be different. One person may not worry about the tickets and continue to drive recklessly, whereas the other person may take the traffic fines to heart and actually change his driving habits. At the experiential level, the reactions of two people who might otherwise appear to be much the same could be quite different. Consequently, understanding people at the experiential level may take some time.

Differences at this level will reveal themselves through different interests, hobbies, developed skills, and much more. How and where a person was raised, and the nature of family relationships and friendships, will certainly affect this area. One person's experiences might leave him or her with a great need for security, whereas another person from the same culture—or even the same family—may have a higher tolerance for risk and a greater need for trying out new things. At the experiential level, understanding a person's language, both verbal and nonverbal, is necessary. Here we must take the time to know people and become their friends.

Long-Term Commitment

The fourth level is that of *core values*. What things are assumed to be true by a group of people? What values are accepted as implicit within that group? This level is the most difficult to understand, in part because few people are consciously aware of their own cultural values. Core values are not overt in such a way that they can be simply stated. We tend to absorb them as we grow up. Perhaps by the age of seven, many of these values are set. They exist primarily in our subconscious, but they affect us at all other levels. Those who have experienced different cultures may understand this level better. For example, space and time are dealt with quite differently from one culture to the next. To understand these deeper issues requires a long-term commitment on the part of the communicator.

Other core values have to do with whether individuals are exalted over the group, or whether the individuals are expected to submit to what is considered to be the group's greater good (individualist versus collective cultures). Do people in authority receive special honor or respect, or is everyone seen as equal (hierarchical versus egalitarian cultures)? Other aspects of culture have been discussed by scholars.[12] When we go to different cultures and language groups, we usually understand that the burden is on us to learn all we can, at every level of involvement, about the people we desire to reach. The need is less obvious when we are dealing with people in or near to our own culture, people to whom we can talk in our own language. Donald K. Smith uses a model called the "cultural onion" to describe these levels of culture. This model corresponds well to culture.[13]

Figure 5 summarizes the similarities and differences of the traditional apologetic approach and the incarnational approach.

---

12. See Geert H. Hofstede, *Culture and Organizations* (New York: McGraw-Hill, 1991), especially part 2, encompassing chapters 2–7.
13. See Smith, *Creating Understanding,* especially chapter 18.

**Figure 5. Comparing Traditional Apologetic and
Incarnational Approaches**

	Traditional Apologetic Approach	Incarnational Approach
Similarities in approach:	1. Goal: Reach people with the gospel/correct error 2. Basis: Biblical and theological truth 3. Requires: Knowledge and skill	
Differences in approach: (these are stated as tendencies not absolutes)	1. Confrontational 2. Propositional 3. Superficial	1. Cultural interaction 2. Personal involvement 3. Long-term commitment

As Christians, it is our desire that "all peoples," including adherents to new religious movements, come to a saving knowledge of our Lord Jesus Christ and grow to maturity in him. They need to be viewed as unreached people groups.[14] As such, our approach must be incarnational and missiological, a combined approach that has yet to be developed in any depth or sustained manner since the Lausanne Committee on World Evangelization identified new religions as unreached peoples in the 1980s. Apologetics is necessary for people in the church to understand error, but merely being trained in apologetics does little to bring people into the kingdom. There are exceptions, of course, but we need a broader-based incarnational approach that follows the model established in the lives of Jesus and Paul, and as seen in the Gospels and the book of Acts.

In essence, a traditional apologetics approach (figure 2) is necessary but not sufficient for reaching followers of new religious movements. The proposed incarnational approach includes traditional apologetics but is more comprehensive and holistic, with multiple levels and steps, covering the various dimensions in the process shown in figures 3, 4, and 5.

---

14. Lausanne Committee on World Evangelization, "The Thailand Report on New Religious Movements: Report on the Consultation on World Evangelization Mini-Consultation Regarding Mystics and Cultists." Electronic document found at www.gospelcom.net/lcwe/LOP/lop11.htm.

STUDY QUESTIONS

1. What attitudes and approaches tend to be developed by users of traditional apologetics? Why are these attitudes and approaches inadequate for reaching the followers of new religious movements?
2. Contrast traditional apologetics with incarnational ministry.
3. What is foundational for an incarnational ministry?
4. What were the levels of Jesus' cultural involvement with other people? Why is each of these levels important?
5. How can traditional apologetics and incarnational ministry be effectively used together?

CHAPTER 2

CONTEXTUALIZED MISSION IN CHURCH HISTORY

HAROLD TAYLOR

The church is called to the continuing task of bringing the good news of Jesus Christ to all the peoples of the world, giving them the opportunity to respond and become part of the universal fellowship of the people of God. This task involves the issue of "contextualization" as an essential requirement of effective missions.

One of the new realities of our time is that the so-called Christian West has now itself become a mission field. In many Western countries, increasing numbers of people have either moved from a "church faith" to no faith, or are seeking for meaning and purpose in "alternative" spiritual paths. As the decline in church involvement continues, there has been a dramatic increase in spiritual and religious experimentation as people develop their own spirituality, sometimes by a return to pre-Christian pagan religions, or by an "amalgam" spirituality that draws on many different sources to provide a personalized do-it-yourself religion. This contemporary search, often described as New Age or "self spirituality," is one expression of the many new religious movements, and it is one of the major frontiers of missions confronting the church in the West.[1] How can the church be faithful in its mission to these new religious movements and offer a gospel that is relevant and contextual?[2]

---

1. L. Newbigin, "Can the West Be Converted?" *International Bulletin of Missionary Research* 2, no. 1 (January 1987): 2–7. Also J. A. Kirk, "Mission in the West," in *A Scandalous Prophet,* ed. T. F. Foust (Grand Rapids: Eerdmans, 2002), 115–27; and M. Robinson, *The Faith of the Unbeliever* (London: Monarch, 1994).
2. A comprehensive overview of such movements is given in John Saliba, *Perspectives on New Religious Movements* (London: Geoffrey Chapman, 1995).

This chapter will focus on the historical development of Christian mission, and will seek to answer the following question: *What can the contemporary church learn from mission history to enable it to present the good news effectively to people involved in new religious movements?*

Following a brief examination of the meaning of contextualization, two examples of contextual mission will be examined—the Celtic mission in the fifth to seventh centuries, and mission to Muslim peoples in the thirteenth and twentieth centuries—and some suggestions offered for the contemporary task of contextualizing the gospel.

THE MEANING OF CONTEXTUALIZATION

Contextualization relates to one of the essential issues of mission: How is the divine word of revelation in Scripture to be made relevant and contextual in the changing patterns of human cultures without distorting the Scriptural message or ignoring the cultural world—without succumbing to the twin dangers of syncretism on the one hand, and cultural irrelevance or "foreign" domination or imposition on the other?

This task of contextualization has received much attention in recent missiological study.[3] Van Engen comments:

> As the gospel crossed cultural barriers over several centuries, the faith assertions of Christendom did not seem to fit the new cultures encountered by the gospel. So a progression of attempted solutions were suggested, with an accompanying succession of words like—persuasion, christianisation, compulsion, accommodation, adaptation, fulfilment, syncretism, indigenisation, transformation and dialogue. The *latest* word, "contextualization," involves theological issues like incarnation, revelation, truth, divine-human interaction, and the shape of corporate religious experience.[4]

Van Engen correctly notes that contextualization includes many essential aspects of mission, including theology, personal and social experience,

---

3. Dean S. Gilliland, ed., *The Word Among Us: Contextualizing Theology for Mission Today* (Dallas: Word, 1989); and D. Bosch, *Transforming Mission* (Maryknoll, N.Y.: Orbis, 1992), chap. 12.
4. C. Van Engen, "The New Covenant: Knowing God in Context," in Gilliland, ed., *The Word Among Us,* 76.

church structure and polity, and communication methodology, among others.

There is no agreed upon definition of contextualization. Dean Gilliland suggests that the goal of contextualization is perhaps its best definition. "That goal is to enable, as far as is humanly possible, an understanding of what it means that Jesus Christ, the Word, is authentically experienced in each and every human situation."[5]

Achieving this goal requires that both the Scriptural revelation and the total human cultural context must be taken seriously—to discover what God is saying to every particular group of people.[6] This approach—"critical contextualization"—involves a three-step process: (1) exegesis of culture, (2) exegesis of Scripture, and (3) response to new insights leading to new practices.[7]

In the past, contextualization was applied to overseas mission-field situations but largely neglected in the home, stateside church. It was often assumed that contextualization did not apply to the "church in Christendom," or had already been dealt with. This perspective is now changing and there is a growing recognition of a new understanding of mission in the Western church. Paul Hiebert suggests that the Western church has largely adopted a "non-contextual" approach in the past 150 years—an issue that demands urgent attention.[8] The presentation of the gospel to contemporary spiritual seekers in new religious movements is one aspect of this challenge.

A true understanding must begin with the biblical emphasis, wherein contextualization has been described as "communication through incarnation," a process in which God is recognized as *the* Contextualizer, who wants to be understood, and who reveals his purposes through people and events. This process reaches its ultimate expression in Jesus Christ, who uniquely communicates the Father's character and purpose—so that the Incarnation becomes "the defining expression of all effective contextualization."[9] The

---

5. Dean S. Gilliland, "contextualization," in *Evangelical Dictionary of World Missions,* ed. A. Scott Moreau (Grand Rapids: Baker, 2000), 225–27.

6. Taber offers a detailed definition and discussion of contextualization in C. R. Taber, "Contextualization, Indigenisation and/or Transformation," in *The Gospel and Islam,* ed. D. McCurry (Monrovia, Calif.: Missions Advanced Research and Communication Center, 1979), 143–54.

7. P. Hiebert, "Critical Contextualization," *International Bulletin of Missionary Research* 2 (July 1981): 104–12.

8. Ibid., 104.

9. C. Kraft, "Contextualizing Communication," in *The Word Among Us,* chap. 6.

Scriptures reveal this process as God communicates through prophets and other people in the Old Testament,[10] and in the New Testament through his ultimate expression in Jesus Christ—which is further articulated and demonstrated in the missionary ministry of Paul.[11]

This "incarnational" principle provides a framework by which contextualization in church history can be described and evaluated.

THE INCARNATIONAL PRINCIPLE IN CHURCH HISTORY

Church history can be described as the attempt to contextualize the gospel in different cultures; that is, to "incarnate" the gospel such that people will "authentically experience" Jesus Christ, be formed into the church, and be enabled to express the truth of the gospel in relevant ways. In evaluating historical examples, the following conditions must be remembered:

- Although church history can be seen as a continuation of biblical history, it lacks the authority of Scripture—demonstrating both inspired understanding and human folly. Therefore, it can offer guidelines but not prescriptions for the task of contextualization.
- Church history reveals a variegated pattern—both positive and negative examples, with many changes in approach—and no one method can be taken as a model for all situations. Contextualization was strongest in the pre-nineteenth century church, but the Western church has largely become non-contextual in its general approach since that time.[12]

Within the variations and ambiguities of history, the church has always been involved in contextualization, whatever the terms used to describe the process.

As the church, with its "Christian culture," related to other cultures, missionaries acted as agents of change to those societies, seeking to "Christianize" each society by a process that was informed and directed by the gospel. This process raised some major questions:

10. A. F. Glasser, "O.T. Contextualization: Revelation and Its Environment," in *The Word Among Us*, 33.
11. A. D. Clarke and B. Winter, "In Public and in Private: Early Christian Interactions with Religious Pluralism," in *One God, One Lord* (Cambridge: Tyndale, 1991), 112–34; and J. D. Charles, "Engaging the (neo) Pagan Mind: Paul's Encounter with Athenian Culture as a Model for Cultural Apologetics," *Trinity Journal*, 1995, 47–62.
12. Based on D. Bosch, *Witness to the World* (London: Marshall, Morgan and Scott, 1980), 87–89.

- What should be *rejected* in the receiving culture as inherently opposed to the gospel?
- What could be *maintained* as consistent with God's revelation, and therefore accepted and transformed by the gospel?
- What new dimensions of truth and goodness could be *incorporated* into the new church—to express the gospel in that cultural situation?

These principles of *rejection, maintenance,* and *incorporation* were variously answered according to the philosophy and purpose of the missionary agents. In some situations, a truly contextual indigenous church was established. In others, the receiving culture was almost completely rejected and a foreign "church culture" imposed. Between these two poles there were many variations.

The process also involved *methods of communication*—words, actions, symbols—and matters of missionary lifestyle and attitude, which influenced and often determined whether the people addressed with the gospel were enabled both to understand and authentically experience Jesus Christ. Sometimes the principles of rejection, maintenance, and incorporation were considered in a relevant way, but the gospel was still experienced as "foreign" because of the non-incarnational approach of the missionary advocate.[13]

CONTEXTUALIZATION IN THE CELTIC MISSION

The name *Celtic* refers to ancient European peoples who shared the family of languages now represented by Gaelic, Irish, and Welsh. By approximately 1000 B.C., these pagan Celts had migrated into the lands now known as Austria, Germany, Switzerland, France, Spain, northern Italy, and the British Isles—especially Ireland and Scotland—where these pagan cultures flourished during the time when the Roman civilization had conquered Europe but had not extended complete control in Britain.

By the fourth century A.D., there were reports of Christians in pagan Ireland. This flame of Christian culture was fanned by the missionary work of Patrick and others, so that the Celtic church became the center and preserver of Christian culture in the period when much of Europe was experiencing the collapse of Roman control. Wilkinson comments:

---

13. A. R. Tippett, *Verdict Theology in Missionary Theory* (Pasadena, Calif.: William Carey Library, 1973), 117–47.

Rooted in those years of Celtic Christian culture's isolation is its uniqueness, its mystery. . . . Nowhere in the history of Christianity is there so clear an instance of the Christian transformation of a pagan culture with so little influence by the culture that brought the Christian message. For as soon as the Roman culture had carried the gospel to Ireland, the carrier collapsed. . . . For several generations there was little influence from the rest of European Christianity and the result was a unique Christian blossoming of a formerly pagan culture.[14]

Today Celtic spirituality enjoys great popularity—and also skepticism and opposition from Christians and non-Christians alike. For some, Celtic spirituality holds the key to church renewal; others rigorously oppose any influence from this tradition. Wilkinson suggests that the truth lies between the extremes of Celtophobia and Celtophilia. There are great riches in the Celtic Christian tradition, but the reconstruction of those traditions must be undertaken judiciously—based not on whether it is appealing but whether it is biblical.[15] Other writers suggest that some aspects of contemporary Celtic spirituality "float on a raft of ideas of comparatively recent construction." These critics speak of "waves of fascination," of "romanticizing the Celts," of a "selective use" of the more positive aspects of the Celtic church, of the peril of "unthinking imitation," and of the use of "abandoned scholarly theory" to justify contemporary expressions of Celtic spirituality.[16]

The Celtic church nevertheless offers a helpful model of effective contextualization, because "the missionary character of the Celtic Church was enhanced by the ability to contextualize mission."[17] Others refer to the "uniqueness of the Celtic mission" and the significance of "the Celtic way of evangelism."[18] Celtic mission involved many complex issues. The fol-

14. L. Wilkinson, "Saving Celtic Christianity," *Christianity Today,* 24 April 2000, 78–85.
15. Ibid., 78.
16. I. Bradley cited in Wilkinson, "Saving Celtic Christianity," 79. See also M. Robinson, *Rediscovering the Celts* (London: Harper Collins, 2000), 165, 183; M. Bowman, "Contemporary Celtic Spirituality" in *Belief Beyond Boundaries: Wicca, Celtic Spirituality, and the New Age,* ed. J. Pearson (Aldershot Hants, England: Ashgate, 2002), 55–102; D. E. Meek, "The Faith of the Fringe: Perspectives and Issues in Celtic Christianity" in Pearson, ed., *Belief Beyond Boundaries,* 251–76.
17. Robinson, *Rediscovering the Celts,* 174ff.
18. G. G. Hunter III, *The Celtic Way of Evangelism* (Nashville: Abingdon, 2000).

lowing aspects are significant in relation to our understanding of contextualization.[19]

Effective Communication of the Gospel

How did the Celtic movement communicate the gospel so effectively to the barbarian populations in Ireland, Scotland, England, and Western Europe? In addressing this question, G. G. Hunter utilizes perspectives from communication theory, especially those enunciated by Aristotle in his *On Rhetoric*, the prevailing model of the communication process for twenty-three centuries.

> Essentially, Aristotle theorized that persuasion takes place in an interplay between the speaker, the message, and the audience, within a cultural and historical context. . . . More specifically he taught that persuasion occurs through the interaction of the *ethos* of the speaker, the *logos* of the message, and the *pathos* of the audience.[20]

The communicator's *ethos* consists of intelligence, character, and goodwill. To be believed, the speaker must be perceived as a person of honesty and integrity—to be seen as "for" the audience, more concerned for their welfare than for self gain. These attitudes were consistently displayed by the Celtic missionaries: they were seen to be both *with* and *for* the people. Because they attempted to understand, adapt to, and identify with their audience, "the continued spread of Celtic Christianity is substantially attributable to the ethos of the Celtic Christian leaders and their communities."[21]

This *ethos* interacted with the *logos* of the gospel message, which was received as meaningful and relevant by the Celtic people. It addressed felt needs in culturally appropriate words, symbols, images, and music, which spoke to the depth of the Celtic consciousness and worldview. It involved both the imagination and the intellect, and used analogies from daily life (for example, fire, wind, water, bread, light, dark) to engage the people through storytelling and

---

19. For the historical development of the Celtic Christian Movement, see S. Neill, *A History of Christian Missions* (Middlesex, England: Penguin, 1986); J. T. McNeill, *The Celtic Churches* (Chicago: University of Chicago Press, 1974); and I. Bradley, *The Celtic Way* (London: Darton Longman Todd, 1993).
20. Hunter, *The Celtic Way*, 56–75.
21. Ibid., 64.

other culturally relevant methods. Essentially, they endeavored to use communication processes that were culturally appropriate and that promoted the development of a deep spirituality and prayerful approach to life.

Ethos and *logos* combined to interact with the *pathos* of the people; that is, their emotional and motivational concerns. The Celts were passionate people who experienced and expressed the full range of human emotions. The gospel message connected with these emotions and concerns as the people discovered that their feelings mattered to the Christian God, that they could experience release from terror and other destructive emotions, and that the Christian way gave them opportunity to express their constructive emotions in culturally appropriate ways.[22]

Much of the unusual communicative power of the Celtic Christian movement is attributable to the presence of these three factors in its communicators and its communities.

The Importance of Community in the Conversion Process

The evangelistic methods used were based on a team approach, rather than an individual one, and emphasized the importance of community in the conversion process.

Whereas much contemporary evangelism focuses on one-to-one, individual approaches, Celtic Christians usually evangelized as teams by identifying with the people of a particular settlement in friendship, conversation, service, and witness. Monastic communities were established and were open to the people of the surrounding settlements, who were invited to participate in some of the personal and communal aspects of faith offered by the monks and other members of these communities. This experience enabled the people to understand more clearly the meaning of the Christian way, and to relate this to their daily lifestyle and social relationships. Monasticism thus became a major factor in the conversion process.

In contrasting the Celtic and Roman way of evangelism, John Finney notes that the Roman model offered a presentation of the gospel, called for a decision, and then welcomed the person into the fellowship of the church. In contrast, the Celtic model began with friendship and fellowship on the basis of ministry and discussion, and this led to an invitation to belief and commit-

---

22. Ibid., chaps. 5–6.

ment. Thus the Celtic way emphasizes *belonging* before *believing,* whereas the Roman way emphasizes *believing* as the primary and essential step.[23]

Attitude to Pagan Religions

While they proclaimed and defended a biblical understanding of the faith as expressed in the teachings of the church, and strenuously opposed paganism, the Celtic Christian leaders maintained a "religious friendly policy." They came to a people deeply influenced by pagan religious traditions that included belief in the divine presence in every part of nature, many gods and spirits, many sacred places, and many rituals and symbols to ensure protection, security, and fertility. These traditions were propagated by powerful religious leaders, most notably the Druids, who guarded their secret knowledge, thus ensuring their power and control over the people.

In confronting pagan religions, Christian leaders sometimes engaged in confrontational "power encounters," but this was not the main policy. Rather, by the use of the spiritual gift of discernment, they were sensitive to the presence of good and evil in people and places. They encouraged the good and combated the evil with prayer, preaching, and teaching.

> They affirmed and built on every positive indigenous feature they could. . . . They affirmed their love for creation. They retained and Christianised some of the prior religious holy days, festivals, ceremonies, and sacred sites, thereby grafting the new onto the old. . . . Celtic Christianity preferred continuity rather than discontinuity, inclusion rather than exclusion.[24]

This religious friendly approach to tribal paganism was very effective.[25] "They understood their adversaries sufficiently well that they knew how to bring the gospel in ways that were powerfully winsome."[26]

---

23. Cited in Hunter, 53–55.
24. Ibid., 92.
25. Cf. Neill, "The Gregorian Mission Policy in S.E. England," in Neill, *A History of Christian Missions,* 59ff.
26. Robinson, *Rediscovering the Celts,* 176.

A Practical Spirituality

Celtic Christianity emphasized the reality of encountering the living God in the normal patterns of daily living, through the following means:

- An experience of community rather than individualism, where account-ability to and participation in the community provided a sense of purpose and belonging to the people of God.
- A spirituality in which God was encountered both in the community experience and in the personal journey within, an encounter which was then expressed in engagement with others in practical service and compassion.
- Liturgy and sacrament, which embraced the natural rhythms and festivals of life, thus enabling people to experience the material world as God's good gift. They also connected the material realm with an external reality that both included and transcended it, and that was revealed both in the grandeur of the creation and in the mystery of the Cross and the Resurrection. Through liturgy and sacrament, all of life was seen as sacred.
- An imaginative vision of Hope—the kingdom of God that they declared and demonstrated was the "core metaphor" for a new social imagination. The kingdom was both the vision and the goal that they prayed for and preached about.[27]

CONTEXTUALIZED MISSION TO THE MUSLIM WORLD

In terms of converts and church plantings, the Muslim world has been and remains one of the most difficult areas of Christian mission. The uneasy relationship between Islam and Christianity has produced economic and social disruption, military and religious domination, and deep pain, resentment, and alienation. However, despite these realities, there has been a steady and extensive Christian influence in the Muslim world, far more than the actual number of converts would suggest.[28] This steady work has been expressed through

27. Ibid., 188–94.
28. For the historical development of Christian mission to the Muslim world, see K. S. Latourette, *A History of the Expansion of Christianity,* vol. 6 (Grand Rapids: Zondervan, 1970); S. Neill, *A History of Christian Mission;* and L. Vander Werff, *Christian Mission to Muslims: The Record* (Pasadena, Calif.: William Carey Library, 1977).

many devoted individuals and groups, offering many examples of a "contextualized missionary approach," such as the work of Francis of Assisi (1182–1226) and Ramon Lull (1235–1315) in the thirteenth century, and Samuel Zwemer (1867–1952) in the twentieth century.

Francis of Assisi

A new dimension in the missionary methods of the church began with the establishment of two great missionary orders, the Franciscans and the Dominicans, replacing the monastery as the primary agent of mission. Until the foundation of the Jesuit order in the sixteenth and seventeenth centuries, the Franciscans and Dominicans held the central place in the missionary practice of the church.

Under Francis's influence, the Franciscans brought a simplicity and joy to mission, which released new forces for the service of the poor and needy. The influence of Dominic (1170–1221) emphasized intellectual competence in missions devoted to the conversion of heretics and pagans, especially through the work of preaching, debate, and discussion.

Francis's understanding of the Muslim people, and his practice of mission as living the gospel, contrasted sharply with that of the church of his day, which was committed to the use of force through the Crusades to combat the threat of Islam.

> Francis' view of the Mohammedan was diametrically opposed to that of his contemporaries. . . . When he read in the gospel that he must love all mankind, he found it impossible to reconcile that with aggression and killing. . . . He felt that the Mohammedan, enemy or not, was his brother and that one didn't kill one's brother to obtain a holy objective. He wanted to bring them his most precious possession, the gospel. He was filled with the conviction, extraordinary for his day, that God loved the Mohammedans more than he loved his tomb. And that possession of the holy land was not worth the death of a single Mohammendan.[29]

Francis's missionary practice was based on the following principles:

---

29. M. Mehren, "Francis of Assisi: Reconciliation with God, Humanity and Creation," *Missionalia* 19, no. 3 (November 1991): 187.

- Missions flowed from a theology that focused on the need for reconciliation—which bound all humanity together, and in which all were equal. Every person needed a fourfold reconciliation: with God as Creator and Savior, with others (that is, with humanity), with the creation, and with oneself. The recognition of our sinful condition, our "dark shadow," and the experience of salvation, healing, and forgiveness, led to a freedom to accept the dark shadow of others without indulging the need to project our shadow—our conflicts and hurts—onto others. That freedom allowed those so forgiven to reach out to others, and to allow God's unconditional love to flow through them to the world. All are "brothers and sisters"—people; animals; the elements of fire, water, air; the sun, moon, stars—all declare the glory of God and are to be respected and honored, and should not be possessed or exploited.[30] This "universal fraternity," in which reconciliation is more important than division, was an invitation to be open to a universe of sharing, and produced a very practical "earth-centered and people-focused" missionary methodology.
- Missions as a work was practiced as "presence and witness," with a strong emphasis on actions and attitudes that revealed the love of God in Jesus. Over against the prevailing mode of "communication through preaching," the rule of Francis was that "all the brothers should preach by their deeds with a minimum of words," because "it was in a few words that the Lord preached while on earth." Words were valuable but could also turn people to "a religion and holiness outwardly apparent to people." Instead, Francis exemplified and pointed people to "a religion and holiness in the interior spirit."[31]
- Mission was based on respect for the Muslim people as those who submit to Allah. Francis recognized the Muslim "other" as brother or sister, and sought to understand what was best and central in their religion, rather than focusing on the negatives. The prevailing mode of witness to Muslims was through verbal disputation in which both Christians and Muslims sought to convince the other of the truth of their respective religion. This often resulted in rancor and separation rather than strengthening and healing relationships.
- Mission was to be conducted in love and nonviolence, rather than the

---

30. Ibid., 188–89.
31. A. Dries, "Mission and Marginalisation: The Franciscan Heritage," *Missiology* 25 (1998): 6.

"battle mentality" of the Crusaders. Repudiating *force* as a means to either destroy the Muslims or bring them to Christian conversion, Francis offered the path of lowly service and a message of indiscriminate love and salvation for all. Whereas the powerful church offered rewards to all warriors for Christ, and promised that the Muslim darkness would be overcome by the power of the Cross as exercised through the sword, Francis offered the Cross as a symbol of reconciliation and divine love for all. Whereas the church supported mercenaries, Francis offered messengers of mercy.[32]

• Presence and witness was taken literally, so Francis traveled to and met with Muslim leaders. On Whitsun 1219, after a failed military assault by the Crusaders, Francis came to the enemy camp, with a single companion and no weapon but the power of love, to persuade the Sultan of the truth of the Christian faith. This meeting profoundly influenced both men, as well as Christian-Muslim relationships, beginning a process that would lead to the declaration by Pope Innocent IV (1243–1250) that "war should not be declared to the Saracens with the goal of converting them to Christianity." The actual presence of Francis "in the camp of the enemy" pointed to a new approach that was a radical departure from the accepted missionary practice of the church. It was a reaffirmation of the policy of going to those outside the church, not with a sword to destroy, but with the power of love to serve and show the way of Christ.[33]

Ramon Lull

Ramon Lull lived in a period when the military Crusades as a missionary weapon were being replaced by a new spiritual emphasis and methodology. While the Franciscans continued to expand their ministries according to the characteristics of their founder, the Dominicans emphasized "missions by controversy," in which doctrinal preaching and debate were the main weapons. To do this effectively required a methodical and intense study of Muslim culture, language, and religion. But this emphasis on learning and "intellectual combat"

---

32. A contemporary evaluation of Francis's methodology and its significance for contemporary Christian-Muslim relationships is given by C. A. Mallouhi in *Waging Peace on Islam* (London: Monarch, 2000).

33. Ibid., chap. 8.

did not replace the continuing need for truly spiritual character. Echoing Francis, Dominic exhorted his followers, "The adversaries of truth must be convinced by examples of humility, patience, religion, and all the virtues."[34]

Lull, a gallant and frivolous courtier, experienced a profound conversion when he was thirty, and devoted his life to missions among the Muslim people. Like Francis, he was convinced of the need for a spiritual crusade, and his great desire was to win the Muslim leaders to faith. To do this effectively, Lull became a disciple of the Dominican pattern and recognized the need for rigorous intellectual training. However, such training was not his main weapon. Overriding all other factors was the experience of divine love that had saved him, which required a total response, even to the point of martyrdom, in a consuming missionary concern for all people.

Lull vowed himself to the conversion of all the nations, emphasizing the ideal of the peaceful conquest of souls.[35] He was a living synthesis of the best of Franciscan and Dominican missionary thought and practice and propounded a theology and methodology of evangelization that included many of the ideas and practices included in "contextualization." His methodology included apologetic, educational, and evangelistic approaches, and was expressed in the following principles:[36]

- Conversion must be a work of love, an overflowing of our love for Christ and others. Love must be based on understanding, because nothing can be truly loved until it is first known.
- Conversion must be an act of freedom, not coercion. Missionaries will convert the world, not by force but "by preaching the gospel, and also shedding tears and blood, and with great effort and a hard death."
- The gospel must be presented in a manner and language that is meaningful to those who receive it. Hence, the need for a thorough understanding of people's beliefs, customs, and philosophy; that is, their worldview. To this end, Lull was instrumental in establishing several language schools in Europe.

---

34. R. Sugranyos de Franch, "The Springtime of Missions in the 13th Century," *History's Lessons for Tomorrow's Mission* (Geneva, Switzerland: World's Student Christian Federation, 1960).
35. Details of Lull's conversion and missionary endeavors given in Latourette, *A History of the Expansion of Christianity*, 6.321f.; R. Tucker, *From Jerusalem to Irian Jaya* (Grand Rapids: Zondervan, 1983), 52–57; and Neill, *A History of Christian Missions*, 114–17.
36. de Franch, "The Springtime of Missions in the 13th Century," 80–81.

- Methods of presentation must be related to the people's way of reasoning, and this meant acquiring an expertise in the use of dialogue, debate, and preaching in the Muslim context. But these must be infused by an attitude of love and respect for all people.

Samuel Zwemer

Designated as "a prince among missionaries," and "the apostle to Islam," Zwemer's advocacy of missions and his example left a powerful legacy for the church. His long missionary career covered four main periods:

1888–1912	Founder and pioneer in the Arabian Mission
1912–1928	Literary and preaching evangelist and ecumenical leader
1929–1938	Professor of the History of Religion and Christian Mission at Princeton Theological Seminary
1939–1952	Retired from Princeton "to go into active service" of writing, preaching, and teaching[37]

Zwemer followed the paths of Francis and Lull, combining an intense love for the Muslim people with a rigorous intellectual understanding of Muslim religion and culture. He had a prodigious literary output, believing that "no agency can penetrate Islam so deeply, abide so persistently, witness so daringly, and influence so irresistibly as the printed page." During his lifetime he wrote more than fifty books, and hundreds of articles, and his major accomplishment was *The Moslem World,* a journal dedicated to "promote understanding in missions to Muslims," which he edited for more than thirty-six years.[38]

Zwemer's missionary practice and methodology can be summarized as follows:[39]

---

37. Details of Zwemer's life and missionary career given in Tucker, *From Jerusalem to Irian Jaya,* 276–80; L. Vander Werff, "Our Muslim Neighbours: The Contribution of Samuel Zwemer to Christian Mission," *Missiology* 10 (April 1982): 185–97; C. J. Wilson, "The Epic of Samuel Zwemer," *The Muslim World* 57, no. 2 (1957): 79–93; and idem, "The Legacy of Samuel Zwemer," *International Bulletin of Missionary Research* 10 (July 1986): 117–21.
38. Wilson, "Epic of Samuel Zwemer," 88–90; and Vander Werff, "Our Muslim Neighbours," 191.
39. Vander Werff, "Our Muslim Neighbours," 188–97.

- Missions must be church-based; that is, the church is the *agent* of mission. Through its life as the covenant people of God, the church must exhibit the gospel of reconciliation and seek to be the incarnational presence of Christ. The church, the local manifestation of the kingdom of God, must also be the goal of missions. Evangelism must result in the visible presence of the church; therefore, the aim of all Zwemer's missionary endeavors was to establish a truly indigenous "contextual" church.

- Knowledge of the Muslim people is vital. Following the example of Lull, Zwemer emphasized that the church must "study those to whom it is sent." Consequently, he sought to understand all aspects of Muslim culture that would promote effective transmission of the gospel.

- Develop a sympathetic approach to Muslim religious beliefs and practices. In his early missionary career, Zwemer advocated the goal of "radical displacement," which placed Christianity over against all non-Christian systems. He argued for the supremacy of Christ over Muhammad, and for the disintegration of Islam. From 1916 onward, his approach became more people-centered and Christocentric. Without in any way compromising his critique of Islam as a system, he wrote empathetically of Muslims as people seeking after God. He saw Islam as offering partial truths, which can only be fulfilled in Christ, who satisfies the hunger and aspirations expressed in the Muslim "way." But this respect did not lead to an acceptance of Islam as the true way of salvation. This was found only in Jesus Christ, who is God's measure to evaluate all religious activity.

- Dialogue and discussion are valuable methods for clarifying the gospel to Muslim people, and for comparing and contrasting Muslim and Christian beliefs. Zwemer encouraged the use of writings from Muslim poets and mystics as connecting points or starting points for the gospel. He sought out and used every possible "key" in Muslim writing, beliefs, and styles of reasoning to open the way for a presentation of the "surpassing grandeur and beauty of the character of Jesus Christ."

- The key to Muslim evangelism is an "affectionate person-to-person relationship." Confrontation, debate, apologetics, books, and other literature were all helpful resources and methods, but "the human personality remains the best bridge for communicating the gospel."

The missionary principles of Francis, Lull, and Zwemer continue to influence contemporary missionary theory and practice, and offer a solid foundation for a truly contextual ministry.[40]

CONCLUSION

Missions history on all continents is replete with efforts to contextualize the gospel. Many of these efforts are recorded in the pages of missionary biographies and missions histories. Many more are yet to be recorded. These efforts have produced both affirmation and opposition as the church struggles with the tension of protecting the truth of the gospel and the church, and the need for a relevant contextual communication of the good news.

In reviewing the examples given, several common factors emerge: respect, understanding, identification, appropriate communication, cultural and religious sensitivity, empathy, and a consuming desire to understand other people, among others. These principles are expressed in an ancient Chinese poem that aptly summarizes many of the main factors of effective contextualization:

> Go to the people
> Live among them
> Learn from them
> Love them
> Start with what they know
> Build on what they have[41]

Today, new religious movements present a challenge to the church to "contextually incarnate" the gospel to enable people to authentically experience Jesus Christ. Church history offers the contemporary church many guidelines for encouragement and action.

---

40. Contemporary contextual approaches to Islam are given in P. Parshall, *New Paths in Muslim Evangelism* (Grand Rapids: Baker, 1980); idem, *Beyond the Mosque* (Grand Rapids: Baker, 1985; and idem, *The Last Frontier* (Quezon City, Philippines: Open Doors with Brother Andrew, 2000).
41. Cited in Hunter, *The Celtic Way,* 120; and D. Whiteman, *Melanesians and Missionaries* (Pasadena, Calif.: William Carey Library, 1983).

STUDY QUESTIONS

1. Discuss the significance of *ethos, logos,* and *pathos* for contemporary missions. Which of these are either overemphasized or underemphasized in the church?
2. Choose either Francis or Lull or Zwemer and discuss their relevance for "contextual" missions to new religious movements.
3. Evaluate the ancient Chinese poem as an "adequate guideline" for contextual missions. What action would be required to make this approach a reality in your own church or fellowship?
4. Investigate your local or regional area for the presence of alternative spiritualities or new religious movements, and evaluate the response of the church to these groups.
5. How would you apply the principles of *rejection, maintenance,* and *incorporation* to the presentation of the gospel in your own cultural situation?
6. To what extent is your local congregation, fellowship group, church denomination, or missions agency actively involved in a process of "critical contextualization"? How could understanding the history of your particular church or missions help in this?
7. Over the centuries, many missionaries have adopted a "religious-friendly" or "empathetic" approach to other spiritual paths, affirming and using any aspects of the other faith that could become "channels" or "keys" for the gospel, and seeking continuity rather than discontinuity (compare, for example, the approach of the Celtic missionaries or Samuel Zwemer). Is this a valid approach in the contemporary setting of religious pluralism, or a dangerous compromise that obscures the uniqueness of Jesus Christ and the truth of the gospel? Why?

Part 2

METHODOLOGICAL ISSUES

CHAPTER 3

HISTORY OF RELIGION AND MISSIOLOGY

Complementary Methodologies

TERRY C. MUCK

INTRODUCTION

The nineteenth century has been called the Great Century of Protestant missions.[1] During these roughly one hundred years, English, German, Scandinavian, and North American Protestant Christian missionaries fanned out across the world,[2] establishing successful missions agencies, both denominational and nondenominational, geographically local and worldwide.[3] This missions effort was truly an ecumenical endeavor—agreed upon in principle by the different denominations, though they differed in their execution of it.[4] Theoretical support for this catholic effort led to the founding of the scholarly discipline of *missiology*, called variously the *science of missions, study of missions,* or *philosophy of missions.*[5] By the end of the Great Century, missionaries, missions agency officials, and missiologists were meeting regularly to discuss issues of

---

1. Kenneth Cracknell, *Justice, Courtesy, and Love: Theologies and Missionaries Encountering World Religions 1846–1914* (London: Epworth, 1995), 2, 3.
2. Stephen Neill, *A History of Christian Missions* (New York: Viking-Penguin, 1986).
3. Kenneth S. Latourette, *A History of the Expansion of Christianity*, 7 vols. (New York: Harper and Brothers, 1937–45).
4. Wayne Detzler, "Seeds of Missiology in the German Erwekung," *Journal of the Evangelical Theological Society*, June 1995, 231–38.
5. J. H. Bavinck, *An Introduction to the Science of Missions* (Philadelphia: Presbyterian and Reformed, 1961). Bavinck popularized in missions circles the theological term "elenctic" to describe a theology that calls to repentance.

strategic and theoretical interest.[6] The Edinburgh Missions Conference in 1910 culminated this enormously productive activity.[7]

The nineteenth century also saw the founding of the so-called "scientific study of religion."[8] Led by Max Müller (1823–1900), the German-born Oxford professor of modern languages, and a Dutch religion scholar named C. P. Tiele, university scholars began theoretical and field work looking at the world's religions from historical and comparative points of view instead of a strictly theological point of view. These studies took an objective approach based on scientific naturalism, instead of a confessional approach based on a theistic understanding of the world.[9] At first, this science of religions methodology was shaped and practiced in the more traditional university departments of linguistics, archaeology, anthropology, biblical studies, and theology.[10] Eventually, it became a standard subdiscipline of the emerging social sciences of sociology and psychology.[11]

These scholars of religion produced an immense amount of work, ranging from linguistic studies of Hindu, Buddhist, and Confucian religious classics;[12] to anthropological studies of South Sea islanders that focused heavily on religion;[13] to history of religion studies of Middle Eastern religions such as Islam.[14] These scholars became at first an interdisciplinary fraternity of researchers, and by the end of the century had developed enough separate identity to hold the first worldwide conference of historians of religion in Paris in 1900.[15]

These two emerging scholarly disciplines, missiology and the scientific study of religions, did not develop independently, however. Indeed, many of

---

6. J. Verkuyl, *Contemporary Missiology: An Introduction* (Grand Rapids: Eerdmans, 1978), 341–68.
7. The book produced at this conference was titled, *The Missionary Message in Relation to Non-Christian Religions* (New York: Revell, 1910).
8. Eric Sharpe, *Comparative Religion: A History* (London: Duckworth, 1986).
9. Donald Wiebe, *The Politics of Religious Studies* (New York: St. Martins, 1999).
10. See, for example, the list of authors in the anthology by Jacques Waardenburg, *Classical Approaches to the Study of Religion: Aims, Methods and Theories of Research* (The Hague, Paris: Mouton, 1973).
11. Walter H. Capps, *Religious Studies: The Making of a Discipline* (Minneapolis: Fortress, 1995).
12. For example, James Legge, *The Chinese Classics* (Taipei, Republic of China: SMC, 1991).
13. For example, Bronislaw Malinowski, *Magic, Science and Religion* (New York: Doubleday, 1954).
14. For example, Nathan Soderblom, *The Living God* (London: Oxford, 1933).
15. Wiebe, *The Politics of Religious Studies*. The International Association of Historians of Religion (IAHR) traces its roots to this meeting.

the first proponents of the scientific study of religions held prestigious academic chairs of theology and biblical studies.[16] Their early writings reveal an interesting dipolar focus—on the one hand scientific, on the other hand theological.[17] To be sure, some of these early scholars of religion saw themselves as merely creating a scholarly alternative to missiology, either preparatory to or complementary with more confessional approaches.[18] Others, however, considered the scientific study of religion a replacement for missiology, and the proper way to study religion, at least when such study takes place in the context of the secular university[19] (even though the secular university of the day was practically a cloister compared with the secular university of today).[20] For their part, a small but increasingly outspoken group of missionaries and missiologists believed that the theological rationale of much missions practice was fatally flawed and that missiology itself needed a theological overhaul.[21] This spectrum of understanding about the science of missions (which was just becoming focused) and the study of religions (which had at last been articulated) produced an ambiguity about each that is impossible to deny and difficult to define—especially in the area of how they related to one another.

Arguably, this ambiguity produced a third approach to non-Christian religions, the interreligious dialogue movement. Because of its uncertain parentage and methodology, the dialogue movement has never achieved discipline status, but is better defined as a movement within both missiology and the science of religions—something of an extra-academic outworking of either.

---

16. There are many examples of this, but one who particularly exemplified the combination of religious-studies scholar, theologian, and even "denominational" official, was Nathan Soderblom. See Eric Sharpe, *Nathan Soderblom and the Study of Religion* (Chapel Hill, N.C.: University of North Carolina Press, 1990).

17. As Donald Wiebe has pointed out, Gerardus van der Leeuw exemplifies this in his two-volume *Religion in Essence and Manifestation* (London: George Allen and Unwin, 1938).

18. In this category, we might include early pioneers like William Robertson Smith, *Lectures on the Religion of the Semites* (n.p., 1889); and Friedrich C. G. Delitzsch, *Babel and Bible* (LaSalle, Ill.: Open Court, 1906).

19. For example, Roman Catholic theologian Wilhelm Schmidt, *The Origin and Growth of Religion* (New York: Cooper Square, 1972).

20. George Marsden, *The Outrageous Idea of Christian Scholarship* (New York: Oxford, 1997).

21. See especially Kenneth Cracknel, *Justice, Courtesy, and Love: Theologians and Missionaries Encountering World Religions 1846–1914* (London: Epworth, 1995). Particularly in need of change, Cracknel opines, are millennialism, millenarianism, radical intellectualist anti-idolatry, Calvinism, radical anti-intellectualist revivalism, and revivalism.

As a movement distinguished by the absence of either committed sectarianism or rigorous scholarship,[22] it eschews either blatant proselytizing or idealized but unobtainable objectivity in favor of dialogue when adherents of different religious traditions meet.[23] It argues that neither salvation nor publicly demonstrable truth is the most satisfactory goal of interreligious interchanges. Instead, the proper goal (the only achievable goal, some would say) is peaceful, productive coexistence with the religions of the world—pursuing harmony and unity with one another instead of competition, at least on some levels. If one reads the missiological and science of religion texts of the nineteenth century, one can often see signs of this third way—signs both endorsing and condemning it—bubbling up through the cracks.[24] Missiologists and scholars of religion rarely identified themselves fully with the interreligious movement, at least as a primary affiliation, but hundreds of them implicitly endorsed it through their attendance at the World's Parliament of Religions held in Chicago as a part of the World's Fair in 1893.[25]

Twentieth century scholars were interested in the increasingly common interchanges brought about by economic globalization, political interdependence, United Nations-mandated religious freedom, and pervasive multiculturalism. Theological missiology, scientific study of religions, and pragmatic/political interreligious dialogue offer discrete ideological, methodological, and sociological options that seem on some levels mutually exclusive but on other levels enticingly complementary. Their interaction has created within each discipline and movement a fundamentalist reaction that attempts to force a choice

---

22. One could make the argument that Chicago theologian David Tracy in his hermeneutical works such as *Plurality and Ambiguity* (San Francisco: Harper and Row, 1987) and *Blessed Rage for Order* (Minneapolis: Seabury, 1975) is providing philosophical support for the interreligious dialogue movement.

23. See Donald Swearer, *Dialogue: The Key to Understanding Other Religions* (Philadelphia: Westminster, 1977); and Leonard Swindler, ed., *Toward a Universal Theology of Religion* (Maryknoll, N.Y.: Orbis, 1987).

24. Max Müller, the founder of the science of religion, expressed regret at missing the Parliament: "There are few things which I so truly regret having missed as the great Parliament of Religions held in Chicago." From "The Real Significance of the Parliament of Religions," *The Arena*, December 1894, 1.

25. Richard Hughes Seager, *The World's Parliament of Religions: The East/West Encounter, Chicago, 1893* (Bloomington, Ind.: Indiana University, 1995); John Henry Burrows, ed., *The World's Parliament of Religions*, 2 vols. (Chicago: Parliament Publishing, 1893); and Eric Ziolkowski, ed., *A Museum of Faiths: Histories and Legacies of the 1893 World's Parliament of Religions* (Atlanta: Scholars, 1993).

in favor of pure missiology,[26] objective science of religions,[27] or humanistic interreligious dialogue.[28] To choose one of these options is seen as necessarily excluding the other two. None of these arguments can be dismissed out of hand. Yet the areas of possible complementarity are much more intriguing. Without dismissing the fundamentalist or foundationalist emphases out of hand, the possibility of complementarity is also worth exploring.

One way to initiate this exploration is to take serious note of the waxing and waning relationship between missiology and the science of religion. We should ask two primary questions, focusing especially on issues of method:

1. Why is there methodological ambiguity between missiology and the science of religion? How can they appear to be so similar, yet so different?
2. How should we deal with this ambiguity?

The ambiguity comes, I think, because it is difficult to draw distinct lines between how missiologists and religious studies scholars approach interreligious interchanges.[29] *Good* missiologists and *good* scientists of religion[30] both seek reliable and accurate information about the religious traditions they study. Both create explanatory theories about how that information—the history, beliefs, and practices of the religious tradition—influence and direct intra- and extra-group behavior and individual behaviors. Representatives from both disciplines write about how these psychological and sociological patterns of behavior have and are affecting the cultures in which the religious traditions exist. In addition, they do much more than merely gather information and create theory. Both missiologists and science of religion scholars vigorously defend the accuracy of their information and the explanatory power of their theories. And they are fervent champions of the legitimacy of the ways in which they have collected and

---

26. James Borland, "A Theologian Looks at the Gospel and World Religions," *Journal of the Evangelical Theological Society,* March 1990, 3–11.
27. Wiebe, *The Politics of Religious Studies.*
28. Swindler, *Toward a Universal Theology of Religion.*
29. The phrase "interreligious interchange" we began to use as co-chair of an American Academy of Religion consultation 1993–1996, "Issues in Interreligious Interchange," to describe the full range of contacts among the world's religions including mission, evangelism, dialogue, and social and political action.
30. By "good" I mean to acknowledge that there is no single way to describe either all missiologists or all scientists of religion.

analyzed their information. (Just try to disagree with either one.) Finally, both would argue for the implications of their work as they express themselves in the moral and ideological realms. These arguments may be implicit or explicit, and either in narrative form or simply by the way they structure their work (including especially the presuppositions they bring to the work in the first place). Yet it would be inaccurate, even foolish, to deny that there are distinct differences between what missiologists and science of religion scholars do. It will help to summarize what each does.

MISSIOLOGICAL METHODS

In examining *missiological methods*, we are limiting ourselves strictly to how missiologists study other religions. It seems that anyone who writes about missiology and its scholarly method must accept four verities as fact. First, that missiology as a scholarly exercise has "a long past but only a brief history."[31] Second, that defining the term *missiology* is problematic.[32] Third, that to speak of missiological methods at all is to run the danger of enervating the subject matter (the gospel).[33] Fourth, that modern missiologists are in ever present danger of having a "failure of nerve"[34] when it comes to following through on their discipline's presuppositions. As a way of attempting to summarize missiological methods vis-à-vis non-Christian religions, let's consider each of these four in turn.

---

31. Olav Myklebust used this phrase to describe missiology but says he borrowed it from Ebbinghaus's remark about the history of the psychology of religion. Olav Myklebust, *The Study of Missions in Theological Education*, 2 vol. (Oslo: Egede Instituttet, 1957), 285. Arthur Glasser uses a version of the phrase in his article on missiology in the *Evangelical Dictionary of Theology*, ed. Walter Elwell (Grand Rapids: Baker, 1984).
32. See Myklebust, *The Study of Missions in Theological Education*, 28–29.
33. Paul Hiebert makes the point this way: "We must move from discussing theology and the social sciences to a discussion of a biblical world view." Paul Hiebert, "Missiological Education for a Global Era," in *Missiological Education for the Twenty-first Century*, ed. J. Dudley Woodbery, Charles van Engen, and Edgar Elliston (Maryknoll, N.Y.: Orbis, 1996), 37.
34. As David Bosch quotes Max Warren in Bosch's *Transforming Mission: Paradigm Shifts in Theology of Mission* (Maryknoll, N.Y.: Orbis, 1991), 7. See also Paul Hiebert: "We in the West are in danger of losing our missionary nerve" ("Missiological Education for a Global Era," 36).

Early Development of Missiology

The church by its very nature is missions-centered.[35] In practice, it has always been missionary.[36] There has never been a shortage of thinking and writing on the missionary enterprise.[37] Still, it is only since the nineteenth century that the church has done second-order reflection on the history, theology, and practice of missions—that is, has practiced missiology.

The two thinkers who are most commonly given the titles "father" and "founder" of missiology are Joseph Schmidlan (1876–1944), professor of missiology at the University of Münster, who is widely recognized as the father of Roman Catholic missiology;[38] and one of his teachers, Gustav Warneck (1834–1910), who is considered the founder of Protestant missiology.[39] Thus, missiology as a scholarly discipline is, at most, 150 years old.

Use of the Term Missiology

A discipline that is only a century-and-a-half old will often have not worked through all of its methodological issues. Such is the case with missiology. Even something as basic as what to call the discipline has been rigorously debated. One term for it in German is *missionwissenschaft;* in French it is rendered *missiologie,* and in the Latin-based languages of Italian, Spanish, and Portuguese it is *missiologia.* But there are variations. Gustav Warneck called it *missionapologetik,*[40] Abraham Kuyper called it *elenchtik,*[41] Emil Brunner called it *eristik,*[42] and Paul Althaus called it *evangelische religionskunde.*[43] English

---

35. To paraphrase the Second Vatican Council's *Ad Gentes* (Decree on the Church's Missionary Activity of the Church): "The pilgrim church is missionary by her very nature." Walter Abbott, ed., *The Documents of Vatican II* (New York: Guild, 1966), 585.
36. "The Christian faith, I submit, is intrinsically missionary." Bosch, *Transforming Mission,* 8.
37. Histories of missions always go back to the Great Commission in Matthew, and to the apostle Paul. Some of the great writings on missiology include Thomas Aquinas's *Summa Contra Gentiles,* Raymond Lull's early writings, and many others before the great centuries of Christian mission ever began.
38. As he is called in the *Biographical Dictionary of Christian Mission,* ed. Gerald Anderson (New York: Macmillan, 1998).
39. Gustav Warneck's great works include *Modern Missions and Culture: Their Mutual Relations* (Edinburgh: James Gemmell, 1888).
40. Warneck, *Modern Missions and Culture,* 16.
41. Abraham Kuyper, *Encyclopedia of Sacred Theology* (New York: Scribners, 1898), 389ff.
42. Emil Brunner, *The Christian Doctrine of the Church, Faith, and the Consummation* (Philadelphia: Westminster, 1962), 106ff.
43. Paul Althaus, *The So-Called Kerygma and the Historical Jesus* (Edinburgh: Oliver and Boyd, 1959).

translations of these terms have included *study of missions, science of missions, philosophy of missions,* and *missiology.* Olav Myklebust recounts the above history in his two-volume *Study of Missions in Theological Education,* and finally settles on *missiology.*[44]

The most common definitions of the term seem easier: "The science of the cross-cultural communication of Christian faith."[45] Or a more elaborate definition: "The field of study which researches, records, and applies data relating to the biblical origins and history of the expansion of the Christian movement to anthropological principles and techniques for its further advancement."[46]

The Nature of Method in Missiological Research

One could question whether there is a characteristic method involved in missiological research vis-à-vis non-Christian religions. If *method* is "a normative pattern of recurrent and related operations yielding cumulative and progressive results,"[47] then it appears that missiological research has one. Most missiologists would acknowledge that their method begins at the point of faith in God—a faith that acknowledges God's initiating activity in creating and sustaining human life, including scholarly activity. God's initiating activity creates a sense of responsibility that precedes and sets bounds for all subsequent activity. It provides a mandate that precedes sensing, perceiving, thinking, and theorizing.

Missiologists often describe this in terms of "call." Perhaps the closest nontheological equivalent is Immanuel Levinas's description in philosophical terms of pre-reflective contact with the Other, a contact that in itself contains a responsibility for action. Karl Barth spoke of the mandate in revelatory terms: "Scripture always speaks of the commissioning and sending of the called man."[48]

Thus it is with a deep sense of responsibility, created by a God-initiated engagement and defined in large measure by the perceived needs of the church, that the missiologist begins to work. That mandate focuses the scholar's attention on the context. In our particular case, context involves analyzing the ex-

44. Myklebust, *The Study of Missions in Theological Education,* 28.
45. Walter Elwell, ed., *Evangelical Dictionary of Christian Theology* (Grand Rapids: Baker, 1984).
46. Ibid.
47. Bernard J. F. Lonergan, *Method in Theology* (Minneapolis: Seabury, 1972), 4.
48. Karl Barth, *Church Dogmatics* 14.3.D (Edinburgh: T. and T. Clark, 1972), 592.

pressions of non-Christian religions by individuals and communities of adherents. Scholars need to understand what the other religious tradition teaches and practices, as well as why and how. What purpose do the beliefs and practices serve? All this information must be collected and classified. These data constitute a large share of the "stuff" of missiology and make the missiologist an authority, as Andrew Walls notes: "The authority of the missionary expert as a writer lay in his eventually descriptive method."[49] Walls gives other examples of the superior descriptive quality of the work of missiologists regarding non-Christian religions.[50]

Once data is collected, the missiologist can begin *theory construction*. Actually, this is the most specifically theological step, in that it determines systematically what is true or false. It is worth noting that theology proper does not come into the effort until this point. As Paul Hiebert has noted, "Theology is the daughter of missions, not its mother."[51] Or as Martin Kahler has said, all theology is in the end missionial, born in the crucible of contact with other religions.[52]

The Responsibility of the Missiologist

The work of missiologists is shaped both in form and content by the context of the missions setting, and the missions setting in turn influences the particular method a missiologist will either develop or appropriate from other missiological sources. However, theology itself emerges from God's revelation in the world. The potential for missionary zeal to weaken is always a possibility, and such an occurrence can adversely affect the degree to which a missiologist places confidence in human effort and rationality, which is a condition referred to in some scholarly circles as the "failure of nerve."[53]

---

49. Andrew Walls, *The Missionary Movement in Church History* (Maryknoll, N.Y.: Orbis, 1996), 202.
50. Ibid., 200.
51. Actually he quotes Harvie Conn. See Hiebert, "Missiological Education for a Global Era," 38.
52. See Carl Braaten, "Martin Kahler on the Historical Biblical Christ," in *The Historical Jesus and the Kerygmatic Christ,* ed. and trans. Carl Braaten and R. A. Harrisville (Nashville: Abingdon, 1964), 79–105.
53. Hiebert, "Missiological Education for a Global Era," 36.

HISTORY OF RELIGIONS

Max Müller (1823–1900), an Oxford philologist, along with C. P. Tiele (1830–1902), a historian of religion at the university of Leiden and author of *Elements of the Science of Religion*,[54] founded the "science of religion" as a sociological discipline. Anyone who writes about this study must accept four verities: First, it is closely tied to the study of language. From Müller comes the paraphrase of Goethe that "He who knows one language, knows none."[55] Second, no one is quite sure what to call the scholarly study of religion.[56] Third, the science of religion is constantly in danger of slipping back into confessionalism, theology, or missiology.[57] Fourth, the modern discipline is experiencing its own "failure of nerve."[58]

Surveys of the history of this young discipline[59] always note that the scholarly study of religion may have only a brief history, but it has a long past, including writings on the plurality of religions from all the major cultures of the world.[60] Still, the study of a multiplicity of religions without predetermining whether they are true is a modern manifestation that can be credited specifically to Müller and Tiele's initiative.

The Scholarly Study of Religions

Both Müller and Tiele were partial to calling this new discipline the "science of religion," as shown by the titles of their books. *Science* had become for both the epitome of scholarly method. Tiele's chair at Leiden, however, was called a "history of religion" position, and Müller often used the term "comparative religion" to refer to his work.[61] In addition, one of Tiele's Dutch coun-

---

54. C. P. Tiele, *Elements of the Science of Religion*, 2 vols. (London: William Blackwood, 1897).
55. Max Müller, *Introduction to the Science of Religion* (London: Longmans, Green, 1873).
56. See Eric Sharpe, *Comparative Religion: A History* (London: Duckworth, 1986).
57. Robert Segal, *Religion and the Social Sciences* (Atlanta: Scholars Press, 1989).
58. Donald Wiebe uses the phrase in an article "The Failure of Nerve in the Academic Study of Religion" in *The Politics of Religious Studies*, 141–62. Wiebe says he borrowed the term from Gilbert Murray, author of *Five Stages of Greek Religion* (New York: Columbia, 1925). For Murray the "failure of nerve" was a loss of confidence in human effort and rationality. This use is consistent with how Wiebe uses it, but, as he notes, other religious studies scholars, such as Carl Raschke, Eric Sharpe, and J. C. McLellan, use it in varying ways.
59. Walter Capps, *Religious Studies: The Making of a Discipline* (Minneapolis: Fortress, 1995).
60. David George Mullan, *Religious Pluralism in the West* (Oxford: Blackwell, 1998).
61. See, for example, Max Müller, introduction to *Chips from a German Workshop*, vol. 1, *Essays on the Science of Religion* (Chico, Calif.: Scholars Press, 1985), 1:vii–xxxiii, where he uses "science of religion" and "comparative religion" interchangeably.

trymen, Gerardus van der Leeuw, adopted from philosopher Edward Husserl a methodology called phenomenology and applied it to religious studies (a common modern term).[62] The phenomenology of religion attempts to study the essence of religious events in and of themselves by bracketing (epoch) one's own beliefs and feelings about those events.[63] The most common way of referring to the discipline today is religious studies.

Often, however, "history of religion" is used as an umbrella term, as in the *HarperCollins Dictionary of Religion* definition: "The academic study of religion from either a comparative, a phenomenological, or a historical point of view."[64] Although we have chosen to use the term history of religion in this chapter, it is interchangeable with the science of religion, religious studies, or even the scholarly study of religion.

Method in the Study of Religions

One can easily get the sense from reading in this nascent field that method is all there is to it. I think the reason for this is that scholars of religion do many of the same things that missiologists (and theologians) do when it comes to examining other religions. However, in their concern to be seen as distinct from missiologists, they point to their well-defined method as a distinguishing feature.

Historians of religion begin with the presuppositions of modern science: the reality of the material world, the reliability of time and space, and the rationality of the human observer. Religion intrudes upon the human senses as an important, universal element of human existence. If one is paying attention at all, one pays at least some attention to religion.[65]

As part of the phenomenal world, religion raises questions about origin, function, and purpose that the scholar of religion attempts to answer. The data collected by our senses are processed by our minds. Classification leads to hypothesis. Hypothesis leads to testing. Results lead to theory formation.

---

62. Gerardus van der Leeuw, *Religion in Essence and Manifestation,* 2 vols. (New York: Harper Torchbooks, 1963), 2.671–79.
63. Ibid., 683–89.
64. Jonathan Z. Smith, ed., *HarperCollins Dictionary of Religion* (San Francisco: Harper Collins, 1998).
65. Bernard Lonergan, *Insight: A Study of Human Understanding* (San Francisco: Harper Collins, 1978), xxv–xxvi.

Theories are evaluated according to standards of truth and error. In short, scholars of religion do what scientists do.[66]

Like scientists, historians of religion see their work as contributing to the flourishing of humanity, especially in the arena of education. They are vigorous in preaching the truth of their theories and advocating the value of the knowledge that their method produces. They feel responsible for acting on the basis of their discoveries, although the nature of that action varies widely from scholar to scholar and finding to finding.[67] Responsibility for the historian of religion is not only shaped by his or her findings, but is created by them.

It is common at this point in the discussion of religious studies methodology to stop and note that the real difficulty of using the scientific method to study religion comes from the unique nature of religious transcendence. Because God (or some other transcendent principle) is by definition not amenable to scientific examination, God cannot be evaluated—only the behavioral effects of human belief in God can be observed.[68] Some scholars advocate an agnostic approach to this question.[69] Others consider an acceptance of an *a priori* understanding of the truth of the transcendent realm a basic requirement for the proper understanding of religion.[70] Still others advocate a subjective methodology that emphasizes human experience of the transcendent.[71]

Although this is an important issue,[72] it is not as methodologically significant as is often suggested. All scholarly methods, in choosing to measure certain features of reality, devise procedures that measure those features but cannot measure other features. A chemical laboratory experiment, for example, measures the interaction of molecules but not the effect the cost of laboratory equipment has on the overall design of the experiment. There's nothing remarkable about this observation, really, but it is sometimes overlooked. In developing a methodology for the scientific study of religion, the question is not *whether* certain features of religion are unmeasurable because of the methodology adopted but *which* features are eliminated by each method. Again,

---

66. See especially Wiebe, *The Politics of Religious Studies.*
67. Lonergan, *Method in Theology,* 8–15.
68. Segal, *Religion and the Social Sciences.*
69. Ibid., 5–29.
70. Mircea Eliade, *Sacred and Profane: The Nature of Religion* (New York: Harcourt, Brace, 1959).
71. Rudolf Otto, *The Idea of the Holy* (London: Oxford, 1923).
72. And it generates other important issues such as the *sui generis* character of religion and the social construction of the concept of religion itself.

this is not unique to religion but is true of any methodology designed to measure anything. It is simply a fact of the limits of human observation.[73]

The Problem of Conflicting Methods

Of course, certain scholars become very attached to methods and will argue for them. This is appropriate, at least to some extent. The range of method is not infinitely elastic; method must bridge the gap between what is being measured and the kind of information sought. One cannot interview molecules, for example, to gather information about their nature. Still, when a particularly powerful method—usually some version of the scientific method—has been successful in producing reliable data and useful theory and someone proposes an alternative method to explore neglected aspects of a subject, the innovators are often accused of having a failure of nerve. Such is the case in religious studies.[74]

As with religious studies, resistance to new innovations exists within missiology, stirring what can best be described as "method wars," differences over what methods to use in doing scholarly work. In a sense, these *internal* battles do more good than harm in that they force adjustments in methodological approach.

However, in spite of the positive benefits that come out of methodological disagreements, such conflicts do inflict damage to the overall missiological enterprise when they occur between disciplines where they escalate into all-or-nothing battles.[75]

One solution to help us avoid methodological bias would be to find some

---

73. Lonergan, *Insight.*
74. Ninian Smart, *The Religious Experience of Mankind* (New York: Scribners, 1969).
75. As an example of this phenomenon, consider the difficulties that sending agencies often encounter in knowing how to position themselves vis-à-vis the religious groups to which they are sending missionaries. When one of the great figures of Christian mission history, August Hermann Franke, was head of the Danish-Halle Mission at Tranzebar, he refused to allow a fine piece of scholarly religious study, a manuscript titled "Genealogy of the Malabarian Gods," by one of his agency's missionaries, Ziegenbalg, to be published in Germany: "While I commend the zeal devoted to this study of 'pagan theology,' it is not necessarily commendable or useful to make this subject matter available in print to the Christian public in Europe." The study was eventually published 152 years later in Madras. Hans-Werner Gensichen, "Daring in Order to Know: The Contribution of Christian Missionaries to the Understanding of Hinduism 1550–1850," *Indian Church History Review,* December 1986, 84.

universal methodological principles against which competing methodologies could be measured and affirmed, denounced, or adjusted. One pattern of such universals is offered by Roman Catholic theologian Bernard Lonergan.[76]

Lonergan's beginning two premises include the observations we have already made that methods differ according to the nature of their subject matter and that methods must be both conscious and intentional. As "normative patterns of recurrent and related operations yielding current and progressive results," methods are not true in and of themselves but only to the extent that they open a defined body of subject matter to systematic examinations that yield well-defined information. Methods must be custom-made to fit their subject matter.

Still, method construction must be generated within certain parameters. It is not an unrestricted intellectual potluck. The structure and capacity of human rationality limit both what we can know and how we can know it. As Lonergan analyzes it, these human structures and limitations can be discussed in terms of four elements of what he calls "transcendental method."

The first of these four elements he calls intention/attention.[77] Human beings are conscious and thus experience the world. Our senses and the impressions they produce demand attention.[78] Although we, like the animals, can and do know subconsciously, without attending, one can talk about method *per se* only in the context of conscious, intentional activity.

Second, our attention demands that we ask questions of the data we receive. (We might call this intelligence, or seeking to understand.) We ask basic questions, such as the classic who, what, when, where, and why.

Third, after we have "understood" the data, we judge them as true or false, useful or not, coherent or nonsensical. We sometimes call this element *reasonableness*. We ask the questions concerning the reality of our "experienced experience and understanding."[79]

Fourth, we decide on a course of action appropriate to our experience, understanding, and reasonableness. Lonergan calls this *responsibility*. Experiencing, understanding, and deciding create the need for action, even if the action is purely mental. Knowledge is not inert.

---

76. Lonergan, *Method in Theology*, 3–25.
77. Ibid., 15.
78. Simone Weil, "Reflection on the Right Use of School Studies with a View to the Love of God," in *Waiting on God* (London: Fortana, 1950), 66–76, talks about attention as a spiritual discipline.
79. Lonergan, *Method in Theology*, 15.

It is important to emphasize that these four elements are not in and of themselves a method of knowing. Although we can attempt to describe them theoretically, as we have in the last four paragraphs, they are meaningless apart from historical/cultural expressions. Method can only be context- or discipline-specific.

It is also important to emphasize that these four elements are not strictly hierarchical in occurrence; instead, they must be considered as a simultaneous, interactive unity. When they are made concrete within a context, a specific order may be appropriate for teaching purposes, or even distinctive for that particular methodology. But that does not mean that the reality to which they refer is so ordered. As Gordon Kaufman points out in *An Essay on Theological Method*, there is a difference between the "order of being" and the "order of knowing."[80]

Finally, it is important to emphasize that the true key to "knowing" about these four elements of transcendental method is to observe and reflect on them in our own mental processes. Although this may appear to rank subjective knowing over objective knowing, it is really "prior" to either. Because Lonergan emphasizes the most basic elements, to reflect on them either naturally or effectively would be to create a prior method, a meta-method.[81]

How can insight into these four elements and three conditions help us understand the relationship between missiological methodology and history of religions methodology? Let's assume for a moment that both methodologies contain all four elements of Lonergan's transcendental method. In other words, let's stipulate Lonergan's argument. We can see some immediate benefit to this in beginning an answer to the first of our questions: Why do missiological methodology and history of religion seem so similar and yet so different? If we accept Lonergan's argument, the two methodologies are *similar* because they are valid methods, each containing the four universal elements of the transcendental method. I would like to further suggest, however, that they appear so *different* because when the four universals—attention, intelligence, reasonableness, and responsibility—are operationalized in a concrete methodology, the relative emphasis on the order of the four elements changes dramatically.[82]

---

80. Gordon Kaufman, *An Essay on Theological Method*, 3d ed. (Atlanta: Scholars Press, 1995), 5.
81. Lonergan, *Method in Theology*, 16.
82. It may also be obvious that this is the point at which I move beyond Lonergan in a way he does not go (although I don't know that he would be opposed to it), but in case it is not obvious, I state it here.

Whereas for historians of religion they move pretty much in the order that Lonergan discusses them, for missiologists the fourth responsibility seems to become the first—the demands of God's initiating revelatory activity creates a course of action that then determines the nature of attending, understanding, and judging.

This observation would be consistent with Longeran's statements that the four elements in the abstract have no specific hierarchical order and that context alone determines how they are objectified and operationalized. And obviously it would allow us to account methodologically for what seems an *a priori* Christian demand for faith in the knowing process.

Further, I think this way of looking at the two methodologies allows us to create the conditions under which both could be seen as productive forms of knowing, in theory compatible with one another. But before we address the question of compatibility, we must first take a short excursus to explore the various ways in which missiology and history of religion have been seen as relating to one another.

MISSIOLOGY AND THE HISTORY OF RELIGION

There have been different views of how missiology and the history of religion fit together—or don't fit together. Three main opinions have emerged: epistemological exclusivism, qualified compatibility, and complementarity. We will discuss each in turn.

Exclusivism

Some consider the relationship between history of religion and missiology to be either-or: There is only one way to study and understand religion, and one either chooses the missiological method or the history of religion method.

Fundamentalist understandings of missions usually fall in this either-or category.[83] They advocate approaching all knowledge through a biblical worldview that relies heavily on a revelatory model of truth. Little attempt is made to incorporate into this understanding the findings of either the hu-

---

83. Karl Barth's theology is often cited as justification for this approach. See Bruce McCormack, "Revelation and History in Transfoundationalist Perspective: Karl Barth's Theological Epistemology in Conversation with a Schleiermacherian Tradition," *Journal of Religion*, January 1998, 18–37.

manities or social sciences, both of which are suspect largely because of their methodological refusal to acknowledge the Bible as God's primary mode of communicating truth to us.[84] In an either-or approach, any attempt to understand other religions sympathetically or objectively is seen as either misguided or missing the point. There are numerous missiologists who take this position. But there are also historians of religion who take this basic oppositional stance.

A religious studies scholar who seems to argue against the very idea of a rationally defensible religious methodology is Russell T. McCutcheon.[85] In a suggestively titled book, *Manufacturing Religion: The Discourse on Sui Generis Religion and the Politics of Nostalgia*, McCutcheon uses an approach that relies heavily on sociology of knowledge and critical school arguments by Michel Foucault to argue that religion itself, including Christianity, is a socially constructed reality, an ideology created not to espouse truth but to defend the status quo.[86] In such an understanding, any conception of religion as a unique *(sui generis)* field of study that demands a methodology matching its unique subject matter is simply disguising its real intent, which is "privileging" itself.[87] Although he spends more time unmasking the duplicitous nature and role of so-called theological understanding than he does in identifying his own understanding, he seems to be basically defending Western Enlightenment rationality: If it cannot be shown by the scientific method, it isn't true.[88]

---

84. A fascinating and scholarly approach to this, especially in relation to the social sciences, is John Milbank's work in *Theology and Social Theory* (Oxford: Blackwell, 1990). And although the theory is less developed, an ecclesiastical version of this approach is taken by the Gospel and Our Culture Network movement in the United States.

85. Many other versions of this general argument exist, of course. A fascinating way to gain insight into the issue is to follow the discussion as represented in *The Council of Societies for the Study of Religion Bulletin*, especially the April 1993, February 1994, November 1994, and September 1997 issues, which contain articles by Francis Schussler Fiorenza, Donald Wiebe, Arvind Sharma, Eric Sharpe, Jonathan Smith, Robert Segal, Delwin Brown, and Ninian Smart.

86. Russell McCutcheon, *Manufacturing Religion: The Discourse on Sui Generis Religion and the Politics of Nostalgia* (Oxford: Oxford University Press, 1997).

87. See Michel Foucault, *The Archaeology of Knowledge and the Discourse on Language* (New York: Pantheon, 1972).

88. In a rather feisty review of this book ("Some Confusions about Critical Intelligence," *Journal of the American Academy of Religion* 66, no. 4, 893–95), Paul Griffiths makes this very point.

Qualified Compatibility

Others have seen the relationship between missiology and history of religion to be somewhat analogous to Martin Luther's "two spheres" theory of church and state. Each methodology is appropriate for measuring different things in different realms. The founder of the science of religion, Max Müller, would fall into this category.[89] Although Müller was unquestionably an advocate of a new way of looking at the religions of the world, he never lost sight of the relationship, for the Christian, of the science of religion to missions. In the introduction to the first volume of his *Chips from a German Workshop*, Müller lists five reasons the science of religion is important.[90] First is the knowledge gained of the other religions—knowledge for knowledge's sake. Second is the help it will give to missionaries to place Christianity in the context of all the world's religions. Third is the empathy for and solidarity with all the world's peoples that the study will create. Fourth is recognition that all religions go through processes of decay in spite of their highest ideals. Fifth, one learns by studying the world religions that all are seeking to find the truth. In four of these five reasons, Müller specifically mentions how this knowledge might affect missionaries. In so doing he accomplishes three things: (1) He does not disavow a missionary's advocacy work; (2) he makes it clear that the science of religions is not in the business of advocating Christianity, but instead seeks for truth; and (3) he makes it clear that even though the science of religions is quite different from missions, the science of religions provides missionaries with valuable information to make them more faithful.

Hendrik Kraemer, the dominant voice in missions theology from 1938 to 1960, was a missiologist who would fall in the two-spheres category. Kraemer was a Dutch missiologist who wrote an important book, *The Christian Message in a Non-Christian World,* for the meeting of the International Missionary Conference at Tambaram (Madras) in 1938.[91] In *The Christian Message,* Kraemer distinguishes sharply between the two spheres, calling one "biblical realism," and the other the worldview of the world's religions. Theologically,

---

89. As do Rudolf Otto, Mircea Eliade, Ninian Smart, and others, although each takes a very distinctive approach. For a popular treatment of one possible variety of this position, see Patrick Ryan, "Homage to a Mule and a Secretary," *America,* 1 March 1997, 12–18.
90. Müller, *Chips from a German Workshop,* vol. 1, *Essays on the Science of Religion,* vii–xxxiii.
91. Hendrik Kraemer, *The Christian Message in a Non-Christian World* (Grand Rapids: Kregel, 1938).

both Karl Barth and Emil Brunner, two prominent theologians of his day, heavily influenced Kraemer. However, he also echoed many of Müller's themes, calling for dispassionate understanding of other religions by Christian missionaries, and searching for "points of contact" between and among the religions.[92] He was a strong advocate of interreligious dialogue.

The two-spheres theory of the relationship between missiology and history of religion has been extremely popular. Setting out spheres offers an alternative to the either-or position of scientists of religion like McCutcheon and the separatist missiologists.[93] It has the advantage of incorporating, to some degree, religious commitment with a dedication to scientific objectivity and the empathic understanding of the historians of religion. It allows dialogue. Neither of these positions, however, has proved to be adequate in light of the radical turns of twentieth century philosophy and epistemology—namely subjectivity, language determinism, multiculturalism, and, most recently, postmodernism. In order to cope with these intellectual and cultural pressures, a third alternative is needed.

Unifying Complementarity

It may be that the relationship between missiological and history of religion methodologies is complementary in a much more radical sense than the complementary leanings of the two-spheres theorists. I would like to briefly outline a position that I call complementarity, a way of looking at seemingly irreconcilable methodologies in a way that does justice to both and—more importantly—to truth. In outlining this position, we move toward attempting an answer to our second main question of this chapter: How should we deal with the apparent ambiguity between missiological method and history of religion method?

---

92. Ibid., 130–41, 299–307.
93. One could argue for another version of the two-spheres theory, which we might call the "multi-methodological view," a position that argues that the more methodologies the better. We haven't described this specific position, which is really the position of the American Academy of Religion in the United States, because just as arguments in favor of polytheism are much the same in form as arguments for dualism, so the arguments for multi-methodologies run along pretty much the same lines as arguments for the two-spheres approach.

COMPLEMENTARITY: DEALING WITH THE AMBIGUITY?

Complementarity is a methodological principle inspired by a physics phenomenon first articulated by Niels Bohr in the 1920s. Let me take just a minute to describe Bohr's discovery, with the caveat that I am not at all sure that what I end up with in talking about complementarity in this hermeneutical sense is really true to Bohr's hypothesis/discovery.

In 1927, Bohr, a world-renowned quantum physicist, gave an address at Lake Como, Italy, in an attempt to describe a difficult problem of measurement having to do with the nature of light.[94] Valid, sophisticated experiments had been done and repeated that showed that light behaved both as a wave and as particles. These are incompatible findings. Neither classical nor quantum physics allowed this kind of ambiguity. Bohr's conclusion was that the ambiguity came from not factoring in the energy and understanding provided in the mechanisms of the measurement itself; that is, the scientist and the scientist's tools. When one sets up an experiment to measure the wave properties of light, the scientist, the experimental design, and the equipment used in the experiment become integral parts of the phenomenon to be observed. The experiment itself changes the phenomenon being measured.

The experimental design and the changes imposed in the phenomenon allow certain properties of the phenomenon to be measured, but other properties can no longer be objectively studied. One can observe (and measure) the wave properties of light with one type of experimental design; and with another experimental design, one can observe and measure the particle properties of light; but one cannot measure both wave and particle properties at the same time. Bohr called this phenomenon *complementarity*.

I have read Bohr's 1927 address, and I have read a good deal of the commentary written about his theory.[95] Although I am not a quantum physicist, I have understood this much: Physicists after Bohr agree that he was talking about something important, but disagree over exactly what it means. In addition, a good deal of non-physicist commentary has been written about complementarity—by theologians, philosophers, social scientists, and psy-

---

94. See Niels Bohr, *Atomic Theory and the Description of Nature* (New York: Macmillan, 1934); and J. Kalikar, ed., *Niels Bohr Collected Works*, vol. 6, *Formulations of Quantum Physics I* (New York: North-Holland Physics Publishing, 1985).
95. See H. J. Folse, *The Philosophy of Niels Bohr: The Framework of Complementarity* (New York: North-Holland Physics Publishing, 1985) for a good summary.

chologists—and they too seem to recognize that the extra-science implications of this discovery are profound, but there is little agreement about the exact nature of those implications.[96]

As a historian of religion and sometime theologian, I think that Bohr's discovery has important implications beyond the strictly scientific setting. I think it has important implications for the relationship between history of religion methodology and missiological methodology. To look at those implications, it is necessary to discuss three applications that are often made in the name of complementarity: (1) complementarity as a way of relating theology and science; (2) complementarity as an easy answer to multiculturalism, religious pluralism, and political fragmentation; and (3) complementarity as proof of one of several versions of philosophical monism.

Complementarity as a Way of Relating Theology and Science

In order for complementarity to work as a way of relating theology and science, it must be assumed that there is a fundamental split, real or perceived, between the two.[97] Usually, this split is described in terms of a Kantian division between the noumena and phenomena.[98] Occasionally, however, the structure built between the two is based on a distinction between God and God's creation.[99] Both arguments correctly identify complementarity as having something to do with epistemology rather than with ontology. The Kantian argument purports to solve the problem of the apparent incompatibility between empirical knowing and rational knowing; the theological argument or the difficulty of the created knowing and the creator. This locating of complementarity in the epistemological realm is essentially correct. However, in order to make

---

96. See R. Moore, *Niels Bohr: The Man, His Science and the World They Changed* (Cambridge, Mass.: MIT Press, 1966); Mara Beller, "The Birth of Bohr's Complementarity: The Content and the Dialogues," *Studies in the History and Philosophy of Science,* March 1992, 147–80; and Gerald Holton, "The Roots of Complementarity," *Daedalus,* summer 1988, 151–97.
97. See K. Helmut Reich, "A Logic-Based Typology of Science and Theology," *Journal of Interdisciplinary Studies,* 1996, 149–67; ibid., "The Relation Between Science and Theology: The Case for Complementarity Revisited," *Zygon,* December 1990, 369–90.
98. David Kaiser, "More Roots of Complementarity: Kantian Aspects and Influences," *Studies in History and Philosophy of Science,* June 1992, 213–39; and G. Holton, "On the Roots of Complementarity," *Daedalus,* 1970, 1015–55.
99. Mark Wynn, "From World to God: Resemblance and Complementarity," *Religious Studies,* 1996, 379–94; and John Losee, *Religious Language and Complementarity* (New York: University Press of America, 1992).

this argument, a certain ontological understanding of reality must be presupposed: the essential unknowability of the noumena (God) and the observability of the phenomena (the creation).[100] This assumption limits the universal application of complementarity to too narrow a range of philosophical/theological understandings. I think the application can be much broader. So, as I am using the term in this chapter, I am not talking about the specifically Kantian statement of it.

Complementarity as an Easy Answer to Multiculturalism, Religious Pluralism, and Political Fragmentation

There has never been a greater need for unity amid diversity than in the world today. Even as globalization draws us together in tighter and tighter economic and scientific webs, fragmentations based on ethnic identities and individual human rights pull us apart. Complementarity is often championed as a way to rationalize the call for greater and greater unity. Arguments of this sort have been in the arenas of social psychology,[101] gender studies,[102] political science,[103] economics,[104] and sociology.[105] These may all be important studies and valid applications, but they are not how I am using the concept here.

100. This is the basic position of philosopher of religion John Hick. See his *Interpretation of Religion* (New Haven: Yale University Press, 1989).

101. Christopher Dryer and Leonard Horowitz, "When Do Opposites Attract? Interpersonal Complementarity Versus Similarity," *Journal of Personality and Social Psychology*, March 1997, 592–603; and Douglas Snyder, "On Complementarity and William James," *American Psychologist*, October 1994, 891–92.

102. See A. M. Allchin, *A Fearful Symmetry? The Complementarity of Men and Women in Ministry* (London: SPCK, 1992); and Jennifer Aube and Richard Koestner, "Gender Characteristics and Relationship Adjustment: Another Look at Similarity-Complementarity Hypotheses," *Journal of Personality*, December 1995, 879–904.

103. See Erik Rasmussen, *Complementarity and Political Science* (Odense, Denmark: Odense University Press, 1987); Gregory Raymond and Charles Kegley, "Polarity Polarization, and the Transformation of Alliance Norms," *Western Political Quarterly*, March 1990, 9–38; and David Bloomfield, "Towards Complementarity in Conflict Management: Resolution and Settlement in Northern Ireland," *Journal of Peace Research*, 1995, 151–64.

104. See Richard Anderson and John Moreney, "Superstition and Complementarity in C.E.S. Models," *Southern Economic Journal*, April 1994, 886–95; and Henry False, "The Environment and the Epistemological Lesson of Complementarity," *Environmental Ethics*, winter 1993, 345–53.

105. See Mark Aldendorfer, *Domestic Architecture, Ethnicity and Complementarity in the South Central Andes* (Iowa City, Iowa: University of Iowa Press, 1993); and Walter Wallace, "Max Weber's Two Spirits of Capitalism," *Telos*, fall 1989, 86–90.

Complementarity as Proof/Description of One of Several Versions of Philosophical Monism

Complementarity may have only a brief history in the way Niels Bohr articulated it, but it has a long past as a way of coming to grips with one of the most perplexing and enduring of philosophical issues, the relationship of the particular to the universal. The Eastern way of dealing with this problem has been to posit an enduring single universal reality—particulars are illusions, mistaken human perceptions, temporary postulates that ultimately, when understood correctly, lead back to unity.

As articulated in Western philosophy, this monism has always appeared as a minority view, and has often used some form of complementarity in its exposition. One of the earliest Western philosophers to take this approach was the fifth century B.C. Greek, Heraclitus, who began his argument by identifying/postulating a basic unity underlying a world of change.[106] Natural transformations (changes) necessarily involve contraries such as hot and cold, wet and dry. These contraries are required in order for the real world to exist. But they exist only in the dynamic of time and in their very conflict lies hidden a harmony that sustains the world. In *Fragments,* his book of epigrammatic remarks, Heraclitus describes it as follows: "Opposition brings concord. Out of discord comes the fairest harmony."[107] "To God, all things are beautiful, good, and right; men, on the other hand, deem some things right and others wrong."[108] "In the circle, the beginning and end are common."[109] For Heraclitus, complementarity is a way of describing the real world, a world of constant change. His understanding of complementarity is an ontology of time.

Nicholas of Cusa, a fifteenth century German philosopher and theologian also gives an ontological understanding of complementarity, but an ontology of space, not time.[110] His central insight may be summed up this way: All oppositions are united in their infinite measure; they are contrary in finite space,

---

106. Philip Wheelwright, *Heraclitus* (Princeton, N.J.: Princeton University Press, 1959).
107. Heraclitus, *Fragments* (London: Heinemann, 1948), 98.
108. Ibid., 106.
109. Ibid., 109.
110. Jasper Hopkins, *A Concise Introduction to the Philosophy of Nicholas of Cusa Trialogus De Possent* (Minneapolis: Banning, 1986).

but complementary in infinite space; that is, in God. Nicholas called this the *coincidentia oppositorum,* the coincidence of opposites.[111]

Although Nicholas is usually described as a philosopher, his main work in which he develops the implications of *coincidentia oppositorum, On Learned Ignorance (De Docta Ignorantia)* reads more like theology than philosophy, but theology of a monistic, emmanentist sort.[112] "God is the enfolding of all things, even contradictories," writes Nicholas. In order to illustrate this, at one point, he uses the example of a top: the faster the top rotates the more motionless it appears.[113] "God is free of all opposition—to see how it is that these things which seem to us to be opposites are identical in Him, how it is that in Him negation is not opposed to affirmation and other such things."[114] For Nicholas, God includes everything, so at this highest level of reality, all is God—that is, the same.

Neither of these understandings of complementarity passed the tests of the twentieth century—neither the theological tests of Christian orthodoxy, which find that they blur or do away altogether with the distinction between God and God's creation, nor the philosophical tests of adequately taking into proper account the role of the knower in attempting to understand the relationship between the particular and the universal. A third way of understanding complementarity has been the postmodern move to absolutize epistemology— the process of knowing is all there is. For postmoderns like Jacques Derrida, there is no "known" (no ontological reality) and no "knower" (the self also disappears) but only endless knowing.[115]

In some ways, this understanding of "understanding" comes closer to the radical implications of Niels Bohr's discovery of complementarity in the process of scientific methodology. Although some of the aspects of his discovery have deep ontological implications (that reality is bounded by the human capacity to know), it really is an epistemological insight and says little about the

---

111. Kevin McCarron, *The Coincidence of Opposites* (London: Sheffield Academic Press, 1995). See also, Kent Emery, "Mysticisms and the Coincidence of Opposites in Sixteenth and Seventeenth Century France," *Journal of the History of Ideas,* January 1984, 3–23.

112. Jasper Hopkins, *Nicholas of Cusa on Learned Ignorance: A Translation and an Appraisal of De Docta Ignorantia* (Minneapolis: A. J. Benning Press, 1981).

113. Ibid., 88–89.

114. John Valk, "The Concept of the Coincidentia Oppositorum in the Thought of Mircea Eliade," *Religious Studies,* March 1992, 31–42.

115. Arkady Plotnitsky, *Complementarity: Anti-Epistemology After Bohr and Derrida* (Durham, N.C.: Duke University Press, 1994).

nature of reality.[116] That is why it has such potential usefulness in comparing methodologies (knowing schemas), particularly missiological and history of religion methodologies. As we have seen, both are human ways of knowing, both reveal valid aspects of truth. But I don't think the way to harmonize them is some form of philosophical monism. Juxtaposed to the aforementioned applications, I am committed to the creation/creator distinction. This complementary way of looking at the relationship between missiology and history of religion produces three insights.

Complementarity and Hermeneutic Fallibility

In effect, the theory of complementarity says that multiple methodologies are required in order for human beings to begin to understand any single phenomenon. Even then, we can never fully know or exhaust all the aspects of a single fact, event, or being. Once we set up our metaphorical "experimental apparatus" in order to study something, we are limiting ourselves to studying certain features. This does not disparage the quality or truthfulness of our findings; it simply means that there is always a remainder, what Paul Harvey calls "the rest of the story," that some other methodological apparatus must discover.

Thus, any time a single methodology is championed as the only methodology—whether scientific, social scientific, aesthetic, or moral—truth is being needlessly constricted. Conversely, multiple methodologies produce better pictures of phenomena than do single methodologies; it is inconceivable in this day and age to claim absolute knowledge for a single methodology when so much else is available.

I think this understanding of complementarity and hermeneutic fallibility comports very well with biblical anthropology. Human beings are limited. Now we see only dimly through a clouded mirror.[117] Complementarity emphasizes that we are not perfect knowers but rather imperfect ones.

The Importance of Collective Epistemology

The search for truth is not an individual affair but a collective one. Each of us as individuals comes at problems with a certain mind-set. We are "wired"

---

116. A point clearly made by many. See Kaiser, "More Roots of Complementarity: Kantian Aspects and Influences," 213.
117. 1 Corinthians 13.

by our cultural and historical experiences to view the world from certain perspectives. In many ways, the way we come at problems as theologians, historians, and scientists is a matter of choice—how we choose to build on certain
presuppositions and understandings; how we choose to embody our attention, understanding, rationality, and responsibilities; how we define the problems we choose to study (which, in turn, demands certain methods). In many
other ways, however, how we come at certain problems is, in effect, determined
for us by our culture and history. Thus, many of us contribute to truth as a
collective.

This understanding of collective epistemology is not reducible to cultural
relativism, however. It is not a way of saying that all methods and all cultures
and all individuals' knowledge are equal. Each method and culture, and each
individual "experiment," must still be judged and evaluated. All will produce
both truth and error.

I think this understanding of complementarity and collective epistemology
accords very well with orthodox ecclesiology—that revelation is best understood by the whole church, not by isolated theologians. The work of discovering God's truth is a task of the growing, developing kingdom of God, not of
individual human kings.

Postsuppositionalism as an Alternative to Presuppositionalism

Much of the argument in studies of comparative methodologies seems to
focus on proving the uniqueness and validity of one's presuppositions. This is
a fruitless task. Presuppositions must be clearly stated, but they cannot be
proved.[118] In very general terms, a fundamental cause of conflict in the world
today is the battle between dueling presuppositions. The only way to win this
battle would be unscriptural—authoritarian imposition of falsely universal
presuppositions. Big brother as philosopher king.

Still, some kind of common ground is required. Instead of presuppositions,
I suggest the following *post*supposition: faith that the little truths discovered
by all of our methodologies and validated collectively by all our normative
standards—from revelation to human flourishing to societal viability—will
dovetail together in the reality of God. There are many corridors to the central
hall of truth and all of them contribute to the central task of being human: to
know and glorify God.

118. Michael Polyani, *Personal Knowledge* (Chicago: University of Chicago Press, 1958).

Missiology *begins* by acknowledging the truth of God's creative work, and history of religions *ends* there. But along the way, both turn on lights that illumine, at least in part, the transcendent God that created us, watches over us, and calls us forward to the *eschaton.*

The segment of the church in America identified as evangelical has been slow to embrace the findings of the history of religion. Perhaps the talk of "science of religion" and "objective studies," raises echoes of other battles fought, especially regarding historical-critical methods of Bible study. And perhaps those echoes make the findings of this other discipline suspect. But as world events continue to show, missiological engagement with the world can no longer be done with the increasingly "missions-minded" religion of the world, including the new religions. The history of religion perspective is indispensable to the missiologist in the cultural plurality of religions that characterizes most of the world's nations and ethnic groups. It is a tool we can no longer afford to ignore.

STUDY QUESTIONS

1. In your ministry context, identify three ways in which missiological methodology can help you in your ministry tasks. In your ministry context, identify three ways in which history of religion methodology can help you in your ministry tasks.
2. What are the limits of the history of religion methodology when it comes to ministry? What are the limits of missiological methodology when it comes to ministry?
3. Imagine that a person of non-Christian religion comes as a visitor to your church. Over time you begin to develop a personal relationship with this person. Clearly articulate how some knowledge of missiology and some knowledge of history of religion can be an aid in your personal interactions with this visitor.

CHAPTER 4

NEW RELIGIONS AS GLOBAL CULTURES

IRVING HEXHAM AND KARLA POEWE-HEXHAM

This chapter summarizes the core ideas found in our book *New Religions as Global Cultures,*[1] in which we explore the complex relationship between global cultures and new religions—specifically how new religions selectively combine aspects of many traditions to create new cultures. To illustrate our case, we examine the European origins and American development of new religions, as well as the Asian and African response to new religions.

By "new religions" we mean spiritual movements that have emerged as self-consciously new religions since the era of the Enlightenment. These are not simply revitalization movements within an existing religious tradition, nor are they the result of missionaries planting an existing tradition in a new cultural environment.

GLOBAL CULTURE

In *Charismatic Christianity as a Global Culture,*[2] Karla traces the worldwide growth of Pentecostalism as a renewal movement within the Christian tradition. Pentecostalism traveled the globe with awakened or renewed missionaries who related their spiritual experience of the work of the Holy Spirit among diverse local peoples. The work of these missionaries was soon reworked in

---

1. Irving Hexham and Karla Poewe, *New Religions as Global Cultures* (Boulder, Colo.: Westview, 1997).
2. Karla Poewe, ed., *Charismatic Christianity as a Global Culture* (Columbia, S.C.: University of South Carolina Press, 1994).

accordance with the cultural predilections of the peoples among whom they labored.

Theorizing about these developments, Karla argues that a global culture is a tradition that travels the world but takes on local color. As such, global cultures have both a global (or meta-cultural) dimension and a local (or situated distinct) cultural dimension.

New religions complicate this picture, although the global aspect of new religions is there for all to see. The *globality* of new religions differs from charismatic Christianity in some very important ways. *Globality* refers to how the global natures of different religions and cultures vary. For example, the global culture of Christianity is the religion's culture before it picks up numerous local adaptations. The global tradition travels the world and takes on local color.

New religions are global in a different way. Their essential idea is a fragment of a tradition that has become so colored that it is largely a new tradition altogether. Multiple fragments can combine in the local setting to create a new religion. That new religion takes on a global tradition and travels the world to pick up local cultural expressions.

Essentially, the ideas that help create new religions travel as fragments of traditions, not distinct traditions, and these ideas continue to fragment and unite with other fragments in order to bear new fruit in the form of distinct folk religions. Like charismatic Christianity, these new religions have both global and local aspects. However, unlike charismatic Christianity, they lack clear historical roots. The recombination of fragments makes such religions global; rooting the recombined fragments in local folk religions makes them authentic.

Adolf Bastian (1826–1905), the nineteenth century German anthropologist, said that folk religions arise everywhere from the deep yearnings of people. We are in the presence of just this phenomenon when we approach the study of new religions that are authenticated by specific local folk religions forming a response to the deep yearnings of urban sophisticates for a global spirituality. Their worldview aspects, and the newness of their recombination, turn local folk religions into new religions with global cultures.

THE EMPIRICAL ROOTS OF A THEORY

Our understanding of the global nature of new religions came about as a result of empirical research in Africa. While living in the Black township of

Katatura, Namibia, in 1981, Karla observed that local Black religious movements prided themselves in their global links, which they saw as a source of
inspiration and legitimacy. At the same time, Irving was working in South
African archives on the Afrikaner visionary Johanna Brandt (1876–1964),
whose books *The Millennium* (1918) and *Paraclete, or Coming World Mother*
(1936) talked about such things as the coming Age of Aquarius, feminist spirituality, and "the Coming World Mother."[3] Like the African prophets that Karla
interviewed, Brandt treasured her global vision through contacts with America
and Germany, which she established with the help of various theosophical
organizations. These empirical observations made us aware of the role played
by global visions in the work of individuals intent on creating their own new
religions.

In 1987, we began to develop our own theory of global cultures while researching new religions and charismatic movements in South Africa. This research led Karla to organize a conference on global culture at the University of
Calgary in 1991. At the same time, and quite independently, Roland Robertson
and other scholars were developing their own theories of globalization and
global culture.[4] As a result, the terms *globalization* and *global culture* came into
use among academics.

THE GLOBAL DYNAMICS OF RELIGIOUS CULTURES

Instead of taking a conspiratorial view of so-called cults and new religions
as being the result of sinister plots by unscrupulous leaders or organizations
such as the CIA,[5] we concentrate on the cultural give-and-take of new religions.
However, before we discuss the global nature of new religions, we must have a
general sense of what a global culture might be. It is best to think of global
cultures as "transnational" or "trans-societal" networks of cosmopolitan people
who self-consciously cultivate "an intellectual and aesthetic stance of openness
toward divergent cultural experiences."[6] As Ulf Hannerz points out, global
cultures "are carried as collective structures of meaning by networks" that are

3. Johanna Brandt, *The Millennium* (Johannesburg, South Africa: privately published, 1918);
   and idem, *Paraclete, or Coming World Mother* (Pretoria, South Africa: privately published,
   1936).
4. Mike Featherstone, ed., *Global Culture* (London: Sage, 1990).
5. Cf. Paul Gifford, *The Religious Right in Southern Africa* (Harare, Zimbabwe: University of
   Zimbabwe, 1988).
6. Featherstone, *Global Culture*, 1, 239.

transnational, rather than being territorially defined.[7] People belonging to new religions, for example, may be "somewhat footloose"—they are as ready to move on as they are to stay on in order to immerse themselves temporarily within other cultures and religions.[8]

Buddhism, Christianity, and Islam have always been global cultures. The ideal of these religions, however, was to spread a religious meta-culture that was perfectly capable of remaining identifiable while yet being absorbed by local cultures. A meta-culture consists of a bare minimum of elements of a faith "that are reasonably consistent and uniform," and are recognizable even when the meta-culture is absorbed into cultures to become movements, denominations, or cultic processes.[9]

For example, in 601, Roman Catholic missionaries from Italy to England asked Pope Gregory (540–604) for advice in their efforts to convert the heathen English. Gregory's reply was recorded by Bede (673–735) in his *Ecclesiastical History of the English People*.[10] Put simply, the pope advised his missionaries to find points of common ground with the English that would allow them to absorb pagan celebrations into Christian festivals. The aim, however, was not to create a new synthesis of Roman Catholic and pagan thought. Rather, the goal was to accommodate the uncompromised meta-culture of a world religion from a cosmopolitan culture to the folk religion of a local culture. As those who have researched renewal aspects of world religions know, the accommodation is always mutual. Not infrequently, indigenous and non-Western spiritual practices were the spark that renewed dry traditions or threw new light on old interpretations of ancient religious texts.

NEW RELIGIONS AS GLOBAL CULTURES

As indicated earlier, the global nature of new religions is significantly different from that of charismatic Christianity. The strict accommodation between a local religious culture and the meta-culture of a world tradition is absent in new religions. Instead, new religionists revel in diversity itself so that

---

7. Ibid., 239.
8. Ibid., 240, 241.
9. Kenelm Burridge, *In the Way* (Vancouver, B.C.: University of British Columbia Press, 1991), xiv, 36.
10. Saint Bede the Venerable, *A History of the English Church and People*, trans. [from the Latin] and with an introduction by Leo Sherley-Price (Harmondsworth: Penguin, 1965), 86–87.

cultures coexist "in the individual experience."[11] This results in the sense of having created a new world culture that is more than a recombination of experiences and fragments from numerous great and small traditions. Furthermore, the success of new religions depends on their finding the proper mix between spiritualizing science and scientizing the exotic. It depends on finding a new buzz phrase, such as "trance channeling" for the old practice of "spirit possession."

In practice and theory, the creators of new religions selectively extract and combine elements they find significant from numerous local cultures spread around the world. Although one great tradition may predominate, such as Buddhism, Christianity, Hinduism, Islam, or even the scientific tradition, all new religions incorporate, often indiscriminately, insights from other cultures and traditions. They also use the idea of lost civilizations and relics from ancient cultures that no longer exist to create their claims to authenticity. People living anywhere can be incorporated into this type of global culture, but not everyone is necessarily allowed to participate.

New religions, as we have observed, are the product of modernity. They have emerged since the eighteenth century as one response to the technological innovations that virtually shrank the world. Speaking metaphorically, mind-boggling innovations in communications and travel allowed people to mine traditions in order to produce shining ideas for a growing religious market. It is only recently that Native Americans began to complain that their traditions were being strip-mined. A kind of protectionism or ecology of tradition is now emerging. It is unlikely, however, that such moves will change the stance of openness of those who practice new religions. How can one expunge the sense that cultures coexist in individual experience? And how can one prove, much less stop, the appropriation of ideas in a computer-linked world?

It is the vision of creating a radically *new* world culture that energizes new religions. To succeed in today's religious market, new religions attempt to convince their followers that they offer a global vision. From this description it might be thought that all new religions are catholic in the sense of including everyone. But as our comments on charismatic Christianity made clear, such an assumption would be a mistake. The stance of including all people anywhere within one distinct tradition is Christian. The stance of including people for whom the coexistence of ideas from diverse cultures, traditions, and practices is an inner experience is new religionist. In other words, creating a new

---

11. Featherstone, *Global Culture*, 239.

religion does not prevent people from adopting hierarchical forms of organization or restricting membership. Absolute tolerance is a chimera.

To be catholic means to be inclusive. A catholic movement is one that is universal in scope and membership. For this reason, the early Christian creeds incorporated the expression "the holy catholic church" to convey the belief that Christianity, like Buddhism and Islam, is open to all people regardless of race, class, or gender. Many new religions share this vision; others are deliberately exclusive. Such groups draw from numerous world traditions but purposely exclude certain people.

THE EUROPEAN ORIGINS OF NEW RELIGIONS

Europe was the home of industrialism. It took root in Britain and spread to Germany and America. Only later was the impact of industrialization felt by the rest of the world.[12] This explains why, during the nineteenth century, the growth of new religious movements coincided with the spread of Christian missions that exported the gospel and modernity and imported other religious texts and exotica.[13]

In Europe there is a long history of religious revitalization movements stretching back to Roman times. The Reformation, for example, began in technical sociological terms as a cult movement proclaiming a novel interpretation of Scripture. It quickly developed into a sect and then became a church throughout most of northern Europe. Similarly, the Puritan movement and Lutheran Pietism developed as sects within Protestant churches. All of these movements sought to revive the Christian tradition through spiritual awakenings.

Only in the late eighteenth century did religious movements emerge that were self-consciously modern. These movements no longer sought to revive the Christian tradition. Rather they sought to create new traditions that merged old Christian themes with exotic elements from other sources. In these movements we find the origins of today's new religions.

---

12. Peter Laslett, *The World We Have Lost* (New York: Charles Scribner's Sons, 1984); Douglass C. North and Robert Paul Thomas, *The Rise of the Western World* (Cambridge: Cambridge University Press, 1980); and Dorothy Marshall, ed., *Industrial England: 1776–1851* (London: Routledge and Kegan Paul, 1973).
13. Andrew Porter, "Commerce and Christianity: The Rise and Fall of a Nineteenth-Century Missionary Slogan," *Historical Journal* 28, no. 3 (1985): 597–621.

The person who prepared the way for the growth of new religions in seventeenth- and eighteenth-century Christian Europe was Benedict de Spinoza (1632–1677), whose biting criticisms of the Bible and revealed religion helped to usher in a revolution in Western thought. His *Theologico-Political Treatise* (1670)[14] sent shock waves through educated European society where Latin still provided a common language of scholarly discourse. Emanuel Swedenborg (1688–1772) read Spinoza's Latin text. Later Thomas Paine (1737–1809) read one of the growing number of English-language editions. Both men were profoundly influenced by Spinoza. His work led them to abandon faith in the Bible and seek consolation in what were to become new religions. Swedenborg and Paine laid the foundation for all that followed.

After an excellent education and extensive travel, Swedenborg embarked on a brilliant career as a natural philosopher—in modern terms, a scientist. In this capacity he became Inspector of Mines for the whole of Sweden. After publishing a series of scientific books on various subjects, including medical topics, he turned to the spiritual in 1749. At first, his writing was published anonymously, but later he published under his own name.[15]

Swedenborg's spiritual writings, which stretch over twenty years, purport to be expositions of the Bible and descriptions of spiritual truths that he learned through dreams, visions, and communication with spirits. They are cast in a semi-Christian mold, yet they repudiate most of the beliefs of traditional Christianity. Most important, they launched a massive spiritual movement throughout Europe.

Behind his work lay the conviction that science and the growth of rational thought had created a religious crisis.[16] It was this crisis that he sought to overcome through direct revelations from God.[17] We know little about the roots of Swedenborg's theories. Although he never left Europe, he read widely, took a keen interest in Africa and China,[18] and was an avid reader of mythology, both ancient and modern.[19]

---

14. Benedict de Spinoza, *A Theologico-Political Treatise,* trans. R. H. M. Elwes (New York: Doubleday, 1951). First published in Latin, 1670.
15. Marguerite Block, *The New Church in the New World* (New York: Octagon Books, 1968), 3–18.
16. Cyriel Odhner Sigstedt, *The Swedenborg Epic* (New York: The New Church, 1952), 166.
17. Ibid., 182–83.
18. Ibid., 119; Block, *The New Church in the New World*, 54–55.
19. Block, *The New Church in the New World*, 427.

Swedenborg appears to have had contact with Swedish or Finnish shamans. This fact is not brought out by his biographers but appears in a footnote of Gloria Flaherty's book *Shamanism and the Eighteenth Century* (1992).[20] Flaherty points out that at least one eighteenth-century writer of religion, who set out to debunk shamanism, specifically mentions Swedenborg's work on the topic.[21] If this is so, it is an important link between Swedenborg and later spiritual figures. Although Swedenborg did not found a new religion, his followers did. On December 5, 1783, the first meeting of a group of devotees took place in London. From this group, the New Church, which was originally called the Theosophical Society, was born.[22] Swedenborgian societies quickly spread through Britain, and in 1784, its first missionary arrived in America, where the new faith quickly took root.[23]

The influence of Swedenborg's teachings was immense. In the United States, the popular folk hero John Chapman (1774–1845), better known as Johnny Appleseed, was a Swedenborgian preacher who spread religious tracts far and wide.[24] Joseph Smith (1805–1844), the founder of Mormonism was strongly influenced by Swedenborgian teachings, as was Mary Baker Eddy (1821–1910), the founder of Christian Science, New Thought, and "mind cure."[25]

Even more telling is the discovery by Hennie Pretorious that at least one African Independent Church in South Africa's Transkei openly admitted its dependence on Swedenborg's writings, as did some Nigerian groups observed by Rosalind Hackett.[26] Further afield, Sun Myung Moon, the founder of the Unification Church, was also influenced by Swedenborgian ideas.[27] Finally, many terms used in new religions, such as "New Age" and "theosophy," as well as doctrines such as celestial marriage were first popularized by Swedenborg and his followers.[28]

---

20. Gloria Flaherty, *Shamanism and the Eighteenth Century* (Princeton, N.J.: Princeton University Press), 1992.
21. Ibid., 97–113; cf. n. 2 page 227.
22. Block, *The New Church in the New World*, 62–63.
23. Ibid., 64–111.
24. Ibid., 115–17.
25. Gail Thain Parker, *Mind Cures in New England: From the Civil War to World War I* (Hanover, New Hampshire: University Press of New England, 1973).
26. H. L. Pretorius, *Sound the Trumpet of Zion* (Pretoria, South Africa: University of Pretoria, 1985), 54–55. Cf. Rosalind Hackett, *Religion in Calabar* (New York: de Gruyter, 1989), 156–57.
27. Conversation with Dr. Young Oom Kim, June 1979.
28. Edmund A. Beaman, *Swedenborg and the New Age* (1881; reprint, New York: AMS Press, 1971).

The extent to which Swedenborg influenced Helena Blavatsky (1831–1891) is unclear. What has now been proved beyond reasonable doubt, however, is that Blavatsky based her first major work, *Isis Unveiled*, on the novels of Edward Bulwer-Lytton, whose works were influenced by Swedenborg.[29] Later, the psychologist Jung, who had a major impact on the New Age movement, drew many of his ideas from Swedenborg.[30]

Finally, Gerald Gardner (1884–1964), who is generally acknowledged as one of the founders of modern witchcraft, or Wicca, was influenced by Swedenborg and the nineteenth-century occult revival. After moving to Sri Lanka in 1900, he worked in Malaya as a colonial civil servant and traveled throughout Asia. After taking a close interest in Malay folk religion and occult practices, he returned to England in 1938 where he joined a theosophical group run by the daughter of Annie Besant. Through this group he met Dorothy Clutterbuch, who encouraged his interest in witchcraft and initiated him into ritual magic. His books *Witchcraft Today* (1954) and *The Meaning of Witchcraft* (1959) laid the foundation for the contemporary witchcraft revival.[31]

Thomas Paine's writings were the scourge of religious thinkers in the nineteenth century. More than any other author he popularized free thought and attacked contemporary arguments for Christian belief. Paine's writings are remarkable, because his work, in embryo, contains all the themes used by later critics of Christianity. He presents a radical critique of the Bible, comments on the implications of comparative religion, and even offers a crude sociological approach to religious ideas that is similar to ideas later developed by Ludwig Feuerbach (1804–1872) and Karl Marx (1818–1883).

Paine was born in Thetford, England, the son of a Quaker corset maker. In 1774, he emigrated to colonial America where he joined the revolutionary movement and published *Common Sense*, a forty-seven-page pamphlet urging an immediate declaration of independence. He also wrote *The Rights of Man* (1791–92), which defended the measures taken in revolutionary France and appealed to the English people to overthrow their monarchy and organize a republic. In England, he was tried, convicted of treason in absentia, and

29. B. F. Campbell, *Ancient Wisdom Revived: A History of the Theosophical Movement* (Berkeley and Los Angeles: University of California Press, 1980), 14, 56.

30. Gerhard Wehr, *Jung: A Biography* (Boston: Shambala, 1987), 62; Richard Noll, *The Jung Cult* (Princeton, N.J.: Princeton University Press, 1994), 86, 297.

31. Margot Adler, *Drawing Down the Moon* (Boston: Beacon Press, 1986), 46, 56, 60–66; and T. M. Luhrmann, *Persuasions of the Witch's Craft* (Cambridge, Mass.: Harvard University Press, 1989), 42–54.

outlawed in 1792. After going to France, he was arrested and imprisoned in Paris as an English spy in December 1793, and remained in prison until November 1794. He was then released at the request of the American minister, James Monroe, who said Paine was an American citizen. In prison he began to write *The Age of Reason*, part one of which was published in 1794, followed by part two in 1796. He returned to America in 1802, and died there in 1809.

Thus, more than two hundred years ago, Tom Paine nuked the advance of evangelical Christianity with his *Age of Reason*.[32] Like a cruise missile, his book struck home with deadly effect. Everywhere it was read, believers lost their faith and skeptics were convinced they held the truth. British sociologist Susan Budd, in her article "The Loss of Faith: Reasons for Unbelief among Members of the Secular Movement in England, 1850–1950,"[33] writes that Paine "remained a dominant influence" on unbelief because of "the enormous circulation" of *The Age of Reason*.[34]

Why scholars writing about religion should ignore Paine's work, and his immensely valuable insights, is an interesting question in itself. Secular historians certainly recognize his importance as both a political and religious writer. But, in theology and religious studies, there is almost a conspiracy of silence.

Nevertheless, Paine is important, and secular historians recognize this. The claim that Paine did not influence nineteenth-century religious thinking has been completely refuted by George Spater, who shows that this claim is based on the fact that Paine's influence was in decline for a few years toward the end of his life and after his death. However, it revived strongly after 1810, and continued to be influential at least until the end of the century. George Jacob Holyoake (1817–1906), Charles Bradlaugh (1833–1891), Abraham Lincoln (1809–1865), Ralph Waldo Emerson (1803–1882), and Joseph Smith (1805–1844) all studied Paine's works, as did thousands of others.[35]

Most importantly, Paine's writings profoundly influenced Ludwig Feuerbach, who described Paine in a private letter as "the famous American philosopher Tom Paine."[36] Paine's ideas are clearly embedded in Feuerbach's *Essence of Chris-*

32. Tom Paine, *The Life and Works of Tom Paine*, ed. William M. van der Weyde (New Rochelle, N.Y.: Tom Paine National Historical Society, 1925), 8:3.

33. Susan Budd, "The Loss of Faith: Reasons for Unbelief Among Members of the Secular Movement in England, 1850–1950," *Past and Present*, no. 36 (1967): 106–25.

34. Ibid., 110.

35. Ian Dyck, ed., *Citizen of the World* (London: Christopher Helm, 1987), 129–40.

36. Ludwig Feuerbach, *Sämtliche Werke* (Stüttgart, Germany: Günther Holzboog Verlag, 1959), 8:173.

tianity (1846),[37] although he makes no mention of Paine in the book itself. (He probably wanted to avoid a conflict with state censors who had banned Paine's work.) Feuerbach begins his essay by suggesting "it is not I, but religion, that worships man, although religion, or rather theology, denies this. . . . I have only found the key to the cipher of the Christian religion, only extricated its true meaning from the web of contradictions and delusions called theology. . . . Let it be remembered that atheism—at least in the sense of this work—is the secret of religion itself."[38] Here, he is clearly echoing Paine's statement, "As to the Christian system of faith, it appears to me a species of Atheism—a sort of religious denial of God. It professes to believe in a man rather than in God."[39]

The importance of the Paine–Feuerbach connection is that Feuerbach, through Paine's suggestion that Christianity is a form of anthropomorphism, developed a far more elaborate theory that formed the basis of a new religious consciousness.[40] Feuerbach's ideas were later taken up by Nietzsche,[41] Freud,[42] and even Richard Wagner.[43] Although there seems little evidence that Feuerbach sought to create a new religion,[44] unlike D. F. Strauss, it does seem that his views had a direct effect on the creation of new religions that centered on the human and sought immortality in a racial memory rather than a literal afterlife.

From this brief overview, we see that a well-established tradition of rationalist and occult writings—originating with Swedenborg and Paine, and later boosted by writers like Blavatsky and the rationalist turned theosophist Annie Besant (1847–1933)—gave birth to numerous new religions. Now, we need to examine the way in which these traditions developed and expanded in America.

---

37. Ludwig Feuerbach, *The Essence of Christianity,* trans. George Elliot in 1854 (1846; reprint, New York: Harper and Row, 1957).
38. Ibid., xxxvi.
39. Tom Paine, *The Age of Reason* (1794; reprint, Secaucus, N.J.: n.p., 1974), 72–73.
40. Udo Kern, *Der Adere Feuerbach: Sinnlichkeit, Konretheit und Prazis als Qualität der "neuen Religion" Ludwig Feuerbachs* (Münster, Germany: LIT Verlag, 1998).
41. Wolfgang Wahl, *Feuerbach und Nietzsche* (Würzburg: Ergon, 1998).
42. Van A. Harvey, *Feuerbach and the Interpretation of Religion* (Cambridge: Cambridge University Press, 1995), 239 n. 10.
43. Paul Lawrence Rose, *Revolutionary Anti-Semitism* (Princeton, N.J.: Princeton University Press, 1990).
44. D. F. Strauss, *The Old Faith and the New,* trans. Mathilde Bline (London: Asher and Co., 1873).

AMERICA'S CONTRIBUTION

Throughout the nineteenth century, the United States was a hotbed of new religions. Swedenborgianism, mind cures, and various forms of new thought created a climate for the growth of spiritualism. Theosophy eventually emerged out of this rich occult mix. Before it did, however, Mormonism was the most successful of all new religions.

It may surprise some readers that we would classify the Church of Jesus Christ of Latter-day Saints as a new religion. Surely, some will argue, the Mormons are a Christian sect; but this is not true, as their early literature shows. Jehovah's Witnesses, Christadelphians, and similar groups are considered sects because they remain part of the Christian tradition, however heretical their views. By contrast, Joseph Smith made it quite clear that his movement represented a complete break with the Christian tradition. Of course, he claimed that he was "restoring" the original teachings of Christ. But unlike Charles Taze Russell of the Jehovah's Witnesses, Smith did not do this on the basis of biblical exposition. Rather, his "restoration" was based on "new revelations" found in *The Book of Mormon* (1830) and, even more importantly, *The Doctrine and Covenants* (1835).

Early Mormon theologians, such as Parley P. Pratt (1805–1859), understood the revolutionary nature of Smith's revelations. In his *Key to the Science of Theology* (1855),[45] Pratt argues that the original knowledge of God and the gift of prophecy were lost among the Jews at the time of the fall of Jerusalem. Later, after a brief period when it flourished, it was also lost among other nations. Therefore, from the time of the early church until the revelations of Joseph Smith, true religion was completely lost on earth.

Smith ushered in a new era with teachings that were completely different from those of the historic Christian churches.[46] Included in the "new" or "restored" doctrine was the idea that the earth was created by a "Grand Council" of gods, and that evolution—what Pratt called "endless progression"—is the basic law of the universe.[47] Accordingly, "gods, angels, and men are all of one species, one race, one great family,"[48] and all humans originally existed as spirit

---

45. Parley P. Pratt, *Key to the Science of Theology* (1855; reprint, Salt Lake City, Utah: Deseret Book, 1973), 19–33; 166–67.
46. Ibid., 34–81.
47. Ibid., 53, 61.
48. Ibid., 40–41.

beings before being given bodies on earth.[49] Finally, the ultimate goal of humans is to govern other planets that will be populated by their own gods.[50] This theology is totally different from anything found in traditional Christian churches. It incorporates ideas—preexistent souls, for example— taken from many traditions, which are bound together by a science-fiction vision of the universe that reflects nineteenth century ideas of modernity. Lest one think Pratt was eccentric, it should be noted that he merely expounded ideas found in *The Doctrine and Covenants.* These ideas have been reaffirmed by Mormon theologians ever since.[51]

If Mormonism is the most successful new religion that originated in America, then Theosophy must be regarded as the most creative. Like Mormonism, Theosophy grew out of the Swedenborgian revival that inspired new thought movements and the growth of spiritualism. Its founder, Helena Blavatsky, was an extraordinary Russian who founded the Theosophical Society in 1875, in cooperation with Henry Olcott (1832–1987), an American. Blavatsky's first major work was *Isis Unveiled* (1877).[52] Later, she and Olcott traveled to India where they imbibed the religious ethos of Hindu society.[53]

The teachings of Theosophy are a curious mix of occult wisdom, late Victorian fiction, and bits of doctrines culled from the great world religions. In this mix, Buddhist and Hindu ideas eventually predominated, although at the beginning of her career Helena Blavatsky seemed drawn to Egyptian themes.[54] As a movement, the Theosophical Society never succeeded in attracting more than a few thousand members.[55] However, the importance of Theosophy was not reflected in its growth rates. Rather, its significance is found in the spread of Theosophical ideas that stimulated both Buddhist and Hindu revitalization movements and numerous new religions.[56]

49. Ibid., 50–57; 125–31.
50. Ibid., 62–65; 150–59.
51. Cf. James E. Talmage, *A Study of the Articles of Faith* (London: Church of Jesus Christ of Latter-day Saints, 1962).
52. Helena Blavatsky, *Isis Unveiled* (1877; reprint, Pasadena, Calif.: Theosophical University Press, 1960); idem, *The Key to Theosophy* (1888; reprint, Pasadena, Calif.: Theosophical University Press, 1972).
53. Marion Meade, *Madame Blavatsky: The Woman Behind the Myth* (New York: G. P. Putnam's Sons, 1980), 111–89; 206–10.
54. Campbell, *Ancient Wisdom Revived,* 31–74.
55. Ibid., 175.
56. C. Wessinger, *Annie Besant and Progressive Messianism* (Lewiston, N.Y.: Edwin Mellen, 1988), 323–44; Peter Washington, *Madame Blavatsky's Baboon: Theosophy and the Emergence of the Western Guru* (London: Secker and Warburg, 1993); and Milton Singer, *When a Great Tradition Modernizes* (New York: Praeger, 1972), 29.

NEW RELIGIONS IN ASIA

The nineteenth century saw a religious renaissance in Asia. This arose in reaction to the outreach of Christian missions and gave birth to hundreds of new religious movements.[57] There seems little doubt that Ram Mohun Roy (1774–1833), founder of the Brahmo Samajin in 1828, and Maharishi Dayananda Sarswati (1824–1883), who founded the Arya Samaj fifty years later, set out to create a new religious consciousness. Both men bitterly attacked the Hindu tradition. Their common aim was to create a new religious synthesis incorporating elements from Christianity and Islam within a scientific framework.[58]

The Hindu Renaissance was given a strong impetus through Blavatsky and Olcott's sojourn in India. In India, Blavatsky published *The Secret Doctrine* (1889),[59] in which she claimed to have had telepathic contact with spiritual teachers, known as Mahatmas, who dwelt in Tibet. These enlightened beings were said to be part of a hierarchy of enlightened teachers that was leading mankind to a new age of enlightenment.[60]

One of Blavatsky's more prominent converts was the English freethinker and political activist Annie Besant (1847–1933), who became a Theosophist in 1889.[61] More than any other European, Besant encouraged the growth of Hindu revitalization movements and political nationalism by her tireless efforts to spread Theosophy in India. Were it not for Besant and other likeminded individuals, Theosophy might have remained an insignificant new religion. Instead, it played a major role in modern history.[62]

Some of Blavatsky's and Besant's successors later cooperated with British and American Unitarians in the hope of creating a new global religion.[63] Many others

57. Stephen Neill, *A History of Christian Missions* (Harmondsworth: Penguin, 1969), 261–80, 255–366. Madathilparampil M. Thomas, *The Acknowledged Christ of the Indian Renaissance* (London: SCM Press, 1969).

58. Vinod Kumar Saxena, *The Brahmo Samaj Movement and Its Leaders* (New Delhi, India: Anmol, 1989), 53; and Dattatrey Vable, *The Araya Samaj: Hindu Without Hinduism* (Delhi, India: Vikas, 1983), 9.

59. Helena Blavatsky, *The Secret Doctrine* (1888; reprint, Pasadena, Calif.: Theosophical University Press, 1974).

60. Vable, *The Araya Sama,* 217–60.

61. Rosemary Dinnage, *Annie Besant* (Harmondsworth: Penguin, 1986).

62. Ibid., 109–14. Arthur Nethercot, *The Last Four Lives of Annie Besant* (Madras, India: Theosophical Society Press, 1963), 213–304; 413–22; 468–69.

63. Saxena, *The Brahmo Samaj Movement and Its Leaders,* 16–25, 54–63; Robert D. Baird, ed., *Religion in Modern India* (New Delhi, India: Manigar, 1981), 2–6, 20–23.

were attracted to the political vision of the founders of these movements, while retaining a deep commitment to the Hindu religion. Consequently, these and similar attempts to create a new religion were quickly superseded by numerous revitalization movements that swept through nineteenth-century Indian society.

The founders of many of these movements freely admitted the intellectual debt they owed Roy and Sarswati. However, instead of attempting to create new religions, they sought to revive the Hindu tradition. Probably the most important of all such figures is Sri Ramakrishna whose movement, the Ramakrishna Path and Mission, began in 1880. It was a Ramakrishna disciple, Vivekananda (1863–1902), however, who successfully blended traditional Hindu religious teachings and practices with modern Western ideas.[64]

Vivekananda's greatest triumph came when he spoke at the World's Congress of Religions in 1894. In his speech he argued that the Hindu tradition was a dynamic one that valued "being and becoming" over dogma. This, he believed, made the ancient scriptures of India far more relevant to the modern world than the Christian Bible. Hindu scriptures, he argued, were in harmony with modern science.[65] Following Vivekananda's example many gurus have since tried to bring traditional forms of Hindu religion to the West. The best known of these today is Sri Prabhupada, the founder of the International Society for Krishna Consciousness, also known as the Hare Krishna Movement.[66] It is very important to note, however, that these expressions of Hindu religion are revitalization movements, not new religions, according to our definition.[67]

Other movements, like that of Bhagwan Shree Rajneesh, are truly new religions.[68] So too is Transcendental Meditation.[69] But these movements are small indeed, by comparison with Hindu revival movements in India and the West.

64. Rolland Romain, *The Life of Vivekananda and the Universal Gospel*, trans. F. Malcolm Smith (Calcutta, India: Advaita Ashram, [1931] 1965); and Baird, *Religion in Modern India*, 197–98, 209–21.

65. J. W. Hanson, ed., *The World's Congress of Religions: The Addresses and Papers* (Chicago: Mammoth Publishing, 1895), 366–76.

66. Satsvarāpa Dās Goswami, *Prabhupada* (Los Angeles: Bhaktivedanta Book Trust, 1984).

67. J. Stilson Judah, *Hare Krishna and the Counterculture* (New York: John Wiley and Sons, 1974); Raymond B. Williams, ed., *A Sacred Thread: The Modern Transmission of Hindu Traditions in India and Abroad* (Chambersburg, Penn.: Anima Books, 1992).

68. Vasant Joshi, *The Awakened One: The Life and Work of Bhagwan Shree Rajneesh* (San Francisco: Harper and Row, 1982); Judith Thompson and Paul Heelas, *The Way of the Heart: The Rajneesh Movement* (Wellingborough, Northamptonshire: Aquarian Press, 1986).

69. Una Kroll, *TM: Signpost to the World* (London: Darton, Longman and Todd, 1974); and Jack Forem, *Transcendental Meditation* (London: George Allen, 1973).

The new religions of Korea also developed in response to modernity and Christian teachings, which entered Korea in the second half of the nineteenth century.[70] The first major new religion, founded in 1860, was the Religion of the Heavenly Way (Ch'ondogyo). It was named after its founder, Ch'oe Che-u, who received "heavenly manifestations" calling him to restore true spirituality.[71] Other new religions combined ancestral practices with elements of traditional Shamanism, Confucian philosophy, Buddhism, and Christianity in the name of science and progress.[72]

In Western society, the best known of these groups is the Unification Church of the Reverend Sun Myung Moon. Identified by its enemies as one of the more dangerous cults, the Unification Church blends Korean traditions with Christianity and science in a unique manner, which raises many important questions for students of religion.[73] It is also a self-consciously global religion.

Moon was originally influenced by Southern Baptist missionaries in Korea.[74] He later studied in Japan, where he received an excellent scientific education that enabled him to become an engineer. The Korean War and exposure to communism forced him to study Marxist works.[75] As a result, his teachings about the nature of religion reflect a complex interaction between Korean religious traditions, Christianity, science, and secular philosophies.[76]

Moon created a religion that not only cultivated a global consciousness but also made it an integral part of its theology. The basic text of the Unification Church is *The Divine Principle*. Most members of the Unification Church regard this book as a new revelation.[77] In this work, "Providence" is that power

---

70. Spencer J. Palmer, ed., *The New Religions of Korea* (Seoul, Korea: Royal Asiatic Society, 1967); and James Huntley Grayson, *Early Buddhism and Christianity in Korea: A Study in the Emplantation of Religion* (Leiden: E. J. Brill, 1985), 187–93; 234–54.

71. Palmer, 92–100; and Benjamin Weems, *Reform, Rebellion and the Heavenly Way* (Tucson, Ariz.: University of Arizona Press Weems, 1964), 7–13, 21–35.

72. Spencer J. Palmer, *Korea and Christianity* (Seoul, Korea: Hollym Corp., 1966); and Grayson, *Early Buddhism and Christianity in Korea*, 234–39.

73. Park Chull, Hang Lee Nyong, Sheen Doh Sung, and Yoon Se Won, *Sun Myung Moon: The Man and His Ideal* (Seoul, Korea: Mirae Munhwa Sa Chull, Nyong, Sung and Won, 1981); George Chryssides, *The Advent of Sun Myung Moon: The Origins, Beliefs and Practices of the Unification Church* (New York: St. Martin's Press, 1991), 46–107.

74. Chryssides, *The Advent of Sun Myung Moon,* 70–80.

75. Chull, Nyong, Sung and Won, *Sun Myung Moon,* 67–75.

76. Eileen Barker, *The Making of a Moonie* (Oxford: Basil Blackwells, 1984), 74–93.

77. Richard Quebedeaux and Rodney Sawatsky, eds., *Evangelical-Unification Dialogue* (New York: Rose of Sharon Press, 1979), 241–55.

of management that makes possible the comfortable coexistence of Shaman-ism, Confucianism, Judaism, and Christianity in individual experience.[78]

In Japan, following the defeat of the empire in 1945, new religions appeared to mushroom. Many observers attribute the origins of these movements to the shock of military defeat and the impact of the atomic bomb. As a result, they are seen as pseudo-political reactions, in terms of deprivation theory.[79] Others view these movements as interesting but superficial.[80] Finally, some studies show that the roots of these movements are far deeper than generally thought and genuinely religious in nature.[81] Nevertheless, all agree that the rapid growth of new religions, from the middle of the nineteenth century, followed Western intrusions that began to disrupt the Tokagawan Shogunate. During the Meiji Restoration, new religions flourished as science, technology, and Christian missions flooded into Japan.[82] Thus, in Japan—as in India and Korea—modernization, the impact of the West, and the activities of Christian missions stimulated the growth of new religions.[83] It is also clear that some modern Japanese religions, such as Sikai Kyuseikyo, the Teaching of World Salvation, founded by Mokichi Okada in 1882,[84] and Sukyo Mahikari, the True-Light Super Religious Organization, founded by Okada Yoskazu in 1960,[85] are new religions. Other movements, such as Rissho Koseikai, the Association of Truth and Fellowship, founded by Mrs. Myoko Naganuma (1899–1957) and Nikkyo Niwano (1906–1999) in 1938; and Soka Gakkai, the Value Creation

78. Young Oon Kim, *Unification Theology* (New York: Holy Spirit Association for the Unifica-tion of World Theology, 1980), 241–55.

79. H. Neil McFarland, *The Rush Hour of the Gods* (New York: Harper, 1970), 11–13, 37–70; Mark R. Mullin, "Japan's New Age and Neo-New Religions: Sociological Interpretations" (unpublished paper, Society for the Scientific Study of Religion, Annual Conference, Vir-ginia Beach, 1990); cf. Mark R. Mullin, ed., "New Religions and Indigenous Christianity," special edition of *The Japan Christian Quarterly* 57, no. 1 (winter 1991): 4–11.

80. C. B. Offner and H. van Straelen, *Modern Japanese Religions* (Leiden: E. J. Brill, 1963), 268–75.

81. Ian Reader, *Religion in Contemporary Japan* (Honolulu: University of Hawaii Press, 1991).

82. Emily Groszos Ooms, *Women and Millenarian Protest in Meiji Japan* (Ithaca, N.Y.: Cornell University; 1993); and Hori Ichiro, Ikado Fujio, Wakimoto Tsuneya, and Yanagawa Keiichi, *Japanese Religion* (Tokyo: Kodansha International, 1972), 24–27, 89–104.

83. Ichiro, Fujio, Tsuneya, and Keiichi, *Japanese Religion,* 84–86; Richard Fox Young, "The 'Christ' of the Japanese New Religions," *The Japan Christian Quarterly* 57, no. 1 (1991): 115–31.

84. Offner and van Straelen, *Modern Japanese Religions,* 76–78.

85. Winston Davis, *Dojo: Magic and Exorcism in Modern Japan* (Stanford, Calif.: Stanford University Press, 1980).

Society, of Tsunesaburo Makiguchi, founded in 1937, are genuine revitalization movements within Japanese Buddhism.[86]

AFRICA'S NEW RELIGIONS

New religious movements abound in Africa, where they are usually called
African Indigenous or Independent churches. As John Buchan's classic novel
Prester John[87] shows, African new religions were initially seen as dangerous
political movements opposed to white rule. A modified version of this view,
popular among scholars, is that African new religions began as a reaction to
colonialism. Consequently, it is often said that the first Independent church of
any consequence was born in the Transkei around 1883, the Thembu Church,
led by Nehemiah Tile.[88]

Recently, however, this analysis has been shown to be false. In fact, new
religions are part of African life and must be interpreted as genuine expressions of African spirituality, not simply as a negative reaction to Europeans. In
South Africa, for example, the earliest reported mass religious movement
among Blacks was that of the prophet Ntsikana early in the nineteenth century.[89] He combined elements of traditional religion with a form of Christianity to develop a new religion suitable for a rapidly changing society. Other
recent research makes it clear that although racism may have played a role in
the development of African Independent churches, the drive to create genuine
religious innovation had its source in African dreams and visions.[90]

For many Africans, Ethiopia became the symbol of liberation because it
was never under colonial control. Various secessions from missions churches
led to an Ethiopian Independent Church movement and later a Zionist
movement. By 1913, there were thirty-two new religions in South Africa. This
number had grown to 800 by 1949, to 2000 in 1960, 3270 in 1980, and 6000 by

---

86. Offner and van Straelen, *Modern Japanese Religions,* 95–109; cf. Peter B. Clarke and Jeffrey
    Somers, *Japanese New Religions in the West* (Sandgate, England: Japan Library, 1994).
87. John Buchan, later Lord Tweedsmuir, the Governor General of Canada, *Prester John* (Lon-
    don: Thomas Nelson and Sons, 1910).
88. Christopher Saunders, "Tile and the Thembu Church," *Journal of African History* 11, no. 4
    (1970): 553–70.
89. Janet Hodgeson, *Ntsikana's Great Hymn* (Cape Town, South Africa: Centre for African
    Studies, 1980).
90. Karla Poewe and Ulrich van der Heyden, "The Berlin Mission Society and Its Theology:
    The Bapedi Mission Church and the Independent Bapedi Lutheran Church," *South Afri-
    can Historical Journal,* no. 40 (1990): 21–50.

1993. Of these 6000 groups, about 90 percent have between twenty-five and sixty members. In other words, some 35 percent—or 8 million—South African Blacks belong to Independent or Indigenous churches, which is more members than the largest missions churches, the Roman Catholics and Methodists, combined.

The oldest of the larger new religions is the ama-Nazarite movement of Prophet Isaiah Shembe. Founded in 1912, this movement has approximately 750,000 followers, mainly Zulus. Shembe drew upon the Bible, his own insights, and revelations to create a new religion that met the needs of traditional people in the modern world.[91]

It is both complicated and academically dangerous to try to decide whether particular African Independent churches are Christian sects or new religions. Many early attempts to identify African groups as new religions were undertaken simply to dismiss them as unworthy of serious consideration. Understandably, a strong reaction set in, suggesting that critics of Independent churches were explicit or implicit racists. Consequently, when G. C. Oosthuizen published his pioneering *Theology of a South African Messiah*[92] in 1976, it was quickly dismissed by many authors as inadequate.[93] Ironically, both Isaiah Shembe's son, Amos Shembe, and his grandson, Londa Shembe, agreed with Oosthuizen against his critics that Isaiah Shembe was a Black Christ.[94]

The religion that Isaiah Shembe created is arguably the best known of all African religious movements. Anyone who has seen the BBC film *Zulu Zion* or read Sundkler's books knows that it preserves the essence of traditional Zulu culture. Nevertheless, a close look at the BBC film shows a scene in which dancers are wearing Scottish kilts and pith helmets. Isaiah Shembe was acutely aware of the need to integrate tradition and modernity. To do this, he reached out to Europeans and Indians, encouraged education, and used a combination of traditional, modern, and biblical ideas to prepare for a new world.[95]

---

91. Inus Daneel, *Quest for Belonging* (Harare, Zimbabwe: Mambo Press, 1987), 35–67.

92. G. C. Oosthuizen, *The Theology of a South African Messiah* (Leiden: E. J. Brill, 1976).

93. Bengt Sundkler, *Zulu Zion and Some Swazi Zionists* (Oxford: Oxford University Press, 1976), 190–92; and Absolom Vilakazi with Bongani Mthethwa, and Mthembeni Mpanza, *Shembe: The Revitalization of African Society* (Johannesburg, South Africa: Skotaville, 1986), 88–110.

94. Irving Hexham, ed., *The Scriptures of the amaNazaretha of Ekuphakameni*, trans. Londa Shembe and Hans-Jürgen Becken (Calgary: Calgary University Press, 1994, 1996), xix.

95. Ibid., sec. 10, 19, 22, 33, 91, 92, 115, 118; and Absolom Vilakazi, *Isonto Lamanazaretha: The Church of the Nazarites* (unpublished M.A. dissertation, Hartford Seminary, Hartford Conn., 1954), 85–94, 101–12.

The perplexing question that remains is whether the amaNazaretha are a new religion or a Christian sect. Oosthuizen presents evidence that they should be regarded as a new religion, and he was torn apart by academic colleagues for daring to suggest that the amaNazarite movement was not Christian. Now it is clear that Oosthuizen was probably correct in his analysis.[96] However, this admission does not solve the issue. Londa Shembe, who was brutally assassinated in 1989, believed that his grandfather had deliberately created a new religion with roots in Christianity, Judaism, and even Hinduism.[97] On the other hand, his uncle, Amos Shembe, who led a rival branch of the church, believed that although Oosthuizen's interpretation was essentially correct, the ama-Nazarites were becoming increasingly Christian. So we are left with a puzzle that applies not only to the amaNazarites, but also to many similar movements in Africa.

CONCLUSION

The study of new religions is in its infancy. For it to be carried out successfully, and for the challenge presented by new religions to be met by Christian theologians, a revolution must occur in theological thinking and training. Christian theologians who aspire to engage members of new religions must be well grounded in the traditions from which these movements draw inspiration. Thus, they need a basic education in the major religious traditions simply to understand the terminology and concepts used by new religions.

However, merely knowing the history of religions is not enough. The ways in which this history is fragmented, selectively incorporated, and synthesized by the leaders and ordinary members of new religions also require attention. This necessitates a basic understanding of world cultures and history. Here, anthropology and the techniques associated with participant observation are invaluable. Before anyone can theorize about the significance or beliefs of a new religion it is necessary to know what they believe and how those beliefs function in practice.

---

he Scriptures of the amaNazaretha of Ekuphakameni, xix; and Irving Hexham,
l History and Sacred Traditions of the Nazareth Baptist Church: The Story of
nafa Shembe, trans. Becken, Hans-Jürgen (Lewiston, N.Y.: Edwin Mellen,

nda Shembe, August 1987, *Ekuphakameni.*

The maxim "understanding precedes criticism" must become the watchword of all Christians who feel called to evangelize members of new religions. As Goethe said, *"Wer die Heiligen will verstehn, mu ins Land der Heiligen gehen,"*[98] (whoever wants to understand saints, must enter the land of saints). Similarly, those who want to understand converts to new religions must take the risk of entering into the world of those religions to understand their appeal so that they can speak to the believer in terms that the believer will understand. If this sounds strange to modern evangelicals, we suggest that it is asking no more than what Paul did when he said, "I am made all things to all men, that I might by all means save some" (1 Corinthians 9:22 KJV).

STUDY QUESTIONS

1. Discuss the role of empirical research using anthropological methods in understanding new religions. What dangers, if any, does this approach pose for practicing Christians?
2. How did Tom Paine affect the development of new religions? What is meant by the statement, "He nuked the advance of Evangelical Christianity"?
3. How would you describe a "global culture"? Discuss ways in which this concept helps us to understand the growth of new religions.
4. How should we revise the curriculum of theological seminaries and Christian colleges to reflect our emerging multireligious and multicultural society?
5. What is the difference between a "new religion" and a "revitalization movement" or "missionary movement"?

98. Hendrik Birus, hg., *Johan Wolfgang Goethe West—Östlicher Divan* (Frankfurt-am-Main, Germany: Deutscher Klassiker Verlag, 1994), 266.

CHAPTER 5

PAUL'S AREOPAGUS SPEECH IN ACTS 17

A Paradigm for Applying Apologetics and Missions
to Non-Christian Religious Movements

STEPHEN ROST

INTRODUCTION

"Is the apologist primarily a gate-keeper who fends off false doctrine, or can an apologist also actively seek to make disciples from the ranks of new religions?"[1] The answer lies in how we apply Matthew 28:18–20, in which Jesus tells his disciples to go into all the world, make disciples of all peoples, baptize them, and—finally—teach the converts to observe all of his commands. Christians have aggressively sought to evangelize the lost worldwide. Yet, for all the work being done in missions, the Christian community has not, until recently, placed much missiological emphasis on those groups commonly identified as "cults" or new religious movements (hereafter NRMs).

Fortunately, the twentieth century saw the rise of ministries dedicated to dealing with NRMs, each with its own unique approach to dealing with non-Christian religious groups. However, the emphasis was primarily on apologetics, consisting of a more confrontational and boundary-maintenance stance. Today, more voices in apologetics and missiological circles are trying to shift the emphasis away from a predominantly apologetic emphasis and balance it with a missiological thrust as well.

---

1. Philip Johnson, "Apologetics, Mission and New Religious Movements: A Holistic Approach," pt. 1, *Sacred Tribes: Journal of Christian Missions to New Religious Movement* (summer/fall 2002), http//www.sacredtribes.com/issue1/apolog1.htm.

According to Christian missionary-apologist John Morehead, "The counter-cult methodology tends to view the new religions primarily as heretical systems in need of refutation. Broader elements of a new religion's culture, world view, and epistemology are rarely considered."[2] Philip Johnson has done extensive research in this area and he identifies six common methodologies, the most popular being what he calls the heresy–rationalist apologia, which focuses primarily on defending the faith and contending for the truth as set forth in Jude 3.[3] Morehead comments that the heresy–rationalist approach "has conditioned apologists to be more focused on dealing with doctrinal errors, with minimal attention given to an evangelistic or missiological strategy."[4] Though the heresy–rationalist approach has been effective in *defending* orthodoxy, it has failed to adequately *pursue* with missiological zeal the adherents of NRMs as unreached people who need to be *evangelized*.

The challenge before us is to develop a paradigm that will equally and consistently combine apologetics (boundary-maintenance) and evangelism (missions). Acts 17 provides such a model, because it describes Paul's brief but effective ministry in Athens in which he applied a balance of both apologetics and evangelism to an environment saturated with intellectual sophistication and unparalleled religious diversity. Though the Areopagus narrative is not a *conclusive* missiological paradigm, it does exemplify the application of a holistic approach to adherents of NRMs.

PRELUDE TO PAUL'S AREOPAGUS SERMON: THE RELIGIOUS CULTURE OF ATHENS (ACTS 17:16–21)

Athens was synonymous with the intellectual life and culture of the Hellenistic world. Here could be found great poets, philosophers, scientists, playwrights, and historians.[5] Although these Athenian attributes had waned by Paul's time, Athens nevertheless retained its distinctive intellectual and religious attractiveness. According to F. F. Bruce,

---

2. John W. Morehead, "Transforming Evangelical Responses to New Religions: Missions and Counter-Cult in Partnership" (unpublished paper presented at the Annual Meeting of the Evangelical Missiological Society in Orlando, Florida, 3–5 October 2002).
3. Johnson, "Apologetics, Mission and New Religious Movements," 1.
4. Morehead, "Transforming Evangelical Responses to New Religions."
5. "Athens," in *Eerdmans' Atlas of the Bible* (Grand Rapids: Eerdmans, 1988).

Although Athens had long since lost the political eminence which was hers in an earlier day, she continued to represent the highest level of culture attained in classical antiquity. The sculpture, literature, and oratory of Athens in the fifth and fourth centuries B.C. have, indeed, never been surpassed. In philosophy, too, she occupied the leading place, being the native city of Socrates and Plato, and the adopted home of Aristotle, Epicurus, and Zeno.[6]

Religious diversity was another strong point of the city, evidenced by the presence of the Metroon, the abode of the mother of the gods, the temple of Apollo Patroos, the stoa of Zeus Eleutherios, and the temple of the Ares. Other sites included the temple of Wingless Victory, a statue of Athena, the temple of a demigod named Erechtheus, the unfinished temple of Olympian Zeus, the music hall of Pericles, the theater of Dionysos, and the temple of Hephaistos.[7]

Paul was greatly disturbed by the rampant paganism that saturated Athens (Acts 17:16).[8] He responded by taking the gospel to the Jews in the synagogue,[9] to God-fearing Gentiles, and to the pagans in the marketplace,[10] reasoning[11] (*dialegomai*) with them regarding Jesus and the resurrection, as was his method.[12] Though his initial approach is missiological, challenges to the gospel message, particularly the resurrection, require a defense.

6. F. F. Bruce, *The Book of Acts,* New International Commentary on the New Testament, rev. ed. (Grand Rapids: Eerdmans, 1988), 329.

7. D. H. Madvig, "Athens," in *International Standard Bible Encyclopedia,* ed. G. W. Bromiley, rev. ed., 4 vols. (Grand Rapids: Eerdmans, 1979–88), 1:351–52.

8. "It was certainly not the first time Paul will have encountered pagan cults. R. E. Wycherley tones down the word to translate it as 'a veritable forest of idols.' He takes the prefix *kata* to mean 'covered with' or 'luxuriant with.'" David Gill, "Achaia," in *The Book of Acts in Its Graeco-Roman Setting,* vol. 2 of *The Book of Acts in Its First Century Setting,* ed. David Gill and Conrad Gempf (Grand Rapids: Eerdmans, 1994), 443.

9. Paul goes to the monotheistic religious community, namely, the Jews (Judaism).

10. This audience consists of the pagan community, comprised of idolaters and the competing schools of philosophy. "Paul debated in the agora. This, the main public space in the city, was the economic, political and cultural heart of the city," Gill, "Achaia," 2:445.

11. Walter Bauer, "*dialegomai*," in *A Greek–English Lexicon of the New Testament and Other Early Christian Literature,* trans. W. Arndt and F. W. Gingrich (Chicago: University of Chicago Press, 1979), 18.

12. Cf. Acts 17:2; 18:4, 19; 19:9.

Paul's Primary Opponents

We cannot fully appreciate the intellectual challenge Paul faced in Athens unless we understand the fundamental beliefs of the Epicurean and Stoic philosophers. These two rival schools of thought were very influential during the New Testament era. Both embraced worldviews that conflicted with what Paul taught, so they would naturally be quick to dispute the credibility of Paul's message (Acts 17:18).

Epicureanism

"Epicureanism, being a philosophy of salvation, was primarily interested in offering for a fading religious faith and a failing traditional morality a philosophical substitute founded upon reason and natural sanctions."[13] Epicureans believed that religion was a detriment to man in two ways: First, it promoted an unhealthy fear of the uncertainties of the afterlife. Second, there was the everpresent "spying, prying eye and heavy, interfering hand of the gods. These terrors are the arch-destroyers of man's happiness."[14]

According to Epicurean epistemology, knowledge is derived from and truth is tested by the senses; namely perceptions, concepts, and feelings. *Perception,* by means of sense organs, is the source of what is true and real. *Concepts* are member images acquired from perceptions, and *feelings* are the criteria of conduct. Whatever feels good is desirable; pain is undesirable.

> The locus of moral judgment therefore must be the pleasure or pain any particular accidental unity, which we call a "human being," might feel. As a consequence, no sexual act is intrinsically evil, for as Epicurus himself said, "every pleasure is a good thing." Since only the individual can affirm or deny whether something gives him a pleasing sensation, then no other individual can deny the "goodness" of what someone else finds pleasant. No one can be wrong about what happens to *feel* good.[15]

---

13. B. A. G. Fuller, *A History of Philosophy,* 2 vols. (New York: Henry Holt, 1945), 1:237.
14. Ibid., 1:240.
15. Benjamin Wiker, *Moral Darwinism: How We Became Hedonists* (Downers Grove, Ill.: InterVarsity, 2002), 86.

Epicurean cosmology was strictly materialistic and taught that the world was made up of atoms that are constantly in motion. Objects are formed when the atoms collide. As for teleology, there is neither destiny nor divine providence. Though the gods do exist, they have nothing to do with the affairs of this world, so Epicureanism taught what could be labeled hard deism. Eschatologically, death is the end of human existence, hence no afterlife or judgment.

Stoicism

According to philosopher Joseph Owens, the Stoics were similar to the Epicureans in that they believed life was to be lived according to nature, because the individual is a part of the whole. The basic impulse of life was self-preservation, not pleasure. Pleasure was merely a by-product of self-preservation. Of the three aspects of life, the contemplative, practical, and rational, reason was the preferred approach.[16] Ronald Nash identifies three periods of Stoic development as follows: the Early Stoa (300–200 B.C.), Middle Stoa (150–1 B.C.), and Later Stoa (A.D. 1–180).[17] The Later Stoa was that which flourished during the first century and was encountered by the apostle Paul. Significant Stoics of this period include Seneca, Epictetus, and Marcus Aurelius.[18]

The Stoics were monists who held to a pantheistic worldview, in contrast to the deism of Epicureanism. "God may be called the Soul of the universe, the universe the body of God. But because neither can be conceived or exist without the other, the two are essentially identical. God is the universe, and the universe is God."[19] As for immortality, the general consensus was that at death the individual soul was "reabsorbed into the ever-living Fire, in a world conflagration";[20] ergo, no judgment in the afterlife. Stoic cosmology, like that of Epicureanism, posited an eternal universe.

In response to Paul's message, the philosophers showed their contempt by calling him an "idle babbler," which is to say he was "an inferior speaker or

16. Joseph Owens, *A History of Ancient Western Philosophy* (New York: Appleton-Century-Crofts, 1959), 390–91.
17. Ronald Nash, *Christianity and the Hellenistic World* (Grand Rapids: Zondervan, 1984), 67–68.
18. Ibid., 73.
19. Fuller, *History of Philosophy,* 1:253.
20. Ibid., 1:254.

writer who picks up and uses as his own ideas that he has found in others."[21] Later, possibly upon reflection of his Athens experience, Paul draws a contrast between the wisdom of this world and the "foolishness" of the gospel (1 Corinthians 1:18–31). Rhetorical questions such as "Where is the wise man? Where is the scribe? Where is the debater of this age?"[22] would serve as a rhetorical rebuke of the pagan intelligentsia.

Paul was also accused of promoting "strange deities"[23] (Acts 17:18), which interestingly enough was reminiscent of the charge brought against Socrates. Nevertheless, the Athenians were known for their interest in new things, so Paul's message aroused their curiosity to the extent that he was invited to discuss it further before the Areopagus (Acts 17:19–21), an institution that had jurisdiction over religious and ethical matters.

THE AREOPAGUS MESSAGE (ACTS 17:22–31)

In his book titled *Frameworks,* Douglas Walrath explains that "different cultures hold different assumptions about what is real and what is not real, as well as why things happen the way they do."[24] He cites Michael Polanyi's observation that "cultures, like individuals, develop mechanisms to protect themselves against challenges to their frameworks."[25]

Regarding Paul's sermon, D. A. Carson notes that it begins with the primacy of biblical theology, which "refers to the theology of the biblical corpora as God progressively discloses himself, climaxing in the coming of his Son

---

21. C. K. Barrett, *The Acts of the Apostles,* International Critical Commentary, 2 vols. (Edinburgh: T. and T. Clark, 2000), 2:830.

22. Gordon Fee understands the wise to be philosophers, and scribes to be rabbis, but the debater is not identifiable. Gordon Fee, *First Epistle to the Corinthians,* New International Commentary on the Old Testament (Grand Rapids: Eerdmans, 1991), 70–71. Given the fact that rhetoric was an important part of Greek education, and the Epicurean and Stoic philosophers were evidently unimpressed with Paul's public speaking skills, it is possible the debater is someone well schooled in rhetoric.

23. The word translated "deities" is the Greek word *daimoniwn,* from which we get the English term *demon.* Unlike the New Testament concept of demons as fallen, evil spirit beings, the Greeks understood demons in a different way. In Plato's Cratylus 398, demons, according to Socrates' understanding of Hesiod, were noble and good. Hermogenes agrees with Socrates and goes on to say that Hesiod's use of *daimone* in reference to the noble and good men defined their nature. *Dahmone,* therefore, meant "knowing and wise." Plato *Dialogues,* "Cratylus" 398–99.

24. Douglas Walrath, *Frameworks* (New York: Pilgrim, 1987), 7.

25. Ibid.

Jesus Christ."[26] The sermon contains five doctrinal categories, which flow in logical sequence: God (theology proper), man (anthropology), salvation (soteriology), Christ (Christology), and final judgment (eschatology). These five categories are developed within three distinct parts. First is the introduction, in which Paul sets the tone of his message by building a rapport with his audience: "I observe that you are very religious" (Acts 17:22 NASB). Second, he gives both a philosophical and theological presentation of the Unknown God. Finally, in his conclusion, Paul conveys to the Athenians that God declares that "all everywhere should repent" (Acts 17:30 NASB). Karl Sandnes observes that Paul's aim was to get the audience to respond to what he was teaching.[27]

Paul begins his message by acknowledging the fact that the Athenians are "very religious" people (Acts 17:22). Simon Kistemaker comments that Paul's statement could be taken as either a derogatory response, or simply a compliment on their devotion to a god about whom they know nothing. He concludes that, given the context of the speech, Paul is complimentary.[28] Next the apostle acknowledges the Athenians' ignorance of the Unknown God, and uses this as an opportunity to give a detailed explanation of who this God really is.

The Doctrine of God

Paul introduces his audience to the metaphysics of monotheism by presenting God's cosmological relationship to the world, that of Creator who is distinct from the created. Paul's monotheistic cosmology naturally posits a God who is ontologically distinct from creation, self-existing, and his aseity[29] is explicitly stated (Acts 17:25). Paul's worldview is philosophically superior to that of the pantheistic and polytheistic worldviews of the Greeks, and it is squarely grounded in the Old Testament (Acts 17:24–25).

---

26. D. A. Carson, *The Gagging of God* (Grand Rapids: Zondervan, 1996), 501–2.
27. Karl Sandnes, "Paul and Socrates: The Aim of Paul's Areopagus Speech," *Journal for the Study of the New Testament* 50 (1993): 15.
28. Simon Kistemaker, *Exposition of the Acts of the Apostles*, New Testament Commentary (Grand Rapids: Baker, 1991), 631. F. F. Bruce and C. K. Barrett believe that Paul merely acknowledges the fact that the Athenians are religious, without any hint of approving or being complimentary of their religious behavior.
29. This is a theological term that has unfortunately been lost in modern discussions about God. It speaks of God's self-existence; his total lack of dependence on anything outside of himself for existence. God is the uncaused First Cause of all contingent things. See "Aseity" in *Pocket Dictionary of Theological Terms*, Stan Grenz, David Guretzki, and Cherith Nordling, eds. (Downers Grove, Ill. InterVarsity, 1999), 16.

This is the very language of biblical revelation: God Most High is "maker of heaven and earth" (Genesis 14:19, 23); "the earth is the Lord's and the fulness thereof" (Psalm 24:1). No concessions are allowed to Hellenistic paganism; no distinction is made between the Supreme Being and a "demiurge" or master-workman who fashioned the world because the Supreme Being was too pure to come into polluting contact with the material order.[30]

Paul's proclamation of God's nature and attributes is in direct response to the ideas taught by the Epicureans and Stoics. "The Christian doctrine of creation *ex nihilo* (from or out of nothing) strikes directly against Epicurus's contrary doctrine that the universe, atoms, and the void are all eternal."[31] Interestingly, Greek Cynics described God in ways comparable to that of Paul's theology proper. Adams points to a Cynic epistle by Heraclitus in which his description of God is comparable to the one given by Paul.

> . . . O you ignorant men, first teach us who God is so that when you speak of committing impiety you may be trusted. (2) *Where is God? Locked up in temples?* Pious indeed, are you who set up God in darkness! A man feels insulted if he is called a person of stone, but is a god truly spoken of when the honored name, "Out of the cliffs he was born," is applied to him? You ignorant men! Don't you know that *God is not made by hands,* that he has not from the beginning had a pedestal, and that he does not have a single enclosure but that the whole world, adorned with animals, plants, and stars is his temple? . . . Am I, then, not pious, Ethycles, I who alone know God, while you are rash and impious, for while you think that he exists, you suppose he is what he is not? If an altar of a god is not erected is there then a god? Are the stones witnesses of gods? His works, such as those of the sun, must testify to him. Night and day testify to him. *The seasons are his witnesses. The whole earth is a fruit-bearing witness.* The cycle of the moon, his work, is his heavenly testimony.[32]

---

30. F. F. Bruce, "Paul and the Athenians," *The Expository Times* 88 (1976): 8.
31. Benjamin Wiker, *Moral Darwinism: How We Became Hedonists* (Downers Grove, Ill.: InterVarsity, 2002), 78.
32. Marilyn McCord Adams, "Philosophy and the Bible: The Areopagus Speech," *Faith and Philosophy* 9 (1992): 139–140. The citation by Adams is taken from Abraham Malherbe, *The Cynic Epistles: A Study Edition* (Missoula, Mont.: Scholar's Press, 1977), 191–93 (emphasis in original).

Heraclitus's statement regarding God echoes the words of Psalm 19, though it is safe to say he didn't get his ideas from the Old Testament.

Biblical Anthropology

The Greek notion that man is alone in the universe to manage his own affairs is contradicted by Paul's cosmology, which states that man is not only created by God, but God has also determined when and where man will take his place in the world (Acts 17:26). Paul's theistic determinism is an important aspect of his argument, for it responds to the deistic, self-determinism of the Epicureans. According to Frederick Copleston, "While not denying the existence of the gods he [Epicurus] wished to show that they do not interfere in human affairs and that man need not therefore occupy himself with propitiation and petition and 'superstition' in general."[33] Epicurus also taught that the world was mechanically caused by the collision of atoms. Thus the world and the life it contains have no teleology.[34] Yet it is clear that behind Paul's metaphysical and theological arguments lays an irrefutable teleology (Acts 17:27).

> The human race was disposed in areas of the earth's surface, and under climatic conditions, calculated to make human life possible; but physical existence was not the final purpose for which men were made. They were intended to seek God, whom (it is implied) they would know only if they sought him; the search itself had value and was willed by God.[35]

Humanity's struggle in his search for God is not in vain. As the apostle explains, God is near and imminent, and his imminence bridges the gap between man the finite, contingent, and created, and God the eternal, transcendent Creator. God seeks a relationship with humanity, which is ultimately accomplished through repentance, contrary to the Epicurean notion that the gods have no involvement or interest in human affairs.[36]

Paul's familiarity with Stoic literature is used strategically in his argument

---

33. Frederick Copleston, *Greece and Rome*, vol. 1 of *A History of Philosophy* (Westminster, Md.: Newman Press, 1966), 403–4.

34. Ibid., 1:405.

35. Barrett, *Acts of the Apostles*, 2:844.

36. Copleston, *Greece and Rome*, 1:406.

to show the Stoic philosophers that even their own poets held to similar ideas regarding the relationship between God and humanity. For example, Paul's statement in Acts 17:28 (NASB), "In Him we live and move and exist," is drawn from the "fourth line of a quatrain attributed to Epimenides the Cretan."[37] In the same verse, his assertion that "we also are His offspring" comes from the poem "Natural Phenomena," "by Paul's fellow Cilician, Aratus, a poet deeply influenced by Stoicism."[38]

These citations from Stoic poets in no way constitute a sympathetic view of Stoic metaphysics. On the contrary, Paul's theology of God contradicts the very notion of a pantheistic deity. Ronald Nash points out that Paul, being an educated man, would have knowledge of Stoic literature, and his use of it in dialogue with the Stoics would at least gain their attention.[39] This is particularly true given that educated, cultured Greeks were influenced more by Stoic thought than by any other philosophy.[40]

Kistemaker says that "by quoting these poets, Paul is not intimating that he agrees with the pagan setting in which the citations flourished. Rather, he uses the words to fit his Christian teaching,"[41] and he cites Stoic authorities to corroborate his particular view of God.[42] The Hellenistic Greeks, though ignorant of the Old Testament, would certainly be familiar with Stoic thought.

> Some of the motifs of this speech have appeared earlier in the short summary of Barnabas and Paul's protest to the people of Lystra who were preparing to pay them divine honors (Acts 14:15–17), but the *Areopagitica* is fuller, more detailed and adapted to the intellectual climate of Athens. At Athens, as formerly at Lystra, the Paul of Acts does not expressly quote Old Testament prophecies which would be

---

37. F. F. Bruce, *Paul: Apostle of the Heart Set Free* (Grand Rapids: Eerdmans, 1979), 242. In this same section comes the quote, "The Cretans, always liars," which is cited by Paul in Titus 1:12. The text in which these statements appear reads as follows: "The Cretans carve a Tomb for thee, O Holy and high! Liars, evil beasts, and slow bellies; for thou art not dead for ever; thou art alive and risen; for in thee we live and are moved, and have our being." Kistemaker, *Exposition of the Acts of the Apostles*, 636.
38. Bruce, *Paul*, 242.
39. Nash, *Christianity and the Hellenistic World*, 74.
40. Ibid., 67.
41. Kistemaker, *Exposition of the Acts of the Apostles*, 637.
42. Bruce, *Paul*, 243.

quite unknown to his audience: such direct quotations as his speech
contains are from Greek poets.[43]

The logical conclusion to our existence and movement within God's sovereign purview is introduced by the statement, "Being then the offspring of God"
(Acts 17:29 NASB), from which Paul is able to establish a clear distinction between the Creator and the created. Because the divine nature is not the product of human thought or purpose, all physical representations of God are to
be abandoned. Not even by analogy can God be represented by the idolatrous
use of gold, silver, and stone. God is to be worshiped in spirit and truth, and
any attempt to represent him in tangible form compromises who he is.

Paul's Soteriological Appeal

Athens was an extremely pluralistic society, so the idea of one absolute truth
would not be well received by the Athenians, particularly with respect to
religious truth claims. The problem would be especially problematic
soteriologically, because the apostolic proclamation that Jesus is the only way
would negate all other non-Christian epistemologies. In response to the question, "Is salvation available to adherents of non-Christian religions via a special work of God?" the Pauline answer, in light of the Areopagus sermon, would
be no.

This problem was addressed in the twentieth century by Catholic theologians Karl Rahner and Bernard Lonergan. George Lindbeck observes:

> [Both Rahner and Lonergan] identify the prereflective, inarticulate
> experience of the divine, which they hold is at the heart of every reli-
> gion, with the saving grace of Christ. Those non-Christians who re-
> spond to the inward call already share in the same justification, the
> same salvation, that is at work in Christians even though, unlike Chris-
> tians, they have no conscious adherence or visible sacramental bond
> to the historical Jesus Christ who is both the ultimate source and the
> only fully and finally appropriate objective correlate of their inner
> experience of salvation. Their faith . . . is wholly implicit, yet one might
> speak of them, Rahner suggests, as "anonymous Christians," for their
> subjective appropriation of salvation may be as ontologically genuine

---

43. Bruce, "Paul and the Athenians," 8.

even in this life as in the case of those who have explicit faith or are manifestly members of the people of God.[44]

In the evangelical community, this same issue has been the source of extensive debate. Evangelical inclusivists contend that God saves people who respond to what revelation they have, without a conscious knowledge of Christ. Evangelicals who embrace exclusivism argue that there is no salvation in other religions and one must explicitly confess the merits of Jesus Christ in order to be saved.

Given the content of the Areopagus speech, what did Paul preach in his pluralistic environment? For apologists, this question is important because it affects how the beliefs and practices of other religions are addressed. Though sensitivity is an important part of the apologetic endeavor, protecting and proclaiming the truth is equally important.

It appears from Paul's argument that he preached an exclusivist soteriology grounded in the person and work of Jesus Christ, namely his resurrection. Furthermore, Paul's admonition for the Athenians to repent has an inherent implication: if repentance is required, then there must be a reason for one's need to repent. If God is calling me to repent, then evidently I am not in a right relationship with him. Furthermore, my repentance is linked to an explicit object of belief: Jesus Christ. Though Luke does not record in exact detail everything that was said on the Areopagus, we know that Paul's gospel was not shallow or inconsistently preached.

Paul's soteriology was particularly difficult for the Epicureans, because they denied immortality. "Moreover, by rejecting immortality he [Epicurus] hoped to free man from fear of death—for what reason is there to fear death when it is mere extinction, absence of all consciousness and feeling, when there is no judgment and when no punishment awaits one in the afterworld?"[45] This is especially significant because the Resurrection is the focus of Paul's gospel (Acts 17:18, 31–32), and it is this issue that compels the philosophers to seek further dialogue with Paul. However, this central teaching of the Christian faith is also the object of ridicule. In this particular case, the resurrection of Jesus Christ poses a serious intellectual obstacle to the mechanistic cosmology of the Epicureans, who would naturally reject miracles because of their denial of immortality. Furthermore, their deistic view of the gods would render

---

44. George Lindbeck, *The Nature of Doctrine* (Philadelphia: Westminster, 1984), 56–57.
45. Copleston, *Greece and Rome*, 1:404.

miracles such as the resurrection incompatible with their naturalistic worldview.

> Undoubtedly, one of the major stumbling blocks to becoming a Christian for many people today is that Christianity is a religion of miracles. It asserts that God became incarnate in Jesus of Nazareth, being born of a virgin, that he performed various miracles, exorcised demonic beings and that, having died by crucifixion, he rose from the dead. But the problem is that these sorts of miraculous events seem to belong to a world view foreign to modern man—a pre-scientific, superstitious world view belonging to the ancient and middle ages.[46]

Philosophers Douglas Geivett and Gary Habermas observe:

> [The] removal of the miraculous eviscerates the Christian faith. So much of the strength and vigor of Christianity depends on the factuality of miracles. As the apostle Paul wrote, "if Christ has not been raised, then our preaching is in vain. . . . If Christ has not been raised, your faith is also in vain. . . . If Christ has not been raised, your faith is worthless; you are still in your sins." At the very least, then, the apologist must answer the charge that the presence of miracles within the New Testament Gospels cancels their claim to historical reliability.[47]

Christianity is a faith that is inextricably connected to the miraculous. Throughout the Old and New Testaments, miracles provided evidence that the truth claims of the people of God were indeed legitimate. Like Paul, Christians today run up against stiff opposition from those who embrace a naturalistic view of the world, which rejects miracles. Ironically, the evolutionary model that is enthusiastically embraced by naturalism posits an explanation for the origin of life and the universe that is no less miraculous than the miracle stories found in the Scriptures. So it is fair to say that the naturalistic worldview, which has historically repudiated the miraculous, is inescapably bound to the miraculous.

---

46. William Lane Craig, *Reasonable Faith: Christian Truth and Apologetics* (Wheaton, Ill.: Crossway, 1994), 127.

47. R. Douglas Geivett and Gary Habermas, eds., *In Defense of Miracles: A Comprehensive Case for God's Action in History* (Downers Grove, Ill.: InterVarsity, 1997), 281 n. 2.

When this happens, a reasoned response is not only in order, but is potentially crucial to helping the unbeliever see the deficiencies in his or her worldview. Therefore, one can conclude that belief in miracles is not an irrational escape into the supernatural.

Eschatological Warning

Paul's gospel concludes with a warning to his audience that they will eventually face God, so now is the time to prepare for the day of judgment by repenting, regardless of the false Epicurean notion that "men may honor the gods for their excellence and may even take part in the customary ceremonial worship, *but all fear of them is out of place and also all attempts to win their favour by sacrifice*" [emphasis added].[48] What is out of place is the notion that there is not accountability to God. The deistic implications of Epicurean theism and Stoic pantheism are systematically dismantled by the apostle's philosophical and theological apologetic, culminating in an evangelistic appeal to turn to the formerly Unknown God who is now known.

For the very religious Athenians, as for adherents of non-Christian religions today, the metaphysical and theological implications of the Areopagus message require an epistemological departure from the framework they have embraced, and replacement with the gospel of Jesus Christ. The difficulty in making such a shift is evident in the remaining passages of Acts 17, where we find Paul's proclamation of the Resurrection to be the source of mockery. Nevertheless, people did embrace the gospel message and follow him. Though some may argue that Paul's efforts failed in the long run, one must keep in mind the fact that it is God, not Paul or modern day apologists, who causes the growth (1 Corinthians 3:6).

RESPONSE TO PAUL'S MESSAGE (ACTS 17:32–34)

The negative reaction that Paul receives to his restatement of the Resurrection is not unusual, given the fact that the crowd to which he was speaking was comprised predominantly of Epicureans, Stoics, and those sympathetic to these two schools of thought. His audience certainly was influenced by Greek thought concerning the afterlife. For example, in the *Eumenides* of Aeschylus, we read

---

48. Copleston, *Greece and Rome*, 1:406.

that "once a man dies and the earth drinks up his blood, there is not resurrection."[49] The Epicureans would certainly look at Paul's ideas as nothing more than misguided disturbances in thinking, attributable to irrational fears of the afterlife.[50] For the Epicurean, there is no immortality of the soul[51] and no resurrection. Death is the end of one's existence.[52] This being the case, Paul's statements regarding the future judgment of humankind by a resurrected man seemed utterly absurd. Likewise, since the Stoic view of the afterlife denied the existence of the soul beyond the grave, they would also reject the idea of a resurrection.[53]

THE APOLOGETICAL AND MISSIOLOGICAL IMPLICATIONS OF THE AREOPAGUS SERMON

Assessing Our Categories: The Use and Misuse of Labels

Paul's irenic approach to the Athenians shows how to establish rapport with adherents of NRMs.[54] Although Paul was fervently committed to the defense of the faith, he was equally passionate about missions, and he saw the unregenerate as opportunities for evangelism. Unlike the categorization that exists today with respect to NRMs, there is no evidence that Paul made such distinctions between adherents of non-Christian religions and people without any strong religious convictions. He saw all non-Christians, regardless of their associations or lack thereof, as opportunities for spiritual harvest. His attitude should be noted by contemporary Christian apologists, who tend to be oriented toward maintaining boundaries and rooting out error in their approach to NRMs. They should seriously consider a paradigm shift away from these methods toward a balanced Pauline strategy of defending the faith and evangelizing the lost souls entangled in NRMs.

---

49. Bruce, *The Book of Acts*, 343.
50. N. Clayton Croy, "Hellenistic Philosophies and the Preaching of the Resurrection (Acts 17:18, 32)," *Novum Testamentum* 39 (1997): 29.
51. Epicureans believed the soul was material, therefore corporeal, so at death it, like the body, would dissolve.
52. Frederick Copleston, *Greece and Rome*, vol. 1, bk. 1 of *A History of Philosophy* (New York: Doubleday, 1985), 402–4.
53. Croy, "Hellenistic Philosophies and the Preaching of the Resurrection," 32, 33, 34.
54. Dean Flemming, "Contextualizing the Gospel in Athens: Paul's Areopagus Address as a Paradigm for Missionary Communication," *Missiology: An International Review* 30 (2002): 202.

Another way to foster an environment conducive to responsible dialogue is to reexamine the use of labels which are used to identify groups that are not considered theologically orthodox. The popular term *cult* is a case in point. Within the evangelical community, the use of this term is cause for concern, and rightly so, for it has become increasingly pejorative, offensive, and counterproductive to establishing a meaningful dialogue with these groups that have been labeled as such. Moreover, the term is ambiguous,[55] and, as sociologist Douglas Cowan rightly notes, the scholarly community has had difficulty defining it. Cowan also points out that the term is not used in a value-free manner today.[56]

Attempts to define *cult* are at best subjective, and the criteria may well apply to any religious system, including Christianity. Alan Gomes acknowledges the problems associated with defining the term, and he offers his own preferred definition:

> A cult of Christianity is a group of people, which claiming to be Christian, embraces a particular doctrinal system taught by an individual leader, group of leaders, or organization, which (system) denies (either explicitly or implicitly) one or more of the central doctrines of the Christian faith as taught in the sixty-six books of the Bible.[57]

In his book *The Kingdom of the Cults,* Walter Martin cites approvingly Dr. Charles Braden's definition of a cult: "By the term 'cult' I mean nothing derogatory to any group so classified. A cult, as I define it, is any religious group which differs significantly in some one or more respects as to belief or practice, from those religious groups which are regarded as the normative expressions of religion in our total culture."[58] Martin expands on Braden's definition by adding, "A cult might also be defined as a group of people gathered about a specific person or person's interpretation of the Bible."[59]

---

55. Morehead, "Transforming Evangelical Responses to New Religions."
56. Doug Cowan, "Cult Apology: A Modest (Typological) Proposal" (unpublished paper presented to the 2002 Society for the Scientific Study of Religion Conference, Salt Lake City, Utah, 1–3 November 2002).
57. Alan Gomes, *Unmasking the Cults,* in *Zondervan Guide to Cults and Religious Movements,* ed. Alan Gomes (Grand Rapids: Zondervan, 1995), 7.
58. Walter Martin, *The Kingdom of the Cults* (Minneapolis: Bethany, 1976), 11.
59. Ibid.

Though each of these definitions may satisfy the evangelical understanding of the term *cult,* they are fraught with elements of subjectivity which create a false dichotomy between groups that are labeled "cults" and those that are given the designation "world religion." For example, the Church of Jesus Christ of Latter-day Saints has historically been labeled a cult, whereas Islam typically falls under the category of world religion. Though both hold views that are contrary to the historic Christian faith, Mormonism tends to receive more attention from Christians than does Islam. This, in my estimation, minimizes one group's presence and accentuates the beliefs and actions of the other.

Historically, *cult* has been used in both popular and scholarly writings dealing with groups considered incompatible with the distinctives of the historic Christian faith, primarily in the Western context. However, "new religious movement" is the preferred designation for non-Christian or aberrant Christian groups.

Contextualization

The debate over contextualization raged for years within the evangelical community. Missiologists David Hesselgrave and Edward Rommen, aware of concerns over contextualization, rightly warn against its misuse.

> The missionary's ultimate goal in communication has always been to present the supracultural message of the gospel in culturally relevant terms. There are two potential hazards which must be assiduously avoided in this endeavor: (1) the perception of the communicator's own cultural heritage as an integral element of the gospel, and (2) a syncretistic inclusion of elements from the receptor culture which would alter or eliminate aspects of the message upon which the integrity of the gospel depends.[60]

With respect to the Areopagus speech, a common observation among New Testament specialists, theologians, and philosophers is that it differs from other sermons given by Paul.

---

60. David J. Hesselgrave and Edward Rommen, "The Historical Background of Contextualization," in *Contextualization: Meanings, Methods, and Models* (Grand Rapids: Baker, 1989), 1.

The form and style of the Areopagus speech are ably adapted to persuade a sophisticated Gentile audience. In contrast to the frequent use
of language and quotations from the Old Testament that we find in
sermons preached to Jews in Acts (e.g., 2:14–36; 13:16–40), this discourse reflects a more Hellenized style that is suited to its occasion
and hearers.[61]

Paul's contextual approach to the Greeks, though mildly Hellenized, was
rigidly controlled by his unwavering commitment to apostolic doctrine and
the unconditional requirement of every person listening to explicitly affirm
the person and work of Jesus Christ for salvation. Philosopher Mark Hanna
makes an excellent point regarding the cross-cultural communication of the
Christian message:

> One must learn the thought patterns and language of the culture which
> he addresses. Both relevance and freshness of expression must be val-
> ued and cultivated. Maintaining the balance between the moorings of
> biblical language and the need for cultural relevance is demanding,
> but the apologist must make that his special concern. This requires
> intense listening, wide reading, painstaking analysis, deep reflection,
> persistent questioning, and profound resolve.[62]

Dialogue with NRMs

A paradigm that utilizes the resources of both apologetics and missions
entails the use of dialogue when dealing with NRMs. Unfortunately, among
many evangelicals the idea of dialoguing with NRMs is associated with pluralism and therefore deemed unacceptable. In response to such apprehensions,
missiologist David Hesselgrave's comments are instructive:

> The Christian mission in the closing decades of the twentieth century
> challenges both the ecumenist and the evangelical to make a reap-
> praisal of their attitudes toward, and participation in, interreligious
> dialogue. Now is the time for ecumenists to review the direction that
> dialogue has taken and subject it to the standards of the revealed will

---

61. Fleming, "Contextualizing the Gospel in Athens," 201.
62. Mark Hanna, *Crucial Questions in Apologetics* (Grand Rapids: Baker, 1981), 63.

of God in the Scriptures. Any form of dialogue that compromises the uniqueness of the Christian gospel and the necessity that adherents of other faiths repent and believe it should be rejected and supplanted by forms of dialogue that enjoin conversion to Christ. Now is the time for evangelicals to review their attitude of disinterest and non-participation in dialogue. To insist upon the uniqueness of the Christian gospel and the need of all people for salvation in Christ is not tantamount to engaging in biblical dialogue. Something new is needed. While it may be in the interest of the Christian mission to participate in those types of dialogue that have positive benefits and do not require abandonment or obfuscation of the Christian message, it definitely would be in the interest of the Christian mission to participate in those types of dialogue that enable evangelicals to enter the forums of the world with the understanding, commitment, and courage that characterized the apostolic era.[63]

In light of Paul's example in Acts 17, contrasted with contemporary evangelical approaches to new religions, it seems that new strategy and applications are in order. John Morehead proposes several approaches. First, think of NRMs as unreached people groups. This is clearly in line with what Paul does in Acts 17, where he forthrightly addresses the Greeks by first proclaiming sound doctrine and then calling them to repentance. Another option is to think holistically. That is, consider all the ways in which NRMs can be better understood and reached. It is a mistake to conclude that Morehead and others like him are in some way compromising the gospel message or minimizing the heretical nature of Bible-based NRMs, for example. On the contrary, his proposal is to develop more effective ways of approaching NRMs in order to better influence them to abandon their views and embrace orthodoxy.[64]

The Use of Philosophy

The Areopagus sermon has received considerable attention by historians, philosophers, and Bible scholars, and opinions vary as to the extent of Paul's

---

63. David Hesselgrave, "Evangelicals and Interreligious Dialogue," in *Ministry and Theology in Global Perspective: Contemporary Challenges for the Church,* eds. Don Pittman, Ruben Habito, and Terry Muck (Grand Rapids: Eerdmans, 1996), 427–28.

64. Morehead, "Transforming Evangelical Responses to New Religions."

success in Athens, or lack thereof. Philosopher Marilyn McCord Adams summarizes some of the negative interpretations that have been leveled against Paul:

> They [commentators] note that, by contrast with other speeches in Acts, (i) Paul's Areopagus oration contains no references to God's special providences towards His chosen people; instead His role as creator and sustainer and His relations with humankind generally are underscored. Moreover, (ii) its proof texts (17:28) are taken, not from the Bible, but from Greek poets. (iii) Finally, this speech nowhere mentions the names "Jesus" and "Christ"; the death of Jesus is entirely passed over, while His resurrection is referred to only in connection with His appointment as eschatological judge. These features suggest to such commentators that the Areopagus speech was an attempt to meet the Epicurean and Stoic philosophers (17:18) on their own ground. But, they conclude, this missionary strategy was a failure, because it won few converts (17:32–34).[65]

Two of the three objections McCord identifies warrant a response. First, the objection that Paul uses Greek poets as proof texts is essentially a *genetic fallacy;* it assumes such sources are illegitimate because they are pagan in origin. Given the fact that Paul was well educated, it would be normal for him to express biblical truths from a variety of sources. In Titus 1:12 and 1 Corinthians 15:33, Paul cites pagan sources to show agreement between himself and those authorities compatible with the views of his audience. In Romans 1:19–20, he firmly establishes the fact that from natural revelation (cosmology) one can derive a natural theology of God sufficient to hold all of humanity accountable to God.

Paul's detractors argue that his methodology, specifically his use of philosophical reasoning and pagan sources, contributed to his alleged ineffectiveness in Athens. According to Sir William Ramsey, "Paul was disappointed and perhaps disillusioned by his experience in Athens. He felt that he had gone at least as far as was right in the way of presenting his doctrine in a form suited to the current philosophy; and the result had been little more than naught."[66]

---

65. Adams, "Philosophy and the Bible," 135.
66. Sir William Ramsey, *St. Paul the Traveller and Roman Citizen* (Grand Rapids: Baker, 1962), 252.

Historian Henri Daniel-Rops says that "on his arrival in Athens . . . Paul was to experience the most resounding defeat of his whole career."[67] However, the conversions of Dionysius the Areopagite, Damaris, and others constitute a successful, though brief, missiological endeavor. Furthermore, Paul successfully countered Stoic and Epicurean metaphysics with a thoroughgoing Christian alternative, thus demonstrating the use of apologetics.[68]

J. D. Charles points out that Tarsus was the native city of such famous Stoic philosophers as Zeno, Antipater, Athenadorus, and Nestor.[69] The fact that Paul was from Tarsus suggests such an environment thoroughly prepared Paul for ministry in a Hellenistic culture.[70] This would include training in and familiarity with philosophy and philosophical reasoning. "Given the fact that Athens was home to several prominent schools of philosophical thought, it is not incidental that Paul's address touches core philosophical assumptions of both Stoics and Epicureans."[71]

With this background, Paul contextualized his message in accordance with his audience of Greek philosophers and those who were philosophically astute. Unfortunately, in some quarters, there is apprehension over the study and use of philosophy, in part due to a mistaken understanding of Colossians 2:8, in which Paul warns people not to be deceived by philosophy. According to R. C. Lucas, "the word *philosophy* has no reference to the work of Greek philosophy, which neither the visitors nor Paul were extolling or disparaging. It was commonplace for contemporary sects and cults to offer a deep knowledge of divine mysteries, and the visitors must have been making some more or less pretentious claims along these lines."[72]

New Testament scholar N. T. Wright concurs with Lucas: "[The] NIV well expresses the fact that Paul was not opposed to (what we would call)

---

67. Henri Daniel-Rops, *The Church of the Apostles and Martyrs* (London: J. M. Dent and Sons, 1960), 72.

68. Mark Hanna distinguishes between "pure" and "applied" apologetics. The former is "concerned with the objective justification of the Christian faith" irrespective of any response, whereas the latter is geared more for persuasion and eliciting a response from the receptor. Mark Hanna, *Crucial Questions in Apologetics,* 60.

69. J. Daryl Charles, "Engaging the (Neo) Pagan Mind: Paul's Encounter with Athenian Culture as a Model for Cultural Apologetics (Acts 17:16–34)," in *The Gospel and Contemporary Perspectives,* ed. Douglas Moo (Grand Rapids: Kregel, 1997), 49.

70. Ibid.

71. Ibid., 54.

72. R. C. Lucas, *The Message of Colossians and Philemon,* Bible Speaks Today, ed. John R. W. Stott (Downers Grove, Ill.: InterVarsity 1980), 96.

'philosophy' in general."[73] James D. G. Dunn points out that "the term as it is used here . . . is in no way disparaging or specific in its reference in itself. It is a term which many apologists for all sorts of religious and pseudo-religious teaching would use because of its distinguished pedigree, as subsequently in relation to the mysteries."[74]

In his book *Handmaid to Theology: An Essay in Philosophical Prolegomena,* Winfried Corduan writes, "All too frequently the theological task is carried on without taking the proper philosophical roots into account, whether they be from first-century or twentieth-century thought. . . . The theologian cannot ever get away from the fact that philosophical thinking is an integral part of the way that we understand and disseminate revealed truth."[75]

Charles rightly points out that Paul's sermon "conforms to a pattern of Hellenistic discourse, with its epistemological and teleological emphasis. Paul's preaching thus cannot be confined narrowly to a normative OT pattern as some commentators have sought to do. Rather, it wraps universal truth in the language and idiom of the day, culminating in a uniquely Christian expression of biblical revelation, and inviting the listeners to a higher metaphysical ground."[76]

Though Paul does not use specific philosophical terms, the concepts are present. In Romans 1:20, the cosmological argument is implied.[77] According to Paul, man is able to deduce, by means of general revelation, the existence of the supreme being, God. Furthermore, from general revelation flows natural theology, by which two important truths about God are made evident, namely His eternal power (omnipotence) and divine nature.[78]

---

73. N. T. Wright, *Colossians and Philemon,* Tyndale New Testament Commentaries, ed. Leon Morris (Grand Rapids: Eerdmans, 1999), 101.

74. James D. G. Dunn, *The Epistles to the Colossians and to Philemon,* New International Greek New Testament Commentary (Grand Rapids: Eerdmans, 1996), 147.

75. Winfried Corduan, *Handmaid to Theology: An Essay in Philosophical Prolegomena* (Grand Rapids: Baker, 1981), 9, 10.

76. Charles, "Engaging the (Neo) Pagan Mind," 55.

77. The cosmological argument simply states that God is the self-existing, eternal First Cause of all finite, contingent things. Aristotle acknowledged the need for a first cause, or unmoved mover.

78. "Natural theology, then, is dependent upon a prior revelation or self-disclosure from God. This prior revelation is a revelation in nature. Natural theology refers to a knowledge of God acquired from God's revelation of Himself in nature." R. C. Sproul, John Gerstner, and Arthur Lindsey, *Classical Apologetics: A Rational Defense of the Christian Faith and a Critique of Presuppositional Apologetics* (Grand Rapids: Zondervan, 1984), 26.

In the Areopagus sermon, not only is the cosmological argument implied, but two other areas of philosophy—ontology and epistemology—come into play as well. Paul's Greek audience would be familiar with Aristotle's idea of a first cause, even if they didn't follow Aristotelian philosophy. Paul doesn't use direct biblical quotations, but his argument is biblically sound, theologically rich, and philosophically tight. Unfortunately, some interpreters of Paul's sermon question his approach, especially his use of Greek literature.

CONCLUSION AND APPLICATION

Paul's Areopagus sermon is an exceptional example of how apologetics and evangelism can be applied in partnership to NRMs without compromising either the defense of the gospel or its content. His tactful yet bold combination of the two approaches enabled him to contextualize his message and establish a dialogue with his Hellenistic audience, without compromising either his defense or proclamation of the gospel. However, the apologist and missionary must never forget that in the final analysis, it is God, not man, who convicts and regenerates. Harold Netland observes:

> To be sure, apologetics in and of itself will not result in the salvation of anyone. Apologetics, just like the simple proclamation of the Gospel, evangelism, is ineffective without the power and work of the Holy Spirit. For ultimately it is only the Holy Spirit who can bring about conviction of sin (John 16:8–11) and liberate the spiritually blind person from the grasp of the adversary to new life in Christ (John 3:5; 1 Corinthians 2:14–16; Titus 3:5). . . . Both evangelism and apologetics must be carried out with much prayer and conscious dependence upon the power of God. Christian apologetics is not the same thing as evangelism, nor should it ever take the place of evangelism.[79]

Netland's final comments on this point express exactly what Paul practiced and establish what should be the goal of Christians today: "In our witness to an unbelieving world primacy must always be given the simple, direct, Spirit-anointed proclamation of the Gospel (Romans 1:6; Hebrews 4:12). . . . Properly

---

79. Harold Netland, "Apologetics, Worldviews, and the Problem of Neutral Criteria," *Trinity Journal* 12NS (1991): 57–58.

construed, apologetics is ancillary to evangelism and is unavoidable in effective proclamation of the Gospel."[80]

STUDY QUESTIONS

1. How does an ignorance of theology, philosophy, and missiology adversely affect a Christian's ability to adequately defend the faith and evangelize adherents of NRMs?
2. How did Paul establish a good rapport with the Greeks, and how would you apply his example to your own witnessing strategy?
3. What takes place when a strictly apologetic approach is used on an adherent of an NRM?
4. What is the disadvantage of using a strictly evangelistic approach on an adherent of an NRM?
5. Explain how combining apologetics and evangelism contributes to the application of Matthew 28:18–20.

---

80. Ibid., 58.

CHAPTER 6

TRADITIONAL RELIGIONS, NEW RELIGIONS, AND THE COMMUNICATION OF THE CHRISTIAN FAITH

DAVID J. HESSELGRAVE

Discussions relating to religion and to particular religions old and new often encounter roadblocks early on. Few subjects are fraught with a higher degree of passion on the one hand, and a greater diversity of opinions on the other. Open discussions, therefore, often generate more heat than light. Scholarly dialogues easily become mired in minutiae and often yield little that is conclusive or helpful.

As for Christian missions to people of other faiths, in the public arena the very idea of missions is challenged by a pervasive relativism and loss of absolutes, a general misunderstanding of what it means to be "tolerant" of other faiths, and repeated appeals to be appreciative of religious diversity. In the theological arena, missions is challenged by a diversity of views as to the relationship between Christianity and other world religions. Lesslie Newbigin classifies the three main views and their representative advocates as being pluralism (John Hick), inclusivism (Karl Rahner), and exclusivism (Hendrik Kraemer). These categories are far from airtight, however. Newbigin describes his own view as being basically exclusvistic but containing aspects that can be thought of as inclusivistic and even pluralistic.[1]

---

1. Lesslie Newbigin, *The Gospel in a Pluralist Society* (Grand Rapids: Eerdmans, 1989), 182–83.

Given this state of affairs, one must ask how it might be possible to do justice to the present topic within the scope of one brief chapter.

Two ideas appeal to me and I can only hope that they will serve to satisfy my readers. First, as for recent and reasoned defenses of the kind of biblical exclusivism espoused here, I will defer to the works of Harold A. Netland[2] and Ajith Fernando.[3] They take quite different, and yet complementary, approaches and their works should be appealing to my readers.

Second, I propose to devote the first part of this chapter to an elucidation of certain pre-understandings, descriptions, and definitions that will allow for, or even necessitate, the kind of communication strategies and methodologies I will advocate later. I believe that these pre-understandings are quite capable of adequate defense, but I will do little more than hint at a defense here. My reason in dealing with them at all is to make clear the theoretical foundation on which practical communication guidelines will be constructed.

PRE-UNDERSTANDINGS AND STIPULATED DEFINITIONS

Religion and Religions

Thinking in generic terms, and because the Bible does not use the word *religion* (we inherited it from Cicero), I will adopt Lactantius's and Augustine's understanding of religion in terms of the linking or binding idea inherent in the Latin word *religare*. In the broad sense, then, religion has to do with linking, re-linking, or binding persons to the Divine, supernatural, or transcendent, however conceived. And particular religions, whether old or new, can be thought of as the various systems of faith and worship that attempt to make this linkage possible.

So far so good, but exclusivist Christians are immediately confronted with questions having to do with *true* religion and *false* religion, and with the presence or absence of truth in non-Christian religions. The basic view adopted here is that of Edmund Perry:

---

2. Harold A. Netland, *Dissonant Voices: Religious Pluralism and the Question of Truth* (Grand Rapids: Eerdmans, 1991); and idem, *Encountering Religious Pluralism: The Challenge to Christian Faith and Mission* (Downers Grove, Ill.: InterVarsity, 2001).
3. Ajith Fernando, *The Christian Attitude Toward World Religions* (Wheaton, Ill.: Tyndale House, 1987).

Since from the viewpoint of Gospel faith the one only True and Living
God is the God of Abraham, Isaac and Jacob, the Father of our Lord
Jesus Christ, and since the Gospel alone brings men to this God, all
other faith claims and systems lead men away from him. Religion is
therefore, first of all, the *generic* term comprehending the universal
phenomenon of men individually and collectively being led away from
God in manifold ways by divers claims and systems. Religion in this
generic sense exists of course only in the *specific* religions, each of which
is a concrete manifestation or actualization of a particular people being led away from God in a particular way by a particular schema, but
as a descriptive term "religion" expresses the unity of human life being oriented and organized away from the God of Gospel faith through
the diversity of creeds, codes, myths, cults and ways of worship.[4]

Perry's lines will no doubt raise eyebrows and, perhaps, blood pressures.
But they accord well with the words of the psalmist, "For all the gods of the
nations are idols, but the LORD made the heavens" (Psalm 96:5), as well as with
the general tenor of Scripture. In agreeing with Perry at this point, the words
of C. S. Lewis come to mind: "I was not writing to expound something I could
call 'my religion,' but to expound 'mere' Christianity, which is what it is and
was what it was long before I was born and whether I like it or not."[5]

Perry's words do entail a semantic problem, however, because according to
his definition, Christianity does not qualify as a religion. But for Perry himself
that is no problem at all, because it is Christ himself (not Christianity) who
actually provides the linkage or relationship with God that religions as such
only purport to provide.

Traditional Religions and New Religions

Solomon observed that "there is nothing new under the sun" (Ecclesiastes
1:9), and a study of so-called new religions would seem to confirm what he
said. For example, in an article on emerging religious movements in North
America, J. Gordon Melton treats them not so much in terms of newness but
more in terms of theological and behavioral deviation from the dominant

4. Edmund Perry, *The Gospel in Dispute: The Relation of Christian Faith to Other Missionary
Religions* (Garden City, N.Y.: Doubleday, 1958), 88 (emphasis in original).
5. C. S. Lewis, *Mere Christianity* (New York: Macmillan, 1960), viii.

host culture religious consensus.[6] In other words, their teachings and rituals are almost always inextricably tied to the religious traditions from which they emerged. Add Melton's emphasis on the strong tendency of these groups to proselytize and his understanding is in agreement with my experience with the so-called new religions of Japan, as well as with the findings of various colleagues who analyzed a variety of new religions that became prominent during the post-World War II world era.[7]

Though not really new, these religious movements nevertheless manifest new points of departure in terms of emergent leadership, unusual happenings, unique emphases, and zeal. The word *cult* drew attention to these more or less unique characteristics and in that sense had a certain validity. The newer terminology *(new religion* or *new religious movement),* however, seems preferable in at least two respects. First, it is less odious and does not immediately assume a combative posture. Second, it encourages researchers to start earlier and dig deeper, rather than merely inquiring into modern origins and developments. All of this is of vital importance to communication strategy and methodology.

The Christian Faith

As indicated by the title of this chapter, and implied in previous paragraphs, our present concern has to do with communicating Christ and the Christian *faith,* not with communicating the Christian *religion.* That distinction is easily made, but what does it mean?

One way to answer the question is to examine the word *faith.* In the New Testament, faith (Gr. *pistis*) is both objective and subjective. Faith in the objective sense can be seen in Jude 3, where Jude admonishes believers to "contend earnestly for the faith which was once for all delivered to the saints" (NASB). A more subjective sense of the word can be found in Hebrews 11:1: "Now faith is being sure of what we hope for and certain of what we do not see." In the final analysis, the "faith once for all delivered" and the "faith that hopes and makes certain" are not to be divorced from each other. Just as hydrogen and oxygen combine to make water, *objective* faith and *subjective* faith together make up what we're referring to here as the *Christian* faith.

6. J. Gordon Melton, "Emerging Religious Movements in North America: Some Missiological Reflections," in *Missiology* 28, no. 1 (January 2000): 85–98.
7. David J. Hesselgrave, ed., *Theology and Mission: Papers Given at Trinity Consultation No. 1* (Grand Rapids: Baker, 1978).

Another way of responding to the question is to examine the various words that New Testament writers employ with reference to the Christian message, such as *gospel* or *good news (euaggelion), proclamation, preaching,* or *announcement (kerugma),* the *word*(s) of Christ or Scripture *(rhema),* and so on. All such words have nuances beyond those that can be explored here. But all of them must be taken into account in communicating what we succinctly refer to as "Christ and the Christian faith." When employed sincerely and wisely, imaginative stories, personal testimonies, creative art, and so on are not to be ignored or demeaned. At the same time, none of these (and nothing at all) takes the place of the incarnate Son and inscripturated Word. Adherents of the world's religions, whether old or new, have no mandate to open ears, minds, and hearts to any other word. Nor do we as Christ's representatives have a mandate to preach any other word.

Missions and Evangelism

Two other concepts require at least preliminary consideration. The word *mission* has become such an omnibus term, even in Christian circles, that it now seems to encompass everything from opposition to the Muslim requirement that women wear veils to encouraging Indian fakirs to become more devout Hindus. The word *evangelism* carries not quite so much baggage, but is often ambiguous, especially when related to missions. Both concepts cry out for clarification.

We agree with Harold Netland when he takes exception to the notion that "our task . . . is not to proselytize but rather humbly to recognize and cooperate with God's presence and work through the other great religions."[8] We disagree with Lesslie Newbigin who says that our task "will simply be the telling of the story, the story of Jesus, the story of the Bible" and not "the converting of others."[9] Although it is true that, like illumination of the Word and conviction of sin, conversion must ultimately be accomplished by the Holy Spirit, New Testament missionaries strove to work with the Holy Spirit to that end. Though we may err at that point today, we can be sure that the apostle Paul did not. In a well known but seldom quoted passage, he writes, "Therefore knowing the fear of the Lord, we persuade men" (2 Corinthians 5:11 NASB). If our hearers misconstrue our intentions at this point, Paul's auditors did not.

---

8. Netland, *Dissonant Voices,* 278.
9. Newbigin, *Gospel in a Pluralist Society,* 182.

After a brief Pauline peroration, King Agrippa rejoined, "Do you think that in such a short time you can persuade me to be a Christian? (Acts 26:28).

As understood here, then, evangelism has to do with communicating the gospel in such a way as to make Christ known and prompt Christian conversion. Christian missions has to do with discipling the world's peoples by winning them to Christ and incorporating them into his church. That being the case, whatever else might legitimately be done in the name of missions, evangelism takes priority.

COMMUNICATING CHRIST AND THE CHRISTIAN FAITH TO ADHERENTS OF TRADITIONAL AND NEW RELIGIONS—BASIC GUIDELINES FOR STRATEGY AND METHODOLOGY

Guideline #1: The disposition and attitude of the missionary is the indispensable point of contact in interreligious communication of the gospel.

Missionaries often think in terms of "points of contact," as if there were many. There may be multiple points of contact, but unless they grow out of one quintessential point of contact, they will tend to be ineffective. Why? Perhaps because that quintessential point of contact has to do with spirituality and ethics as much or more than it has to do with knowledge and insight. Hendrik Kraemer stated it in a way that should leave an imprint upon the soul of every missionary:

> There is only one point of contact, and if that one point really exists, then there are many points of contact. This one point of contact is the disposition and attitude of the missionary. . . . Such is the golden rule, or, if one prefers, the iron law in this whole matter. The way to live up to this rule is to have an untiring and genuine interest in the religion, the ideas, the sentiments, the institutions—in short, in the whole range of life of the people among whom one works, *for Christ's sake and for the sake of those people.*[10]

---

10. H. Kraemer, *The Christian Message in a Non-Christian World* (Grand Rapids: Kregel, 1963), 140 (emphasis in original).

Kraemer's "golden rule" of missionary communication might seem better suited to his mid-twentieth-century era when missionary work tended to be thought of in terms of a life commitment to the adherents of a particular region, people, or (traditional) religion. But is it not true that "incarnational missions," as currently proposed, entails something similar? "Incarnationalism" has various connotations, but it certainly includes the idea that missionary communicators will identify with respondent peoples and their ways, needs, and aspirations. Missionaries of most every stripe—whether to adherents of religions old or new—would assent to this approach, at least in principle.

Exclusivists are often, and usually unjustly, accused of disregard for everything but the souls of their respondents. However, I believe that Ajith Fernando, strict exclusivist that he is, is actually quite representative when he makes a case for coupling a strong conviction for truth as revealed in Christ and Scripture with a profound respect for respondents as endowed by their Creator with the "privilege and responsibility to accept or reject the gospel."[11] To illustrate what is involved, Fernando points to the apostle Paul who was "greatly distressed" (NIV) and even "provoked" (NASB) by the idolatry all around him in Athens (Acts 17:16). Nevertheless, Paul responded with a reasonableness and logic sufficient to merit an invitation to speak at the Areopagus. His message may have been considered quite contemptible, but not so Paul the messenger. He was only considered foolish for believing and preaching it.

Whether or not past criticism has been justified, conservative evangelicals today, in dependence on the Holy Spirit, must learn how to maintain the integrity of the gospel while demonstrating a respect for those of other faiths. In communicating the gospel to those of other faiths, they may well be tempted to feelings of pity in some cases, arrogance in others, and animosity in still others. But pity can be self-defeating and attitudes of superiority (vis-à-vis "inferior religions") or resentment (vis-à-vis "diabolic cults") are unchristian. What is to be coveted is *respect* for adherents to other faiths and a genuine interest in them, in their culture, and—yes—in the system(s) that lead them away from their Creator. Genuine respect and interest are the *sine qua non* of effective Christian communication.

---

11. Fernando, *Christian Attitude Toward World Religions*, 26.

Guideline #2: Self-exposure constitutes the common ground for missionary communication.

As with "point of contact," a variety of approaches have been taken in the search for common ground on which missionaries might stand alongside non-Christians, whether primal religionists, Hindus, Buddhists, Muslims, Jews, Jehovah Witnesses, Scientologists, New Spirituality adherents, or what have you.

One method can be called the "similarity approach" to establishing common ground. In order to build bridges of understanding, proponents of this very popular method seek out teachings and practices in the various religions that appear to be the same or similar to presumed counterparts in Christianity. For now, we will simply say that we reject this avenue of establishing common ground, for reasons we will explain under Guideline #3 below.

Another means of finding common ground, and the one we will evaluate here, can be categorized as the "search approach." The underlying idea is that missionaries should embrace non-Christian religionists as fellow pilgrims in some kind of common or cosmic search for God, truth, meaning, fulfillment, or (now in the third millennium especially) unity and just plain survival. This approach is not new, but it does have a special attraction in urgent times such as these—as is evident in the writings of Willard Oxtoby, Leonard Swidler, and Hasan Askari. Swidler, for example, if I understand him correctly, thinks of humans as evolving a kind of utopia in which freedom of thought and action is somehow guided by mutual love and respect. Religion, then, serves both as the expression of and the vehicle for achieving that kind of culture and society.

> Human nature is directed at an open-ended, endless, in-finite [sic] all-embracing, comprehensive knowing and loving and knowing freely acting. That total knowing and loving and knowing freely acting that humans, both individually and communally, have created over the centuries is Religion, and the Culture that matches it.[12]

Though somewhat cryptic, Swidler's lines suggest that he believes that Religion (with a capital R) somehow enlists adherents of all religions old and new,

---

12. Leonard Swidler, *The Meaning of Life at the Edge of the Third Millennium* (Mahwah, N.J.: Paulist Press, 1992), 115.

and involves them in this common effort to create a "Global Culture" based on knowledge, love, and freedom.[13]

Ultimately, the "similarity" and "search" approaches to the discovery of common ground between Christian faith and non-Christian systems prove to be either inadequate or unbiblical. The search approach, especially, is in stark contrast to biblical teachings, because all such searches and endeavors must end in despair unless and until men and women find God himself. People may indeed be searching, but in a profound sense they are not really searching for God. Contrary to human philosophy, mankind has been running *away* from God ever since Eden. The truth is that God is the one who is doing the searching and we are the objects of his search. We are the ones who have been hiding; he is the one who has been seeking. We are the rebellious sinners; he is the loving God.

At that precise point, we find the common ground between Christian and non-Christian. "The Son of Man came to seek and to save what was lost" (Luke 19:10). "God demonstrates his own love for is in this: While we were still sinners, Christ died for us" (Romans 5:8). We did not first love *him; he* first loved *us!* (1 John 4:10). The common ground upon which Christian missionaries and their non-Christian counterparts stand is their common *sinfulness!*

Some may be tempted to reply, "That may be true, but to say it is to make our non-Christian respondents out to be sinners right away. How can such a negative approach be an effective way of establishing common ground?"

The objection is understandable, but it fails to take into account the sober reality that the missionary (though saved by grace) is just as much a sinner as the non-Christian. "Sinner status" constitutes the common upon which the missionary source and non-Christian respondent stand. This is so for at least three reasons.

First, an important part of the attraction of almost all religions, old and new, is the impact of very important personages (founders, prophets, and various other holy men and women) who are granted status that may broadly be described in terms of "saintliness" or "sainthood." True believers look to such persons and become converted and/or committed without ever having seen a "sinner." That is, they have never seen a sinner *in the biblical sense of the word.* But we know that, to be saved, they must first see themselves as sinners. Now, if the missionary comes as a saint, they may never actually "see" what a sinner really is. How then can they be expected to repent and believe the gospel?

---

13. Ibid., 115–16.

Logically as well as biblically, then, it follows that it is in "sinnerhood," not sainthood, that common ground must first be established.

Second, as in the case of Christ himself, skeptical unbelievers are constantly on the lookout for the foibles and failings of anyone who lays claim to being "good" or possessing the "truth." Christ's contemporaries could find no fault in him. That occasioned their frustration and anger. However, the auditors of missionaries today will have little difficulty in discovering even egregious failings. Unless, and until, missionaries humbly and sincerely expose themselves as being subject to temptations and failings, and in need of divine forgiveness and grace, they may easily become their own worst enemies. Of course, this is not an argument to sin more so that grace may abound. But it is an argument for self-exposure, so that respondents understand that God in Christ has been searching for them and now invites them to join missionaries as saved sinners on a pilgrimage that truly leads onward and upward.

Finally, Paul proved himself to be a model missionary in this respect. He always made it clear that he preached Christ and not himself; that he himself was weak and unworthy of being Christ's ambassador; and that he was, in fact, foremost among sinners (1 Timothy 1:15 NASB). Invariably, the common ground between Paul and his hearers—whether in Athens, Berea, Corinth, or Ephesus—was this: all alike were sinners; once saved, all alike were sinners saved by grace.

We are on safe ground, then, in concluding that it makes little difference whether we are dealing with New Dehli Hindus or Los Angeles Hare Krishnas; Ahmadiyyas in Karachi or Black Muslims in Detroit. It makes little difference whether our hearers seek the ministrations of gurus or godlings; of medicine men or magicians; of astrologers or angels. *Human nature* is the problem and Divine grace is the solution. Sooner or later, the religious world—no, the whole world—will discover that its sickness is sin and the remedy is Christ. As part of that world, missionaries should be able to identify with that truth.

Guideline #3: Understanding of the Christian faith is greatly enhanced by an emphasis on dissimilarities between that faith and its rivals.

It is difficult to compare the various religions, especially when the Christian faith is involved. Consequently, the study of comparative religions has tended to give way to history of religions. Nevertheless, comparisons continue to be made out of differing motives and with varying degrees of success.

In an oft-referenced smaller work, Eric Sharpe attempts to define and explain fifty words that have special and correlative meanings in the world's religions. His objective is to promote understanding of comparative religion in general and the several major religions in particular.[14]

Leonard Swidler takes a quite different tack. He selects seven words (*redemption, liberation, enlightenment, nirvana, heaven, communism,* and *salvation*) that he believes to be descriptive of the "goal of religion" and proceeds to explain how these words are used and what they mean within the contexts of the various religions.[15] Swidler's objective is to bring to light commonalities and complementary aspects of religions so as to promote unity and a new society.

In works that have become evangelical missions classics, Don Richardson concentrates on the discovery of "redemptive analogies" and "eye openers" (e.g., the peace child idea and ritual among the Sawi) that will enable non-Christian peoples to understand the gospel.[16] His goal is the conversion of non-Christians.

It seems fair to say that Sharpe, Swidler, and Richardson are of the opinion that there are similarities between Christian and non-Christian faiths that, properly understood and exploited, will facilitate both understanding and the fulfillment of "missions" as they understand it. However, even though there may be some truth to this approach, the proposition is problematic—especially if one holds to the absolute uniqueness of the Christian faith. Both philosophically and theologically, a method of communication that is overdependent on the discovery and utilization of similarities is open to question. In the long run, the *dissimilarities* between beliefs and practices may be more important and utilitarian.

From a philosophical perspective, Aristotle, in his "chain of being" illustration, long ago attempted to demonstrate that we come to know that which is outside our experience (or "above" it, from Aristotle's viewpoint) by virtue of analogy to that which is experienced. For example, we understand the nature of angels that we have not seen by analogy or comparison to the nature of human beings that we do see. Such comparisons, however, reveal both similarities and differences. As Aristotelian logic makes clear, analogies are to be considered valid only to the degree that similarities outweigh dissimilarities.

---

14. Eric J. Sharpe, *Fifty Key Words: Comparative Religion* (Richmond, Va.: John Knox, 1971).
15. Swidler, *Meaning of Life at the Edge of the Third Millennium,* 12–17.
16. Don Richardson, *Eternity in Their Hearts* (Ventura, Calif.: Regal, 1981).

From a theological perspective, the perceptive Hendrik Kraemer points out that attempts to catalogue similarities "on such subjects as the idea of God and of man, the conception of the soul or of redemption, the expectation of an eternal life or the precedence of the community over the individual, etc., [are] an impossible thing."[17] He offers two reasons for this conclusion. In the first place, no religion is an assortment of spiritual commodities that can be "compared as shoes or neckties."[18] On the contrary, every religion is a unity or individual whole in which every myth, rite, and teaching must be understood in relationship to all else. Secondly, when exposed to the light of God's revelation in Christ and the Scriptures, even those parts of another religion that might appear to be lofty and uplifting prove to be parts of a whole that is under the judgment of God.[19]

Kraemer's words are in accord with Edmund Perry's definitions of "religion" and "specific religions" stipulated at the beginning of this chapter. Moreover, what Kramer says is quite easily demonstrated by the kind of holistic examination advocated by both authors. For example, even though Shang-ti is conceived of as a "high god" in Chinese religion, Shang-ti hardly qualifies as being analogous to the God of the Bible if one takes all of Chinese religion into account. The same could be said of the "three bodies of Buddha," the mercy of Amida, and the faith displayed in Mahayana—each so dimly reflects its supposed counterpart in Christianity as to be entirely misleading if construed as anything approaching a mirror image. Likewise, even if we agreed that the Allah of the Qur'an has been divested of the qualities of the pre-Islamic moon god of Muhammad's Quryash tribal people (which in itself would be quite a stretch) and is therefore the same or similar to the God of the Bible, Allah's very nature (and not just Muhammad's misapprehension of the Trinity) would make the deity of the world's only Savior and true King impossible.[20]

---

17. Kraemer, *Christian Message in a Non-Christian World*, 134.
18. Ibid., 135.
19. Ibid., 136.
20. I am not arguing so much for the validity of one particular name for God as compared with another. Words themselves are neither absolute nor absolutely arbitrary. As names for the Divine, *Elohim* and *Yahweh* might seem to take precedence over the Greek *Theos*, Latin *Deus*, and English *God*. But even that is somewhat beside the point. The point is that, whether examined logically or theologically, when one extrapolates critical words from their native religious systems and compares them with corresponding Christian words— in much the same way as one might compare the hearts, lungs, and livers of a monkey or mouse and a man in a laboratory—certain characteristics and functions are indeed similar. But as soon as one restores each to the system from which it has been extracted, it

Readers will have to judge for themselves the validity of redemptive analogies such as the well-known peace child comparison. It seems beyond question that, early on in the communication of the gospel to the Sawi, that particular analogy functioned well. However, the peace child of Sawi tribalism is light years removed from the Prince of Peace of biblical revelation. Sooner or later—and better sooner than later—the difference must become as crystal clear to the Sawi believers as it is to the missionaries themselves. To the degree that it does not, the Sawis will inevitably be more syncretistic and less Christian.

To the extent that Christ and the Christian faith are sui generis, they become more and more knowable by virtue of differentia. As we proposed early on, the Christian faith (not as practiced, but as revealed) *is* absolutely unique. There is no other faith like it—no other God; no other Christ; no other Calvary; no other empty tomb; no other redemption; no other salvation; no other heaven; and so on. That being the case, our communication of the Christian faith is made increasingly effective through comparison and *contrast*—for example, by pointing out differences between the teachings of the Bible and those of other sacred books. If one's objective is to convert and disciple, the number and importance of these differences will far outweigh the number and importance of supposed similarities. Whether we are comparing sin in Scripture to Shinto *tsumi;* Pauline grace to *karuna* in Mahayana; Trinity in Christian faith to *Trimurti* in Hinduism; biblical inspiration to Islamic *wahy* and *ilham* revelation; or evil in Scripture to engrams in Scientology, all such contrasts will serve to explain what the Christian faith is and what it is not.

Implicit in Christ's method of teaching—"You have heard it said . . . but I say unto you"—is a "formula" we can utilize effectively: "Your tradition (or teaching) says . . . but God's Word, the Bible, tells us . . ." By respectful use of this technique, nominal adherents of traditional religions will be instructed on two counts: (1) what their religion really teaches (which will often surprise them), and (2) how Christian teaching differs—both from their own religion and from what they might have been led to believe about Christianity. Adherents of new religions may well discover that, as compelling as their leader's or prophet's perorations might appear, they are a far cry from the principles

---

functions to sustain *that* system, not some other system. Append it to some other system and it functions imperfectly, if at all. A pig's liver may or may not sustain the life of a person temporarily; but, very providentially, no human being will ever be born with a pig's liver.

propounded by the Christ of the New Testament. The more clearly Eastern adherents understand who Christ really is in contrast to the bodhisattvas and avatars of history and myth, the fewer syncretisms and the more conversions we can expect. The more clearly Western adherents understand what the Scriptures really teach in concrast to the teachings of such books as the *Pearl of Great Price* or *The Book of Mormon*, the less defections from and the more conversions to Christ there will likely be.

Guideline #4: "Storying the gospel" is a most effective method of communicating the Christian faith.

There are various ways of referring to the method of gospel communication in view here: storying the gospel (Tom Steffen), chronological Bible study (Trevor McIllwain), communicating the "divine drama" (Harry Wendt), showing the "big picture," (Timothy George), "chronological Bible storying" (James Stack and J. O. Terry), and others. The method can be termed "applied biblical theology" when biblical theology is thought of in the more technical sense of the unfolding record of God's dealings with mankind in Scripture from Genesis to Revelation.

Though narrative was not one of the more popular evangelization proposals of the last half-century, it was employed effectively by Hans-Reudi Weber shortly after World War II when he was faced with the daunting task of bringing biblically illiterate Dutch Reformed churches in Indonesia to a new level of understanding and maturity.[21] In the 1970s, almost as a last resort, Australian Trevor McIllwain introduced narrative with significant success to stumbling New Tribes Mission churches in the Palawan area of the Philippine Islands.[22] In the 1980s, Harry Wendt began to hold seminars for Lutheran clergy and laity throughout the United States,[23] and Lesslie Newbigin proposed narrative as a communication strategy for reaching pluralist societies.[24] In the 1990s, Biola's Tom Steffen published his helpful *Reconnecting God's Story to Ministry*

21. Hans-Ruedi Weber, *The Communication of the Gospel to Illiterates: Based on a Missionary Experience in Indonesia* (London: SCM Press, 1957).
22. Trevor McIllwain, *Notes on the Chronological Approach to Evangelism and Church Planting* (Sanford, Fla.: New Tribes Mission, 1981).
23. Harry Wendt, *The Divine Drama* (Indianapolis, Ind.: Shekinah Foundation, 1986).
24. Newbigin, *Gospel in a Pluralist Society*, 95–102, 183.

(1996) and other works.[25] As a result of these and other similar works, chrono-logical Bible teaching has come to be widely used by New Tribes Mission, South-ern Baptists, and various missions from Korea, among others. It has also served as a guide to translation priorities among Bible translators, and has been foun-dational to the monumental Insight curriculum instituted by William Carey International University and now offered by various Christian colleges and universities in the United States.

Even more importantly, this method was used by the Lord Jesus himself when he instructed two errant disciples on the road to Emmaus (Luke 24:13–32). It must forever challenge the minds of Christian communicators that those two disciples were literally walking with the resurrected Christ but did not recognize him until they were introduced to the Christ of Moses and the prophets.

The apostle Paul also used a narrative method when he attempted to con-vert the Athenian philosophers on the Areopagus to a Christian view of his-tory and to the person of Christ (Acts 17:22–31). Missionary commentaries on Paul's discourse tend to give special emphasis to his references to Greek religiosity—to the altar to an "Unknown God"—and Greek poetry. Further reflection, however, would seem to indicate that Paul's recitation of the his-tory of God's dealings with mankind beginning with life-giving creation and ending with judgment at the bar of the resurrected Christ was of far greater significance given the larger context of Greek mythology and religion. Chro-nological storying, if one chooses to call it that, seems to have represented an early stage in Pauline contextualization.

It is also worth noting that, even when Paul summarized the gospel in terms of Christ's death, resurrection, and post-resurrection appearances, he twice used the phrase "according to the Scriptures" (1 Corinthians 15:3–8). Even the rudiments of Paul's gospel did not stand alone. Instead, they were nested in a much larger "his-story" and rested on the authority of divine revelation.

Though, at first blush, teaching the "big story of Scripture" appears to be a formidable and almost impossible task, it offers many advantages over alternative approaches that begin by selecting texts, topics, and stories that grow out of a missionary's or respondent's experiences and interests. First, it exploits the full potential of narrative—that form of communication most prominent not only

---

25. Tom A. Steffen, *Passing the Baton: Church Planting That Empowers* (La Habra, Calif.: Cen-ter for Organization and Ministry Development, 1993); and idem, *Reconnecting God's Story to Ministry: Crosscultural Storytelling at Home and Abroad* (La Habra, Calif.: Center for Organizational and Ministry Development, 1996).

in Scripture but also in tribal and developed religions generally. Second, it lends itself to the avoidance of syncretism by keeping the little stories and distinct teachings of the Bible within the larger story or big picture that lends their true significance and meaning. Third, because the larger story of Scripture constitutes the "frame" for understanding any and every individual part of it, the "mere" telling and retelling of the whole involves the kind of contrasts we have already spoken of as prods to conversion. Fourth, the method provides the best foundation for what is often called "follow-up" but is better thought of as discipling and maturation. Finally, as we have implied previously, the method lends itself to a continuation of witness and evangelism by virtue of the fact that most inhabitants of the Third World especially—though they are not prepared to construct and communicate structured formulae such as "six things God wants you to know," for example—nevertheless tend to be master storytellers and unusually capable when it comes to telling God's stories, as well as their own.

Guideline #5: The full potential of biblical dialogue should be utilized in communicating the Christian faith.

Missionaries to adherents of both traditional and new religions are generally most comfortable with monological communication, and least comfortable with dialogical communication. The same could not be said with reference to either Jesus or Paul. Both excelled in the give-and-take of dialogical communication, whether in conversations on the city street, discussions in the halls of academia, or in defense of truth at the bar of first-century tribunals. A case could be made that the two primary reasons for the reticence of contemporary evangelicals to enter into meaningful and productive interreligious dialogue have to do with (1) a limited understanding of religions new and old, and (2) confusion as to the nature and objectives of dialogue as a means of communicating the Christian faith.

It would seem to be unnecessary to urge fellow evangelicals to give more attention to the study of competing belief systems. But it isn't. Too many leaders seem to think that missionary communication has everything to do with discovering new ways to deliver Christian truth, and relatively little to do with investigating non-Christian error. Too often, evangelicals are so overwhelmed by the advances of indigenous sects and the inroads of foreign religions that they are quite content to communicate the gospel in opportunistic ways and leave it at that.

I hope that what has already been written in this chapter and in the rest of this book will be sufficient to encourage professionals to undertake a more thorough study of religions in general and of target audience religions in particular. The evangelical laity, however, merit special attention. To challenge them to faithfulness in evangelism without channeling their witness is self-defeating. Church leaders should see to it that all believers, and especially young believers, have the kind of instruction that will strengthen their own faith in the face of false teachings so as to make them less vulnerable to aggressive non-Christian sects on the one hand and better witnesses for Christ on the other. More than that, Christian leaders would do well to take a page from the manuals of many of the newer religious organizations by encouraging qualified laypersons to study the various religions and make themselves available in situations where special expertise in this or that sect or NRM would be especially helpful. Most people find dialogue to be less intimidating when they don't feel they must "have all the answers" and can call upon others for advice and even involvement.[26]

But let us turn from the laity back to the "specialists." What about interreligious (sometimes called interfaith) dialogue as a strategy for communicating the Christian faith? The problem here is that there are various kinds of dialogues, some of which not only fail to promote Christian objectives but actually conspire against them. These latter types are often designed to "promote unity," based on the notion that "doctrine divides while humanity unites." Some dialogue is undertaken in order to achieve a common religious experience. Some is entered into with the hope of sharing perspectives in order to enhance participants' "knowledge of the Divine." Some simply proposes to promote a more incisive understanding of other faiths.

---

26. My own experience with ordinary Soka Gakkai believers in Japan is illustrative. They did not hesitate to talk about their faith, even with American missionaries, because they had been informed that they were free to offer the services of "experts from headquarters" when faced with objections or questions they themselves were not prepared to answer. In such cases, therefore, the adept would invariably say something like, "I do not know much about that, but we have teachers who would be happy to visit and talk to you at your convenience if you would just give me your name and telephone number." I, for one, soon discovered that this was not a ploy but a genuine offer. Officials were happy to send representatives to engage missionaries or other inquirers in dialogue, but always with one stipulation. Namely, on no occasion would they send only one representative, no matter how expert, and the number of representatives would equal (or exceed) the number of inquirers. The laypeople seem to have more confidence in their instructors than their instructors had in themselves, but, of course, the rationale for their approach was a bit subtler than just the strength of numbers.

Dialogue in the Bible is fundamentally different from the foregoing types. In the New Testament, *dialogue* appears almost exclusively in verb forms *(dialegomai* and *dialogizomai).* Though the Gospels make it clear that Jesus never hesitated to enter into the give-and-take of two-way conversation, there is no clear example of Christ's use of dialogue in connection with what we would call interreligious communication. However, the cognate verb *dialogizomai* ("to converse or discuss with," but with emphasis on the discussion aspect) is used in the case of one confrontation between Jesus and the scribes and Pharisees (Luke 5:21–24).

The apostle Paul used dialogue *(dialegomai* and *dialogizomai)* much more prominently. He engaged in dialogue in the synagogues (Acts 17:2, 17; 18:4, 19), in the marketplace (Acts 17:17), in the school of Tyrannus (Acts 19:9), and in the church at Troas (Acts 20:7, 9). It is interesting to note that when defending himself before Felix, Paul made special note of the fact that his Jerusalem accusers did not find him "dialoguing" or causing riots in that city or in its temple or synagogues (Acts 24:12).

All of this suggests three things: First, dialogue (including interreligious dialogue) in the New Testament (especially in Acts) includes the distinct possibility—if not the likelihood—of debate, disputation, and even dissension. Second, dialogue played an important role in the ministries of both Jesus and Paul, and interreligious dialogue was especially important to Paul's missionary ministry. Third, though dialogue by its very nature involved debate and often ended in disagreement, it was entered into judiciously so as not to arouse unnecessary opposition.

In summary, it is important to understand that biblical dialogue was not calculated to be a method of *discovering* truth but of *disseminating* it. As Gottlob Schrenk writes:

> In the New Testament there is no instance of the classical use of *dialegomai* in the philosophical sense. In the sphere of revelation there is no question of reaching the idea through dialectic. What is at issue is the obedient and percipient acceptance of the Word spoken by God, which is not an idea, but the comprehensive declaration of the divine will which sets all life in the light of divine truth.[27]

---

27. Gottlob Schrenk, "Dialogue," in *Theological Dictionary of the New Testament,* 9 vols., ed. Gerhard Kittel; trans. and ed. Geoffrey W. Bromiley (Grand Rapids: Eerdmans, 1964), 2:94.

Significantly, John R. W. Stott—writing at a time when both interecclesiastical and interreligious dialogue was being strongly advocated by ecumenists as ways of promoting understanding, unity, and world peace—noted that there are numerous examples of dialogue in both the Old and New Testaments in addition to the ones we have cited. Taking all into account, Stott insisted that biblical dialogue was designed to declare God's truth, not to discover truth or to achieve peace. At the same time, and in a sentence to which evangelicals would do well to give attention, he reminded us that our Lord Jesus "seldom if ever spoke in a declamatory, take-it-or-leave-it style. Instead, whether explicitly or implicitly, he was constantly addressing questions to his hearers' minds and consciences."[28]

If Schrenk's analysis speaks volumes concerning dialogue to theological liberals, Stott's observation should be allowed to do the same in the case of theological conservatives. Adherents of religions old and new deserve more than monologue; they deserve at least the offer of dialogue, but with the understanding that it is the nature of Christian dialogue to respectfully advocate and advance the cause of Christ and the Christian faith.

CONCLUSION

If Christ and the Christian faith are as unique as we claim, we conservative evangelicals would do well to rethink our communication approaches to adherents of the world's religions, including the new religions. The primary point of contact may be more dispositional and attitudinal than propositional and cerebral. Our "sinnerhood" may constitute a more realistic and meaningful common ground than would some type of human spiritual search. It may well be that highlighting differences between the Christian faith and competing faiths would be more instructive than attempting to catalogue and describe similarities. In the final analysis, a chronological storying of God's dealings with mankind in accordance with the whole of Scripture would seem to be superior to topical treatments growing out of missionary interests and/or respondent needs. And though both monological and dialogical communication patterns are viable, dialogue deserves more attention than it ordinarily receives. Let us not forget, however, that the type of dialogue enjoined in Scripture is designed more to disseminate truth and encourage conversions than it is to discover new ideas and promote unity among the several religions.

---

28. John R. W. Stott, *Christian Mission in the Modern World: What Christians Should Be Doing Now* (London: Falcon Press, 1975), 61.

STUDY QUESTIONS

1. Analyze and evaluate Edmund Perry's understanding of "religion" and "particular religions." Locate five Scripture passages that deal with particular religions (other than that of Jews and Christians). Do these passages support Perry's understanding or run counter to it?

2. What is "new" and what is "old" about the "new religions"? Illustrate your understandings by referring to at least three "new religions."

3. Evaluate Hendrik Kraemer's "golden rule" of missionary communication. Do you agree or disagree? Why?

4. What are the advantages of "storying the gospel" as compared with articulating a shorter or longer list of Christian teachings when communicating a biblical faith?

5. Interfaith dialogue has both significant potential and serious pitfalls. How does "dialogue" as understood and practiced biblically maximize its potential while helping us to avoid pitfalls?

Part 3

PRACTICAL APPLICATION

CHAPTER 7

BRIDGING THE DIVIDE

Cross-Cultural Missions to Latter-day Saints

KENNETH MULHOLLAND

When the International Olympic Committee announced that the 2002 Winter Olympics Games would be held in Salt Lake City, many in the Utah evangelical community were filled with a mixture of excitement and dread—excitement at the wonderful opportunity God had given us to share the love of Christ with visitors from around the globe, and dread that Christians from outside Utah would come here, attack the Church of Jesus Christ of Latter-day Saints (popularly called Mormons) and its members, and call this "evangelism." Utah Christian leaders quickly decided that we had a responsibility to provide a positive model for those who were coming. Salt Lake Theological Seminary was asked to produce an evangelism training tool that conveyed the philosophy of area pastors. The final product was a video-based training tool titled *Bridges: Helping Mormons Discover God's Grace.*[1] *Bridges* was used with considerable success during the 2002 Winter Games and continues to offer Christians an effective method of outreach to Mormons.

The basic philosophy of the *Bridges* approach is built around three core beliefs: first, a commitment to relational evangelism rather than confrontation; second, a commitment to understanding the unique culture of Latter-day Saints and finding points of contact within that culture in which the gospel can be understood; and, third, a commitment to church-based evangelism. Church-based evangelism seeks to lead LDS adherents beyond a biblically based faith in Jesus Christ to a strong commitment to the local church.

---

1. Additional information on *Bridges* is available at the Salt Lake Theological Seminary Web site, found at www.slts.edu.

THE BIG PICTURE

Before we discuss the *Bridges* philosophy in more detail, it is important that we understand the big picture—the context in which the *Bridges* approach is needed.

First, we must understand that there is a deep theological divide between traditional Christianity and the LDS faith. This can be traced in part to the earliest days of the LDS Church when its founder, Joseph Smith Jr., claimed that God had told him that he should not join any of the existing churches because all their members were "corrupt" and "all their creeds were an abomination." Instead, Smith claimed, God had selected him to restore true Christianity to the earth. These statements, along with his claim that God had given him a new book of scripture, *The Book of Mormon*, incited the frontier evangelicals against Smith and his followers.

This initial encounter between Latter-day Saints and traditional Christians was extremely negative, but it took decades for the worldview of the LDS Church to come into clearer focus. The key doctrinal distinctive and unifying thread that holds Mormon doctrine together is "eternal progression," the teaching that Heavenly Father was once a human being who, along with his wife, "progressed" to become a god. The doctrine of eternal progression promises that the potential for godhood also lies within the grasp of every person. To use another LDS description, every human is "god in embryo." In short, LDS doctrine rejects the traditional Christian belief that God is ontologically of a different order than humans. The most famous summary of this teaching is captured in the statement, "As man is, God once was; as God is, man may become."[2]

The average Christian is confused about the LDS faith. After all, there is a common religious vocabulary that is shared between Latter-day Saints and traditional Christians, and the LDS Church is careful to identify its teachings with Jesus Christ. In recent years, several major denominations felt that it was important to provide guidance to their members on this subject. The South-

---

2. Trying to define current LDS doctrine has proven to be an exceedingly difficult task because direct references to LDS Scriptures and references to the teachings of the president of the LDS Church, who is viewed as a living prophet, are often said to be cited out of context or to be misinterpreted. The most direct way to discern what the LDS Church considers current basic doctrine is to turn to one of its publications, *Gospel Principles* (Salt Lake City: The Church of Jesus Christ of Latter-day Saints, n.d.), which is used to introduce its own members to the essentials of LDS doctrine.

ern Baptist Convention, the largest Protestant denomination in North America, held its annual convention in Salt Lake City in 1998. In preparation for this meeting, they produced a video titled *The Mormon Puzzle,* which politely but firmly declared LDS doctrine to be beyond the pale of Christian teaching. The Presbyterian Church (USA) and the United Methodist Church, two of the larger mainline denominations, have also provided position statements. The Presbyterian document says, in part, "The Church of Jesus Christ of Latter-day Saints is a new and emerging religion that expresses allegiance to Jesus Christ in terms used within the Christian tradition. *It is not, however, within the historic apostolic tradition of the Christian Church.*"[3] The United Methodist statement concludes with almost identical words: "[The] LDS Church is not a part of the historic, apostolic tradition of the Christian faith."[4] The Roman Catholic Church concluded that they would not accept Mormon baptism as a valid baptism.[5] Thus, three Protestant denominations and the Roman Catholic Church have declared with one united and unambiguous voice that the teachings of the LDS Church are outside biblical, apostolic, and historic Christianity. The obvious conclusion would be that traditional Christians are thus under an obligation to share the message of God's grace with Latter-day Saints.

A second element of the big picture is that evangelistic outreach to Latter-day Saints has been dominated in recent decades by a "heresy–rationalist apologetic."[6] This approach, widely popularized by Walter Martin's *The Kingdom of the Cults,* now provides the basic modus operandi for the majority of people involved in the "counter-cult movement," as well as for the average Christian who has read and absorbed the methods and assumptions of those who advocate this approach.

An apologist or evangelist using the heresy–rationalist apologetic begins by presenting a biblically orthodox understanding of core theological categories:

---

3. From *Minutes of the Presbyterian Church (USA),* 1995, pt. 1 (Office of the General Assembly, 1995), 64 (emphasis mine).

4. E. Bryan and Jennifer L. Hard-Diggs, *Sacramental Faithfulness: Guidelines for Receiving People from the Church of Jesus Christ of Latter-day Saints* (Nashville: General Board of Discipline of the United Methodist Church, 2000), 14.

5. The Vatican's Congregation for the Doctrine of Faith answered the question "Whether the baptism conferred by the . . . Church of Jesus Christ of Latter-day Saints called 'Mormons' in the vernacular is valid." Their answers were "negative." The ruling was a departure from the Catholic Church's usual practice of recognizing the baptisms of converts from most other churches. *L'Obseratore Romano,* English ed. (1 August 2001), 4.

6. See John Morehead's analysis of the heresy–rationalist apologetic in the concluding chapter of this volume.

the doctrine of God, of Christ, and of salvation. The teachings of the LDS Church are then set side-by-side with traditionally orthodox biblical teaching in order to show that the LDS faith fails to square with them. Having demonstrated that the Mormon faith is "something other than Christian," the evangelist appeals to the Latter-day Saint to leave the LDS Church and embrace biblical Christianity. For reasons we will explore later, such an approach almost always receives a hostile response from Latter-day Saints.

A third component of our understanding is that, despite the dedication of those who employ the heresy–rationalist apologetic, the LDS Church continues to grow at an amazing rate, at least according to LDS statistics. It is now an international religious movement of 12 million members, with sixty thousand missionaries. If present growth trends continue, according to Baylor University sociologist Rodney Stark, by 2080 the LDS Church will be the first full-fledged new world religion since Islam, with 265 million members.[7]

These three facts—the heretical nature of LDS doctrine, the dominance of the heresy–rationalist approach to evangelism, and the general failure of this approach to adequately meet the challenge of reaching Latter-day Saints—call for serious and prayerful reflection among traditional Christians who are committed to sharing the gospel of God's grace with the Mormons. Clearly, something needs to change if we are to be effective witnesses.

A NEW MODEL

During the 1990s, a few evangelical churches in Utah experienced considerable growth and effectiveness in reaching Latter-day Saints. For example, Washington Heights Baptist Church in Ogden has thirteen hundred people attending on a typical Sunday, and more than four hundred are former Mormons. Christ Evangelical Church, located only a few miles from Brigham Young University, has six hundred people attending weekly, with half coming from a LDS background. These two churches represent a growing number of Utah congregations that have taken a fresh approach to reaching Latter-day Saints. This approach—the one advocated by *Bridges*—is bearing considerable fruit.

The essential and critical characteristic of the *Bridges* approach is the assumption that Latter-day Saints should not be viewed as members of a *cult*, but rather as members of a *culture*. In the Great Commission (Matthew 28:18–

---

7. Richard N. and Joan K. Ostling, *Mormon America: The Power and the Promise* (San Francisco: HarperSanFrancisco, 1999), 374–75.

20), Jesus commanded his disciples to take the gospel to all nations. We often read this as a command to take the gospel to nation-states, such as China or Nigeria. However, the word that is translated "nations" is *ethne,* and the meaning is closer to what we now call ethnic groups. An even better translation would be "people groups." Some might resist the idea that Latter-day Saints should be considered a people group, but interestingly, the *Harvard Encyclopedia of American Ethnic Groups* identifies "Mormons" as a unique American ethnic group that emerged within the American context.[8] Put simply, "ethnicity" is defined by a cluster of characteristics that leads a group to see itself as "us" and those outside to see the group as "them."[9] Thus Jews, Armenians, and Gypsies fall within the category of ethnic groups—and so do the Latter-day Saints.

The first (and also the most obvious) of these cultural markers is that Latter-day Saints have a shared worldview that flows from their unique religion. Religion is not accidental to Mormon ethnicity, but causative. Converts choose to enter this new community and in so doing, they also embrace a worldview. For example, the belief in a "Living Prophet"—the president of the LDS Church, who is believed to be God's spokesman—is the central belief from which all others flow. Latter-day Saints also have their own scriptures and their own unique religious practices (e.g., baptism for the dead and temple marriages).

A second marker of Mormon ethnicity is the shadow cast by the early Mormon practice of polygamy. Even though polygamy was disavowed more than a century ago, Latter-day Saints still endure the smirks and jokes about this practice that sets them apart from their non-Mormon neighbors. A third marker is the "word of wisdom" that prohibits faithful Latter-day Saints from using alcohol, tobacco, and caffeinated drinks. Thus, something as basic as ordering a meal becomes a statement of their religious identity. Yet another marker is the two-year proselytizing mission, undertaken by many young men and some women, that serves as a special rite of passage within their culture. Such cultural markers (and these are but a few examples) are continual reminders to Latter-day Saints that they are indeed a unique people—even for those who

---

8. Stephan Thernstrom, ed., *Harvard Encyclopedia of American Ethnic Groups* (Cambridge, Mass.: Belknap Press, 1980), 720–31.

9. For example, Jews are an ethnic group, but the ethnic markers are not as obvious as one might think. They are not racially defined—some are White (European and North American Jews), some are racially Middle Eastern, and some are Black. Neither are they religiously defined—some identify themselves with the "denominations" of the Jewish faith, Orthodox, Conservative, or Reform, whereas others are agnostic, atheists, or even "Jews for Jesus." Yet, despite the differences, we see them all as "Jews."

no longer believe the doctrines of the LDS Church.

TWO CRITICAL ISSUES

Once Mormons are seen as a people group, then those who seek to share the gospel with them must decide which parts of LDS culture are the most important to address. Specifically, what is the major cultural barrier that prevents Mormons from "hearing" the gospel, and what is the major cultural bridge that would make the good news sound like good news to them? The *Bridges* approach offers a two-prong strategy for overcoming the barrier and building a bridge.

The Barrier

Mormons view themselves as a persecuted people. Unless this is understood and taken seriously, it will be very difficult or impossible to communicate the gospel with them in a meaningful way. A short history lesson should give some insight into this cultural reality. Beginning in Missouri in 1838, the Latter-day Saints were involved in the "Missouri War" with their non-Mormon neighbors. There were casualties on both sides, but the Latter-day Saints were badly beaten and became refugees in mid-winter.[10] They fled back to Illinois, where the settlers received them with open arms. However, once established in Nauvoo, their new city settlement on the Mississippi River, a new cycle of conflict began with their neighbors. At issue this time was the presence of a huge LDS militia, which terrified the other settlers; rumors of polygamy; and the destruction of a newspaper that was critical of Joseph Smith. He was arrested and moved to Carthage, Illinois, where he was murdered by a mob in 1844.

Soon the Latter-day Saints were forced to abandon Nauvoo, and they struck out for the Great Basin (then in Mexican territory) where their new leader, Brigham Young, believed they would be beyond the reach of the United States government. Many went through enormous physical hardship in their trek across the plains. Ironically, the United States acquired what would later be called the Utah Territory from Mexico the following year, and Brigham Young's

---

10. The importance of this persecution is reinforced by the retelling of an especially grisly story of the Haun Mill Massacre in the long-running movie *Legacy*, which is produced by the LDS Church and shown to tens of thousands of visitors each week at the Joseph Smith Memorial Building in Salt Lake City.

hostile attitude toward the authority of the United States government eventually led to the "Utah War" of 1857, in which no one was killed but federal
authority was tentatively established. A "cold war" ensued between the United
States and the LDS Church, in which many LDS leaders eventually were arrested, many Mormons were disenfranchised, and LDS property was seized by
the federal government. In 1890, when the pressure to submit was overwhelm-
ing, the LDS Prophet officially renounced the practice of polygamy. With this
step, the period of antagonism ended, but the impact of this experience is *still*
felt by LDS people.

Latter-day Saints, like most people, are selective readers of history. For many,
the essence of LDS history is that they are a people that has endured great and
undeserved persecution. Any fault that might be placed at the feet of the LDS
Church is unrecognized, dismissed, or ignored. Only particular fragments of
history—those telling the story of Mormons as the victims of unjust
persecution—remain in their collective memory. These stories are still very
much alive within LDS circles, and the sense of being persecuted for their faith
is an integral part of the Mormon psyche.

The perception of persecution has a huge impact on how twenty-first-
century Latter-day Saints respond to comments about their Church, their
beliefs, their culture, their history, and their leaders. Their sense of what
constitutes criticism generally has an extremely low threshold. This sensitivity
is especially pronounced when such comments come from evangelical
Christians, who are seen as the chief critics and persecutors of Latter-day Saints.
Ironically, this sense of being persecuted confirms their LDS faith.

Consider, then, in light of this sense of being a persecuted people, the likely
effectiveness of standard "counter-cult" approaches. Should it surprise us that
one particular tactic—calling the LDS Church a "cult"—sets off the persecution
fire alarm? How many traditional Christians would respond positively to
someone calling their church a cult? Another tactic, insisting that the LDS
Church or Mormon people are not "Christian," has the same effect. Most Latter-
day Saints attach a moral/behavioral meaning to the word *Christian*, rather
than a theological meaning, so any statement that Latter-day Saints should
not call themselves Christians will likely be heard as an accusation of
immorality. No wonder they are offended! Efforts to discuss the theological
implications of the name "Christian" are likely to be fruitless. Here is the typical
LDS response to this claim: "What do you mean we're not Christians? Jesus
Christ is the center of our faith, his name is in our church's name; therefore,

we are Christians."

Yet another tactic that backfires is that of handing out tracts or preaching in front of LDS temples. Because Mormons see their temples as their most sacred places, these acts are viewed as showing blatant disrespect and intentional persecution. Although this is not necessarily the intention of most who utilize this strategy, it is nevertheless the message that is conveyed and received. Again, how would most of us respond to LDS missionaries standing in front of our churches with tracts and signs, preaching as we enter and leave the building? Each of these tactics backfires, causing even agnostic and unbelieving Mormons[11] to "circle the wagons" and defend their culture and heritage against people whom they see as hateful and provocative. If we desire to communicate the gospel of God's grace with Latter-day Saints, we must take seriously their sense of being a persecuted people and allow this insight to inform our strategies.

The greatest antidote to the belief that they are a persecuted people is to get to know them as individuals and demonstrate that we like them. One pastor in a solidly LDS city coaches a community youth football team, and this single activity has opened countless doors with parents and young people, because it communicates that he *likes* his neighbors and *values* their children. This single act makes him, in the eyes of his LDS neighbors, a person with whom they will consider talking about their spiritual concerns. The word also gets out in the tightly knit LDS community that here is a Christian who does not hate them.

Another Utah church hosts a Christmas dinner theater to which members invite LDS neighbors. They are treated to a nice meal, served on fine china, and a well-acted play with a Christian message. Thousands attend these events. There is no overt evangelistic appeal, but the Mormons are left with the pleasant and indelible impression that these traditional Christians honor Christ, they actually pray, and they seem to enjoy being with their LDS neighbors. These Latter-day Saints remember this church as a "safe place," and many come back to seek and find answers.

Once a church is considered someplace where they will be welcomed, many Mormons will come like Nicodemus came to Jesus—discreetly, hoping not to be found out by their fellow ward members. It is surprising how many Latter-day Saints are deeply dissatisfied with the LDS Church and beliefs. Churches

---

11. Latter-day Saints who are unconvinced of LDS doctrine may be as high as one-half of all church members.

that take a strategically low-key approach are experiencing rapid growth and seeing large numbers of Latter-day Saints confessing faith in Jesus through Christian baptism.

The Bridge

The cultural bridge that allows evangelicals to make the good news sound like good news to Mormons is found in the LDS emphasis on personal experience. I first discovered this reality more than thirty years ago. As a young man, I had great confidence in the power of argument to persuade Latter-day Saints that their truth claims were false. I was dedicated to knowing as many facts as I could so that I would be well equipped to tear down the foundational LDS beliefs. I believed that if I could just show them that their confidence in Joseph Smith, in their new revelations, or in their church was ill-founded, they would quickly accept my beliefs in the authority of the Bible, the triune God, and salvation by grace through faith alone. I'm not sure why I assumed this, but I did.

Eventually, I became convinced that I had found an unassailable argument that would overthrow any "reasonable" Mormon's confidence in LDS doctrine. I shared this argument with two Latter-day Saints, who listened with great interest. After I had finished what I thought to be a compelling presentation, I asked them for their response. They looked at me with sincerity and said thoughtfully that my argument was solid and good, but, in the final analysis, they could not accept its conclusion because they had both prayed about the Mormon faith and they had a "testimony" that it was true. I was stunned by their response. I could see that they really did understand the intellectual power of my argument. However, they rejected it with a quiet confidence that forever changed my life. Their response was that they *knew* the LDS Church was true because they *felt* it to be true.[12]

It was at this point that I stopped trying to argue Latter-day Saints out of their belief in LDS doctrine or leadership. Instead, I prayed that the Lord would open *my* eyes and *my* heart and show me how to communicate with Mormons

---

12. The text that is most often cited to support this appeal to feelings comes from *The Book of Mormon* (Moroni 10:3–5): "Ask God . . . if these things are not true . . . he will manifest the truth of it unto you, by the power of the Holy Ghost." Mormons are taught that God will confirm the truth of the LDS gospel by a "burning in the bosom." For Latter-day Saints, this warm feeling is the ultimate way of knowing truth.

in ways that they could—and would—hear. A major insight came via an article in the Brigham Young University campus newspaper, which described the story of a nominal Roman Catholic's conversion to the LDS faith. The potential convert was a doctoral student in psychology who had been exposed to intensive missionary efforts while at BYU. He finally decided, once and for all, to determine if Mormonism was true.

> It had become kind of a game with him. "Mormon" he would say, and a consuming tingling would immediately follow. . . . If he asked if he should remain a Catholic the manifestation would immediately stop. After doing this for four days, "He [finally] concluded that he had not been earnestly seeking an answer when the white stone slab naming the Provo Temple appeared a brilliant white." Tingling from head to foot, he felt his vision narrow. Stars and city lights paled in comparison. He could see nothing but the white stone slab. . . . "I knew then that the church was true and I should become a Mormon. . . . I knew in no uncertain terms that this was the word of God."[13]

This young man's story is very helpful in understanding the Mormon way of knowing truth. Even though he had been confronted with the LDS message for months, his decision to convert to their faith was not based on understanding the relative claims of Catholicism and Mormonism. His *feelings* provided the basis by which he *knew* that the LDS Church was true. He believed that God spoke to him quite independently of the Bible or LDS scripture, and he believed this because he felt a tingling and had a vision. This young man's reliance on an emotional proof is typical, and in some senses is the rule for the vast majority of Latter-day Saints. Understanding the importance of such a feeling-based "testimony" is critical if we hope to communicate with Latter-day Saints.

In philosophical terms, we are discussing epistemology—*how do you know what you know?* The LDS way of knowing spiritual truth based upon feelings is something I call a romantic epistemology. The extent and importance of this romantic approach to epistemology can be seen at work in many areas of LDS experience. For example, the first encounter most people have with the LDS Church comes through the Mormons' beautifully produced and emotionally charged television commercials. One memorable ad portrays a frazzled housewife who is desperately waiting for her husband to relieve her at the end

---

13. "Non-Mormons Have Varied Experiences at BYU," *Daily Universe*, 2 November 1981.

of a difficult day. However, when he arrives home, rather than seeing his wife's needs, he is distracted by a business call. Viewers watch the wife struggling not to crumble under the weight of her disappointment until her husband recognizes his mistake, hangs up the phone, and embraces her. Who could fail to be moved by this scene? Then the tag line says, "Brought to you by the Church of Jesus Christ, *the Mormons*." Like all good marketing, links are made between the "product" of the Latter-day Saints and the feelings of the "market." Thus, the way is prepared for Mormon missionaries.

Another indication of the importance of feelings to LDS faith is the tradition of testimony meetings, held one Sunday each month in LDS congregations all around the world. At each testimony meeting, a number of church members stand before their local congregation and "bear their testimony," saying such things as that their Church is true, that Joseph Smith is a prophet, that *The Book of Mormon* is true—often with tears in their eyes. The evident expression of feeling has a powerful impact of affirming the faith. Latter-day Saints who may have begun to doubt certain doctrinal beliefs of the LDS Church will ask themselves, "How can I doubt when others seem so sure?"

Traditional Christians may feel put off, or may ridicule Latter-day Saints for confusing "heart burn" with genuine faith. Such a reaction, however, is a serious mistake. Although this feeling-based method of knowing God's truth is not the same as faith based on the biblical truth, it is still a deeply rooted *cultural* fact. The reality is that we must learn to speak "Mormonese"—the language of spiritual experience—if we are to communicate with LDS people. Some traditional Christians fear that by speaking the language of experience they will compromise the gospel message, because the reliability of God's truth is found not in feelings but on God's unchanging truth revealed in the Bible. However, by following some basic suggestions, it is possible to speak the LDS language and remain faithful to the truth of Scripture.

The following are just a few ways in which we can use the LDS language of experience as a bridge to make the good news sound like good news to Mormons.

Listen to Their Stories

As obvious as it sounds, the first step is to realize that there is a wide variation in what individual Mormons believe. Although many sincerely believe the basics of traditional LDS doctrine, others are simply cultural Mormons, who appreciate their upbringing and heritage but do not believe, or perhaps even know, the teachings of the LDS Church. Some of these people are agnostic, others hold New Spirituality beliefs, and still others hold beliefs that may be close to traditional Protestant Christian orthodoxy. Indeed, some have a genuine faith in Christ, but for one reason or another choose to remain associated with the LDS Church. Therefore, we need to listen carefully to each person's story as an essential aspect of authentic friendship and the first step of relational evangelism.

We should begin by simply asking "getting to know you" questions about background, family, and work. When it is appropriate, we should ask questions about their faith as well. "Tell me, how did you come to be LDS?" Some people might tell you that they were converted after a serious spiritual quest, whereas others might say they were raised Mormon but now have little use for the LDS Church. Their answers may reveal that "missionary dating" drew them in: They began dating a Mormon, who insisted on their conversion before marriage. Another helpful question might be, "What is important to you about being LDS?" Some come from broken homes and they look to the LDS Church to help them develop strong and stable families. Others are attracted by the strong moral values, healthy lifestyle, or social structure. If we listen to Latter-day Saints, they will tell us what we need to know to apply the good news to their special need.

Present Our Story

We must move beyond simply listening. Evangelism, in the final analysis, involves sharing the story of God's grace. Many Latter-day Saints are very surprised and intrigued to find that traditional Christians have personal spiritual experiences with God. If we are indeed disciples of Jesus, we should have many stories about how God has worked in our lives. These stories are our own testimonies, and we should share them.

However, we need to connect the experiential to the biblical by showing how our experiences are tied to God's promises in the Bible. For example, whenever I share my conversion story, I always include a brief exposition of Romans 10:9–10. I make it clear that when I came to faith in Jesus, it was because I believed what God promised, even though my feelings were unmoved. I did not *feel* that my sins were forgiven, but I *believed* what the Bible promised, that if I have faith in Jesus, believe in his resurrection, and confess Christ as my Lord (my Ruler and my God), then I am forgiven and accepted by God.

In effect, I offer my Mormon friends and contacts a "gospel sandwich," a text of Scripture surrounded by my personal experiential testimony. In doing this, the timeless truth of God's word is presented in a way that makes sense to experience-based Mormons.

We should also tell of our ongoing experiences with God. We should tell of answered prayer (mentioning the scriptural promises we claimed) and of how the Holy Spirit encouraged us (or confronted us) as we read certain passages of Scripture. We can tell something of our struggles with sin and of our growth in godliness. This kind of openness is not the Mormon way, but it is extremely attractive to many Latter-day Saints who simply want to be honest about their struggle with sin. Many Mormons are hungry for a personal relationship with Jesus and many will welcome someone who is willing to speak openly about God's work in their lives.

Expose Them to Christian Worship

One of the best ways to communicate God's grace to Latter-day Saints is to take them to worship with a traditional Christian congregation. Many Mormons believe that because the LDS Church is the only true church, God is not present in our worship and they may feel guilt attending a traditional Christian service. Christian worship is very different from Sunday meetings in an LDS ward. A Mormon might see what many Christians would consider an average service as an amazing and meaningful event. For many Latter-day Saints, the turning point of faith comes as a result of experiencing Christian worship and *feeling* God's presence in a place where they did not expect to feel God.

It is critical to choose the right church and service. It should be a church where Latter-day Saints will not be made to feel unwelcome with negative comments about the LDS Church from the pulpit or church members. Latter-day Saints (even those who are looking for answers outside of Mormonism) react negatively to criticism of the LDS Church and culture. Mormons who agree to attend worship are often afraid that they will be found out by fellow Mormons, that traditional Christians will mistreat them, that they will stand out, or that they may be taking the first step to apostasy. We must do everything in our power to make them feel safe and welcome.

Introduce Them to God's Promises in the Bible

If we want to see Latter-day Saints begin to be transformed by God's grace, we need to introduce them to God's promises in the Bible. Mormons have a basic respect for the Bible as one of their scriptures, though most have little actual knowledge of its message. Most Latter-day Saints know only a handful of proof-texts. Consequently, many Latter-day Saints are loaded down with guilt because they know they are not "worthy" to progress to the highest of the three LDS heavens. Rather than rebuking them for a false view of the afterlife, it is much more effective to point them to God's answer to guilt. For example, Romans 8:1 speaks to *any* person who is weighed down by guilt: "There is now no condemnation for those who are in Christ Jesus." Latter-day Saints need to *hear* the good news. Extending God's promises to them is a good way to start.

It is critical that Latter-day Saints begin to study the Bible for themselves at some point, but this is no easy task. Mormon culture resists the idea that God speaks today through written words—even the words of the Bible. Instead, most Latter-day Saints look for immediate personal guidance either directly from God or through the voice of their Prophet. Yet, they must study the Bible if they are to know about God's grace that will set them free from a works-based religion that offers only frustration for the spiritually sensitive person who truly seeks to please God. If Latter-day Saints are open to Bible study, it is a good idea to point him or her toward the Gospels to discover who the biblical Jesus is and what he has done for them, apart from their self-effort. The book of Acts tells the story of the early church, Galatians and Romans provide a clear presentation of the message of God's grace, and the early chapters of Genesis are important to help them gain an understanding of some basic biblical doctrines, such as Creation and the Fall. Do not browbeat your Mormon friends or attempt to correct them at every turn. Give them time to listen to God's Word. After all, they must learn a new way of knowing God—by faith in Christ alone—despite what their feelings tell them.

THE FIELDS ARE WHITE UNTO HARVEST

The traditional understanding of evangelism aimed at Latter-day Saints is that it is extremely difficult and one can expect to see little fruit. However, the *Bridges* approach flatly declares that this is not true. Mormons *are* spiritually hungry, and many long to know that God can accept them—yet, for many, that spiritual hunger is not being satisfied within the LDS Church. If we extend ourselves to them in genuine friendship, are respectful of their culture, demonstrate by our lives that *we* love and follow Jesus, then we will have their ear. If we will do these things, we will experience a wonderful harvest.

STUDY QUESTIONS

1. What are your impressions of the LDS Church, its people, and its teachings—both positive and negative?
2. What do you think about the argument that Latter-day Saints constitute a "people group?" Is there any evidence to support this contention?
3. Is the Mormon concept that they are a persecuted people an important insight into their mind-set? Does this self-perception have any implications for outreach to them?
4. How do Latter-day Saints determine religious truth? How can this be a bridge to making the good news sound like good news to them?
5. How can you begin to build a relationship with a Mormon?

CHAPTER 8

REACHING THE CHRISTADELPHIANS

PHILIP JOHNSON

> When they describe Christadelphians as a cult, it is because Bible teach-
> ings as explained by Christadelphians are unacceptable to them. It is
> easier to dismiss a group by describing them as a threat to vulnerable
> members of society, than to address the challenge of their teachings.[1]

With the above remarks, Michael Ashton, a Christadelphian apologist, rejects
the classification of *cult*. Instead, he argues that Christadelphians are
nonconformists who comprise a valid Christian sect. Ashton feels that the critics
misunderstand Christadelphian beliefs and misread the Bible. Of course,
evangelicals insist that it is the Christadelphians who misunderstand the Bible.
This is where an impasse is often reached as apologists on both sides pass each
other like ships in a fog. Yet Ashton leaves evangelicals with a truism about
addressing the challenge of Christadelphian teachings. Remarkably, of all the
Bible-based groups that have been examined in evangelical counter-cult
literature, the Christadelphians have received far less attention than that devoted

---

1. Michael Ashton, *The Danger of Cults: From Fervour to Fanaticism,* retrieved 31 December
   2002, from www.christadelphia.org/pamphlets/cults.htm. Ashton has also written booklets on spiritualism and Satanism, see www.christadelphia.org/pamphlets/. Cf. Duncan
   Heaster's booklets *Bible Basics for Jews, Bible Basics for Buddhists,* and *Bible Basics for Muslims,* see www.bbie.org/chbooks/heaster/index.html. Also cf. "Mormonism of God—Or
   Men?" *Herald of the Coming Age* 30, no. 2 (January 1981). "Jehovah's Witnesses Refuted By
   the Bible!" *Herald of the Coming Age* 20, no. 3 (October 1969) (reissued *Herald of the Coming Age* 31, no. 2 [August 1982]). R. W. Abel, *Christadelphianism of God or Men?* Retrieved
   from www.antipas.org/books/christadelphianism/cism_book.html.

to Jehovah's Witnesses and Latter-day Saints (Mormons).[2] The latter two groups numerically outstrip the Christadelphians' worldwide membership. Perhaps it is because the Christadelphians are not very active in door knocking and are numerically small that evangelicals have not made it a priority to produce much apologetic literature addressing them. This lack of apologetic resources has meant that very little effort has been made to understand them, and certainly no conscientious attempts to disciple them. Clearly there is an urgent need for some missional reflection and action. A comprehensive apologia is a project waiting for apologists to pursue.

This chapter however cannot fill that gap, nor is it constructed as a summary apologia debunking their beliefs. Instead, after sketching some background data, we will profile the Christadelphians' hermeneutical and apologetic tools. With these insights we can best understand why they read the Bible the way they do and why they reject orthodox Christianity. From this context, some proposals are presented as fresh trajectories for missions and apologetics with Christadelphians.

BACKGROUND

The Christadelphians derive their name from a combination of two Greek words *Christou* (Christ) and *Adelphoi* (brothers), which literally means "brethren of Christ." It is premised on passages such as Matthew 12:50 and Hebrews 2:11.[3] The name was coined in 1864 as a means of identifying those people who had aligned themselves with the preaching of John Thomas (1805–1871) and as conscientious objectors seeking exemption from military service in the

---

2. Counter-cult books dealing with the Christadelphians include Wm. C. Irvine, ed., *Heresies Exposed* (Neptune, N.J.: Loizeaux, 1921), 61–65. J. Oswald Sanders, *Heresies Ancient and Modern* (London and Edinburgh: Marshall, Morgan and Scott, 1948), 97–104. Maurice C. Burrell, *Some Modern Faiths* (London: InterVarsity, 1973), 58–69. Richard Kyle, *The Religious Fringe* (Downers Grove, Ill.: InterVarsity, 1993), 90–92. Branson Hopkins, *Unmasking Christadelphianism: The Hopelessness of "The Hope"* (Wellington: Jubilee Publishers, 1996). John Ankerberg and John Weldon, *Encyclopedia of Cults and New Religions* (Eugene, Ore.: Harvest House, 1999), 92–104. H. Wayne House, *Charts of Cults, Sects, and Religious Movements* (Grand Rapids: Zondervan, 2000), 35–43.
3. "Introducing the Christadelphians: Modern Revival of Apostolic Faith," *Herald of the Coming Age* 28, no. 6 (n.d.): 2. Cf. Rob Hyndman, *The Christadelphians (Brothers and Sisters in Christ): Introducing a Bible-Based Community* (Hyderabad, India: Printland Publishers, 2000), 4.

U.S. Civil War. Prior to this, adherents had been known informally as "in the truth," "Thomasites," and "Royal Association of Believers."[4]

Although their early history dovetails with the life and ministry of John Thomas, neither his teachings nor those affirmed by the Christadelphians arose in a vacuum. After the War of Independence, the establishment of American democracy brought the whole social order into question. Nathan Hatch points out that the notion of popular sovereignty took hold in politics, law, and religion. Hatch argues that as the ideal of an egalitarian society gained currency in parts of North America, so too did the idea that an individual's conscience was paramount in deciding religious matters in certain segments of the churches.[5]

Although the Reformers asserted the supremacy of Sola Scriptura—the Bible alone as the authoritative source of faith—Hatch maintains that a populist hermeneutic of one's right to privately interpret the Bible unfettered by creeds and systematic theology took root between 1780 and 1820.[6] He believes that the best illustration of this is the Christian Restorationist Movement spawned by Barton Stone, Alexander Campbell, and Thomas Campbell that culminated in the Disciples of Christ and Churches of Christ. The tenets these men espoused centered on the Bible alone—or more specifically the New Testament—a plea to bypass the denominational strife of church history in favor of New Testament simplicity, and following one's conscience from Scripture without having one's views judged.[7]

This populist hermeneutical approach to Scripture suited well the mood of the day where anti-papal and anti-clerical sentiments and eschatological speculation about Christ's Second Advent abounded. Hatch remarks:

The hermeneutic of the Christian Movement had considerable appeal early in [sic] nineteenth century for at least two reasons. It proclaimed a new ground of certainty for a generation perplexed by sectarian rivalry. If people would only abandon the husks of theological abstraction and return to the Bible, the truth would become plain

4. Charles H. Lippy, *The Christadelphians in North America* (Lewiston, N.Y.: Edwin Mellen Press, 1989), 49, 52.
5. Nathan O. Hatch, "Sola Scriptura and Novus Ordo Seclorum," in *The Bible in America: Essays in Cultural History,* ed. Nathan O. Hatch and Mark A. Noll (Oxford: Oxford University Press, 1982), 65.
6. Ibid., 66–71.
7. Ibid., 71–72.

for all to see. A second appeal was that common folk using this method could easily confound the most erudite clergymen. Any Christian using New Testament words could fend off the most brilliant theological argument by the simple retort that he was using God's word against human opinion.[8]

One other important intellectual current of the day was the Scottish philosophy, associated with Thomas Reid (1710–1796), known as Common Sense Realism.[9] Common Sense philosophy emphasized a correspondence theory of realism allied to Baconian induction. American evangelical apologetics reflected Common Sense Realism, though this was mostly in "the broader habits of mind or reassuring conventions of thought."[10] Common Sense became a catch cry for those advocating being one's own interpreter of Scripture.

EMERGENCE OF THE CHRISTADELPHIANS

It was in the wake of this religio-cultural ferment that John Thomas, an English medical practitioner and son of the manse, emigrated to the United States in 1832.[11] He immediately encountered Alexander Campbell's Christian Restorationist teachings, then met Campbell and made his debut as a Campbellite preacher. In 1834, he married Ellen Hunt, and edited a Campbellite magazine known as the *Apostolic Advocate*. He soon found that his doctrinal views were diverging from Campbell's. Two key issues were Thomas's insistence on the need for rebaptism of people who had participated in other denominations, and the resurrection only of "true believers." By 1837, the breach had widened as Thomas espoused conditional immortality, and Campbell disfellowshipped him. Two years later, Thomas drifted away from his religious

---

8. Hatch, "Sola Scriptura and Novus Ordo Seclorum," 72.
9. Mark A. Noll, "Common Sense Traditions and American Evangelical Thought," *American Quarterly* 37 (1985): 220. Sydney E. Ahlstrom, "The Scottish Philosophy and American Theology," *Church History* 24 (1955): 257–72. Alvin Plantinga indicates that Reid's position may have derived from the French philosopher Claude Buffier (1661–1737), see his *Warrant and Proper Function* (New York: Oxford University Press, 1993), x.
10. Noll, "Common Sense Traditions and American Evangelical Thought," 220.
11. Thomas's biography was composed by fellow Christadelphian, Robert Roberts, *Dr. Thomas: His Life and Work*, 3d ed., rev. C. C. Walker and W. H. Boulton (Birmingham, England: Christadelphian, 1954). Cf. Lippy, *Christadelphians in North America*, 27–56; and Bryan R. Wilson, *Sects and Society: A Sociological Study of the Elim Tabernacle, Christian Science and Christadelphians* (London: Heinemann, 1961), 236–66.

concerns, but his religious fervor was reignited after encounters with both Universalists and Mormons.[12]

Thomas then studied William Miller's eschatological teachings. In 1847, he again reflected on the issue of baptism and arranged for an unnamed male acolyte to rebaptize him. Thomas's preaching coalesced into his first major monograph, *Elpis Israel,* published in 1848. He evangelized throughout Britain that year and two years later returned to the United States. In 1852, he established his base in New York City and it was there that his first congregation was known as the Royal Association of Believers. Congregations became known as *ecclesias* (assemblies) rather than churches as a way of maintaining an exclusivist stance toward mainstream Christianity.

The Christadelphians spread in North America and the British Empire, first under Thomas's guidance and then by acolyte Robert Roberts (1839–1898). Thomas's status as the founder and leader of the Christadelphians differed from that of Joseph Smith (Mormons). Thomas did not view himself as a specially commissioned apostle or prophet. He was an exhorter and polemicist toward mainstream churches, but did not intervene in the affairs of local Christadelphian ecclesias. Christadelphians concede that Thomas was a fallible yet diligent Bible student.[13] The status of his books is comparable to that of John Calvin in Reformed circles. The Christadelphians do not claim to have been inaugurated by any charismatic vision or extra-biblical revelation.[14]

After Thomas's death, Roberts emerged as a significant apologist but not as an official successor. Because Thomas's theology was anti-clerical, he did not conceive of the need for a sectarian leader. Roberts provided direction for the sect and was widely respected.[15] Yet, in the ensuing years, internal dissent over doctrinal issues arose that resulted in extensive schisms throughout the United States, Britain, Australia, and elsewhere. An early example was the "Free Life" or "Clean Flesh" controversy concerning Jesus' immaculate flesh. Opinion was

---

12. Lippy, *Christadelphians in North America,* 40–41.
13. See Aleck Crawford, introduction to *"The Hope of Israel," or "No Hope"? A Critique of the Book* Christadelphianism: The Hopelessness of "The Hope," retrieved from http://users.chariot.net.au/~aleck/index.html. Crawford rebuts Hopkins's book op. cit. and correctly points out that it is an *ad hominem* diatribe.
14. "Introducing the Christadelphians": 2.
15. Christadelphians concede that Robert Roberts erred in his eschatological conjectures about current events. See the publisher's foreword to Robert Roberts, *Christendom Astray* (London: Dawn Book Supply, 1965), 11–14.

divided over whether Jesus had inherited Adam's sinful flesh, because he died, or he was not subject to sinful flesh, because God was his Father.[16] The "orthodox" Christadelphian position holds to the former view, while the latter view became that of the Berean or Old Paths Christadelphians. Some of these ecclesias still exist.

Perhaps the greatest dispute concerned the resurrection of the dead—namely, whether only those who have been baptized are resurrected or if those who have heard the gospel but have not been baptized are included in the resurrection. Two protagonists in this debate were John J. Andrew, who espoused the former position, and Robert Roberts, who espoused the latter. Although the two men were on cordial terms, the debate was unresolved when Roberts died in 1898. A schism occurred when the South London and Birmingham ecclesias amended their doctrinal statements to reflect Roberts's position. A ripple effect occurred worldwide and two camps came into existence: Unamended Christadelphians, whose theology followed Andrew's position, and Amended Christadelphians following Roberts's views. These camps still exist, although reunion between some ecclesias has taken place in Britain and elsewhere.[17]

HETERODOX DOCTRINES AND HERMENEUTIC

Although the Christadelphians eschew creeds, they nonetheless have a declaratory statement about what they believe. The document is known as *A Declaration of the Truth Revealed in the Bible,* with Amended and Unamended versions expressing the beliefs of the two major camps.[18] The Christadelphians believe in and worship God the Father, but reject the doctrine of the Trinity as spurious. They accept the historicity of the creation narratives—hence rejecting evolutionary theories—and maintain that sin entered the world through Adam's disobedience. Central to their theology is an understanding of the promises God made to Abraham (Genesis 12:1–7; 13:14–17; Galatians 3:16). In this legal contract, God promised Abraham that he and his offspring would inhabit the land forever. For Christadelphians this means that the future hope

---

16. See Lippy, *Christadelphians in North America,* 61–63, 74–77.
17. See Wilson, *Sects and Society,* 251–261; and Lippy, *Christadelphians in North America,* 68–73.
18. Both Amended and Unamended camps have these declaratory statements, see J. Gordon Melton, ed., *The Encyclopedia of American Religions: Religious Creeds* (Detroit: Gale Research, 1988), 523–41 and 541–63 respectively.

lies in the resurrected Abraham and his descendants, who will inherit the ancient lands promised to them. Also wrapped up in this is the promised seed of Messiah. John Thomas maintained that to have a true faith one must adopt Abraham's mode of thought about the future hope of the people living in the Promised Land.

Some other distinctive teachings include the following:

- Jesus was only a human being. He did not exist before the virginal conception. He was Israel's Messiah. Because he had the Holy Spirit from birth, Jesus was God's Son, yet he was only human.
- Jesus' death on the cross was a sacrifice for sin but was not a substitutionary death. It brought justification because people can now be restored to the covenant relationship God made with Abraham.
- Salvation requires that one have accurate knowledge of the gospel first and that upon repentance one is baptized for the remission of sin. Obedience to the Lord's commandments is essential.
- The Holy Spirit is not a personage of spirit, but rather God's creative energy or power.
- The devil has no ontological reality, but instead is the personification of sin.
- Man is mortal and there is no such thing as an immortal soul that survives death.
- At death, the human being's soul is asleep, there being no intermediate state between one's earthly sojourn and the day of resurrection.
- Immortality is a conditional gift bestowed at the resurrection.

We must also note their hermeneutical principles. For Christadelphians, the keys for unlocking Scripture are these:

- "The Old Testament lays the foundation of all that is involved in the New. The New Testament is simply an appendage to the Old, valuable beyond all price, and indispensable in the most absolute sense; but in itself, apart from the Old Testament, far from being sufficient to give us that perfection of Christian knowledge which constitutes a person 'wise unto salvation.'"[19]

---

19. Roberts, *Christendom Astray*, 32.

- The ordinary rules of speech apply to understanding what is written in Scripture.
- One will find correspondence between its words and the events it describes.
- Prophecy is to be understood literally, although it is recognized that both metaphor and symbol are sometimes used in the Bible.

Christadelphian theology is systematically organized and argued in Robert Roberts's *Christendom Astray* and H. P. Mansfield's *Key to the Understanding of the Scriptures.* Their doctrine begins with proving the mortal nature of humanity, then soul sleep, and then immortality as a resurrectional gift, which is then followed by the doctrine of God, Christology, and so forth.[20] That logical structure means that their understanding of mortality and soul sleep shapes their doctrines concerning Jesus this was evident in a debate held in Melbourne in 1905, which was titled *Are the Dead Extinct?*[21] Remarkably, apologists who have written against the Christadelphians have overlooked the centrality of this point. No wonder evangelical apologias have fallen on deaf ears.

CHRISTADELPHIAN APOLOGETICS

The Christadelphians' approach to apologetics is bibliocentric. The Bible speaks for itself. "The Bible is its own witness" and Christadelphians accept "the view of the Bible put forth by Christ and the apostles, for the Bible is not otherwise intelligible."[22] One approach they follow is the juridical style of presenting a tightly reasoned argument using jural vocabulary such as "case," "testimony," "eyewitnesses," and "evidence."[23] Christadelphians are also keen on public debates where the juridical goal of reaching a verdict is either explicit

---

20. H. P. Mansfield, *Key to the Understanding of Scripture* (West Beach, South Australia: Logos Publications, 1968). Mansfield plagiarized great chunks of Roberts's *Christendom Astray* without any acknowledgment.
21. Debate between R. A. Miller-Argue (Christian Evidence Society) and B. F. McGibbon (Christadelphian) held in Melbourne on 9 and 16 August 1905, *Are the Dead Extinct? Or the Final Verdict,* 2d ed. (Sydney: Commonwealth Christian Evidence Press, 1911).
22. "The Certainty and Significance of Christ's Resurrection Established by Logic and Scripture," *Herald of the Coming Age* 27, no. 4 (November 1977): 10.
23. On juridical apologetics see Philip Johnson, "Juridical Apologists 1600–2000 A.D.: A Bio-Bibliographical Essay," *Global Journal of Classical Theology* 3, no. 1 (March 2002). Retrieved from www.trinitysem.edu/journal/philjohnsonpap.html.

or implicit.[24] The bodily resurrection of Christ is defended with appeals to the scriptural evidences.[25] The honesty and integrity of the apostles is upheld, and circumstantial evidence, such as the existence of the church, is used as proof that Christ must have risen.[26]

Their principal approach is to argue from fulfilled prophecy to demonstrate that the Bible is trustworthy.[27] Prophetic apologias focus on three areas. The first covers prophecies against ancient nations like Tyre and Babylon.[28] The second focuses on fulfilled messianic prophecies.[29] The third examines the restoration of Israel as a nation in 1948 and the signs of Christ's imminent return.[30] Of these three areas, most attention is on eschatological prophecies. Although the Christadelphians believe that Christ shall reign in Jerusalem for one thousand years, they utterly reject dispensational theology.[31]

Another apologetic style is that of refuting "false doctrines" by Scripture, appeals to common sense, and using syllogistic reasoning.[32] Although some

---

24. An explicit call for a verdict is found in the debate between Miller-Argue and McGibbon (see n. 21). An implicit example is the debate between Ross Clifford (Baptist) and Richard O'Connor (Christadelphian), "Bible Teaches That Jesus Is God, Co-Equal with the Father," held in Sydney on 25 October 1987. Audiotapes are available from the Christadelphian Tape and Visual Aid Department, 3 Shackleton Avenue, Birrong, NSW 2143 Australia.

25. Cf. Alan Hayward, "The Evidence of the Empty Tomb" in *God's Truth: A Scientist Shows Why It Makes Sense to Believe the Bible*, chap. 7, at www.godstruth.org/. Hayward's book was originally published by Marshall Morgan and Scott in 1973, but I have only consulted the Internet version. Hayward confesses his Christadelphian commitment in "An Ancient Faith in Modern Dress," in *Great News for the World*, chap. 9, at www.lincolnecclesia.clara.net/gnftw_12.htm. Hayward is also known as the author of *Creation and Evolution* (London: SPCK, 1985), which U.S. evangelical publisher Bethany House released in 1995.

26. "The Certainty and Significance of Christ's Resurrection," 4–8.

27. Ibid., 2.

28. Ibid., 2–5.

29. "Who Is Jesus Christ? Not a Pre-Existent Being but Saviour of Mankind," *Herald of the Coming Age* 32, no. 3 (June 1984): 5.

30. W. Excell, "Prophecy: Its Purpose and Promise," *Herald of the Coming Age* 29, no. 3 (December 1979): 6–8. Cf. "Israel, Egypt, Russia and Christ's Coming," *Herald of the Coming Age* 29, no. 1 (August 1979). "Israel's Revival: Sure Sign of Christ's Coming," *Herald of the Coming Age* 30, no. 5 (December 1981). "The Coming New World Order," *Herald of the Coming Age* 34, no. 6 (March 1988).

31. See "Will the Rapture Ever Occur?" *Herald of the Coming Age* 30, no. 44 (July 1981).

32. The late Richard O'Connor, in his debate with Ross Clifford, used forty-five overhead transparencies setting out syllogistic arguments rebutting the Deity of Christ and upholding Christadelphian Christology. O'Connor's syllogisms, though logical in structure, rested on unverified presuppositions.

Christadelphian apologists have written on certain "cults," they are antipathetic toward "cult buster" ministries and prefer to exposit biblical truth rather than debunking cults.[33]

COMMON SENSE AND RHETORIC

The Christadelphians frequently invoke "common sense" when making their apologetic points:

> The language of the Bible is a model of clarity and simplicity. Anybody, reading it without bias, should be able to comprehend its basic message at least. But, unfortunately, many fail to do so. Equally sincere people draw conflicting interpretations from the Bible. Although they may agree that it is the revelation of God's will, they often disagree as to its meaning and significance. Why is that? Basically because its study has been approached with bias; a bias that distorts its interpretation. Remove that bias, and accept the face value of the Bible's message, and truth will soon be apparent as distinct from prevailing error.[34]

One apologist, in defending the apostles' testimony to Jesus' resurrection, states, "We submit that you cannot get rid of it without doing violence to every principle of logic and of common sense."[35] Educated theologians are depicted as those who obfuscate the plain or obvious meaning of Scripture:

> What a pity, that theologians make mystery out of the God-head, confusing that which is plain and simple, and contrary to Bible teaching, insist that God is three![36]

Within these appeals to common sense, one can detect the two-step gambit that propagandists often take. First, the rejected view is intentionally presented

---

33. Cf. Ashton's remarks on cult buster ministries in *The Danger of Cults*. H. P. Mansfield remarked, "Exposing error does not establish Truth. We prefer to do the latter rather than the former." See "Jehovah's Witnesses Refuted by the Bible," *Herald of the Coming Age* 20, no. 3 (October 1969): 48. Also see note 1 for references to their counter-cult materials.
34. "What the Bible Teaches About Christ's Second Coming," *Herald of the Coming Age* 31, no. 5 (June 1983): 1.
35. "The Certainty and Significance of Christ's Resurrection," 7.
36. "God Is One Not Three!" *Herald of the Coming Age* 25, no. 2 (December 1974): 7.

as ridiculous ("this is silly"). The second step involves contrasting the rejected view ("we would not think like that") with what is reasonable ("this is plain and simple"). The rejected view is deemed intellectually flaccid, whereas the endorsed view is considered mentally robust. Robert Roberts best exemplifies this tendency:

> Words truly fail to describe the mischief the doctrine has done. It has rendered the Bible unintelligible, and promoted unbelief by making the Bible responsible for a doctrine with which its historic and moral features are inconsistent. It has taken away the vitality of religion by destroying its meaning, and investing the subject with a mystery that does not belong to it. It has robbed it of its vigour, and reduced it to an effeminate thing, disowned and unpractised by men of robust mind, and heeded only by the sentimental and romantic. Fling it to the moles and to the bats, and humbly accept the evidence of fact, and the testimony of God's infallible word.[37]

Another common thread is the use of rhetorical questions, as illustrated by the following two quotes:

> If the Bereans were satisfied by a searching of the Old Testament, which were the only Scriptures in existence at the time of their search, that what Paul said was true, is it not evident that what he said must in some form be contained in the Old Testament?[38]

> What has God shown to men? Is it not His omnipotent power, His Supreme Divinity? Has not all this been plain and visible to the eyes of man from the very foundation of the world, in the things that God has made? Look about and consider the manifold wonders of nature, so marvelous in their precision and perfection. They constitute indisputable visible evidence of God's existence. Who can deny it?[39]

---

37. Roberts, *Christendom Astray*, 51.
38. Ibid., 31. The "Bereans" here refers to Acts 17:11 and not the schismatic group within Christadelphian history.
39. R. K. (author's initials only), "Evolution: Modern Myth of Science," *Herald of the Coming Age* 25, no. 5 (August 1975): 2.

Now the grammatology of the Christadelphians parallels that of the Jehovah's Witnesses, who embed rhetorical speech in their literature and daily conversations:

> The rhetorical question is a major linguistic tool used by the Witnesses. So ingrained is its use that even casual conversation around the dinner table is permeated with self-answered questions. . . . [A]mong the Witnesses the stock answers to the stock questions provide a verbal feedback system for consolidating social integration within the faith. It also obviates the necessity of thinking when presented with a question.[40]

Christadelphians do not manifest the same preference for rhetorical speech patterns in ordinary daily discourse; however, it is instructive to note this is an apologetic device.

MISSIONS TO CHRISTADELPHIANS

The standpoint taken in this book is that evangelical responses to new religious movements ought to broaden from debunking beliefs to including cross-cultural missiological methods. Some contributors have charted how contextual approaches work with esoteric forms of spirituality. After digesting those chapters, readers might concede the viability of contextual missions with those groups. However, it might be strongly felt that contextual missions is implausible and unnecessary to tackle heretical Bible-based groups. So this chapter and Ken Mulholland's on the Latter-day Saints constitute "test cases" in contextual missions.

The classic response to the Christadelphians has been a doctrinal apologetic, and that is not being dismissed here. However, two critical observations must be considered. First, this method of refutation is adversarial. It can yield a victorious argument and yet fail to win converts. Could this failure to win converts be connected to our vocabulary when we classify the Christadelphian as an "enemy" or false prophet? We need to be mindful that the Ephesian Christians were experts at heresy hunting (Acts 20:25–31; Ephesians 4:11–16; Revelation 2:1–2), yet they lost their first love (Revelation 2:4). The other point is

---

40. Heather Botting and Gary Botting, *The Orwellian World of Jehovah's Witnesses* (Toronto: University of Toronto Press, 1984), 88.

that, in drafting comparative doctrinal charts, the Christadelphians' herme-neutic is either overlooked or inadequately understood. If we do not know why they read the Bible the way they do, then all communication will degener-ate into a shallow biblical Ping-Pong match between protagonists, with proof texts being hit back and forth. The doctrinal method of refutation needs to be deepened in a way that works through the Christadelphians' own hermeneu-tic. It should have a winsome call to discipleship where we invite them as sin-ners and seekers to discover the fullness of Christ.

So what would a cross-cultural missions approach entail? The foundation of it rests on Christ's kingdom commissions, but especially those concerned with making disciples of sinners. We need to see the Christadelphians first and foremost as people bedeviled by sin. So, the first step is to change the theologi-cal metaphor that solely emphasizes that they are purveyors of false doctrine. It is not being denied that they uphold heretical doctrine. However, their com-mitment to such doctrine has a lot to do with spiritual blindness. That blind-ness arises from their faulty hermeneutic and presuppositions, and translates into a zeal that is confounded and misdirected by their doctrine and their sin. A more helpful metaphor is to see the Christadelphians as God-fearers who do not yet properly comprehend the gospel.

It is instructive to consider how the apostles interacted with people who were God-fearers and yet whose knowledge of Christ was faulty or incom-plete. Philip in his encounter with the Ethiopian did not debunk the man's Judaic doctrines, but conversed with him about the meaning of the prophet Isaiah's words. Philip used an intriguing and thought-provoking question as his commencement point: "Do you understand what you are reading?" (Acts 8:30 NASB). Ananias abandoned his phobias about Saul of Tarsus, who was the great enemy of the early Church. Ananias was God's vessel, through whom both healing and the bestowal of the Holy Spirit came to Saul (Acts 9:17). Paul later reviewed his former life and spoke of himself as having been a zealous heretic (Philippians 3:2–9; Galatians 1:13–14). Peter likewise had to confront his taboos about Gentiles, which he did when ministering to Cornelius the God-fearer (Acts 10). Apollos certainly knew things about Jesus, but his preach-ing was deficient until Priscilla and Aquila took him aside to explain the gos-pel "more accurately" (Acts 18:24–26 NASB). Similarly, Paul treated with courtesy those who knew only John's baptism (Acts 19:1–7).

In depicting the Christadelphians as God-fearers, we must emphasize that their knowledge of Christ is seriously deficient. Yet this is the juncture where we can begin to consider them as an unreached people group or tribe. As they maintain a separatist stance from both society and the churches, Christadelphians cannot help but cultivate their own subculture. To be a Christadelphian, one embraces an all-encompassing way of life that is expressed in family relationships, personal rites of passage, moral behavior, and one's interaction with the external social, political, and religious orders. Christadelphian vocabulary provides the verbal means for demarcating the boundaries between who belongs and who is excluded. There is a dynamic interplay between how members behave and conform to expectations in the ecclesia, how commitment is encouraged and reinforced there, and how their hermeneutic for reading the Bible and interpreting the outside culture binds them to their dogmas. A Christadelphian who strives to be a faithful member will experience acute tensions between loyalty to that commitment and his or her unavoidable interactions with the rapidly changing globalized social order outside the ecclesia.[41]

Because the Christadelphians constitute a tribe with their own subculture, we need to consider what strategies will be appropriate for making disciples. Although personal, one-to-one evangelism is to be encouraged, it must be remembered that the social bonds of each Christadelphian are normally centered in the local ecclesia. So when we exhort repentance and faith, the Christadelphian faces the tension between loyalty to Christ and loyalty to family and friends. Jesus undeniably spoke firmly about making our spiritual priorities uppermost, even when it may cost us dearly (Matthew 8:18–22; Mark 10:29–31; Luke 9:57–62). However, Jesus also exalted family relationships (Matthew 15:3–6; Mark 10:11–12, 29–30; Luke 7:12–15; John 19:26–27).

All too often, Western Christians engage in "extraction evangelism," in which the focus is on converting individuals and drawing them out from their native culture.[42] This no doubt reflects the excessive emphasis on rugged individualism in the West. However, not all cultures operate with such notions, especially those that have tight-knit bonds. Missiologists recognize that when extraction evangelism predominates as the method of outreach, it does not

---

41. For more sociological insights refer to Wilson, *Sects and Society,* and Lippy, *Christadelphians in North America.*

42. Phil Parshall, *Beyond the Mosque: Christians Within Muslim Community* (Grand Rapids: Baker, 1985), 178–80. H. L. Richard, *Following Jesus in the Hindu Context: The Intriguing Implications of N. V. Tilak's Life and Thought* (Pasadena, Calif.: William Carey Library, 1998), 104–5.

yield a church of family relationships. Rather, the local unreached community builds up resentments toward the missionaries for disrupting relational bonds. This is one reason why in cross-cultural circumstances, missionaries seek to woo entire families to Christ, so that social dislocation is lessened and a harmonious church can grow.

These missional insights have direct bearing on how to reach the Christadelphians. They form a close-knit community where growth relies heavily on handing the faith down to the next generation of offspring. A family or group approach should be the priority of those who wish to make disciples among the Christadelphians. A missions team that is specifically committed to reaching Christadelphians can form the nucleus of a new ecclesia. The ecclesia should develop within the bounds of normative biblical faith but in form and basic structure closely resemble the Christadelphians' experience of life in an ecclesia. It might be recalled that Christadelphian ecclesiology has a lot of affinity with that of the Brethren.[43] Literature that explains the gospel and the rudiments of orthodox faith could be composed in the customary style and format of Christadelphian booklets.[44] For apologetic purposes, the missions team should feel comfortable presenting eschatology about Israel that will resonate with Christadelphians, rather than seeking to impose, say, an amillennial or postmillennial position.

To reach inside the Christadelphians' world, a missions team must start by building relationships. However, apart from the people skills, Christadelphians should be addressed in the thought-forms of their world. Because they accept the Scriptures as inerrant and perspicacious, this is an obvious point of contact or common ground. However, as we have already noted, the fundamental problem is in their hermeneutic. The inclination of apologists might be to immediately engage in a debate over hermeneutics by trying to refute the Christadelphians' principles—namely, "I'm right, you're wrong." The difficulty with that line of approach is that apologists are unlikely to get beyond first base. The way forward is to speak gently along rhetorical lines, emphasizing that the Scriptures speak for themselves in plain and intelligible terms. The aim is to assist the Christadelphians in discovering a Christocentric view of

---

43. Another interesting line of study would be to compare and contrast the Christadelphians with the International Churches of Christ, as established by Kip McKean, because this group likewise mirrors the theology of Restorationism.

44. Cf. the careful observations made about contextual ministry with Jews in Faña Spielberg and Stuart Dauermann, "Contextualization: Witness and Reflection Messianic Jews as a Case," *Missiology* 25, no. 1 (January 1997): 15–35.

Scripture. It unlocks Scripture's meaning and avoids the cul-de-sacs created by Christadelphian exegesis.

The launching pad is to agree in principle with John Thomas's assertion that we need Abraham's mode of thought. Here we can start by referring to John 8:56, where Jesus says that Abraham rejoiced at the possibility of seeing Jesus' day. In other words, Abraham's focus was forward looking to Jesus. The second step is to note how Jesus is the fulfillment of the Law, Prophets, and writings (Luke 24:44–45; Matthew 5:17–18; 24:35). Scripture records that Jesus opened his disciples' minds to what the Bible was about, and his word stands forever. The New Testament is the best place to start, because it amplifies what was progressively foreshadowed in the Old Testament. Moreover, Jesus proleptically put his stamp of approval on the then unwritten New Testament. He did so promising that the Comforter would bring to the disciples' remembrance what he had taught (John 14:26). The plain and simple meaning, then, is that we need a Christocentric focus to interpret the Scriptures accurately. The common sense conclusion is that the Scriptures teach that we must look to the Gospels and Epistles first, and only from that vantage point can we fully comprehend what the Law, Prophets, and writings foreshadowed. This leads us to the correct inference that God's revelation was progressive until it reached its fulfillment in Jesus. Here, no doctrine is being examined; instead, we are merely setting the foundational hermeneutic principle from which doctrine can be developed.

The next step is to consider further what Abraham's mode of thought was through the apostle Paul's paradigmatic illustration in Romans 4–5 about faith and justification. This should be followed by a consideration of Jesus' humanity from his birth to death, affirming the genuineness of his experience as a person. At this stage, no apologia should be made for Jesus' deity. The next gambit is to critically examine the issues of mortality, soul sleep, and the intermediate state, because they have an impact on how we understand Jesus' mission. Unless these issues are clarified, no argument for Jesus' deity will make sense to them. Because Jesus died, Christadelphians cannot accept that he was Deity. According to their doctrine, when Jesus died, his soul went to sleep. So who ran the universe while Jesus was asleep? Moreover, God cannot die—and because Jesus did, Jesus could not possibly be God.[45]

The next step is to find appropriate pointers to the unique relationship between the human Jesus and the Father and the Holy Spirit. The recent work of former Christadelphian Julian Clementson can assist us. Clementson argues

---

45. Cf. Robert A. Morey, *Death and the Afterlife* (Minneapolis: Bethany House, 1984).

that popular evangelical explanations of the Trinity make little sense to Christadelphians,[46] and the classic patristic vocabulary about divine persons in the Godhead is beyond the Christadelphians' comprehension. To overcome this obstacle, Clementson suggests that "what we can usefully talk about instead are three distinguishable centres of personhood within the one God, as known through Christian experience."[47] He believes that if we focus on the personal and relational qualities within the Godhead, our description of Jesus' divinity will begin to make more sense to the Christadelphian.

Clementson reminds us that the Father-Son relationship is "an essential part of the revelation of God that Jesus came to bring, and must therefore predate the human Jesus himself."[48] He emphasizes that we must be very precise in our explanations, particularly ensuring that a distinction be made between the preexistent Son and the human being known as Jesus. This is important because, as Clementson has pointed out, the Christadelphians mistakenly think that evangelicals claim that the human Jesus was eternal. The remedy for this, he suggests, is to persuade Christadelphians that Jesus *as the Son of God* had a prior relationship with the Father (John 16:28). In Philippians 2:6–8, a preexisting nonhuman person chooses to become a human being.

Once clarity is established on this point, we can expand on the evidence for Jesus' divinity. The apostles confirm that he was declared to be the Son of God by his resurrection (Acts 13:33; Romans 1:4). Further scriptural support is found in that Jesus is shown to be divine through his miraculous conception (Luke 1:35). His divinity is confirmed by the Father's voice when the Son is baptized (Mark 1:9–11).

In the New Testament, Jesus is included in God's identity. "This is shown by Jesus sharing God's throne and sovereignty over all things, his being given the divine name, his being worshipped, and his participation in the work of creation."[49] Because Christadelphians respond to syllogistic reasoning, Francis Beckwith's helpful model of presenting a syllogism for Christ's deity should be employed as a means of illustrating the point.[50] Here we can also use fulfilled

---

46. Julian Clementson, "The Christadelphians and the Doctrine of the Trinity," *Evangelical Quarterly* 75, no. 2 (April 2003): 174.

47. Ibid., 175.

48. Ibid., 170.

49. Ibid., 167.

50. Francis J. Beckwith, "Of Logic and Lordship: The Validity of a Categorical Syllogism Supporting Christ's Deity," in *See the Gods Fall: Four Rivals to Christianity,* by Francis J. Beckwith and Stephen E. Parrish (Joplin, Mo.: College Press, 1997), 243–45. On syllogistic reasoning generally, see Irving M. Copi, *Introduction to Logic,* 3d ed. (New York: Macmillan, 1968).

prophecies that show the unique relationship between the Messiah and God the Father. Objections will arise, especially a puzzlement as to how Jesus could be our "brother" and be one of us while simultaneously being deity. Another objection will be that God cannot be tempted, yet Jesus was tempted, so how can he be divine? Thereafter we should explore the unique relationship between Jesus and the Holy Spirit and also between the Holy Spirit and the believer.

After examining these two teachings, the Christadelphian can better comprehend what the Scriptures say about the Father, Son, and Holy Spirit. Then systematic Bible studies about salvation, baptism, discipleship, and eschatology need to be developed.

Cross-cultural mission to a Bible-based group like the Christadelphians is feasible. The challenge is to shift from theory to praxis and begin the slow but steady task of sowing and reaping among this unreached people group.

STUDY QUESTIONS

1. Examine the following Bible passages: Philippians 1:20–24; 2 Corinthians 5:1–10; and Luke 23:39–43. What do these passages intimate about there being an intermediate state? What other passages can you find that are concerned with the intermediate state?
2. In the Old Testament, God is referred to as King, Savior, and Judge—and these same titles are applied to Jesus. What other titles does Jesus have in common with God the Father?
3. In this chapter, a missions team model was proposed for reaching Christadelphians. How might a team approach be developed to reach Jehovah's Witnesses? In what ways would the approach be similar to that in this chapter? Would there be any major differences?

CHAPTER 9

REFRAMING A TRADITIONAL APOLOGETIC TO REACH "NEW SPIRITUALITY" SEEKERS

ROSS CLIFFORD

A review of this generation's apologetics indicates the prominent role played by historical–legal apologists in theoretical discourse. In this genre, the resurrection of Jesus, based on the direct evidence of reliable New Testament records and trustworthy eyewitness testimony, is the primary focus. Often one moves to the circumstantial evidence in support: the fact of the empty tomb; that Christians worship on Sunday and not the Sabbath; the fact that the tomb of Christ was not subject to early pilgrimages; the existence of the church, whose existence can be traced to the resurrection of its founder; an unbroken chain of testimony of changed lives, from the disciples to today. Popular apologists who rely on the marshalling of evidence for a historical–legal case include Josh McDowell and Lee Strobel.[1]

Although much of this apologetic paradigm can be traced back to the New Testament documents and the apologetic of the early church,[2] its flowering occurred during the eighteenth century. There are a number of reasons for the growth of the historical–legal argument at that time, including the rise of historical consciousness and historiography, the spread of Deism, and the strength of rationalism.[3] The historical–legal apologetic has survived biblical criticism

---

1. Josh McDowell, *The Resurrection Factor* (San Bernardino, Calif.: Here's Life, 1981); and Lee Strobel, *The Case for Christ* (Grand Rapids: Zondervan, 1998).
2. Allison A. Trites, *The New Testament Concept of Witness* (Cambridge: Cambridge University Press, 1977), 78–135.
3. William Lane Craig, *The Historical Argument for the Resurrection of Jesus During the Deist Controversy* (Lewiston, N.Y.: Edwin Mellen, 1985), 234–35, 317–52.

193

and still flourishes. The findings of Sir Lionel Luckhoo, the "world's most successful lawyer" (according to *The Guinness Book of Records*), are typical of this apologetic genre:

> I have spent more than forty-two years as a defence trial lawyer. . . . I have been fortunate to secure a number of successes in jury trials and I say unequivocally the evidence for the resurrection of Jesus Christ is so overwhelming that it compels acceptance by proof which leaves absolutely no room for doubt.[4]

This style of apologetic clearly attracts a listener or reader who is open to a more reasoned, rational, and cognitive thought-system approach to religious truth claims: a modernity style of thinking. For today's "postmodern" seeker, one would expect to look for another apologetic model. The aim of this chapter is to show that there is still a role for historical and legal evidences in evangelizing adherents to experiential new religious movements such as the New Age movement, provided this traditional apologetic is reframed. It is necessary to reframe these evangelical positive apologetics because, overall, the approach to date has been to continue to churn out arguments for general consumption without paying attention to the issues of the listener or reader who is drawn to new religious movements.

CHARACTERISTICS OF NEW SPIRITUALITY

To date, two primary terms have been used to identify these new religious movements: *New Spirituality* and *New Age*. The term *New Age* is not currently favored. *New Spirituality* has also been called "New Consciousness," "New Sense," "New Edge," and "Postmodern Spirituality."[5] The numerous "name tags" point to the evolving nature of this spirituality. What one can say for certain is that many in the West practice religion differently today. They follow a connected spirituality whose eclectic, evolving nature is very difficult to define— partly because there are few empirical marks (unlike with Christianity), such as a founder-figure, a church, an authoritative text, and a Nicene Creed. How-

---

4. Cited in Ross Clifford, *Leading Lawyers' Case for the Resurrection* (Edmonton: Canadian Institute for Law, Theology, and Public Policy, 1996), 112.
5. John A. Saliba, *Christian Responses to the New Age Movement* (London: Geoffrey Chapman, 1999), vii–ix.

ever, it is important to have some approximate "definition" of a philosophy before considering one's apologetic response to it.[6]

One mark of New Spirituality that meets with common agreement is its eclectic nature. Neville Drury, an occultist and authority on occultism, sees this as one of its major tenets.[7] The leading consumer-predictor, Faith Popcorn, states that people will continue to develop personalized faiths by blending parts of belief systems and rituals. She concludes, "Customised Bibles will be created, merging passages from Animism to Zen."[8] Johannes Aagaard speaks of a "Pacific paradigm," a trans-syncretism that fuses eastern mysticism and Western capitalism. This paradigm places no limitations on human capacity and therefore it fits well with capitalism.[9] Researchers describe Australia's "religious institution" as "postmodern," because people's spiritual expectations do not require a single religious identification or affiliation, and some see no conflict among "consulting the stars, praying, meditating, [or] wearing a cross along with a crystal."[10] Although such eclecticism is particularly attracted to Eastern religion and concepts, it is important to note that on the whole it includes the person of Jesus. Samantha Trenoweth, in her feminist embracing of the goddess and Neo-Paganism, recounts her love of the "myth" of Jesus, even if Christianity is too big a leap of faith.[11]

In *Jesus and the Gods of the New Age*, Philip Johnson and I document other "testimonies" similar to Trenoweth's.[12] Approximately ten years ago, we founded an apologetic ministry at Sydney's twice-yearly Mind–Body–Spirit festival. In a recent survey we conducted with New Spirituality seekers, we found that 76

---

6. Gordon Lewis, "The Church and the New Spirituality," *Journal of the Evangelical Theological Society* 36, no. 4 (December 1993): 434.

7. See interview of Neville Drury, "New Age Journey," *Compass ABC Television* (10 June 2001).

8. Clarissa Bye, "The Future of Popcorn: An Interview," *The Sun-Herald—Tempo*, 21 January 2001, 5.

9. Johannes Aagaard, "Conversion, Religious Change, and the Challenge of New Religious Movements," *Cultic Studies Journal* 8, no. 2 (1991): 91–103.

10. Philip Hughes, Craig Thompson, Rohan Pryor, and Gary D. Bouma, *Believe It or Not: Australian Spirituality and the Churches in the 90s* (Hawthorn, Victoria: Christian Research Association, 1995), 10.

11. Samantha Trenoweth, *The Future of God* (Alexandria, NSW: Millennium, 1995), x–xi.

12. Ross Clifford and Philip Johnson, *Jesus and the Gods of the New Age* (Oxford: Lion, 2001), esp. "Vicky's Story," 196–200: "I have never actually given up on the idea that Jesus died for my sins. . . . But I would also pray with Buddhists and Pagans and Hindus and Muslims if they let me. . . . I like Wicca-style paganism. I find its whole life-affirming, non-bigoted, self-empowering, spirit-in-everything. . . . I will leave the question as to whether I am a Christian or not up to God for s/he alone can judge that one."

percent of respondents believed Jesus could truly empower their lives. This openness to the person and work of Jesus is confirmed by the thousands of pamphlets we have distributed. They include the following titles: "The tarot's message," "Learning from the magi astrologers," "It's true for you, but not true for me," "Did Jesus go to India?" This last pamphlet has uniformly been the most popular choice of those passing our exhibit.

Another commonly agreed mark of New Spirituality is "self-spirituality." As Drury states it, "One should transform oneself before endeavouring to transform others."[13] In a popularist sense, self-spirituality is found in the self-help emphasis of media giants like Oprah Winfrey.[14] Paul Heelas connects self-spirituality with the "detraditionalization" of the person, implying a movement away from hierarchical religions and institutions.[15] He characterizes the autonomous spiritual journey as follows:

> Typically presented as beyond belief, beyond belonging, beyond externally imposed moral commandments, a major factor in the appeal of the New Age—it is now clear—is that it does not require any great leap of faith. Basically, all that one has to do is *participate,* in order, that is, to *experience* one's barriers, one's potential, or the inner wisdom of Buddhism (for example). . . . As a number of my students (for instance) insist, "you don't have to make any truth-commitments or judgments; just try it out—see what it does for you."[16]

Apart from eclecticism and self-spirituality, there is a diversity of opinion as to what other elements should be emphasized. This is due to the eclectic and evolving nature of "New Spirituality." Gordon Lewis typifies evangelical apologetic responses when he claims that, generally, New Spirituality presupposes, "(1) a pantheistic or panentheistic worldview, (2) a noncognitive, mystical view of spiritual experiences, (3) an occult (magical) approach to spiritual knowledge and power, and (4) a vision of future world peace."[17] Irving Hexham

---

13. Neville Drury, *Exploring the Labyrinth* (St. Leonards, New South Wales: Allen and Unwin, 1999), 98.
14. Kate Maver, "Oprah Winfrey and Her Self-Help Saviours: Making the New Age Normal," *Christian Research Journal* 23, no. 4 (2001): 12–21.
15. Paul Heelas, *The New Age Movement: The Celebration of the Self and the Sacralization of Modernity* (Cambridge, Mass.: Blackwell, 1996), 159.
16. Ibid., 173.
17. G. Lewis, "The Church and the New Spirituality," 434. Similar, if at times, more extensive lists are found in other evangelical tomes. For example, Douglas R. Groothuis, *Unmasking*

is critical of such evangelical assessments of the New Spirituality, asserting that there is a tendency toward reductionism in boiling the movement down to "monism, pantheism, relativism, and evolutionary philosophy."[18] John Drane expresses a similar concern about categorizing the New Spirtuality in a way that represents it as a monolithic movement. He points out there are different nuances that expose at least two different philosophies, one monistic and the other strongly dualistic. The latter nuance connects more with hermeticism and Western esoteric and magical traditions such as astrology, alchemy, and the tarot.[19] Drane writes, "These two strands do not share the same heritage: the one has historical roots to a creation-based spirituality which is either pantheistic or panentheistic, which can be traced through Romantic poets such as Shelley, Blake, and Wordsworth, while the other has more in common with people like Swedenborg, Mesmer, Blavatsky, Bailey, and Cayce."[20]

In light of the proper concerns raised by Hexham and Drane, one could be led to believe there are no valid markers of this nebulous spirituality, outside of its eclecticism and self-oriented nature. This is not so. Although New Spirituality is not a unified system or Weltanschauung, there are common indicators. The evangelical markers have some validity, provided one is honest in stating that this is not a uniform movement, and in ensuring that beliefs are not caricatured.

EMERGENT METHODOLOGICAL ISSUES

Although belief patterns of New Spirituality are elusive, the elements that surface for consideration—beyond eclecticism and self-spirituality—are its cosmic view, its openness to occult or "hermetic holism" technologies, and its hope of the divine.[21] The aim of this essay is not to dismantle New Spirituality,

---

the New Age (Downers Grove, Ill.: InterVarsity, 1986), 18–31: "(1) All is One," "(2) All is God," "(3) Humanity is God," "(4) A Change in Consciousness," "(5) All Religions Are One," "(6) Cosmic Evolutionary Optimism."

18. Irving Hexham, "The Evangelical Response to the New Age," in Perspectives on the New Age, ed. James R. Lewis and J. Gordon Melton (Albany, N.Y.: University of New York Press, 1992), 159. Hexham also correctly accuses the more sensational texts of being unscholarly in their methods of research and creating guilt by association.

19. See Clifford and Johnson, Jesus and the Gods, 19–20.

20. John W. Drane, "Methods and Perspectives in Understanding the New Age," Themelios 23, no. 2 (February 1998): 30.

21. Douglas Groothuis, Confronting the New Age (Downers Grove, Ill.: InterVarsity, 1988), 70: look for apologetic common ground, "such as the reality of the spiritual realm, life after death, and the need for spiritual growth and social change."

but rather to engage with it. Hence, in the following pages, it will be emphasized that there needs to be in our methodology an acknowledgment of the place of wisdom and story; an understanding that the average seeker holds personal empowerment and transformation—rather than truth—to be the initial journeying point;[22] and a treatment of "religious others" with respect and dignity (Acts 17:22, 1 Peter 3:15).[23] As Alister McGrath puts it, "Experience is a vital 'point of contact' for Christian apologetics in a postmodern world."[24] This does not mean, as we will see, that the truth question is irrelevant.

THE CENTRALITY OF THE RESURRECTION

The resurrection of Jesus, which is the focus of the historical–legal apologetic, remains a primary apologetic point of interchange even with New Spirituality. In fact, scholars like J. D. Charles argue that in view of Paul's Areopagus address to a "pagan" audience,[25] where the Lukan narrative mentions the resurrection three times (Acts 17:18, 31, 32), one would have to ask whether it is not the central focus.[26] McGrath observes:

> In the end, the debate with the New Age movement will not be won through philosophy, but through the proclamation of Christ . . . Paul's Areopagus sermon sets before us a crisp, concise, and convincing approach, ideally suited to the New Age challenge—both in terms of the movement's ideas, and the opportunities available for confronting it. As for the Athenians, the resurrection of Christ may hold the key to engagement with New Agers.[27]

22. See Neville Drury in David Millikan and Neville Drury, *Worlds Apart? Christianity and the New Age* (Crows Nest, NSW: ABC Enterprises, 1991), 39–43.
23. Harold Netland, *Encountering Religious Pluralism: The Challenge to Christian Faith and Mission* (Downers Grove, Ill.: InterVarsity, 2001), 281–83.
24. Alister E. McGrath, *A Passion for Truth: The Intellectual Coherence of Evangelicalism* (Leicester: Apollos, 1996), 87.
25. Pagan is used here in a general sense and not in the context of the specific subculture of "Neo-Paganism."
26. J. Daryl Charles, "Engaging the (Neo) Pagan Mind: Paul's Encounter with Athenian Culture as a Model for Cultural Apologetics (Acts 17:16–34)," in *The Gospel and Contemporary Perspectives*, ed. Douglas Moo (Grand Rapids: Kregel, 1997), 135.
27. Alister McGrath, "Building Bridges to . . . ," in *Springboard for Faith*, by Alister McGrath and Michael Green (London: Hodder and Stoughton, 1993), 78.

With respect to the resurrection of Jesus, Richard Gaffin claims that in the history of doctrine, especially in soteriology, it has been "relatively eclipsed" by the atonement. Consequently, the soteriological significance of the Resurrection "has been largely overlooked."[28] Although the bodily resurrection of Jesus is a central tenet, it is the soteriological character of the Resurrection, its existential warrant, that the apologists to New Spirituality need to discover. Elsewhere, I have sought to demonstrate apologetically the powerful nature of the message of Jesus' resurrection in transformation of one's "soul sorrow," a transformation that is both spiritually self-oriented and cosmic. This transformation exhibits the holistic nature of our relationship with the truth. In Christ's resurrection, the listener or reader discovers forgiveness (1 Corinthians 15:17), hope (1 Corinthians 15:20–21), a relationship with the Divine (John 2:19; 20:28), and values for living, because a risen Christ brings new meaning to earthly wisdom. The bodily resurrection of Jesus, seen as the "firstfruits," demonstrates God's concern not only for one's "spirit" but also for the totality of the New Spirituality concept of humanness—mind, body, and spirit. It is an Aquarian new world order of cosmic dimensions (1 Corinthians 15:22–28).[29]

THREE APOLOGETIC MYTHS

Before we outline a reframing of the traditional apologetic in light of the above discussion, let's take a look at three myths that need to be debunked, but that are often propagated by evangelical apologists. The first is that New Spirituality has a total aversion to any factual argument. This is not so. The guru of New Spirituality, Deepak Chopra, begins his influential book *How to Know God,* by dipping into a legal analogy: "Although it does not seem possible to offer a single fact about the Almighty that would hold up in a court of law, somehow the vast majority of people believe in God." He goes on to ask what the facts would be like if we had them.[30] Clearly, although Chopra is not aware of a proof at hand for God's existence that would satisfy a historical–legal test,

28. Richard B. Gaffin, "Redemption and Resurrection: An Exercise in Biblical-Systematic Theology," in *A Confessing Theology for Postmodern Times,* ed. Michael S. Horton (Wheaton, Ill.: Crossway, 2000), 230–31.

29. See Ross Clifford and Philip Johnson, *Riding the Rollercoaster: How the Risen Christ Empowers Life* (Sydney: Strand, 1998). This book is based on a number of addresses or sermons shared in "market place" environments where the audience comprised seekers and those exploring New Spirituality.

30. Deepak Chopra, *How to Know God* (London: Rider, 2000), 1.

he does not dismiss such an approach a priori. In fact, he goes on to discuss how indicators such as quantum physics, the big bang theory, and near death experiences give us insights about our unity with God as well as revealing that the universe is not simply mechanistic.[31]

James Redfield in his New Spirituality classic, *The Celestine Prophecy,* takes a similar apologetic course,[32] as does Wayne Dyer in acknowledging that his movement from a "soft" agnosticism was the result of teleological "proofs," even though he still holds that knowledge achieved by "realization" (trusting our own personal experience) is of a higher order than intellectual reasoning.[33] The way some within New Spirituality revert to, or rely on, factual discussions will be highlighted in the case study herein. My experience is that many seekers are both-and and not either-or when it comes to modernity and New Spirituality.[34] In fact, Gus DiZerega speaks of the "enormous blessings" of the Enlightenment and talks of his pagan spiritual perspective in the context of offering a "fitting corrective to the excesses of the Enlightenment and post-Enlightenment modernity."[35]

The second myth relates to metanarratives. It is often claimed that because New Spirituality clearly has postmodern traits, it sneers at an apologetic that enters into worldview stories and metanarratives. However, just because New Spirituality is eclectic does not mean it is averse to all metadiscourse. For example, New Spirituality places a strong emphasis on myth, as will be discussed shortly. The three major influences here are Carl Jung, Mircea Eliade, and Joseph Campbell, who all espouse some form of universalism. Robert Ellwood comments that the essential "point of Jung's archetypes, Eliade's structuralism, and Campbell's one message behind all myths" is that all myths are one, and behind their "thousand faces they had, in effect, one message, based on the psychic unity of humanity, and proclaimed one intrapsychic path to salvation."[36] Such universalism is found in Drury's tale of four occult shamans from

---

31. Ibid., 267–305.
32. James Redfield, *The Celestine Prophecy* (Sydney: Bantam, 1993), 41–43.
33. Wayne W. Dyer, *There's a Spiritual Solution to Every Problem* (Sydney: HarperCollins, 2001), 201–2, also 6–7.
34. See Dan Story, *Christianity on the Offense: Responding to the Beliefs and Assumptions of Spiritual Seekers* (Grand Rapids: Kregel, 1998), 24.
35. Gus DiZerega, *Pagans and Christians: The Personal Spiritual Experience* (St. Paul, Minn.: Llewellyn, 2001), 224.
36. Robert Ellwood, *The Politics of Myth: A Study of C. G. Jung, Mircea Eliade and Joseph Campbell* (Albany, N.Y.: State University of New York Press, 1999), 174.

different corners of the globe who come together at the mythic "centre of the world," to witness a healing of the earth. The healing is based on a common story from the "ancient ones." These "ancient ones" know "that all beings had come from an ancient and timeless place which had always existed even before the creation of the world."[37]

Rather than opposing metanarratives *per se,* New Spirituality is a reaction to *disempowering* metanarratives. And because of its eclectic nature it also struggles with those who do not see good in beliefs other than their own, and/or who show a lack of respect for the religious traditions of others. However in its reliance on myth, New Spirituality clearly shows an appreciation of common psychic life and a common human condition. John Drane puts it this way:

> The Gospel needs to be people-centred and not predominantly idea-centred. We need to listen to what ordinary people are saying, and recognize that in many ways it is not the same as the ideologies of intellectual post-modernity. . . . [P]hilosophers of the post-modern have invested much time and energy in the effort to convince us that people today no longer believe in truth and values, and have no place for metanarratives in their worldview. Christian apologists, for their part, have largely accepted this position. But why, if this is true, did no one respond to those terrorist atrocities (September 11, 2001) in this post-modern way?[38]

The third myth concerns the nature of the apologetic task. The glut of books and seminars teaching negative or defensive apologetics toward New Spirituality has helped to create an evangelical climate of fear. New Spirituality is now viewed as a movement one apologetically holds the cross up to in order to protect the church and our children,[39] rather than being a cultural group to which one takes the cross in order to evangelize. The history of early church evangelism indicates that adherents to pagan religions are open to the gospel.

---

37. Neville Drury, *The Shaman's Quest* (Rose Bay, NSW: Bandl and Schlesinger, 2001), 188.

38. John W. Drane, "Unknown Gods, Declining Churches, and the Spiritual Search of Contemporary Culture," *200th Annual C.M.S. Sermon* (delivered at Westminster College, Cambridge and Blackfriars, London, 2000).

39. The focus is on heresy and spiritual warfare rather than on how to reach New Agers.

REFRAMING THE HISTORICAL–LEGAL APOLOGETIC

Consistent with the theme of this book, the primary apologetic to New Spirituality is "incarnational." It is based on Paul's approach at the Areopagus in Athens (Acts 17:16–34) and on Paul's call to be all things to all people (1 Corinthians 9:22). It is the missionary principle of understanding another culture and its religious beliefs and sharing Christ from within these frameworks. As J. D. Charles puts it, "In sum, Acts 17:16–34 mirrors apologetic Christian contact with pagan culture. It begins with the epistemological assumptions of its hearers, it builds on a common understanding of the cosmos, yet it climaxes in the fullest self-disclosure of the Creator—the resurrection."[40]

The Resurrection is the focus of the apologetic discourse. However, initially it is not the truth of the Resurrection that is significant, but its message of empowerment. It works!

The starting point is usually testimony. Because New Agers are open to story, testimony engages them. However, by keeping the emphasis in one's testimony on the empowerment of the Resurrection, the apologist avoids the danger of de-emphasizing Christ. Testimony is one of the strands of the circumstantial case outlined previously. The role of such circumstantial evidence is not limited to the legal apologetic. Leading historical apologists, such as Paul Barnett, see testimony and historical data being interwoven in today's apologetic.[41]

A fourth component of a reframed apologetic is the introduction of a *new* circumstantial strand of evidence that interconnects with one's testimony: an argument relying on common myths, folklore, and archetypes. In other words, when I tell you my story, you are, in a sense, listening to your own story—which has a commensurate impact.

Leading historical–legal apologist John Warwick Montgomery has advocated for many years a literary apologetic based on myths and archetypes. By *archetypes* he is referring to the Jungian belief in universal patterns in the subconscious life of humanity. These archetypes of the collective consciousness or primordial images disclose universal needs for healing and transformation and manifest themselves symbolically in religions, myths, fairy tales, films, and fantasies. Montgomery calls upon the literary apologist to unlock this hidden treasure. "To achieve a vigorous, sound Apologetic for the twenty-first century," he says, we need to employ the writings of the existentialists and of

---

40. Charles, "Engaging the (Neo) Pagan Mind," 133.
41. Paul Barnett, *Southern Cross* (December 2000–December 2001), 25.

"the depth psychologists and psychoanalysts to point out the misery of the human condition apart from a relationship with Christ."[42] It is an approach that historical–legal apologists should add to their armory. Montgomery explains further:

> Under these circumstances, redemptive knowledge would surface not in a direct fashion but by way of symbolic patterns—visible not only to the sensitive psychoanalyst, but also to the folklorist whose material "bubbles up" collectively from the subconscious of the race. . . .
>
> Jungian analytical psychotherapy has indeed identified such redemptive "archetypes," or fundamental and universal symbolic patterns, which appear equally in the physical liturgies of ancient alchemists and in the dreams of contemporary business men. Religious phenomenologists—the greatest being Mircea Eliade—have discovered these motifs in the most widely diversified primitive and sophisticated religions.[43]

Montgomery typically concludes his case citing J. R. R. Tolkien and C. S. Lewis:

> The gospels contain . . . a story of a larger kind which embraces all the essence of fairy stories. . . . The birth of Christ is the eucatastrophe of man's history. The resurrection is the eucatastrophe of the story of the incarnation. This story begins and ends in joy. It has preeminently the "inner consistency of reality." There is no tale ever told that men would rather find was true, and none which so many sceptical men have accepted as true on its own merits. For the art of it has the supremely convincing tone of primary art, that is of creation. . . .
>
> God is the Lord, of angels, and of men—and of elves. Legend and history have met and fused.[44]
>
> We must not be ashamed of the mythical radiance resting on our

42. John Warwick Montgomery, "Defending the Hope That Is in Us: Apologetics for the 21st Century," http://www.bucer.de/theologyconsultation/Docs/JWMENGLISH.pdf: 1–11.

43. John Warwick Montgomery, "Neglected Apologetic Styles: The Juridical and the Literary," in *Evangelical Apologetics,* ed. Michael Bauman, David Hall, and Robert Newman (Camp Hill, Pa.: Christian Publications, 1996), 127.

44. J. R. R. Tolkien, "On Fairy-Stories," in *Essays Presented to Charles Williams,* ed. C. S. Lewis (n.d.; reprint, Grand Rapids: Eerdmans, 1981), 83–84.

theology. We must not be nervous about "parallels" and "pagan Christs": they *ought* to be there—it would be a stumbling block if they weren't. We must not, in false spirituality, withhold our imaginative welcome. If God chooses to be mythopoeic—and is not the sky itself a myth?—shall we refuse to be *mythopathic?* For this is the marriage of heaven and earth: Perfect Myth and Perfect Fact: claiming not only our love and our obedience, but also our wonder and delight, addressed to the savage, the child, and the poet in each one of us no less than to the moralist, the scholar, and the philosopher.[45]

So whether as apologists we look at psychoanalytical theory, religious phenomenology, or folklore, each portrays a portrait of humanity's common psychic life. In this context, Leon McKenzie, in his illuminating study titled *Pagan Resurrection Myths and the Resurrection of Jesus,* argues that the resurrection of Jesus is not a copying of other religious traditions as liberal scholars claim; rather it reflects the human experience of responding to resurrection archetypes in the world of nature—for example, sleep and wakefulness, climatic and solar cycles, caterpillars and butterflies.[46]

In the case study that follows, there will be a brief illustration of how one can apply this strand in apologetics. It is based on a response to the tarot pack. It is just one approach. One can simply explore common archetypes found in myths such as the magician, the alchemist, the hanged man, and the hero and their connection to the risen Christ. The sum of all this is that as we weave this strand into our testimonies, we are sharing a profound story we have in common (mutual revelation) with the listener or reader.

After addressing the existential need of the listener or reader, the apologist presents the other historical–legal data. As previously indicated, most New Spirituality seekers are not averse to truth claims, they just don't begin there. In any event, one must equip oneself mentally for the questions that will arise about the actuality of the Resurrection.

There is a real benefit to placing the testimonial and other historical–legal evidence into a novel or story form. James Sire reiterates that "stories are in-

---

45. C. S. Lewis, *God in the Dock: Essays on Theology,* ed. Walter Hooper (London: Fount, 1979), 45. Cited in Montgomery, "Neglected Apologetic Styles," 130–31.
46. Leon McKenzie, *Pagan Resurrection Myths and the Resurrection of Jesus* (Charlottesville, Va.: Bookwrights, 1997), 138.

deed a major postmodern way of communicating."[47] Certainly, New Spirituality gurus such as Deepak Chopra and James Redfield have chosen at times to communicate their philosophy of life through narrative.[48] The popularity of historical and legal novels today suggests that a narrative approach is a likely way to move forward. It is not the only approach, but we desperately need a new generation of literary apologists who embrace an apologetic motif.

In a small group environment, a dialogical, person-centered model is appropriate. Here, the historical–legal case is presented conversationally following a discussion about the values grid of those in the group, possible obstacles to faith, and anticipated outcomes. David K. Clark, in his work on dialogical apologetics, affirms that one will still use evidence in this approach, but he highlights the power of a story or testimony in this interactive process.[49]

There is still a role for the historical–legal apologetic to New Spirituality. However, evangelical apologists must rethink and improve their approach. The following actual case study seeks to map out a possible direction.

CONCLUSION: AN APOLOGETIC CASE STUDY APPROACH

Sharon approached our Community of Hope stall at the Mind–Body–Spirit festival. The stall was located opposite the Kirlian Photographic Diagnosis booth and alongside the Vegetarian and Vegan Societies stand. The Community of Hope stall featured as a backdrop a large picture poster of the famous "Face in the Snow." Overhead were the words, "Life is a puzzle. He (Jesus) can make sense of it."[50] The picture in the snow proved to be a highly successful way of attracting people and creating numerous opportunities for conversation.

A conversation began with Sharon, who shared something of her own spiritual journey from fairly normal Catholicism to a commitment to Wicca. We discussed how upbringing, education, and external spiritual experiences had influenced her views on life and faith. I then shared about the influences

---

47. James Sire, "On Being a Fool for Christ and an Idiot for Nobody," in *Christian Apologetics in the Postmodern World*, ed. Timothy R. Phillips and Dennis L. Okholm (Downers Grove, Ill.: InterVarsity, 1995), 112.

48. Deepak Chopra, *The Return of Merlin: A Novel* (New York: Harmony, 1995); and Redfield, *The Celestine Prophecy.*

49. David K. Clark, *Dialogical Apologetics* (Grand Rapids: Baker, 1993), 221–23.

50. The picture is based on a photograph of some burnt coals in the snow that, when developed, appeared to contain the shape of a face that resembles church art portraits of Jesus' face.

that might color my perceptions. Sharon, during the telling of her story, indicated that she appreciated Jesus, but her understanding of life was centered on reincarnation. She then briefly outlined some of her concerns about the church. She asked me, "Do you believe in reincarnation?" I said, "I believe in its understanding that there is more to life than death, but I find the message of the Resurrection more empowering." I then shared the strand of circumstantial evidence for the Resurrection, based on the testimony of changed lives. She listened to my story and others, including those of Lionel Luckhoo and the apostle Paul, that linked the transformation to the resurrection of Christ. In the course of this apologetic discourse, Sharon indicated an openness to the holistic character of the Resurrection. Unlike the denial of the body inherent in reincarnation, the resurrection of Jesus encompasses mind, body, and spirit.

At the Community of Hope stall, we were also interacting with tarot readers and devotees. Sharon and I discussed how the cards mimic archetypes and symbols that reveal our common search for meaning. She had a real interest in the tarot. I explained that many of the images on the cards are taken from the Bible.[51] The "Lovers" card (Genesis 1–2) depicts Adam and Eve before the "Cosmic Mountain" and "Cosmic Tree," in harmony with themselves, the world, and the numinous. The "Devil" card is where we confront the dark lord in Tolkien's *Lord of the Rings* or *Star Wars'* Darth Vader or Jung's Shadow, and it shows the same couple now in bondage to the devil[52] but still with fruits of the "Cosmic Tree" (image of God), though removed from the "Cosmic Mountain" (God's presence). The "Death" card shows us that, whether king, pope, or child, we will confront the Grim Reaper, and there appears to be no path to the eternal celestial city depicted on the card. The "Judgment" card portrays the archangel blowing the trumpet at the end of time and people rising from their graves in joy; and on the pennant connected to the angel's trumpet is a red cross, which is a universal symbol of hope and healing. I said, "Sharon, the image on the card is one of resurrection, not reincarnation."

51. Timothy Betts, *Tarot and the Millennium* (Rancho Palos Verdes, Calif.: New Perspective Media, 1998). See also John Drane, Ross Clifford, and Philip Johnson, *Beyond Prediction* (Oxford: Lion, 2001). We always indicate that divination from the cards is clearly contrary to Scripture, but that the classic A. E. Waite deck is full of biblical images.

52. Joseph Campbell and Richard Roberts, *Tarot Revelations* (San Anselmo, Calif.: Vernal Equinox, 1987), 74: "The Devil, presents an image of the underworld or winter solstice, with the sovereign Lord of the abyss, Saturn/Capricorn. The serpent is of course a form of this so-called Devil."

The "Magician's" card is more than the Jungian archetype of the wise man, because above his head is the symbol of infinity, which shows we need help from one beyond us. The dual sign of the wand in the magician's hand raised toward heaven and the left hand pointing to the earth, is known as a source of grace drawn from above.[53] The key card is the "Fool," which Campbell and Roberts observe clearly symbolizes the dying and resurrected sun god.[54] The "Fool" is also an archetype for the sage or medieval jester, who is not a "natural" fool but an "artificial" fool, who by his antics disturbs the court of human arrogance and self-interest. It is by the dying and rising Christ-"Fool" that one returns to the "Lover's" paradise. "Sharon, this is our universal story."

After a pause in the conversation there was a short dialogue about the other circumstantial evidence—in particular the fact of the empty tomb. Sharon quizzed me about the "swoon" theory. She then said, "But the account of the resurrection of Jesus is in your New Testament Gospels that are really pretty average stuff. Haven't Barbara Thiering and Bishop Spong basically shown that?" I replied, "Sharon, you are not meant to ask such a cognitive question." She laughed. The discourse then turned to the evidence for the Resurrection, including whether it had any historical and legal standing and whether the New Testament narratives could be trusted. The "stories" (testimonies of the apostles John and Paul) were highlighted. A basic historical–legal apologetic for reliability of the New Testament accounts of the Resurrection was fully outlined. Sharon was particularly interested in the role of the women in the Resurrection brief. Her response was to share again something of her own personal hurts and spiritual search. She asked for prayer for faith and healing and for further information on Jesus. She took a pamphlet that set out a list of recommended churches. Not an atypical apologetic discourse had taken place.

STUDY QUESTIONS

1. In what ways does the message of the Resurrection empower life?
2. Why have evangelicals focused on a negative apologetic to New Spirituality? Have we unwittingly portrayed them as "the enemy"?

---

53. See A. E. Waite, *The Key to the Tarot*, rev. ed. (London: Rider, 1993), 67–68. Waite also sees the card signifying the divine motive in humanity, reflecting God.
54. Campbell and Roberts, *Tarot Revelations*, 253–54.

3. What myths, archetypes, and fairy tales do you see having connections with the gospel? Are there films and novels that also connect apologetically?

4. What incarnational apologetic ministries to New Spirituality have you witnessed? Are there other incarnational apologetic approaches to New Spirituality that you believe could be worth exploring?

5. What missionary principles should be the foundation for an apologetic to New Spirituality?

CHAPTER 10

REACHING WICCAN AND MOTHER GODDESS DEVOTEES

PHILIP JOHNSON AND JOHN SMULO

Modern day witchcraft, of which Wicca is a prominent branch, must rank as one of the "spookiest" of all spiritual movements for Christians to study. Mention the word *witch* and it is easy to conjure up many dark images in our minds. So the very idea of Christians undertaking missions with witches probably sounds just slightly less spooky than witchcraft itself. However, as the other contributors to this book have already argued, it is imperative that evangelical Christians recognize the missiological challenges that all new religious movements pose. If we are truly convinced that God is in control of his creation and that the gospel constitutes the power of God to save people, then the resurrected Christ can touch even witches. Jesus would have us issue the call to discipleship to witches as he compels us to do for any sinner.

METHODOLOGY AND PRESUPPOSITIONS

Before we explore what Wiccans believe and practice, we must identify our methodology and presuppositions. First, our *investigation* into Wicca proceeded on phenomenological grounds by delving into primary sources and interviewing practitioners.[1] In the initial process, we endeavored to bracket

---

1. On phenomenology generally, see Terry Muck's essay, "History of Religion and Missiology," chapter 3 in this book. We have conversed with practitioners at the International Festival for Mind-Body-Spirit in Sydney and Melbourne. Other venues include Magick Happens in Sydney, the Winter Magic festival in Katoomba, and in e-groups established by Neo-Pagans. John Smulo has been an invited speaker at the Pagan Pride Day in Queensland in 2003. Philip Johnson was on ABC-radio in 2001 in a panel discussion about Wicca, which

our preconceptions, which means that we withheld making any immediate judgments about Wicca. As we delved the primary sources, we metaphorically put on the Wiccans' shoes to see how they view reality. We then crosschecked our initial findings against other scholarly studies of Wicca.[2]

Next, based on our biblical presuppositions, our *analysis* of Wicca proceeded from the revelation of God in Christ as the unique savior of the world. We believe that Wiccans are human beings, made in God's image, who suffer, like everyone else, from the effects of the Fall—sin, idolatry of self, and the loss of fellowship with God. It is only through the cross and resurrection of Jesus that God provides atonement for sin and that justification by grace through repentance and faith is made possible. We acknowledge that the Scriptures unreservedly prohibit and condemn ancient witchcraft and other occult practices (Exodus 22:18; Deuteronomy 18:10; 2 Chronicles 33:6; Micah 5:12; Nahum 3:4). We do not endorse the fundamental tenets of Wicca, but neither do we exclude devotees from hearing about Christ and his grace.

Our *response* is grounded in a biblical approach to missions and apologetics.[3] We view Wiccans as belonging to a subculture with its own mythology, cosmology, customs, and traditions. Any attempts to communicate, commend, and defend the gospel must be undertaken in terms that Wiccans will best comprehend.[4] We find the best scriptural models of this in the dialogue between Jesus and the Samaritan woman (John 4) and Paul's address to the Areopagus

---

also included the Australian Wiccan Fiona Horne. Wiccan and Neo-Pagan religions are now the fastest growing group of religious bodies in Australia. See Philip Hughes and Sharon Bond, "Nature Religions," *Pointers: Bulletin of the Christian Research Association* 13, no. 2 (June 2003): 1–7.

2. Such as Douglas Ezzy, "The Commodification of Witchcraft," *Australian Religion Studies Review* 14, no. 1 (autumn 2001): 31–44; Charlotte Hardman and Graham Harvey, eds., *Pagan Pathways: A Guide to the Ancient Earth Traditions* (London: Thorsons, 1996); Graham Harvey, *Contemporary Paganism: Listening People, Speaking Earth* (New York: New York University Press, 1997); Lynne Hume, *Witchcraft and Paganism in Australia* (Melbourne: Melbourne University Press, 1997); T. M. Luhrmann, *Persuasions of the Witch's Craft: Ritual Magic in Contemporary England* (London: Picador, 1994); and Michael York, *The Emerging Network: A Sociology of the New Age and Neo-pagan Movements* (London: Rowman and Littlefield, 1995).

3. Cf. the chapters in this book by Mikel Neumann (chapter 1) and Harold Taylor (chapter 2), and Philip Johnson, "Apologetics, Mission and New Religious Movements: A Holistic Approach," *Lutheran Theological Journal* 36, no. 3 (December 2002): 99–111.

4. Cf. Andrew J. Mclean, "Neopaganism: Is Dialogue Possible?" *Lutheran Theological Journal* 36, no. 3 (December 2002): 112–25.

(Acts 17:16–34).[5] We believe there are points of contact between Christian and Wiccan beliefs where a positive apologia can be developed. That apologia builds a bridge from their myths and beliefs and arrives at Jesus Christ and the evidences for his death and resurrection.[6] We have been developing a field-tested model for Christian missions to Wiccans. We acknowledge that there is a role for a philosophical–doctrinal apologia that underscores spiritual deficiencies in Wicca.[7] However, we have found that in the street-life realities of conversing with devotees, Wiccan practitioners generally have little respect for an apologist who simply debunks their beliefs.[8]

One major concern we have is that Christians often stigmatize Wiccans as if they were spiritual lepers, and this view is sustained in books about witchcraft and the occult. Unfortunately, many popular texts suffer from critical drawbacks such as poor documentation, factual errors, and illogical arguments, or they present unsubstantiated testimonies of people who claim they were witches.[9] The stigmas we correlate with being a Wiccan, when combined with the misinformation we often accept at face value about Wicca, are further compounded by the anxieties

---

5. J. Daryl Charles, "Engaging the (Neo) Pagan Mind: Paul's Encounter with Athenian Culture as a Model for Cultural Apologetics," *Trinity Journal* 16NS (1995): 47–62; and Dean Flemming, "Contextualizing the Gospel in Athens: Paul's Areopagus Address as a Paradigm for Missionary Communication," *Missiology* 30, no. 2 (2002): 199–214.

6. On the evidentialist apologetic generally see Steven B. Cowan, ed., *Five Views on Apologetics* (Grand Rapids: Zondervan, 2000).

7. The philosophical–doctrinal apologetic is best expressed in Craig S. Hawkins, *Witchcraft: Exploring the World of Wicca* (Grand Rapids: Baker, 1996). We are not saying that exposing philosophical flaws and detecting doctrinal deviations is wrong, but rather it can be abstruse in the context of personal witness.

8. For general perceptions by former Christians turned pagans see Fiona Horne, *Witch: A Personal Journey* (Sydney: Random House, 1998), 8–9; Anatha Wolfkeepe, "Jesus Is One of Us," *Witchcraft* 12 (1999): 41–44; and Gus DiZerega, *Pagans and Christians: The Personal Spiritual Experience* (St. Paul, Minn.: Llewellyn Publications, 2001); and Ross Clifford and Philip Johnson, "Vicky's Story," in *Jesus and the Gods of the New Age: Communicating Christ in Today's Spiritual Supermarket* (Oxford: Lion, 2001), 196–200.

9. Examples include Rebecca Brown M.D., *He Came to Set the Captives Free* (Chino, Calif.: Chick Publications, 1986); Roger Ellis, *The Occult and Young People* (Eastbourne: Kingsway, 1989); Audrey Harper with Harry Pugh, *Dance with the Devil* (Eastbourne: Kingsway, 1990); Doreen Irvine, *From Witchcraft to Christ* (Cambridge: Concordia Publishing, 1973); Kevin Logan, *Paganism and the Occult* (Eastbourne: Kingsway, 1988); and William J. Schnoebelen, *Wicca: Satan's Little White Lie* (Chino, Calif.: Chick Publications, 1990). Mike Warnke's testimony about Satanists and witches has also influenced a lot of popular Christian impressions. On the problems with Warnke's story see Mike Hertenstein and Jon Trott, *Selling Satan: The Evangelical Media and the Mike Warnke Scandal* (Chicago: Cornerstone, 1993).

expressed about the fictional children's character Harry Potter.[10] It is not our intention here to argue the pros and cons of the Harry Potter stories. However, we are appalled that anyone can seriously believe that these children's books are accurate primary source documents about Wicca. Wiccans find that their spirituality is misrepresented or belittled in films like *The Craft* and television shows like *Sabrina* and *Charmed*. Christians take these stories too seriously; meanwhile, few conscientious efforts have been made by Christian congregations generally to understand what Wiccans believe and practice.[11]

ORIGINS AND CONTOURS

Wicca is a modern nature-based Neo-Pagan spirituality that originated in Britain.[12] It is a contemporary form of western witchcraft, but as Lynne Hume has noted "Wiccans are witches, but not all witches are Wiccan."[13] Many forms of witchcraft, magic, and sorcery have been in evidence from biblical times, in medieval history, and throughout primal cultures.[14] However, Wicca is not synonymous with these other manifestations of witchcraft. There are historical, sociological, cosmological, and cultural differences between ancient witchcraft and modern Wicca.[15]

---

10. Anti-Harry Potter arguments are presented in Richard Abanes, *Harry Potter and the Bible: The Menace Behind the Magick* (Camp Hill, Pa.: Horizon Books, 2001); and idem, *Fantasy and Your Family: Exploring the Lord of the Rings, Harry Potter and Modern Magick* (Camp Hill, Pa.: Horizon Books, 2002). A critical but generally positive perspective is argued in Connie W. Neal, *What's a Christian to Do with Harry Potter?* (Colorado Springs, Colo.: Waterbrook Press, 2001); and idem, *The Gospel According to Harry Potter: Spirituality in the Stories of the World's Most Famous Seeker* (Louisville, Ky.: Westminster John Knox, 2002).

11. A noticeable exception is Pastor Phil Wyman and his Foursquare Church in Salem, Massachusetts, known as "The Gathering." See www.gathering4square.com/.

12. There is no historical evidence for a continuous transmission of witchcraft from biblical times to the present. See Ronald Hutton, *The Triumph of the Moon: A History of Modern Pagan Witchcraft* (Oxford: Oxford University Press, 1999).

13. Hume, *Witchcraft and Paganism in Australia*, 66.

14. On these other forms of witchcraft, start with Frederick H. Cryer and Marie-Louise Thomsen, *Witchcraft and Magic in Europe: Biblical and Pagan Societies* (London: Athlone Press, 2001); Ronald Hutton, *The Pagan Religions of the Ancient British Isles* (Oxford: Blackwell, 1993). Joseph Klaits, *Servants of Satan: The Age of the Witch Hunts* (Bloomington, Ind.: Indiana University Press, 1985); J. Middleton and E. H. Winter, eds., *Witchcraft and Sorcery in East Africa* (London: Routledge and Kegan Paul, 1963); and Jeffrey Burton Russell, *Witchcraft in the Middle Ages* (Ithaca, N.Y.: Cornell University Press, 1972).

15. Cf. Stephen Hayes, "Christian Responses to Witchcraft and Sorcery," *Missionalia* 23, no. 3 (November 1995): 339–54.

Gerald Gardner (1884–1964), who was the principal architect of the craft, originally used the word *Wica*, which means "wise." For Gardner, it denoted "craft of the wise" or "wise people." By the 1960s, the word changed to *Wicca*, which derives from Old Anglo-Saxon and refers to a male witch (*wicce* refers to a female witch). It also has connotations of an adviser or diviner.[16] The term *Wicca* now blends the meaning of *Wica* (wise) with the Anglo-Saxon nuances. Wiccans prefer the term because of the negative connotations attached to the word *witchcraft*.

Gardner established Wicca in the late 1940s but tried to legitimate his creation by claiming he was initiated into a coven that had existed for generations. There is no evidence to support his claims for the coven's pedigree. Ronald Hutton has shown that Gardner adapted material from people such as Margaret Murray and Aleister Crowley; movements such as Theosophy, Spiritualism, Freemasonry; eighteenth century romantic poets; and, finally, liturgical Christianity.[17] The dependency on Christian sources has prompted Charlotte Allen to wryly remark, "Practicing Wicca is a way to have Christianity without, well, the burdens of Christianity."[18]

Wicca now has many traditions. The Gardnerian tradition obviously refers to Gardner's rituals as perpetuated by his disciples. Alex Sanders, a disciple of Gardner's, developed his own approach, which is known as the Alexandrian tradition. The Dianic tradition, represented by Zsusanna Budapest and Starhawk, reflects strong feminist perspectives, with much emphasis on the Mother Goddess.[19] Radical Faery Wicca represents a gay version of the craft. However, it must be emphasized that Wicca does not purport to be a revealed religion with a sacred scripture, creed, or confessional statement. The precepts of Wicca are not organized around the doctrinal constructs of systematic theology. So there are no "sects" or "heresies" in Wicca.[20]

---

16. Its etymology is succinctly discussed in Hutton, *The Triumph of the Moon*, 241.
17. Ibid., 3–201.
18. Charlotte Allen, "The Scholars and the Goddess," *Atlantic Monthly*, January 2001, 22.
19. Cf. Angelo Coco, "Searching for Reflections: Women's Paths to a Feminist Pagan Spirituality Group," *Australian Religion Studies Review* 14, no. 1 (autumn 2001): 19–30; Caitlín Matthews, *The Elements of the Goddess* (Dorset: Element, 1989); and Annabelle Solomon, *Between the Worlds: Women Empowering Ourselves Through Re-Imagining Our Spirituality and Creativity* (Winmalee, NSW: The Author, 1999).
20. On the various traditions see Margot Adler, *Drawing Down the Moon*, rev. ed. (Boston: Beacon, 1986).

Wiccans affirm that a polarity exists in the deity—there is a male horned God and the Mother Goddess. Wiccans believe that this polarity brings balance to what they feel is the lopsided "patriarchal" view of God as Father in Christianity. British Wiccan Vivianne Crowley suggests, "Wicca is a mystery religion."[21] She sees a fusion between old pagan ideas that are reconstituted for today with Carl Jung's psychoanalytic theory about archetypal symbols embedded within us.[22] Fiona Horne, the Australian pop star and Wiccan, avers:

> I felt very attracted to the fact that Wicca acknowledges many different Goddesses and Gods, but most importantly, recognises that they can exist within the individual, not in the sky out of our reach. In fact, the Craft doesn't provide answers as to what the Goddesses and Gods actually are, but emphasises that whichever way the individual relates to them is the right way for her/him. I have always felt that Gods and Goddesses do not exist in their own right but are projections of our consciousness.[23]

Fellow Australian Wiccan Wendy Rule disagrees with Horne's atheism: "I actually believe that they do exist in their own right."[24] Others, like DiZerega, accept that a sole deity exists, but the polarities of God/Goddess are understood in terms of panentheism (all is in God).[25] Wicca may be characterized, then, as a nature-based or eco-spirituality that emphasizes the immanence of the divine in the world. Wiccans express their spirituality in rituals that are meant to attune them with the rhythms of the natural world. They follow a ritual calendar whereby various festivals are observed in conjunction with the seasonal equinoxes, and the full and new moons. The major festivals, known as *sabbats,* are linked to an annual cyclic myth (of which more will be said below).

21. Vivianne Crowley, *Wicca: The Old Religion in the New Age* (London: Aquarian Press, 1989), 18.
22. On Jung's impact on Neo-Pagan spirituality see Richard Noll, *The Jung Cult: Origins of a Charismatic Movement* (London: Fontana, 1996). But cf. Robert Ellwood, *The Politics of Myth: A Study of C. G. Jung, Mircea Eliade and Joseph Campbell* (Albany, N.Y.: State University of New York Press, 1999). David Tacey, *Jung and the New Age* (Hove, East Sussex and Philadelphia: Brunner-Routledge, 2001). For Jung's interaction with various forms of spirituality see Vivianne Crowley, *Principles of Jungian Spirituality* (London: Thorsons, 1998).
23. Horne, *Witch: A Personal Journey,* x.
24. Fiona Horne, *Witch: A Magickal Year* (Sydney: Random House, 1999), 132.
25. DiZerega, *Pagans and Christians,* 6–12.

Practitioners often perform these rituals in forest or parkland settings, or at a private altar in their homes. One may be a solitary practitioner (sometimes known as a hedge witch) or participate in a group (known as a coven).

Wiccans practice what they refer to as natural magic (or magick).[26] Magic does not entail invocations to Satan or demons. As Horne bluntly states:

> How many times do I have to tell you? Witches do not worship Satan! One of the earliest and most common misconceptions about witches is that we worship Satan. Whenever I am asked by individuals or the media if I am a "Devil-worshipper" I always say, "My parents have more to do with Satan than I do—they're Christian."[27]

Síân Reid offers the following definition: "Magic is the art of changing consciousness at will."[28] Graham Harvey amplifies this view:

> Magic is not devil worship but a coherent way of understanding the world in which something within each person—the will—can be used to effect change or affect others beyond the self.[29]

According to Harvey, the application of one's will is an exercise in changing one's perception of reality. The will is the "true self" and it is both within the person but also permeates all of reality. Paul Tuitéan and Estelle Daniels affirm this perspective using psychological jargon: The individual must utilize the Conscious Mind, Subconscious Mind, and Soul (roughly corresponding to Freud's Ego, Super Ego, and Id) in order to work magic.[30] One may work magic on behalf of others, for healing, or for oneself, but the true aim of ritual magic is to align oneself with this ultimate reality called the will.

---

26. The term *magick* was coined by Aleister Crowley to differentiate it from stage illusionist's tricks. Either spelling of the word crops up in Wiccan literature. Crowley was a notorious late-Victorian decadent and quite a few Christians misinterpret him as a Satanist who sacrificed people. For clarification, start with Clifford and Johnson, *Jesus and the Gods of the New Age,* 41–42.
27. Horne, *Witch: A Personal Journey,* 199.
28. Síân Reid, "As I Do Will, So Mote It Be: Magic as Metaphor in Neo-Pagan Witchcraft," in *Magical Religion and Modern Witchcraft,* ed. James R. Lewis (Albany, N.Y.: State University of New York Press, 1996), 161.
29. Harvey, *Contemporary Paganism,* 88.
30. Paul Tuitéan and Estelle Daniels, *Essential Wicca* (Freedom, Calif.: Crossing Press, 2001), 148–49.

A precept that Wiccans espouse as fundamental to working magic, known as the Wiccan Rede, is "do what you will if it harm none."[31] Another precept, known as the Law of Three, is that "whatever you do will return to you three-fold."[32] These twin precepts are meant to direct the thought and path of Wiccans toward harmony with self, others, and the earth. If others are harmed by one's spells, then the practitioner must expect the moral law of cause and effect to rebound on them three times over. Although one can find many examples of Wiccans adhering to harmony and peace, many find it difficult to abide by these precepts.[33] Wiccans can have fractured relationships and sometimes resort to hexing—using binding or negative magic—in certain situations.[34] Wiccans are often interested in complementary healing remedies, shamanism, and in esoteric divinatory arts such as astrology, Qabalah, and tarot.

DIALOGUE WITH WICCANS

When encountering Christians, many Wiccans brace themselves for hostile and vehement denunciations. However, we have found that many are open to serious dialogue when Christians show that they have done their homework, have a listening ear, and share the gospel with gentleness and respect. This does not mean we compromise on matters of biblical truth—especially pertaining to proscribed practices—or downplay the reality of spiritual deception. Yet neither is it fruitful to wage a rhetorical demonizing crusade.

Elsewhere we have indicated that there are several major theological topics where Wiccan thought challenges Christianity.[35] These include: God language, God's immanence, creation stewardship, sexuality and spirituality, and the church as community. We believe that, on several of these points, Wiccan thought provides an imperfect mirror image of things that the church ought to be proclaiming because the original truth is wholly found in the Bible. Space limitations preclude revisiting those issues, but we have found that, through them, very fruitful apologetic lines of communication can open up with Wiccans.

From a different perspective, David Tacey suggests that there is a missing "trin-

---

31. Horne, *Witch: A Personal Journey,* 45. This precept derives from Aleister Crowley's maxim "do what thou wilt shall be the whole of the Law."
32. Tuitéan and Daniels, *Essential Wicca,* 28.
33. See the discussion in DiZerega, *Pagans and Christians,* 149–52.
34. Horne, *Witch: A Personal Journey,* 42–52.
35. Clifford and Johnson, *Jesus and the Gods of the New Age,* 48–55.

ity" in Western Christian churches—women, the body, and nature—that is powerfully reflected in Wicca. Tacey believes that neglect of these three issues is among
the sociological reasons why the Christian church in Australia is in serious decline.[36] In effect, the feminized spirituality of Wicca is filling up a vacuum created by the church, but this need not be the case if we would practice what the
Scriptures teach about the value of women, the human body, and the creation.

MYTHIC APOLOGETICS

A very fruitful method for presenting the gospel to Wiccans is through what
is known as "mythic apologetics."[37] This is a style of apologetic that uses myth
in a variety of ways to communicate the gospel. One approach is through
storytelling as exemplified in the novels of J. R. R. Tolkien and C. S. Lewis.[38]
Another approach is to examine the core stories or myths embraced by people
groups or new religious movements—to locate "altars to the Unknown God"
or biblical analogies in those stories as a contact point—and develop an apologia for the gospel as the fulfillment of those stories.[39] Loren Wilkinson has
re-echoed the importance of myth for apologetics with Wiccans. Wilkinson
has also drawn attention to the positive role that myth played in the conversion of C. S. Lewis, and how Lewis made use of myth in his apologetics.[40]

New religious movements such as Wicca eagerly incorporate myth and story
into their beliefs and rituals, being inspired by Jung's theories about universal
archetypes. As a result, mythic apologetics provides a helpful tool in the
apologist's toolbox where more rational "tools" would otherwise be blunt. Below
we explore a form of mythic apologetics in relation to Wicca.

---

36. David Tacey, *ReEnchantment: The New Australian Spirituality* (Sydney: Harper Collins, 2000), 231–35.
37. See Philip Johnson, "Apologetics and Myths: Signs of Salvation in Postmodernity," *Lutheran Theological Journal* 32, no. 2 (July 1998): 62–72.
38. See John Warwick Montgomery, ed., *Myth, Allegory and Gospel* (Minneapolis: Bethany, 1974). Cf. Royce Gordon Gruenler, "Jesus As Author of the Evangelium: J. R. R. Tolkien and the Spell of the Great Story," in *New Approaches to Jesus and the Gospels* (Grand Rapids: Baker, 1982), 204–20.
39. Cf. Leon McKenzie, *Pagan Resurrection Myths and the Resurrection of Jesus* (Charlottesville, Va.: Bookwrights, 1997); and Ronald Nash, *Christianity and the Hellenistic World* (Grand Rapids: Zondervan, 1984).
40. Loren Wilkinson, "The Bewitching Charms of Neo-Paganism," *Christianity Today*, 15 November 1999, 58–63; and idem, "Circles and the Cross: Reflections on Neo-Paganism, Postmodernity, and Celtic Christianity," *Evangelical Review of Theology* 22, no. 1 (January 1998): 28–47.

GOSPEL PARALLELS IN THE WHEEL OF THE YEAR

Wiccans observe eight festivals, or sabbats, during the year as part of the cyclical Wheel of the Year,[41] which is held by Wiccans to be "one of the principal keys to understanding the religion."[42] Each sabbat entails a specific ritual ceremony that relates to the changing of the seasons. The ceremonies revolve around an altar on which sacred emblems are placed, representing the God and Goddess, as well as sacramental bread and wine. With each sabbat there is an episodic myth that has eight installments. The content of each episode in the myth yields a seamless annual story that Wiccans retell every year. Matthew and Julia Phillips bring the following perspective to bear:

> The Wheel of the Year is a continuing cycle of life, death and rebirth. Thus the Wheel reflects both the natural passage of life in the world around us, as well as revealing our own connection with the greater world. To a Wiccan, all of creation is divine, and by realizing how we are connected to the turning of the seasons and to the natural world, we come to a deeper understanding of the ways in which we are connected to the God and the Goddess.[43]

Wiccans believe that the eight sabbats in the Wheel of the Year observances were all part of the ancient Celtic pagan calendar. However, not all of these festivals can be documented among the Celts. Quite a few events (such as Halloween) have Christian origins, long since de-Christianized and appropriated both in commercial enterprises and in Neo-Paganism.[44] Apologists, of course, must deal with Wiccans in the way they perceive things to be, even when the evidence for their perception may be sparse or contradicted by the data.

---

41. John Smulo originally developed this apologetic construct for an undergraduate paper in theology. For more on the Wiccan view of the Wheel of the Year, see Janet and Stewart Farrar, *Eight Sabbats for Witches, and Rites for Birth, Marriage, and Death* (London: R. Hale, 1981); and Edain McCoy, *The Sabbats: A New Approach to Living the Old Ways* (St. Paul, Minn.: Llewellyn, 1994).
42. Matthew Phillips and Julia Phillips, *The Witches of Oz* (Berks: Capall Bann Publishing, 1994), 65.
43. Ibid.
44. Ronald Hutton, *The Stations of the Sun: A History of the Ritual Year in Britain* (Oxford: Oxford University Press, 1996). For a Wiccan perspective on Halloween see Gerina Dunwich, *The Pagan Book of Halloween: A Complete Guide to the Magick, Incantations, Recipes, Spells, and Lore* (New York: Penguin Compass, 2000).

Because the sabbats are observed seasonally, Wiccans in the Northern and Southern hemispheres follow the calendar differently, as tabulated below:

Northern Hemisphere	Date Observed	Southern Hemisphere	Date Observed
Samhain	31 October	Beltane	31 October
Yule/Winter Solstice	20–23 December	Litha/Summer Solstice	20–23 December
Oimelc/Imbolc	2 February	Lammas/ Lughnasadh	2 February
Ostara/Eostre/ Spring Equinox	20–23 March	Mabon/Autumn Equinox	20–23 March
Beltane	30 April	Samhain	30 April
Litha/Summer Solstice	20–23 June	Yule/Winter Solstice	20–23 June
Lammas/ Lughnasadh	1 August	Oimelc/Imbolc	1 August
Mabon/Autumn Equinox	20–23 September	Ostara/Eostre/ Spring Equinox	20–23 September

The Wheel of the Year myth has many striking parallels with the gospel. Of course, there are also significant divergences. Though the parallels tend to break down if pressed too hard, what follows is suggested in hope of providing some means by which to use the Wheel of the Year myth to communicate the gospel within a Wiccan framework.

During the first sabbat, Samhain, the Goddess is impregnated. From this time, the son to be born grows until the second sabbat, Yule, when the Goddess gives birth.[45] The son represents the Sun in nature, growing brighter and stronger daily.[46] The third sabbat to arrive is Imbolc. During this festival the Goddess appears as the Virgin.[47]

---

45. Horne, *Witch: A Personal Journey*, 77.
46. Ibid., 78.
47. Ibid.

The gospel of Matthew begins with the prophecy that the Virgin Mary would give birth to a Son, Jesus, whom Malachi describes in natural terms as the "sun of righteousness" (Matthew 1:18–22; Malachi 4:2; Isaiah 9:2; Luke 1:78–79).

The fourth sabbat is the Spring Equinox (or Ostara). At this time, the growing son becomes aware of the mysteries of his sexuality and his ability to become a father and—eventually—a wise old man.[48] From this time until the fifth festival, Beltane, the son and the Virgin pursue each other. This pursuit climaxes during Beltane, when they are joined in sacred marriage.[49] From Beltane to the sixth sabbat, the Summer Solstice (or Litha), the child grows within the mother's womb, reflecting the growth of crops and vegetation in nature. The virgin has become Queen along with her partner, now King, and they rule the land together.[50]

The Old Testament describes the intimate relationship God has with believers by using the imagery of a marriage (Isaiah 54:5–7; Hosea 2:19–20). The New Testament describes the church as the Bride of Christ joined in sacred marriage (Matthew 22:2–14; Ephesians 5:25–32). This union is celebrated not only on earth, but will climax at the consummation of history (Revelation 19:7).

Litha is the time of the longest day and shortest night and the sun is said to be at its peak, descending from this time toward winter. According to the Wheel of the Year myth, this foreshadows a challenger who will appear, a dark lord who wants to claim the land and the child within the Queen as his own. The dark lord and the King of Light do battle. The power of the King overcomes the dark lord, but not before the dark lord wounds him with a blow to his side.[51] From Litha to Lammas the force of darkness is growing in the world, though its presence is not immediately apparent.[52]

Scripture speaks of a dark lord, Satan, who challenges the King of Light, Jesus—also known as the Light of the World (John 8:12). Though the dark lord challenges the authority of the King of Light, and even seeks to make Him

---

48. Ibid.
49. This is a time of fertility and great rejoicing. As a result of the consummation of the marriage, a seed is planted into the womb of the bride. Beltane rituals are said to often be the biggest and most fun of the year with plenty of feasting enjoyed by all who take part. See ibid., 78.
50. Ibid, 78–79.
51. Ibid., 79.
52. Ibid.

fall through temptation (Matthew 4:1–11), the most he could do was wound his heel (Genesis 3:15). The King crushed the head of the dark lord through His victory on the cross, and the followers of the King will soon crush Satan under their feet too (Romans 16:20). Nevertheless, for a time, the force of darkness will grow in the world (1 Timothy 4:1).

Finally the eighth sabbat, the Autumn Equinox (or Mabon), arrives. From Lammas to Mabon, darkness is no longer subtly apparent, but firmly and noticeably present. At Mabon, night and day are said to stand equal.[53] The son born at Lammas grows and comes into conflict with the King, because the King has realized that to maintain his hold on the kingdom he will have to fight his son. This is said to reflect the fight of Light and Dark at the Summer Solstice. While fighting, the father and son realize that they are one and the same.[54] The battle continues from this point, with the father and son both lifting their guard and impaling themselves on each other's sword, falling dead to the ground. It is at this point in the myth that the final harvest is said to be reaped.[55]

As with the eighth sabbat, the gospel story ends with a final harvest to be reaped. The followers of the Light of the World will reap eternal life, while the followers of the dark lord will reap eternal punishment (Matthew 13:30; 25:31–46; Revelation 14:15).

From these parallels in the Wheel of the Year, our next step is to demonstrate that Jesus fulfilled these things in history, and validated his unique claims to deity through the Cross and the Resurrection. Here the traditional historical–legal apologetic for the positive evidences for the New Testament documents comes into play.[56] For some Wiccans, this corpus of evidence will challenge their preconceptions. Fiona Horne, for example, states:

> I have to say that I don't relate to Jesus as he's described in the Bible as well as I do to his presentation in alternative writings about him, like the book *Jesus the Man* by Barbara Thiering.[57]

---

53. Ibid.
54. Ibid.
55. Ibid., 80.
56. Paul W. Barnett, *Is the New Testament History?* (Sydney: Hodder and Stoughton, 1986); Ross Clifford, *Leading Lawyers' Case for the Resurrection* (Edmonton: Canadian Institute for Law, Theology, and Public Policy, 1996); and William Lane Craig, *Assessing the New Testament Evidence for the Historicity of the Resurrection of Jesus* (Lewiston, N.Y.: Edwin Mellen Press, 1989).
57. Fiona Horne, *Life's a Witch!* (Sydney: Random House, 2000), 3.

Other Wiccans may adopt the position taken by Timothy Freke and Peter Gandy, namely that Jesus was not a historical personage and that early Christian beliefs were borrowed from the mystery religions.[58] Again, the traditional apologetic for the Gospels' trustworthiness is relevant at this point. Beyond that, we then endeavor to show the practical application of the gospel to all the spheres of life and how we are empowered to live through the risen Christ.[59]

Thin Places

Our apologia is not just a cerebral exercise, but also translates into a missional approach to worship where Wiccans can experientially find the fulfillment of their quest in Christ. Bill Stewart and Steven Hallam have collaborated with us in designing an artistic reinterpretation of the sabbats that visually portrays Christ's mission. This artwork has been used as an evangelistic tool in the context of booth ministry.[60]

Another practical outcome of this apologia is that it has recently (2002) inspired a lay missional experiment known as Thin Places. The creative impetus came from our colleague Matthew Stone, who has for several years been involved in evangelism with New Age and Neo-Pagan devotees. The expression is borrowed from remarks made by George Macleod, founder of the modern Christian community in Iona. Macleod indicated that a "thin place" is one where the physical and spiritual realms are so close together that we sense that God is not far from us. It is a place of pilgrimage. In geophysical terms, a "thin place" can be a *transition point,* such as where the earth and sky touch on a mountaintop, where urban dwellings touch the boundaries of a forest, or the coastline where land and water converge, and can become a sacred place for worship. Another nuance is that of *transition zones* or rites of passage in our

58. Timothy Freke and Peter Gandy, *The Jesus Mysteries* (London: Thorsons, 1999). Their position is briefly evaluated in Clifford and Johnson, *Jesus and the Gods of the New Age,* 161–62. Cf. McKenzie, *Pagan Resurrection Myths and the Resurrection of Jesus;* and Nash, *Christianity and the Hellenistic World.*

59. Ross Clifford and Philip Johnson, *Riding the Rollercoaster: How the Risen Christ Empowers Life* (Sydney: Strand, 1998).

60. On booth ministry refer to Philip Johnson, "Discipling New Age and Do-it-Yourself Seekers Through Booth Ministries," chapter 11 of this volume. A draft of the artwork appears in the illustrated essay by Steven Hallum, "Symbolically Foreshadowed: The Gospel and the Wheel of the Year," illus. John Smulo and Bill Steward in *Sacred Tribes: Journal of the Christian Mission to New Religious Movements* 1, no. 2 (Spring/Summer 2003). See at www.sacredtribes.com.

lives—such as birth, puberty, moving from school to employment, marriage, menopause, and death—where God's presence should also be felt and acknowledged.[61]

Thin Places is a nomadic network of lay evangelical Christians in Sydney (some are theologically educated), who are committed to a missional theology of worship that gathers on each sabbat. By "nomadic network" we mean that the group is geographically scattered and the locale changes each time they convene for worship. This reflects the sociological realities of contemporary urban life where people network with each other across the eight points of the city's compass and do not necessarily associate identity and primary meaning in life with the suburbs in which they live. The motif of the nomad is grounded in the scriptural example of the Patriarchs, who were often mobile, and the wilderness sojourn of the post-Exodus people.[62] In like manner, Thin Places involves a "portable faith" that goes from locale to locale according to the six-weekly cycle of the sabbats. The locales oscillate between private dwellings and open public spaces (e.g., beaches and parks).

Another motif in Thin Places is that of Christians in exile, which draws inspiration from the Israelite experience of exile in Babylon. The exiled Israelites were compelled to face up to what their spiritual priorities ought to be as they found themselves inhabiting a strange place that was multicultural and religiously diverse. Today's Australian evangelical cannot help but feel a spiritual exile because the Church is in a multicultural social context where other religions flourish and Christianity is no longer regarded as the definitive expression of faith.

A multilayered missional theology informs the activities of Thin Places. There is the recognition that, biblically, worship and missions go hand-in-glove.[63] The immanence of God's Spirit within the creation (Acts 17:27) grounds the basis for the notion of there being "thin places," precisely because God is near.[64] This then links into a theology of the creation that acknowledges it belongs to the transcendent Lord (Psalm 24:1; Colossians 1:16–17) and that

---

61. On Macleod and Iona see Ronald Ferguson, *Chasing the Wild Goose: The Story of the Iona Community* (Glasgow: Wild Goose Publications, 1998).

62. On contemporary mission to Third World nomads see the twin "Nomadic Peoples" editions of the *International Journal of Frontier Missions* 17, no. 2, and no. 3 (2000).

63. See John Drane, *Faith in a Changing World* (London: Marshall Pickering, 1997).

64. B. B. Warfield, "The Spirit of God in the Old Testament," in *Biblical and Theological Studies* (Philadelphia: Presbyterian and Reformed, 1968), 127–56; and Wilf Hildebrandt, *An Old Testament Theology of the Spirit of God* (Peabody, Mass.: Hendrickson, 1995).

we are stewards of the earth. It encompasses the awareness that the creation praises God (Psalm 148), and animals are included in the new heaven and new earth (Isaiah 11:6–9; 65:17–25).[65] A Christocentric focus takes center stage, because the incarnation of Christ occurred in the sphere of the creation. By the Cross and Resurrection, we see how the redemption of humanity and the renovation of the creation takes place.

Participants form a circle around an altar dedicated to God in Christ that is erected at each locale as a focal point for a contextual form of worship. Each one contributes with music, art, prayer, devotional and meditative exercises, mutual encouragement through personal storytelling of what God is doing in their life, Scripture, and communion. At these gatherings, the participants also tithe their time and resources to support prophetic practical action on issues such as the degradation of the creation, cruelty to animals, and social injustices.[66]

Matthew Stone has encouraged the participants in Thin Places to cultivate friendships with Wiccans and Neo-Pagans. The aim is to invite them to the sabbat gatherings. As discipleship occurs, it is envisaged that a church for pagan converts will develop. Our Melbourne colleagues, Bill Stewart and Peter Jolly, participate in "Pagans at the Pub," where opportunities for personal witness are unfolding. Mark and Mary Muss have recently settled in the alternate spiritual community at Mullumbimby, where they are establishing themselves as tent-maker missionaries through booth ministry in local markets and permaculture. Our colleagues, Warwick and Dianne Saxby, are tent-maker missionaries with Neo-Pagans in Tasmania.[67]

We believe that God is calling Christians to forsake their phobias and minister grace to Wiccans who are broken by sin. As church history records, pagans are among the easiest people to convert. It was from their ranks that the Gentile church was born and Europe became, for a long time, the world center of Christianity. We have the example from Bede's history of the church in England, particularly Pope Gregory's letter to Abbot Mellitus concerning the treat-

---

65. Calvin DeWitt, ed., *The Environment and the Christian* (Grand Rapids: Baker, 1991). Andrew Linzer, *Animal Thoeology* (Urbana, Ill.: University of Illinois Press, 1994); Robert N. Wennberg, *God, Humans, and Animals: An Invitation to Enlarge Our Moral Universe* (Grand Rapids: Eerdmans, 2003).

66. Web site for the Thin Place is www.thinplaces.info.

67. See Warwick Saxby, "The Little Things," in *Australian Stories for the Heart,* comp. David and Rachel Dixon (Sydney: Strand, 2002), 21–24.

ment of pagans and pagan shrines.[68] Richard Fletcher, in surveying the conversion of Europe's pagans to Christianity, has remarked:

> The conversion of Europe to Christianity certainly had its epic moments, duly highlighted by the hagiographers. There the scenes are unforgettable passages of assertion, of confrontation, of triumph. [69]

Perhaps as Neo-Pagan spirituality surges throughout the Western world, God may indeed be preparing the way open for yet another "epic moment" in the mission of the church.

STUDY QUESTIONS

1. What have been your preconceptions of Wiccans and Neo-Pagans? Where do you believe those ideas originated?
2. A topic that could not be discussed in this chapter concerns the Witch Trials that spanned from the late Middle Ages until the eighteenth century. In that period, it is estimated some 40,000 people were executed. Should the church have sought the death penalty for witches? Would it be appropriate for modern Christians to say "We're sorry" to today's Wiccans for these past misdeeds?
3. In what ways could the Western church positively address the missing "trinity": women, the body, and creation?

---

68. Bede, *Ecclesiastical History of the English People,* bk. 1, chap. 31, trans. Leo Sherley-Price, rev. ed. (London: Penguin, 1990).
69. Richard Fletcher, *The Conversion of Europe: From Paganism to Christianity 371–1386 a.d.* (London: Harper Collins, 1997), 521.

CHAPTER 11

DISCIPLING NEW AGE AND DO-IT-YOURSELF SEEKERS THROUGH BOOTH MINISTRIES

PHILIP JOHNSON

Since 1991, the author and his colleagues have been developing a contextual ministry with devotees of New Age (or more commonly New Spirituality) and "Do-It-Yourself" spirituality (DIY). The ministry operates Christian exhibitor's booths in alternate spiritual festivals in both urban and rural settings in Australia. It is grounded in biblical principles of missions that have already been discussed in this book. In this chapter, we will set the scene by examining the Australian religious template and the emergence of alternate spiritual festivals there. Then the discussion will focus on booth ministry. It is not an apologetic exposé of New Spirituality or DIY spiritualities.[1] Any attempts at replicating this model must necessarily involve critical reflection on one's specific cultural context.

AUSTRALIAN RELIGIOSITY

Australia embraces the paradoxical polarities of antique and youthful cultures. The indigenous first-nation culture is regarded as the oldest surviving one in the world today.[2] Meanwhile, the national anthem, *Advance Australia*

---

1. For apologetic responses see Ross Clifford's, "Reframing a Traditional Apologetic to Reach 'New Spirituality' Seekers," chapter 9 in this book and Ross Clifford and Philip Johnson, *Jesus and the Gods of the New Age: Communicating Christ in Today's Spiritual Supermarket* (Oxford: Lion, 2001).
2. Tony Swain and Garry Trompf, *The Religions of Oceania* (London and New York: Routledge, 1995), 2–3; and David J. Tacey, *ReEnchantment: The New Australian Spirituality* (Sydney: Harper Collins, 2000), 74–78.

Fair, envisages its people as "young and free." The national coat of arms rein-
forces this idea through the kangaroo and emu—neither animal can go back-
ward—so the nation is symbolized as always forward moving. British
colonization began in 1788, at the height of the Enlightenment, as a convict
settlement. Australia was not founded as a haven for religious dissenters.[3] The
colony subsequently metamorphosed into a frontier society of British free settlers, followed later by waves of immigrants from Southern Europe, the Middle
East, and Asia.

Australian churches began with European ecclesiology. From around 1820
until 1965, there were strong sectarian tensions between Roman Catholics and
Protestants, but they subsided with the cultural changes of the late 1960s.[4] The
churches' engagement with skeptics, rationalists, and freethinkers mirrors the
British and North American experiences.[5] Churches have had a significant role
in education, morality, charity, politics, social justice, and military conscrip-
tion debates.[6] Christianity remains statistically the dominant religion. However, Australian religiosity differs somewhat from its American counterpart in
terms of enthusiasm and patronage. Australians have long been ambivalent
about regular church attendance. Among the general populace there is widespread belief in a Supreme Being, but this simply has not translated into high
participation rates in the church. This ambivalence led sociologist Hans Mol
in 1971 to make the following remarks:

> The fact that such a large percentage of the Australian population does
> not worship regularly but still "believes in God without doubt" and
> still holds the churches and the clergy in high esteem fits the picture
> of ambiguity. As in Britain the goodwill towards religion is counter-

---

3. The state of South Australia was convict-free with expatriate German Lutheran settlers
   important in its early development. See David Schubert, *Kavel's People: From Prussia to
   South Australia* (Adelaide: Lutheran Publishing House, 1985).
4. Michael Hogan, *The Sectarian Strand: Religion in Australian History* (Melbourne: Penguin,
   1987).
5. Walter Phillips, "The Defence of Christian Belief in Australia 1875–1914: The Responses
   to Evolution and Higher Criticism," *Journal of Religious History* 9, no. 4 (1977): 402–23;
   and T. L. Suttor, "The Criticism of Religious Certitude in Australia, 1875–1900," *Journal of
   Religious History* 1 (1960): 26–39.
6. Ian Breward, *A History of the Australian Churches* (Sydney: Allen and Unwin, 1993);
   Hilary M. Carey, *Believing in Australia: A Cultural History of Religions* (Sydney: Allen and
   Unwin, 1996); and Stuart Piggin, *Evangelical Christianity in Australia: Spirit, Word and
   World* (Oxford: Oxford University Press, 1996).

balanced by a massive wooliness of thinking about it. Australia seems to be a Christian nation in search of a religion, or a heathen nation in flight from one. Most Australians, like Englishmen, are obviously heathen, but wish they were not.[7]

In the years since, belief in God has remained very high, while overall church membership and attendance rates have been in decline.[8] Some Christians refer to the apparent growth of the Australian Pentecostal churches, but these require sober analysis. Notwithstanding the phenomenon of Hillsong, the statistics are mixed. Part of the growth is composed of membership transference from mainstream denominations, and part of it involves genuine conversions, but it is also accompanied by a substantial revolving door rate of attrition as many affiliates drop out.[9]

The religious landscape is now more obviously pluralist than it was in 1971.[10] Australia's geographical proximity to Southeast Asia has facilitated the flourishing of a minor subterranean thread of religious pluralism. Buddhists have been present since the mid-nineteenth century.[11] Statistically, Buddhism is now the second largest faith and its growth involves a mixture of migrant reproduction and Western converts. Islam ranks third, with its growth overwhelmingly caused by migrant reproduction.[12] The Jewish and Hindu faiths are ranked fourth and fifth respectively, again sustained primarily by reproduction or immigration.[13]

---

7. Hans Mol, *Religion in Australia* (Melbourne: Nelson, 1971), 302.

8. For general sociological treatments see Hans Mol, *The Faith of Australians* (Sydney: George Allen and Unwin, 1985); Alan W. Black, ed., *Religion in Australia: Sociological Perspectives* (Sydney: Allen and Unwin, 1991); Gary D. Bouma, *Religion: Meaning, Transcendence and Community in Australia* (Melbourne: Longman Cheshire, 1992); Philip Hughes, *Religion in Australia: Facts and Figures* (Melbourne: Christian Research Association, 1997); and Peter Kaldor, John Bellamy, Ruth Powell, Merrilyn Correy, and Keith Castle, *Winds of Change: The Experience of Church in a Changing Australia* (Sydney: ANZEA Publishers, 1994).

9. On Pentecostal statistics see Peter Kaldor, John Bellamy, Ruth Powell, Keith Castle, and Bronwyn Hughes, *Build My Church: Trends and Possibilities for Australian Churches* (Adelaide: Open Book Publishers, 1999), 55.

10. Norman C. Habel, ed., *Religion and Multiculturalism in Australia: Essays in Honour of Victor C. Hayes* (Adelaide: Australian Association for the Study of Religions, 1992).

11. Paul Croucher, *Buddhism in Australia 1848–1988* (Kensington, NSW: NSW University Press, 1989).

12. Mary Lucille Jones, ed., *An Australian Pilgrimage: Muslims in Australia from the Seventeenth Century to the Present* (Melbourne: Law Printer, 1993).

13. Purusottama Bilimoria, *Hinduism in Australia* (Melbourne: Spectrum, 1989).

Aside from the world faiths, "religions of informality" have emerged from time to time, ranging from Temperance movements, jingoism (fervent patriotism for the British empire), ANZAC myths (as a form of civil religion), and now the annual Carols by Candlelight (another folk/civil religion).[14] Organized irreligion, like the Humanist Society, has always maintained miniscule patronage.[15] The 2001 national census shows that 15.4 percent of the population has "no religion," but this figure does not equate to atheism or agnosticism. Rather, it reflects the fact that many Australians see themselves as "spiritual" but not "religious." These sorts of people either do not identify with organized forms of religion or see themselves as belonging to more than one faith.[16]

ESOTERIC TRADITIONS

Alternative religious movements have also established their own niches in the culture, with several having originated in the nineteenth century.[17] Between 1890 and 1930, Theosophy, Co-Masonry, the Liberal Catholic Church, and "Esoteric Adventist" groups left their imprint on Australian subterranean

14. See K. S. Inglis, "Anzac and Christian—Two Traditions or One?" *St. Mark's Review* 42 (November 1965): 3–12; Keith Dunstan, *Wowsers* (Sydney: Angus and Robertson, 1974); Peter E. Glasner, "The study of Australian Folk Religion: Some Theoretical and Practical Problems," in *Australian Essays in World Religions*, ed. Victor Hayes (Adelaide: Australian Association for the Study of Religions, 1977), 11–26; and Norman Habel, "Carols by Candlelight: The Analysis of an Australian Ritual," in *Religious Experience in World Religions*, ed. Victor Hayes (Adelaide: Australian Association for the Study of Religions, 1980), 160–73.
15. Alan Black, "Organised Irreligion: The New South Wales Humanist Society," in *Practice and Belief: Studies in the Sociology of Australian Religion*, ed. Alan W. Black and Peter E. Glasner (Sydney: Allen and Unwin, 1983), 154–66.
16. See "Future of Christianity Is in the Cards," *Southern Cross* (July 2002), 1.
17. Nevill Drury and Gregory Tillett, *Other Temples, Other Gods: The Occult in Australia* (Sydney: Methuen Australia, 1980); Ian Gillman, ed. *Many Faiths One Nation* (Sydney: Collins, 1988); Graham Hassall, "Outpost of a World Religion: The Bahá'i Faith in Australia, 1920–1947," *Journal of Religious History* 16 (1991): 315–38; Lynne Hume, *Witchcraft and Paganism in Australia* (Carlton South: Melbourne University Press, 1997); Ian Hunter, "Some Small Religious Groups in Australia: Mormons, Moonies, Hare Krishnas, Scientologists," *Compass Theology Review* 18 (1984): 21–32; Jill Roe, *Beyond Belief: Theosophy in Australia 1879–1939* (Kensington, NSW: NSW University Press, 1986); idem, "Testimonies from the Field: The Coming of Christian Science to Australia, c. 1890–1910," *Journal of Religious History* 22 (1998): 304–19; and F. B. Smith, "Spiritualism in Victoria in the Nineteenth Century," *Journal of Religious History* 3 (1964): 246–60.

spirituality.[18] Theosophy attracted famous Australians such as Alfred Deakin (three times Australian prime minister) and poet Christopher Brennan. Under Charles Leadbeater's direction, an amphitheater was built in 1923 at Balmoral, a northern Sydney beach, in anticipation of the arrival of the World Teacher (Krishnamurti). American architect Walter Burley Griffin, also a Theosophist, designed Australia's capital city, Canberra, as well as the Sydney suburb of Castlecrag, according to geomantic and feng shui principles, in the belief that Australia was destined to be an occult utopia.[19]

Although Griffin's romantic notions were never fulfilled, the last three decades of the twentieth century saw a resurgence of interest in esoteric spiritualities. Major alternate spiritual festivals in Australia began in the 1970s. The first, which was instigated by the National Union of Students, was the Aquarius Festival in May 1973, at Nimbin in northeast New South Wales. It attracted approximately 5,000 youths and heralded the beginning of an alternate community at Nimbin based around New Spirituality and Neo-Pagan spirituality. Nimbin is now the unofficial alternate capital of Australia, with Neo-Pagan shamanic religion and a pro-marijuana lobby predominating the scene.[20]

Other important alternate cultural events include the Down to Earth's ConFest (beginning in 1976); the Homeland Festival of Peace and Healing at Bellingen, New South Wales (beginning in 1985); the Wild and Wise Women's Festival in East Gippsland; the Woodford/Maleny Folk Festival (also beginning in 1985); and Perth's Conscious Living Expo (beginning in 1988).[21] In the state capital cities and major urban and rural areas, we find a plethora of free markets, Neo-Pagan festivals, psychic fairs, and spiritual exhibitions.[22] Magick Happens is a recent Neo-Pagan and Wiccan festival designed to

---

18. Greg Tillett, *The Elder Brother: A Biography of Charles Webster Leadbeater* (London: Routledge and Kegan Paul, 1982); and idem, "Esoteric Adventism: Three Esoteric Christian Adventist Movements of the First Half of the Twentieth Century," in *Cargo Cults and Millenarian Movements: Transoceanic Comparisons of New Religious Movements*, ed. G. W. Trompf (Berlin and New York: Mouton De Gruyter, 1990), 143–77.

19. Peter Proudfoot, *The Secret Plan of Canberra* (Sydney: University of New South Wales Press, 1994).

20. Alan Dearling with Brendan Hanley (Mook Bahloo), *Alternative Australia: Celebrating Cultural Diversity* (Lyme Regis, U.K.: Enabler Publications, 2000).

21. The ConFest has been examined in Graham St. John, "*Alternative Cultural Heterotopia: ConFest as Australia's Marginal Centre*" (Ph.D. Thesis, La Trobe University, 2000). This is on-line at www.come.to/confest. Cf. Hume, *Witchcraft and Paganism in Australia*, 37–39.

22. See the bimonthly periodical *Australian Markets and Fairs Magazine* and their Web site: www.marketsandfairs.com.au/home.html.

demystify the craft. Absolute Alternatives, which began in 2002, sponsors nine spiritual festivals per year throughout Victoria.[23]

Between the mid-1980s and mid-1990s, New Spirituality forms shifted from the social fringe toward acceptance in mainstream society. The shift was characterized as a personal experiential search by individuals for holistic healing and spiritual empowerment, borrowing from many different sources, including alternative healing remedies, astrology, first-nation indigenous cultures, meditation, nature-based pagan religion, reincarnation, tarot, theosophy, and much more. New Spirituality thought is shaped by myths about spiritual evolution and human potential, symbolic correspondences between the cosmos and the inner being of humans, notions of inner gnosis (that the answers lie inside us), and elements of pantheism (all is God) and panentheism (all is in God).[24] Prominent international advocates include Peter and Eileen Caddy, Deepak Chopra, Shakti Gawain, Louise Hay, Shirley Maclaine, James Redfield, David Spangler, Marianne Williamson, Oprah Winfrey, and Neale Donald Walsch.

Robert Ellwood succinctly profiles the trend as follows:

> New Age people by and large give the impression of being 1960s people, now well into middle age and looking for reaccess to the wonders of their youth. But now under new terms: being putatively well established in families and careers, not to mention susceptible to the lassitude of noonday and the skepticism born of a little experience, they are much less likely than they once were to drop out, to commit themselves entirely to a guru or a gospel, to trip out to Katmandu or the antipodes of the mind. On the other hand, they are affluent enough to be able to put down cash in spiritual salesrooms, and self-assured

---

23. On gatherings outside Australia see Colin Broadley and Judith Jones, eds., *Nambassa: A New Direction* (Wellington, NZ: A. H. and A. W. Reed, 1979); Justine Dignance and Carole M. Cusack, "Secular Pilgrimage Events: Druid Gorsedd and Stargate Alignments," in *The End of Religions? Religion in an Age of Globalisation*, ed. Carole M. Cusack and Peter Oldmeadow (Sydney: Department of Studies in Religion at The University of Sydney, 2001), 216–29; Kevin Heatherington, "Stonehenge and Its Festival: Spaces of Consumption," in *Lifestyle Shopping: The Subject of Consumption*, ed. Rob Shields (London: Routledge, 1992), 83–98; Irving Hexham, "The Freaks of Glastonbury: Conversion and Consolidation in an English Country Town," *Update: A Quarterly Journal on New Religious Movements* 7, no. 1 (1983): 3–12; and Michael I. Niman, *People of the Rainbow: A Nomadic Utopia* (Knoxville, Tenn.: University of Tennessee Press, 1997).

24. For further details see Clifford and Johnson, *Jesus and the Gods of the New Age*, 18–23.

enough to want to put together their own redemption kits, with gem-stones, tapes, teachers, doctrines now from this tradition, now from another. The New Age seems to represent a virtually unprecedented level of spiritual independence and commercialism together. People get fragments of Tibet or Chaldea in an enlightenment emporium and practice it on their own at home, apart from any living priest or temple, with a confidence both wonderful and appalling, with an attitude less of credence than of, Let's check it out, and I'll take from it what I can use.[25]

In 1995, David Tacey of La Trobe University (Melbourne) made this provocative comment:

> As the masculinist pubs, churches, convents, and barber shops go broke or close down in Australian cities, new age bookshops and "awareness centres" are popping up everywhere, offering the public a broad range of largely non-Christian, non-patriarchal esoteric arts and sciences.[26]

Sydney journalist Ali Gripper poignantly echoed Tacey's point in 1996:

> Australians buy more self-development and spiritual books per head than the U.S. and Britain. . . . It seems that when Australians are searching for meaning these days, they walk straight past the church and into their nearest bookshop, the shelves of which are starting to sag with how-to-change-your-life tomes.[27]

For a while, seekers used the term *New Age* self-referentially, as reflected in periodicals such as the *New Age Journal*. By the early 1990s, however, James Lewis noted that many North American seekers had dropped the term altogether so that its usage persisted among observers and Christian apologists.[28]

---

25. Robert S. Ellwood, *Islands of the Dawn: The Story of Alternative Spirituality in New Zealand* (Honolulu: University of Hawaii Press, 1993), 245–46.
26. David J. Tacey, *The Edge of the Sacred: Transformation in Australia* (Melbourne: Harper Collins, 1995), 192.
27. Ali Gripper, "Get a Life! (Please)," *Sydney Morning Herald,* 19 August 1996, 11.
28. James R. Lewis, "Approaches to the Study of the New Age Movement," in *Perspectives on the New Age,* ed. James R. Lewis and J. Gordon Melton (Albany, N.Y.: State University of New York Press, 1992), 1ff.

Australian bookstores now designate this literature as "body and soul," "lifestyle improvement," "mind, body, spirit" and "new spirituality." This shift is substantiated by the field research of Adam Possamaï, who in 1996 and 1997 surveyed a small group of New Age seekers in Melbourne. He found that 71 percent of the interviewees were very negative about the term *New Age*, and that 9 percent of those who were positive about it nonetheless did not see themselves as New Agers.[29] Though Possamaï's point is well taken, 0.2 percent of the population surveyed in the Australian national census of 2001 still identified themselves as New Age.[30]

DIY SPIRITUALITIES

Do-It-Yourself spirituality is a descriptive term for alternate or innovative spiritual approaches in the West that operate outside the boundaries of organized, conventional religion. It is a decentralized approach to spirituality. Seekers acquire spiritual knowledge from a range of sources that draw from the major religions and esoteric traditions. Although DIY is a recently applied label, Robert Fuller maintains that creation of a personal or self-spirituality has been an integral part of the American religious landscape since colonial days. He detects these impulses in folk religious practices such as divination, astrology, mesmerism, folk healing, and witchcraft, as well as in alternate spiritual groups such as Swedenborg's Church of the New Jerusalem, the New England Transcendentalists, New Thought religion, and New Spirituality.[31] Its antecedents can be traced to the esoteric traditions of Renaissance Europe.[32] What Fuller has found in U.S. history has its counterpart in Australian history.

Spiritual knowledge is sought for purposes of personal growth, hence a knowledge of self. Consensus to establish a creed is not an essential component of DIY, simply because you "do it yourself." DIY often involves critical discourses about mainstream social and spiritual institutions, and so the church may be viewed unfavorably. There are, of course, various DIY spiritualities. Because New Spirituality is decentralized and heterogeneous, its practitioners

---

29. Adam Possamaï, "Diversity in Alternative Spiritualities: Keeping New Age at Bay," *Australian Religion Studies Review* 12, no. 2 (spring 1999): 111.

30. See "Future of Christianity Is in the Cards."

31. Robert C. Fuller, *Spiritual but not Religious: Understanding Unchurched America* (New York: Oxford University Press, 2002).

32. See B. J. Gibbons, *Spirituality and the Occult: From the Renaissance to the Modern Age* (London and New York: Routledge, 2001).

engage in a form of DIY spirituality, but the terms are not synonymous. Scholars differ with one another over whether New Spirituality is a clearly demarcated social movement or merely a loose network of like-minded seekers.[33] Irrespective of what one decides on that matter, it does not directly impinge on our model of outreach. A second version is discernible among Western seekers who commodify for themselves elements from the disparate Buddhist traditions and sects to create what might be called DIY Buddhism.[34]

A third expression of DIY spirituality has some overlap with what is known as DIY culture. DIY culture is found in countercultural dance subcultures (e.g., raver-dance and Gothic), and among anti-hegemonic or resistance groups such as the new travelers or nomads, ferals, and rainbow tribes, healing-arts and agitation art activists.[35] Some participants in the countercultural dance scene are social anarchists, but include those who are

---

33. There are five major scholarly theories about how to define New Age, and, as space precludes any analysis, we simply make these summary notes. Michael York argues that the structural model of New Age spirituality is that of a segmentary, polycephalous, integrated network (SPIN) that forms a dual movement of New Age and Neo-Pagan strands. See Michael York, *The Emerging Network: A Sociology of the New Age and Neo-Pagan Movements* (London: Rowman and Littlefield, 1995). Paul Heelas characterizes New Age as a movement of "self-spirituality." See Paul Heelas, *The New Age Movement: The Celebration of the Self and the Sacralization of Modernity* (Oxford and Cambridge, Mass.: Blackwell, 1996). Wouter Hanegraaff interprets New Age as a movement that involves cultural criticism of modernity through secularized forms of esoteric thought in, *New Age Religion and Western Culture* (Albany, N.Y.: State University of New York Press, 1998), 520. Steven Sutcliffe denies that New Age meets the mark of a self-defined movement based on a unifying ideology, but maintains that various key identities who have used the term New Age have made aborted attempts to launch a movement. See Steven Sutcliffe, *Children of the New Age: A History of Spiritual Practices* (London and New York: Routledge, 2003). Adam Possamaï postulates there is a new form of spirituality that is syncretic and can be labeled "perennism." Perennism consists of three defining elements: the cosmos is a seamless reality (monism), its participants pursue their own human potential, and their soteriology is grounded in gnosis. These elements are common to New Age, Neo-Pagan, and other alternate expressions of spirituality, see Adam Possamaï, "Not the New Age: Perennism and Spiritual Knowledges," *Australian Religion Studies Review* 14, no. 1 (autumn 2001): 82–96.
34. Peter Oldmeadow, "Tibetan Buddhism and Globalisation," in *The End of Religions? Religion in an Age of Globalisation,* 266–79; and Terry C. Muck, "Missiological Issues in the Encounter with Emerging Buddhism," *Missiology* 28, no. 1 (January 2000): 35–46.
35. See George McKay, ed., *DiY Culture: Party and Protest in Nineties Britain* (London: Verso, 1998); Richard Lowe and William Shaw, *Travellers: Voices of the New Age Nomads* (London: Fourth Estate, 1993); Graham St. John, ed., *Free NRG: Notes from the Edge of the Dance Floor* (Melbourne: Common Ground Publishing, 2002); and Mary Anna Wright, ed., *Dance Culture: Party, Politics and Beyond* (London: Verso, 2002).

clearly committed to a Neo-Pagan or eco-spirituality. Within the networks of this DIY culture, there tends to be a combination of personal development and social-political activism that is aimed at resisting globalization.[36] In Neo-Pagan thought, one can be a solitary practitioner and Wiccan devotee, like Spiraldancer, who encourages readers of *Witchcraft* magazine to pursue a DIY approach to the ritual craft.[37] Other Neo-Pagans participate in loosely affiliated countercultural tribes in rural or urban contexts.

A fourth manifestation of DIY arises in complementary healing modalities that are entwined with spirituality. The DIY approach to healing does not entail a total rejection of scientific medicine, but it does reflect issues that apologists cannot overlook. For example, scientific medicine, like the church, is perceived as patriarchal. DIY healing challenges that hegemony by asserting the central role of the patient, and it reflects the refeminizing of healing generally.[38]

MIND-BODY-SPIRIT FESTIVALS

One of the important conduits for the grassroots impact of New Spirituality and DIY spiritualities has been the International Festival for Mind-Body-Spirit, created by Graham Wilson in London in 1977. Unlike the free markets, this is a commercial exhibition where spiritual entrepreneurs and spiritual groups exhibit their goods, services, and beliefs to the public. The festival has been held in London every year since 1977.[39] In 1989, Wilson brought the festival to Sydney's Darling Harbor Exhibition Center, and then franchised it to Melbourne (1991), Adelaide (1996), and Brisbane (1999). The Sydney festi-

---

36. Cf. Benjamin Shepard and Ronald Hayduk, eds., *From ACT UP to the WTO: Urban Protest and Community Building in the Era of Globalization* (London: Verso, 2001). On value changes generally see Paul R. Abramson and Ronald Inglehart, *Value Change in Global Perspective* (Ann Arbor, Mich.: University of Michigan Press, 1995); Ronald Inglehart, "Globalization and Postmodern Values," *Washington Quarterly* 23, no. 1 (2000): 215–28; and Peter Ester, Loek Halman, and Ruud de Moor, eds., *The Individualizing Society: Value Change in Europe and North America* (Tilburg, Netherlands: Tilburg University Press, 1993).
37. Spiraldancer, "Find Your Magickal Creativity with Ritual Craft," *Witchcraft* 30 (December–January 2003): 44–46.
38. Cf. Ruth Pollard, "Jesus Among the Alternative Healers: Sacred Oils, Aromatherapists and the Gospel," chapter 13 in this book.
39. Malcolm Hamilton, "An Analysis of the Festival for Mind-Body-Spirit, London," in *Beyond New Age: Exploring Alternative Spirituality,* ed. Steven Sutcliffe and Marion Bowman (Edinburgh: Edinburgh University Press, 2000), 188–200. A Christian perspective on the sixth London festival is in "Religions of the New Age," *New Religious Movements Update* 5, no. 2 (1981).

val convened on an annual basis from 1989 to 1995, and since 1996 has been a biannual event (May and November).

Attendance Figures for the Sydney Festival for the Years 1989–1996

1989	17,500
1990	23,500
1991	34,000
1992	42,000
1993	56,000
1994	60,000
1995	62,500
1996	40,000 (May)
1996	46,000 (November)[40]

In 2001, having achieved all that he could reasonably expect from his eleven-year investment, Wilson sold the Sydney festival. Since then, the attendance figures have declined. In the absence of available official figures, a fair estimate would be that, since 2000, approximately thirteen thousand people now attend each festival. This decline reflects four factors. One is the general saturation of Australian society to the point where information and services related to DIY spirituality is accessible in bookshops, local awareness centers, and on the Internet. Second, many smaller festivals and exhibitions now dot the landscape, and the novelty of Mind-Body-Spirit has long since passed. Neo-pagan and neo-Buddhist networks now flourish independent of this festival. Third, the Mind-Body-Spirit festival has a strong commercial ethos; seekers who prefer a countercultural ethos are unlikely to patronize it. Fourth, the exhibition company that now sponsors Mind-Body-Spirit appears to have repositioned the festival as a more mainstream gathering, but thus far has been unable to generate the same passionate interests in the public, as compared with the mid-1990s. This direction differs considerably from Graham Wilson's vision for the festival, as Malcolm Hamilton discovered when researching the London event:

---

40. Figures supplied by the then festival co-coordinator, Erika Elliott, in a letter dated 17 December 1997. No further figures have been disclosed since the May 1997 festival (42,500). This table stands as a correction to those previously cited in Philip Johnson, "Postmodernity, New Age and Christian Mission: Mars Hill Revisited," *Lutheran Theological Journal* 31, no. 3 (1997): 117.

It is important, Graham Wilson feels, that the Festival does not become too mainstream. Part of the appeal of the Festival, and one might add of the alternative scene generally, is precisely that it is alternative and not established, and it is important to preserve a balance in bringing the esoteric to a wider mainstream audience and clientèle.[41]

COMMUNITY OF HOPE—MISSIONS IN FESTIVALS

John Saliba has handsomely surveyed several apologetic responses of Roman Catholic, Protestant, and Eastern Orthodox churches.[42] In England, Daren Kemp has explored what he refers to as the Christaquarians—those who profess Christian faith but also adopt some New Spirituality ideas and practices by way of response.[43] In Canada, some evangelical Christians have participated in outreach ventures at New Spirituality festivals by combining a standard heresy–rationalist apologetic with spiritual warfare techniques.[44] Each of these approaches could be critically compared with our case study, but space limitations preclude this. Instead, let us consider how the Community of Hope ministry began.

In 1990, Ross Clifford and I visited the Sydney Mind-Body-Spirit festival. Afterward, we compared notes about our experiences and observations. The festival brought alternate spiritualities to life for us in a way that the evangelical apologetic literature simply could not do. It was easy to read about this from the safety of one's armchair, and entirely another thing to be face-to-face with devotees. We found ourselves experiencing something akin to culture shock as unfamiliar sights, sounds, aromas, and the sheer mass of the crowd buffeted us. We agreed that this was certainly a spiritual marketplace and it prompted us to think of the apostle Paul's visit to Athens in Acts 17:16–34. Initially, we toyed with the idea of stationing ourselves outside the venue, offering tracts to visitors, but quickly concluded that this approach would be

41. Hamilton, "An Analysis of the Festival for Mind-Body-Spirit, London," 190.
42. John A. Saliba, *Christian Responses to the New Age Movement* (London: Geoffrey Chapman, 1999). Cf. Rachel Sharp and Jan O'Leary, "The Christian Critique of New Age," *Australian Religion Studies Review* 6, no. 2 (1993): 13–18.
43. Daren Kemp, "The Christaquarians? A Sociology of Christians in the New Age," *Studies in World Christianity* 7, no. 1 (2001): 95–110. Our approach certainly does not fit into Kemp's typology of Christaquarians.
44. Gene Wilson, "Reaching New Agers on their own turf," *Evangelical Missions Quarterly* 31 (1995): 174–80.

unfruitful. For one thing, it would engender an "us vs. them" adversarial stance, and because Australians typically support the underdog, we understood that patrons would react unfavorably. Second, tracts distributed outside venues are typically discarded unread. Third, we noticed that this was not the way Paul approached the pagan Gentiles in Athens—he was unafraid of entering their marketplace and conversing with them. We decided that the way forward was to establish an exhibitor's booth inside the festival.[45]

We applied to the organizer's office for a booth and adopted the name Community of Hope. Rather than try to represent a denomination or congregation, we felt it would be prudent to take a more generic title that reflects certain aspects of the faith—namely, that Christians are supposed to constitute a new community, one based in the hope of Christ. After some initial prevarication from the organizers—largely due to their awareness that Christians are generally negative and hostile about New Spirituality—we were accepted as a bona fide exhibitor. Prior to the exhibition, we held a training seminar for fifty booth volunteers. Our baptism of fire occurred at the Sydney festival in November 1991. In June 1996, our colleagues Harold Taylor and Wim Kruithof led a group of lay Christians into the Melbourne Mind-Body-Spirit festival. The operations in Sydney and Melbourne evolved to the point where a formally constituted parachurch ministry was born.

In 1991, our evangelistic emphasis entailed a blending of standard gospel presentations and personal testimonies, dovetailed with a rationalist debunking of New Spirituality beliefs. We persisted with this as our primary approach for the next festival, after which we critically assessed the outcomes. On the positive side, we felt that we had faithfully presented the content of the gospel in the power of the Holy Spirit. We had also distributed Bibles and Christian literature, and were pleasantly surprised to find that many seekers are quite prepared and open to hear about Jesus. On the downside, we reflected that our approach had often put people off from seriously listening to us. Most took umbrage at our being dismissive of their search for meaning and our debunking style of argument. We decided that the problem was not so much the offense of the Cross as it was that we were not winsome in our approach, due to our adversarial and superior attitude. Another acute problem was that we had failed to put in place any means for follow-up with people who might want to investigate Christianity further. We also noticed that our booth was hopelessly overstaffed

---

45. Cf. Clifford and Johnson, *Jesus and the Gods of the New Age*, 30–31.

with male volunteers, whereas at least 70 percent of the festival patrons were female. As contemporary Australian women perceive the churches as patriarchal and with little scope for females to develop spiritually, we were simply reinforcing the negative image of the church as a place that is organized and controlled by men.

As we reappraised our efforts for these two festivals, we began to realize that this was not a static spirituality with fixed dogmas that could simply be debunked with some memorized apologetic arguments. We were dealing with a distinctive audience or subculture that had its own myths, cosmologies, customs, and traditions. Our message was not really being properly understood. The receptor group did not identify with our jargon; therefore, our message was not comprehended. We had to rethink our methodology, because we were dealing with an unreached people group—perhaps not quite identical with the people of the 10/40 window, but a tribe nonetheless without Christ. Our basic paradigm had to be transformed from formulaic evangelism based on a christendom model into a biblically informed approach to cross-cultural missions.

Booth ministry is not a monologue; instead, it involves dialogue—a two-way process of communicating and understanding. Christians who wish to participate must have people skills and be willing to listen first before talking about the gospel. Prayer is essential, and the training of volunteers is a critical exercise. Some Christians have very fixed views about New Age and about how evangelism works, and they can be temperamentally ill-suited for such outreach. In Sydney, we have a small core group of lay volunteers who have committed themselves to this form of missions. The booth trains people in evangelism and contextual ministry, and ordinands for ministry assist on the booth as part of their college assessment. In Melbourne, a much larger core group of laypeople assists. The almost uniform feedback we receive from volunteers is how this training and practice has enlivened their own walk with Christ, empowering them to minister more effectively.

After a festival, a team debriefing is essential. We ask ourselves: What sorts of people attend these festivals? What age groups are represented? Why do these festivals appeal to women? What are they finding here that is possibly missing from the local churches? What are the exhibitors offering from their booths? How are other booths decorated and which ones seem to attract the most patrons? Have we achieved our objective of opening up conversations with people about Christ? Did we convey the content of the gospel to people? Were we people of integrity, demonstrating the love and compassion of Jesus to seekers? What stories can we encourage one another with about our inter-actions with searchers?

The booth must be colorful, with an eye-catching display, and with activi-ties that engage the seekers. Elsewhere we have briefly profiled some of the creative experiments in booth activities used in Sydney and Melbourne.[46] These include a crystal display that symbolically represents all the facets of life, with Christ the Rock at the center; a healing-prayer chair; foot-washing using es-sential oils; samples of Margaret River Rain Water linked to the theme of the living water Jesus offers, and so forth.

Are there any tangible results in terms of seekers listening to the gospel and hearing the call to follow Christ? We have found that booth ministry operates at many levels, depending on the kinds of people who visit. Some sneer, some want to hear more, and some figuratively say, "Show me the water" (cf. Acts 8:36 and 17:34). If we were to classify visitors according to James Engel's clas-sic scale of conversion, the range would encompass people from minus ten to minus four in terms of awareness and response to the Christian message.[47] The booth can be pre-evangelistic insofar as it opens up some individuals for the first time to any meaningful contact with the biblical message of Christ. For others, the encounter may dovetail with other forms of Christian contact occurring in their lives—and the conversations may deepen their awareness of the message and deal with apologetic issues. Still others, as we have found, listen to us, accept our literature, and leave without desiring any further con-tact. Occasionally, we learn later on that the person has come in repentance and faith and entered into Christian fellowship. For yet others, the conversa-tion leads to prayer as the person crosses the threshold of faith in Christ.

Perhaps the Achilles' heel in our model has been in the area of follow-up. Part of this difficulty lies in the sad but stark fact that some Christian congre-gations simply have a mind-set that is unsympathetic to what we do, and they are equally unsympathetic toward those who are searching through New Spiri-tuality and DIY spiritualities. We have had some negative instances where seek-ers have been referred to a local congregation only to be treated as spiritual lepers. Another, broader, issue is that in some respects the New Age critique of the Christian churches' shortcomings are sometimes very true, and so we need

---

46. Ibid, 182–91.
47. See James F. Engel, *Contemporary Christian Communication* (Nashville: Nelson, 1979); and idem, "The Road to Conversion: The Latest Research Insights," *Evangelical Missions Quar-terly* 26, no. 2 (1990): 184–93.

not be surprised that people regard the church as the last place they want to go. Here we ought to wrestle with the issues raised by John Drane in his aptly titled book, *What Is the New Age Still Saying to the Church?*[48]

However, we have not let the matter of follow-up drop. Apart from taking responsibility to make contact with seekers beyond the festival, we have tried convening post-festival seminars on topics concerning spirituality. Some people have participated in discipleship courses like Christianity Explained, but these courses are not suited to the sorts of questions and issues seekers are interested in. Our Melbourne colleagues refer seekers into "recovery" workshops run by a parachurch ministry known as Careforce. A more recent development involves a nomadic network of Christians meeting together known as Thin Places. (This ministry is specifically geared toward those interested in Neo-Pagan spirituality, and further remarks on this are made in the chapter "Reaching Wiccan and Mother Goddess Devotees.")

After more than a decade of booth ministry, we have seen positive outcomes both in the lives of the booth volunteers and also in the lives of seekers who have encountered the risen Christ. Booth ministry is not a panacea for missions to New Spirituality and DIY spiritualities, but it does offer one practical avenue for Christians who want to make disciples of those seekers.

STUDY QUESTIONS

1. What have been your perceptions of the New Spirituality movement? Have you had any experiences in talking with New Spirituality devotees? Relate one of those encounters and then reflect on what you learned from it.

2. Have you ever heard a non-Christian speak scathingly about the defects in Christianity? How did you react to that person's claims? Now put yourself in the shoes of a New Spirituality seeker. How do you think they feel when Christians devalue and debunk their spirituality? Is there a lesson to be learned here about our attitudes toward non-Christians and the way we converse with them about our faith?

3. In this chapter, the model of booth ministry was presented as one way of reaching out to people. What other ways of cross-cultural outreach can you think of that might be suitable for missions with New Spirituality seekers?

---

48. John Drane, *What Is the New Age Still Saying to the Church?* (London: Marshall Pickering, 1999).

CHAPTER 12

REACHING NIETZSCHEAN INDIVIDUALISTS

Toward a Contextualized Apologetic to LaVeyan Satanism

JOHN SMULO

Among the rapidly growing list of new religious movements is Satanism. Contemporary Western Satanism had its origins in the work of the late Anton Szandor LaVey (1930–1997). In 1966, LaVey founded the Church of Satan and subsequently published *The Satanic Bible* (1969).[1] Both of these events, as well as a much-publicized Satanic wedding, baptism, and funeral conducted by LaVey in 1967, brought about a growing interest in the movement.[2]

Contrary to popular stereotypes, the majority of Satanists are atheists who believe neither in Satan nor in God, demons nor angels, hell nor heaven.[3] For most Satanists, the term *Satan* represents satanic ideals such as freedom, indulgence, a rejection of guilt, and individuality.[4]

Though there are several main streams of Satanism, this chapter will focus exclusively on the most influential and widespread form inspired by LaVey, aptly titled LaVeyan Satanism. The following apologetic is divided into two

---

1. Anton Szandor LaVey, *The Satanic Bible* (New York: Avon, 1969).
2. Blanche Barton, *The Secret Life of a Satanist: The Authorized Biography of Anton LaVey* (Venice, Calif.: Feral House, 1992), 87–92.
3. In a survey undertaken by James Lewis, 60 percent of respondents held "that Satan was a symbol, an archetype, myself, nature, or some other antitheistic understanding of Satan. Twenty-five [percent] indicated that Satan was an impersonal force. . . . Nineteen [percent] were theistic Satanists, although even most of these respondents did not have what one would call a traditional view of Satan/god/demons." James R. Lewis, *Satanism Today: An Encyclopedia of Religion, Folklore, and Popular Culture* (Santa Barbara, Calif.: ABC-CLIO, 2001), 329.
4. Gavin Baddeley, *Lucifer Rising: A Book of Sin, Devil Worship and Rock 'n' Roll* (London: Plexus, 1999), 163.

sections. The first seeks to uncover effective entry points for Christian apologists to Satanism. The second provides two representative issues that Christians should critique within Satanism. We note that the first section is largely a positive interaction with Satanism, whereas the second section includes what may be perceived, at least in part, as a negative critique. A holistic incarnational apologetic needs to encompass both aspects and respond to rejoinders that arise.

JESUS, NIETZSCHE, AND SATANIC IDEALS

Friedrich Nietzsche (1844–1900) has been an especially influential source in Satanic thought.[5] For example, his criticism of the majority of humankind's "herd morality" becomes in Satanism a critique of the "herd mentality."[6] Rather than being blind followers, Satanists free themselves from the herd. As Nietzsche writes, "Every superior human being will instinctively aspire after a secret citadel where he is set free from the crowd, the many, the majority."[7] This "superior human being" is for Nietzsche most clearly delineated in his idea of the "overman" or "superman."[8] Following Nietzsche's thought, Satanists view themselves as powerful individuals. Nietzsche held that not everyone could understand what he had to say. It was only the "Higher Men" who could. Such individuals are superior to the herd that believes all individuals are equal. For example:

---

5. At least one Satanist has used Nietzsche's thought to critique other Satanists. Joe Necchi, *Nietzsche and Satanic "Stratification,"* retrieved 24 October 2001, from http://www.churchofsatan.org/nietzsche.html.

6. The Christian, for Nietzsche, is "the domestic animal, the herd animal, the sick animal man." Friedrich Nietzsche, "The Antichrist," in *Twilight of the Idols and the Antichrist* (London: Penguin, 1968), 128. As Robinson notes, for Nietzsche, "Christianity is a 'herd morality' that attracts and produces people who are pessimistic and timid." Dave Robinson, *Nietzsche and Postmodernism* (Duxford, Cambridge: Icon, 1999), 26. In regard to Satanism, "Herd conformity" is one of LaVey's *Nine Satanic Sins,* and a repeated critique that Satanists have of Christians. Anton Szandor LaVey, *The Nine Satanic Sins* (1987), retrieved 11 April 2001 from http://www.churchofsatan.com/Pages/sins.html.

7. Friedrich Nietzsche, *Beyond Good and Evil* (London: Penguin, 1990), 57.

8. Thiele writes that for Nietzsche, "Greatness is the nearing of perfection; the overman is the ideal of human being. He fosters the emergence of greatness." Leslie Paul Thiele, *Friedrich Nietzsche and the Politics of the Soul: A Study of Heroic Individualism* (Princeton, N.J.: Princeton University Press, 1990), 184.

You Higher Men, learn this from me: In the market-place no one believes in Higher Men. And if you want to speak there, very well, do so! But the mob blink and say: "We are all equal." "You Higher Men"—thus the mob blink—"there are no Higher Men, we are all equal, man is but man, before God—we are all equal!" Before God! But now this God has died. And let us not be equal before the mob. You are Higher Men, depart from the market-place![9]

Satanism borrows from Nietzsche in this regard and views itself as a religion for the elite.[10] Satanism is thus a religion for those who have broken away from the herd.

Even these few examples of where Satanism borrowed from Nietzsche become significant when we realize that it appears Nietzsche was influenced at least to some extent by Jesus, and followed him in some of his teachings. In comparing the teaching of Nietzsche with that of Jesus in the synoptic Gospels, Frederick Peterson finds many parallels and "similar doctrines"—suggesting that Nietzsche borrowed from Jesus, who preceded him by nearly two millennia.[11]

Nietzsche was largely positive toward Jesus. For example, he writes:

One could, with some freedom of expression, call Jesus a "free spirit"—he cares nothing for what is fixed: the word *killeth,* everything fixed *killeth.* The concept, the *experience* "life" in the only form he knows it is opposed to any kind of word, formula, law, faith, dogma.[12]

For Nietzsche, "free spirits" were those who rose out of the constructs of the herd. It's important to note that Nietzsche believed that the Christian church went in the opposite direction of Jesus. Whereas Jesus was a free spirit, the church encouraged a herd mentality. Nietzsche held that the church was constructed out of the gospel's antithesis.[13]

---

9. Friedrich Nietzsche, *Thus Spoke Zarathustra* (London: Penguin, 1969), 297.

10. LaVey saw Satanism "developing two circles, an elitist group which I always intended my church to be, and the faddists who are becoming Satanists because it's the thing to do." Blanche Barton, *The Church of Satan* (New York: Hell's Kitchen Productions, 1990), 26.

11. Frederick S. Peterson, *Strange Bedfellows: Nietzsche and Jesus Reconciled,* retrieved 24 October 2001 from http://infonectar.com/nietzsche/nietgod.htm.

12. Nietzsche, "The Antichrist," 156.

13. Ibid., 160.

There are several areas where Nietzsche follows Jesus' teaching. However, it is first necessary to place Jesus in the context of Judaism. Here we see that Jesus was a powerful individual who opposed the herd mentality. Jesus repeatedly lived outside the boundaries of the context in which he lived, often discounting fervently held social and religious customs (Mark 2:1–12; 7:1–15). As Peterson notes, "Jesus, like Nietzsche, had very little regard for the priests and their rule. The gospels are full of the taunts and criticisms of the Pharisees, the priests of Judaism."[14]

Next, we see that Jesus emphasized that the individual would need to come out of the herd to become who they were meant to be. This wasn't something that everyone could do. Although Jesus spoke to the masses, he knew—as did Nietzsche in his day—that not everyone would be able to "hear" what he was saying. The cost to those who did "hear" was leaving the herd and making the informed decision to be Jesus' disciples. Similarly, Nietzsche tells his disciples that they would have to think through what it means to follow his teaching.[15]

The idea of the *overman* in Nietzsche is shown in the individual who strives to "live," to push forward and overcome.[16] Though we would be going too far to assert that Nietzsche based this idea on Jesus, it is nevertheless apparent that it is ultimately fulfilled in him. This is shown clearly in his life and death—and especially in his resurrection. Peterson asks the following question:

> What of the Resurrection? Well, if one accepts that life does not end in death, then returning to this world after the event that separates us from whatever comes after for the love of one's companions, would be the ultimate act of will, of power, of striving, indeed it would be the act . . . of an overman.[17]

To the extent that Satanism is built on Nietzschean concepts, it relies on—and implicitly shows support for—Christian ideals as lived out in the person

---

14. Peterson, *Strange Bedfellows.*
15. Friedrich Nietzsche, *Ecce Homo: How One Becomes What One Is* (London: Penguin, 1979), 6.
16. This idea has been used for evil (but by no means needs to). Cf. "it is well known that National Socialism claimed to find its roots in the doctrines of the *Übermensch,* the will to power, in Nietzsche's apparent validation of cruelty, in his pronouncements on greatness and destiny." Tracy B. Strong, "Nietzsche's Political Misappropriation," in *The Cambridge Companion to Nietzsche,* ed. Bernd Magnus and Kathleen M. Higgins (Cambridge: Cambridge University Press, 1996), 130.
17. Peterson, *Strange Bedfellows.*

of Jesus. Building on this foundation, we can now more clearly explore what an incarnational apologetic to Satanists may entail.

LEFT-HAND CHRISTIAN PHILOSOPHER

In an e-mail addressed to the author on the First Church of Satan e-group, Thomas Potter writes:

> John . . . to tell you, I feel that you may be a Left-hand (thinks for the self, regardless of what peer pressure is applied; focuses on personal development; takes responsibility for the self) philosopher, which I believe the majority of us on this list are.[18]

In this definition of the "Left-hand philosopher," the author believes there is a basic foundation for living out a contextualized apologetic to Satanists. We will briefly explore some of these terms.

It is difficult to know the precise origin of the metaphorical use of the term *Left-hand*. Satanists often refer to Satanism and some occult religions as "Left-hand paths" (LHP), and their adherents as "Left-hand philosophers." Other religions, such as Christianity and Wicca, are referred to as "Right-hand paths" (RHP). The use of this term in Tantra certainly predates its use in Satanism. However, the term LHP is used in a different sense in this context. Leon Wild believes that Helena Blavatsky, cofounder of the Theosophical Society, was influential in the promotion of the term.[19] This interpretation is likely; however, another possible origin of the terms could be found in Matthew's Gospel, where Jesus speaks of placing the sheep (followers of Christ) at his right hand, and the goats (those who didn't follow Christ) at his left hand (Matthew 25:33). In spite of the difficulty of locating the origin of the term *LHP*, its meaning in our context is clear, as defined above.

An important quality of Left-hand philosophers is that they think for themselves in spite of what peer pressure is applied. In other words, Left-hand philosophers push against the herd and come to their own conclusions.

Herd conformity is one of LaVey's "Nine Satanic Sins":

---

18. Thomas Potter, retrieved 15 October 2001, from churchofsatan@yahoogroups.com.
19. Leon D. Wild, *An Introduction to the Left Hand Path*, retrieved 29 October 2001 from http://www.fortunecity.com/meltingpot/chad/208/oit/lhpzin.htm.

It's all right to conform to a person's wishes, if it ultimately benefits you. But only fools follow along with the herd, letting an impersonal entity dictate to you. The key is to choose a master wisely instead of being enslaved by the whims of the many.[20]

It's important to note that there is nothing in LaVey's statement that in-and-of-itself is contrary to being a disciple of Jesus. "Conforming" to Jesus ultimately benefits individuals. Jesus is not an impersonal entity, but personal. He does not dictate to anyone, but instead offers individuals the free choice to make an informed decision to follow him. The "key" here is "to choose" the master Jesus wisely, "instead of being enslaved by the whims of the many."

Some may object to this assertion by pointing to biblical passages that refer to Christians as "sheep," in the sense of "blind followers." However, though the word *sheep* is used metaphorically in a variety of contexts in the Christian Bible, none of them has anything to do with being an unconditional follower.[21] The Bereans also provide an example in the Christian Scriptures of those who didn't follow the herd in believing the gospel, but examined the evidence first before coming to a decision (Acts 17:10–12). Satanism provokes us to reexamine our heritage in this regard.

Left-hand philosophers also focus on personal development. Although this is not the place to define everything that "personal development" in this context would include, it would incorporate such things as sanctification, broadening one's knowledge, and following Jesus' and Paul's example of living incarnationally.

What term would best describe a Christian apologist incarnationally interacting with LaVeyan Satanists? Because the phrase "Christian Satanist" is often used derogatorily by Satanists, and because it has troubling connotations for Christians, we believe it would not be a useful term in this context.[22] However, a second expression, and one that we find acceptable, is "Left-hand Christian philosopher."

---

20. LaVey, *The Nine Satanic Sins.*
21. David H. Johnson, "Shepherd, Sheep," in *Dictionary of Jesus and the Gospels,* ed. Joel B. Green and Scot McKnight, consulting editor, I. Howard Marshall (Downers Grove, Ill.: InterVarsity, 1992), 751–54.
22. LaVey uses the term "Christian Satanist," but in the context of describing those who claim to be Satanists but in reality are not. Barton, *The Secret Life of a Satanist,* 204; cf. idem, *The Church of Satan,* 70–71.

HYPOCRISY AND CHRISTIANITY

A Left-hand Christian philosopher will seek to be incarnational; however, this does not exclude a negative critique where appropriate. This would follow Christ's example of living incarnationally as a Jewish person, yet critiquing Judaism when necessary (Matthew 15:1–9; 23; John 2:14–16). In our discussion here regarding hypocrisy, and below on "Indulgence and Satanism," we will seek to demonstrate two examples where an "incarnational critique" is required in regard to Satanism.[23]

In the third of LaVey's "Nine Satanic Statements," he writes, "Satan represents undefiled wisdom, instead of hypocritical self-deceit!"[24] When LaVey speaks of "hypocritical self-deceit," he is especially referring to hypocrisy within the Christian church. In several passages in *The Satanic Bible*, LaVey speaks of personally witnessing such hypocrisy. For example:

> I would see men lusting after half-naked girls dancing at the carnival, and on Sunday morning when I was playing organ for tent-show evangelists at the other end of the carnival lot, I would see these same men sitting in the pews with their wives and children, asking God to forgive them and purge them of carnal desires. And the next Saturday night they'd be back at the carnival or some other place of indulgence. I knew then that the Christian church thrives on hypocrisy, and that man's carnal nature will out no matter how much it is purged or scourged by any white-light religion.[25]

LaVey notes that Christians confess their sins in order to clear their consciences. Yet once their consciences are clear, they feel free to go out and commit the same sin again. However, LaVey holds that Satanists are different:

> When a Satanist commits a wrong, he realizes that it is natural to make a mistake—and if he is truly sorry about what he has done, he will learn from it and take care not to do the same thing again. If he is not honestly sorry about what he has done, and knows he will do the same

---

23. Other obvious areas that need to be critiqued include Satanism in relation to vengeance, conscience, guilt, and rational self-interest. Due to space restraints, we reluctantly limit ourselves to these two topics.

24. LaVey, *The Satanic Bible*, 25.

25. Ibid., introduction. Cf. Barton, *The Church of Satan*, 38.

thing over and over, he has no business confessing and asking forgiveness in the first place.[26]

What should be the Christian response to LaVey's charge of hypocrisy within
the Christian church? Admission. LaVey perceptively notes that Christians often do sin, ask God's forgiveness, feel their conscience cleared, and start the
cycle of sin once again without sincere repentance.

HYPOCRISY AND LAVEY'S AUTOBIOGRAPHY

However, the dialogue between Satanists and Christians need not stop with
the admission by Christians that they are guilty of hypocrisy. Satanists, too,
are guilty of hypocrisy. LaVey himself is representative of this.[27]

According to Burton Wolfe, who wrote a biography of LaVey called *The
Devil's Avenger,*[28] "All of LaVey's background seemed to prepare him for his
role. He is the descendant of Georgian, Roumanian, and Alsatian grandpar-
ents, including a gypsy grandmother who passed on to him the legends of
vampires and witches in her native Transylvania."[29]

In spite of the fact that these and other biographical details are well-circulated,
it appears that virtually all of the information that LaVey and those close to him
documented are mere myths.[30] LaVey not only tacitly allowed others to repeat
inaccurate details about him, he himself largely created this false persona in
autobiographical material in *The Satanic Bible* and in personal interviews.

In a well-documented article titled "Anton LaVey: Legend and Reality," written by one of LaVey's daughters, Zeena LaVey, and her husband, Nikolas

---

26. LaVey, *The Satanic Bible,* 41.
27. This was held by Satanists themselves early in the history of LaVeyan Satanism. In 1975,
    there was a large exodus of members from the Church of Satan due to what they saw as
    LaVey's hypocrisy in stating in the church's newsletter that in the future all higher degrees
    would be available for contributions in cash, real estate, or valuable art objects. Neville
    Drury, *The History of Magic in the Modern Age: A Quest for Personal Transformation* (Lon-
    don: Constable, 2000), 195–96; cf. Gareth J. Medway, *Lure of the Sinister: The Unnatural
    History of Satanism* (New York: New York University Press, 2001), 21–22.
28. Burton H. Wolfe, *The Devil's Avenger: A Biography of Anton Szandor LaVey* (New York:
    Pyramid Books, 1974).
29. Burton H. Wolfe in LaVey, introduction to *The Satanic Bible.*
30. For examples of other sources that repeat the same largely inaccurate biographical details,
    cf. Barton, *The Secret Life of a Satanist,* 15–16; idem, *The Church of Satan,* 35–38; Drury,
    The History of Magic in the Modern Age, 190–92; and Ted Schwarz and Duane Empey,
    Satanism (Grand Rapids: Zondervan, 1988), 72–82.

Schreck, virtually all of the oft-repeated details about Anton LaVey were shown to be fictitious.[31] The truth about his background is rarely published. According to Lawrence Wright's profile of LaVey, he was born Howard Stanton Levey, of partly Jewish parentage.[32] Autobiographical details supplied by LaVey—such as his job as second oboe with the San Francisco Ballet Orchestra and his employment as a seventeen-year-old lion tamer with the Clyde Beatty Circus— have been discredited.[33] However, according to Peter Gilmore, the current high priest of the Church of Satan:

> Zeena, along with her companion Barry "Nikolas Schreck" Dubin, wanted to ease Dr. LaVey into retirement so that they could assume his position. Neither was suited for this role, and Dr. LaVey was quite firmly in control. So when their efforts failed, they made a big show out of departing the "corrupt" Church of Satan and leaving the United States behind for "Fortress Europa."[34]

Whether or not this was the case is open for debate. However, what is clear is that Zeena and Nikolas's motivation for making public the myths behind LaVey's self-created persona does not in itself provide a case against the accuracy of their information. The lack of adequate refutation of such details by the Church of Satan or anyone else is telling.

As was noted above, LaVey pointed out that he observed the hypocrisy of Christians pretending to be one person on Saturday night and another on Sunday morning. However, the struggle of Christians to live out ethical ideals

---

31. Zeena LaVey and Nikolas Schreck, *Anton LaVey: Legend and Reality*, retrieved 1 March 2001 from http://www.churchofsatan.org/aslv.html (2 February 1998). For further confirmation of this, cf. Lawrence Wright, "It's Not Easy Being Evil in a World That's Gone to Hell," in *Rolling Stone*, 5 September 1991, 63–68, 105–16; and Lawrence Wright, *Saints and Sinners* (New York: Alfred A. Knopf, 1993), 121–56.
32. Referring to the influence that Sir Basil Zaharoff had on LaVey, as opposed to "Stanton" being LaVey's middle birth name, Barton writes, "LaVey's grandson, born in 1978, was named Stanton Zaharoff in his honor." Barton, *The Secret Life of a Satanist*, 24. When referring to LaVey's grandson's first name, Barton says that he was named after a character in William Lindsay Gresham's novel *Nightmare Alley*. Ibid., 42. What Barton fails to mention in both instances is that Stanton was Anton LaVey's middle birth name. Because Barton was LaVey's common law wife, and here the author of his authorized biography, the failure to do so is significant because it further goes to prove a deliberate repression of pertinent information for the purposes of advancing LaVey's self-created "autobiographical" details.
33. LaVey and Schreck, *Anton LaVey*.
34. Peter Gilmore as quoted in Baddeley, *Lucifer Rising*, 226.

is not completely foreign to LaVey. Parallel to Howard Stanton Levey's creation of the name Anton Szandor LaVey was the fabrication of a matching fictional character. One begins to wonder whether LaVey ever actually observed the hypocrisy of the Christians he described, or if, like the rest of his story-bound life, he merely created it out of his active imagination.

HYPOCRISY AND PLAGIARISM

LaVey's hypocrisy extended further than disseminating fictional autobiographical details. It also extended to what he is most well-known for: *The Satanic Bible.* Upon close inspection, it is clear that LaVey did not have many unique ideas. He relied heavily on the ideas of a handful of authors, notably Ayn Rand and Friedrich Nietzsche.[35] It should be said, however, that although LaVey wasn't an original thinker, he should be given credit for his creative synthesis of the thoughts of others into what has become the most influential statement of modern Satanism.

Another source that heavily influenced LaVey's writing is the author who went by the alias Ragnar Redbeard.[36] In *The Satanic Bible,* LaVey wrote a chapter titled "The Book of Satan." However, comparison between this chapter and portions of Redbeard's 1896 work *Might Is Right,* makes it clear that LaVey plagiarized a significant portion of Redbeard without so much as a footnote or bibliographic reference.[37]

---

35. Ayn Rand, *The Fountainhead* (New York: Bobbs-Merrill, 1943); idem, *Atlas Shrugged* (New York: Signet, 1957); and idem, *The Virtue of Selfishness* (New York: Signet, 1964). LaVey stated that his religion was "just Ayn Rand's philosophy, with ceremony and ritual added." LaVey, as cited in Bill Ellis, *Raising the Devil: Satanism, New Religions, and the Media* (Lexington, Ky.: University Press of Kentucky, 2000), 180. For one Satanist's appraisal of Rand's philosophy, objectivism, in relation to Satanism see Nemo, *Satanism and Objectivism,* retrieved 9 May 2001 from http://www.churchofsatan.com/Pages/SatObj.html.
36. There is debate over who Redbeard actually was. Most likely he was a New Zealander named Arthur Desmond (1842–1918). Anonymous, "Arthur Desmond—Ragnar Redbeard and 'Might Is Right,'" in *Radical Tradition: An Australasian History Page,* retrieved 25 June 2001 from http://takver.com/history/desmonda.htm. Some, including LaVey, believe the author was Jack London (1876–1916). Shane Bugbee and Amy Bugbee, *The Doctor Is In,* retrieved 13 October 2001 from http://www.churchofsatan.com/Pages/MFInterview.html. Still others believe that there were two distinct authors of *Might Is Right.* Katja Lane's preface to *Might Is Right,* by Ragnar Redbeard (St. Maries, Ida.: Fourteen Word Press, 1999), x–xi.
37. Ibid.

Though there are much longer sections that LaVey plagiarized, due to space considerations we will compare only a few examples of shorter passages.[38]

1. REDBEARD: "Behold the crucifix, what does it symbolize? Pallid incompetence hanging on a tree."[39]

    LaVEY: "Behold the crucifix; what does it symbolize? Pallid incompetence hanging on a tree."[40]

2. REDBEARD: "'Love one another' you say is the supreme law, but what power made it so?—Upon what rational authority does the Gospel of Love rest?"[41]

    LaVEY: "'Love one another' it has been said is the supreme law, but what power made it so? Upon what rational authority does the gospel of love rest?"[42]

3. REDBEARD: "Can the torn and bloody victim 'love' the blood-splashed jaws that rend it limb from limb? Are we not all predatory animals by instinct? If humans ceased wholly from preying upon each other, could they continue to exist?"[43]

    LaVEY: "Can the torn and bloody victim 'love' the blood-splashed jaws that rend him limb from limb? Are we not all predatory animals by instinct? If humans ceased wholly from preying upon each other, could they continue to exist?"[44]

---

38. For comparisons of longer passages that LaVey plagiarized see Redbeard, *Might Is Right,* 1–2, and LaVey, *The Satanic Bible,* 30; Redbeard, *Might Is Right,* 21, and LaVey, *The Satanic Bible,* 33; Redbeard, *Might Is Right,* 34, 36, and LaVey, *The Satanic Bible,* 34–35.
39. Redbeard, *Might Is Right,* xx.
40. LaVey, *The Satanic Bible,* 31.
41. Redbeard, *Might Is Right,* 20.
42. LaVey, *The Satanic Bible,* 32.
43. Redbeard, *Might Is Right,* 20.
44. LaVey, *The Satanic Bible,* 32–33.

4. Redbeard: "'Love your enemies and do good to them that hate you and despitefully use you' is the despicable philosophy of the spaniel that rolls upon its back when kicked."[45]

LaVey: "Love your enemies and do good to them that hate and use you— is this not the despicable philosophy of the spaniel that rolls upon its back when kicked?"[46]

LaVey wrote the introduction to a later edition of *Might Is Right*.[47] In an interview with LaVey, a question regarding the book arose. LaVey downplayed the seriousness of his plagiarism. In his words:

Might Is Right by Ragnar Redbeard is probably one of the most inflammatory books ever written, so who better to write an introduction? It was only natural that I excerpted a few pages of it for *The Satanic Bible*.[48]

LaVey went on to note, "The book has been so indelibly linked with me, it was felt that any new edition should have my name on it."[49] Oddly, the question of *why* the book had been indelibly linked to him was not brought up.

Though LaVey justly charges that many Christians are guilty of hypocrisy, he himself falls short. The sixth of LaVey's "Eleven Satanic Rules of the Earth" says, "Do not take that which does not belong to you unless it is a burden to the other person and he cries out to be relieved."[50] Unfortunately, when it came to writing *The Satanic Bible*, LaVey hypocritically fell short of following his own rules.

45. Redbeard, *Might Is Right*, 20.
46. LaVey, *The Satanic Bible*, 33.
47. Ragnar Redbeard, *Might Is Right* (Bensinville, Ill.: Michael Hunt, 1996).
48. Anton LaVey as quoted in Bugbee and Bugbee, *The Doctor Is In*.
49. Anton LaVey as quoted in ibid.
50. Anton Szandor LaVey, *The Eleven Satanic Rules of the Earth* (1967), retrieved 19 October 2001 from http://www.churchofsatan.com/Pages.Eleven.html. In LaVey's authorized biography, Barton says that LaVey "attacks most savagely those who ride on his coattails, or who steal his ideas, all the while pretending at originality or innovation—with, at best, a begrudging acknowledgement of their inspiration's very existence." Barton, *The Secret Life of a Satanist*, 222. LaVey's hypocrisy here speaks for itself. Similarly, Barton speaks of those who obviously drew from LaVey's philosophy, but "routinely give not so much credit as a notation in their bibliography." Ibid., 14. However, most of LaVey's books, including *The Satanic Bible*, don't even have a bibliography.

SATANISM AND INDULGENCE

The first of LaVey's "Nine Satanic Statements" is, "Satan represents indulgence, instead of abstinence!"[51] Within Satanism, indulgence is understood to be a natural and healthy means toward personal enjoyment and well-being. Social influences, particularly Christian ones, have been viewed as primary inhibitors to the expression of the human tendency toward indulgence. Satanism claims to provide a corrective to this. LaVey writes:

> For centuries, magnificent structures of stone, concrete, mortar, and steel have been devoted to man's abstinence. It is high time that human beings stopped fighting themselves, and devoted their time to building temples designed for man's indulgences.[52]

LaVey believed that Christianity had caused human beings to seek atonement for behavior that they should have never felt guilty about in the first place. Once again, the religion of Satanism provides the corrective:

> For two thousand years man has done penance for something he never should have had to feel guilty about in the first place. We are tired of denying ourselves the pleasures of life which we deserve. Today, as always, man needs to enjoy himself here and now, instead of waiting for his rewards in heaven. So, why not have a religion based on indulgence? Certainly it is consistent with the nature of the beast.[53]

Rather than denying oneself greed, pride, envy, anger, gluttony, lust, and sloth, LaVey holds that people should indulge in them. "Satanism advocates indulging in each of these 'sins' as they all lead to physical, mental, or emotional gratification."[54] If individuals indulge in natural desires, they will be completely satisfied. If they don't, they will develop frustrations that can be personally and socially harmful.[55]

---

51. LaVey, *The Satanic Bible*, 25.
52. Ibid., 53–54.
53. Ibid., 54. Similarly, Nietzsche, on whom LaVey relies in many respects, writes, "Hatred of *mind*, of pride, courage, freedom, *libertinage* of mind is Christian; hatred of the *senses*, of the joy of the senses, of joy in general is Christian." Nietzsche, *The Antichrist*, 143.
54. LaVey, *The Satanic Bible*, 46.
55. Ibid., 81.

INDULGENCE AND CHRISTIANITY

There is no doubt that Christianity has been associated with abstinence rather than indulgence, especially when it comes to sex. Augustine, for example, whose view of sex was influential for centuries, taught that it would be a matter of praise if a married couple refused to have sex with each other.[56]

Unfortunately, the prominence of Augustine and others who have held similar views led to the inaccurate belief on a popular level that Christianity is antisex. Even a cursory glimpse of the Song of Songs in the Christian Bible shows something quite different. Here we find two lovers who are passionate about their sexual relationship, and there is no hint that the pleasure they derive from one another should be anything other than celebrated.

Another extreme within Christianity has been an overemphasis on asceticism. Henry Chadwick refers to some of the milder forms of asceticism that have been practiced when he observes that some ascetics slept on rough pallets, flagellated themselves, or walked barefoot in winter.[57] Once again, such cases have created a distorted stereotype of the Christian life. Referring to no less of a central Christian figure than Jesus himself, Loren Wilkinson rightly notes:

> Jesus was no ascetic, but joined in the pleasures of food and work and wine to the extent that his critics called him "a wine-drinker and a glutton." Indeed, His first miracle seems to sanctify the principle of pleasure: He heightened the delight of a long wedding party by changing water into wine.[58]

INDULGENCE, PLEASURE, AND CHRISTIANITY

Because Satanists affirm indulgence as an ideal, primarily because of its pleasure value, we will here explore pleasure especially as it relates to Chris-

---

56. Augustine, "The Good Marriage," in *Treatises on Marriage and Other Subjects,* trans. Charles T. Wilcox (Washington, D.C.: Catholic University of America Press, 1955), 12. For a helpful discussion of Augustine's views on sex and gender see John M. Rist, *Augustine: Ancient Thought Baptized* (Cambridge: Cambridge University Press, 1994), 112–21.
57. Henry Chadwick, "The Ascetic Ideal in the History of the Church," in *Monks, Hermits and the Ascetic Tradition,* ed. W. J. Sheils (Oxford: Ecclesiastical History Society, 1985), 15.
58. Loren Wilkinson, "The Problem of Pleasure," in *Christianity for the Tough Minded,* ed. John Warwick Montgomery (Minneapolis, Minn.: Bethany House, 1973), 190.

tianity. Contrary to the view of many Satanists, and apparently of some Christians, Christianity is pro-pleasure. Christianity affirms that human beings were created to enjoy life as it is lived out in relationship with the Creator and his creation.

However, the subject of pleasure itself raises its own questions and difficulties. Wilkinson perceptively notes that one of the difficulties humans experience with pleasure is found in their insatiable desire for it. We seem to be built for something we cannot experience. "Every pleasure we seek is perhaps a quest for that ultimate pleasure hinted at in our moments of deepest longing."[59] The Satanic ideal of indulgence points to the need for personal fulfillment that at best is only ever partially completed in the life of an individual. In part, this is because the pleasure that indulgence creates merely lasts for finite periods of time. For most, this will create frustration and a sense of longing for a source of pleasure that is enduring.

This difficulty was identified at least as early as Epicurus (341–270 B.C.).[60] He emphasized that persons needed to discern the consequences that their actions, including actions that were initially pleasurable, would have long-term. He writes, "No pleasure is a bad thing in itself: but means which produce some pleasures bring with them disturbances many times greater than the pleasures."[61] In other words, certain actions that cause momentary pleasure may cause mental or physical pain over a period of time that is much worse than the initial pleasure.[62] The wise individual will thus approach indulgence and pleasure with caution.

Epicurus provides a helpful corrective to Satanism's view of indulgence. The pleasure that indulgence provides, whether physical or mental, is not an end in itself. Nor is it ultimately fulfilling in itself. However, the question still

---

59. Ibid., 191.
60. Epicurus is often mistakenly associated with an Epicureanism that is synonymous with hedonism. This appears to be an error as old as Epicurus. Though not a Epicurean, Cicero speaks for Epicureans when he writes, "Now I will explain what pleasure is and what it is like, to remove any misunderstandings which inexperienced people may have and to help them to understand how serious, self-controlled, and stern our doctrine is, though it is commonly held to be hedonistic, slack, and soft." Epicurus, *The Epicurus Reader: Selected Writings and Testimonia,* trans. and ed. Brad Inwood and Lloyd P. Gershon (Indianapolis: Hackett, 1994), 60.
61. Epicurus, "Principal Doctrines," in *Epicurus: The Extant Remains,* trans. Cyril Bailey (Oxford: Clarendon, 1926), 97.
62. Cf. Stanley J. Grenz, *The Moral Quest: Foundations of Christian Ethics* (Leicester: Apollos, 1997), 79.

remains as to why there is, in LaVey's words, a "universal trait" among humans toward indulgence, toward pleasure?[63] Why is it that the longing for pleasure, the longing for completion, the longing for wholeness, is apparently innate in humanity? We believe that the question is best answered within a Christian framework. Christianity answers why human beings have such a high capacity for pleasure by showing that humankind was made for pleasure by the same God who invented pleasure.[64] Trying to find lasting pleasure apart from the Creator of pleasure will only lead to frustration and pain.

CONCLUSION

Blanche Barton writes:

> LaVey saw there must be a new representative of justice—not some oppressive, patriarchal, white-bearded God but a new human advocate. Someone who wasn't removed from us and shrouded in "divinity," but who understood the torments of being human, who shared our own passions and foibles yet was somehow wiser and stronger.[65]

The Left-hand Christian philosopher, we believe, provides the ideal way forward in apologetically interacting with Satanism. Acting as Christ's advocate, the Left-hand philosopher will be enabled to point to the fulfillment of LaVey's desire for "Someone who wasn't removed from us and shrouded in 'divinity,' but who understood the torments of being human, who shared our own passions and foibles yet was somehow wiser and stronger" in Jesus Christ. Through the incarnation, Jesus demonstrated his humanity; by his death and resurrection, he demonstrated his divinity. Through incarnating into the world of the Satanist, the Left-hand Christian philosopher is in a strategic position to apologetically defend and communicate the Christian faith to adherents of Satanism.

STUDY QUESTIONS

1. What are common misunderstandings of Satanism? How may these misunderstandings have been established?

---

63. LaVey, *The Satanic Bible,* 53–54.
64. Wilkinson, "The Problem of Pleasure," 191.
65. Barton, *The Church of Satan,* 5.

2. Name at least two literary sources from which LaVeyan Satanism has derived beliefs.
3. How does the apologetic employment of the Left-hand Christian Philosopher make use of contextualization principles?
4. Is admitting genuine fault necessary in certain apologetic encounters? Why or why not?

CHAPTER 13

JESUS AMONG THE ALTERNATIVE HEALERS

Sacred Oils, Aromatherapists, and the Gospel

RUTH POLLARD

Throughout this book, the case has been made for adopting a missiologically informed stance toward new religious movements. In this chapter we shall be developing a contextual model, partly supported by a legal apologetic, for reaching people committed to aromatherapy.[1] One caveat: We are not offering medical advice; readers must always consult with an accredited physician about specific ailments.

COMPLEMENTARY MEDICINE'S APPEAL

The term *complementary medicine* designates therapies that exist alongside conventional medicine. For a while, the term *alternative medicine* was in currency, but it has largely fallen out of use because of the negative perception that it was a competitor with conventional treatments.[2] My research indicates that aromatherapists encourage contact with mainstream doctors.[3]

---

1. On the role of lawyers in apologetics see Philip Johnson, "Juridical Apologists 1600–2000 A.D.: A Bio-Bibliographical Essay," *Global Journal of Classical Theology* 3, no. 1 (March 2002): retrieved from www.trinitysem.edu/journal/philjohnsonpap.html.
2. Catherine Zollman and Andrew Vickers, "ABC of Complementary Medicine: What Is Complementary Medicine?" *British Medical Journal* 319 (11 September 1999): 693. Some Christian apologists persist in referring to it as "alternative medicine."
3. My research comprised interviews with practitioners of aromatherapy, as well as discussions with a local pharmacist, Christian doctor, retired Christian missionary, and an evangelical theologian. Other fieldwork included attendance at the 2002 "Open Day" of the Nature Care College in Sydney, and at the Mind-Body-Spirit festival in Sydney (since 1995), as well as reading primary sources.

Complementary medicine is now widely accepted. Several universities offer courses and many hospitals have complementary therapy clinics. Some health insurance funds pay for certain therapies, and pharmacies sell herbal mixtures, aromatherapy oils, and their accoutrements. With this mainstream acceptance, we cannot ignore the topic.

Catherine Zollman and Andrew Vickers adduce eight reasons why complementary medicine appeals to people: time and continuity, personal attention, patient involvement and choice, hope, touch, dealing with ill-defined symptoms, making sense of illness, and spiritual and existential concerns.[4] People are clearly looking for elements they perceive to be missing from conventional treatments.

AROMATHERAPY AND ESOTERIC SPIRITUALITY

What is aromatherapy? Most of us probably think of oils used in massage. Certainly, the use of aromatic scents and plant oils for cosmetic and medicinal purposes and religious rites is attested cross-culturally in the ancient world.[5] However, Kurt Schnaubelt argues that aromatherapy is technically different from the "general use of aromatic plants throughout history."[6]

Gabriel Mojay defines it this way:

> Aromatherapy can be defined as the controlled use of essential oils to maintain and promote physical, psychological, and spiritual wellbeing. Essential oils are volatile (easily evaporated) substances that occur naturally in a variety of plants growing the world over. Each plant essence is extracted from a single botanical source through a number of possible methods, the most common and generally favoured being that of steam distillation.[7]

---

4. Zollman and Vickers, "ABC of Complementary Medicine: Complementary Medicine and the Patient," *British Medical Journal* 319 (4 December 1999): 1486–88.

5. Gabrielle J. Dorland, *Scents Appeal: The Silent Persuasion of Aromatic Encounters* (Mendham, N.J.: Wayne Dorland, 1993), 205–14; Julia Lawless, *Aromatherapy and the Mind: The Psychological and Emotional Effects of Essential Oils* (London: Thorsons, 1998), 8–71. Lise Manniche, *Sacred Luxuries: Fragrance, Aromatherapy and Cosmetics in Ancient Egypt* (Ithaca, N.Y.: Cornell University Press, 1999).

6. Kurt Schnaubelt, *Medical Aromatherapy: Healing with Essential Oils* (Berkeley, Calif.: Frog, 1999), 9.

7. Gabriel Mojay, *Aromatherapy for Healing the Spirit: Restoring Emotional and Mental Balance with Essential Oils* (Rochester, Vt.: Healing Arts Press, 1997), 10.

Rene-Maurice Gattefossé, the French perfumer, coined the term *aromatherapy* in 1937. Gattefossé was primarily interested in the medicinal properties of essential oils, and during the Second World War he tested their antiseptic properties on wounded soldiers.[8]

Although Gattefossé explored medicinal uses for the oils, others developed a mystic paradigm. Marguerite Maury was a trained nurse who studied Zen, yoga, macrobiology, naturopathy, and meditation. Maury believed that bodily regeneration was feasible through using essential oils, and she advocated the concept of a vital energy or life force: "When we are dealing with an essential oil and its odoriferance, we are dealing directly with a vital force and entering the very heart of the alchemy of creation."[9]

Maury linked aromatherapy with esoteric spirituality. Her approach is just one example of how a subterranean spirituality was attached to a therapy that in the march of time has now become quite mainstream. Over the past one hundred and fifty years, scientific medicine marginalized healing techniques that were premised on esoteric spiritual knowledge. Catherine Albanese has charted how complementary healing techniques emerged into the American mainstream largely through New Age religion.[10]

Aromatherapy holds tremendous appeal for women, and it is an example of the current re-feminizing of healing. Most students at complementary therapy colleges are women, and nurses have been preeminent in bringing these therapies into the hospital system. Women are reclaiming a past social role where the village healer was often a female skilled in the use of herbal remedies. This relates to the wider mosaic of feminizing trends in spirituality.[11]

Many healers conceive of an energetic model of humanity. One model is based on Hindu–Tantric thought that humans have a "subtle anatomy" consisting of five bodies: physical, etheric, astral, mental, and causal.[12] Within the

8. Marcel Gattefossé, "Rene-Maurice Gattefossé: The Father of Modern Aromatherapy," *The International Journal of Aromatherapy* 4, no. 4 (winter 1992): 18–19.

9. Marguerite Maury, *Marguerite Maury's Guide to Aromatherapy: The Secret of Life and Youth: A Modern Alchemy* (Essex: C. W. Daniel, 1990), 80–81.

10. Catherine L. Albanese, "The Aura of Wellness: Subtle-Energy Healing and New Age Religion," *Religion and American Culture* 10, no. 1 (winter 2000): 29–55.

11. Mary Farrell Bednarowski, "The New Age Movement and Feminist Spirituality: Overlapping Conversations at the End of the Century," in *Perspectives on the New Age,* ed. James R. Lewis and J. Gordon Melton (Albany, N.Y.: State University of New York Press, 1992), 167–78.

12. Patricia Davis, *Subtle Aromatherapy* (Essex: C. W. Daniel, 1991), 23–33. Subtle anatomy arose in Tantric Yoga, but Theosophists such as Charles Leadbeater radically reinterpreted the concepts, see Greg Tillett, *The Elder Brother: A Biography of Charles Webster Leadbeater* (London: Routledge and Kegan Paul, 1982), 4.

mental body are energy centers called chakras, and these can be activated through meditation or via healing tools. Illness arises when we are energetically out of harmony with cosmic forces.[13] The aim is to harmonize the energy flow to produce health.

Another model is grounded in Chinese metaphysics: All of the cosmos is permeated with what is called chi or Qi. The human body has energy points known as meridians. Illness arises when chi is imbalanced, and healing techniques are applied to the meridians to restore energetic harmony and hence health.[14] Both energetic models, which crop up in some aromatherapy texts, are cross-referenced to quantum physics to present a new anthropology: humans as energy in material form. The terms *energy, vital force,* and *universal life force* are often used as synonyms for an impersonal God.

Perhaps the most influential contemporary aromatherapist is Robert Tisserand. According to Kurt Schnaubelt, Tisserand succeeded in popularizing the link between medical aromatherapy and esoteric powers.[15] Some practitioners claim that the oils work as a result of cosmic energy—and because all elements in the cosmos partake of it, when we activate this energy then healing occurs.[16] For example, when crystals are used with oils, they can balance and restore energy through the body. Oils can supercharge crystals or be used to drain crystals of accumulated negative energy. Others suspend a pendulum (dowsing) over oils to determine by the swing which oil is suitable for use on a particular patient.[17] Schnaubelt boldly asserts, "Aromatherapy is shamanism for everyone."[18]

Other practitioners combine aromatherapy with astrology, crystals, magic, vibrational therapy, colors, chakras, and dowsing, and with Chinese, Tibetan, Ayurvedic, and herbal healing paradigms.[19] Neo-pagan writer Scott Cunningham advocates a do-it-yourself magical aromatherapy:

13. Davis, *Subtle Aromatherapy,* 12.

14. Ted J. Kaptchuk, *Chinese Medicine: The Web That Has No Weaver,* rev. ed. (London: Rider, 2000).

15. Schnaubelt, *Medical Aromatherapy,* 4.

16. J. Kusmirek, "Perspectives in Aromatherapy," in *Fragrance: The Psychology and Biology of Perfume,* ed. S. Van Toller and G. H. Dodd (Essex: Elsevier Science Publishers, 1992), 282–84.

17. Davis, *Subtle Aromatherapy,* 83–94.

18. Schnaubelt, *Medical Aromatherapy,* vii.

19. See Davis, *Subtle Aromatherapy*; Judith White, Karen Downes, and Leon Nacson, *Aromatherapy for Meditation and Contemplation* (Sydney: Nacson, 1998); and Farida Irani, *The Magic of Ayurveda Aromatherapy* (Sydney: Subtle Energies, 2001).

To me, *magic is the movement of subtle, natural energies to manifest needed change* . . . visualization is maintained while inhaling the fragrance of aromatic plant materials or essential oils.[20]

Gabriel Mojay links essential oils to harmonizing the flow of chi or Qi in the body with that in the cosmos.[21] As regards Qi, Ted Kaptchuk brings this insight to bear:

Qi has frequently been identified with the western concept of vital energy. . . . To characterize Qi as energy is to invoke a world view the Chinese never had.[22]

Not all aromatherapists believe and practice the same things. Some use the oils only to assist in relaxation through massage. The latest innovation is in hydrosols, which uses the residual water and plant mix produced during the distillation of the essential oils.[23] There are Christians who reject the esoteric but affirm that God has given us the oils as a blessing.

SCIENTIFIC CLAIMS AND MEDICAL STATUS

My survey of popular aromatherapy literature revealed that extravagant claims, sweeping statements, and anecdotal reports are often presented as if they constitute valid evidence. Although patient testimony cannot be summarily dismissed (a basic legal principle), neither does it qualify as conclusive medical proof. The fundamental problem is that patients' anecdotes need empirical verification through rigorous clinical tests. Another difficulty is the logical leap made from quantum theory (concerned with subatomic matter) to the whole cosmos interfused with cosmic energy.[24]

Both skeptics and Christian apologists challenge the claims of aromatherapists. Skeptics tend to dismiss aromatherapy on the grounds that: (a) the steam distillation method of extracting oil removes many active ingredients, (b) massage and the inhalation of oils has limited practical effects,

20. Scott Cunningham, *Magical Aromatherapy: The Power of Scent* (St. Paul, Minn.: Llewellyn, 2000), 5–6 (emphasis in original).
21. Mojay, *Aromatherapy for Healing the Spirit*, 7, 26.
22. Kaptchuk, *Chinese Medicine*, 69–70 n. 3.
23. Suzanne Catty, *Hydrosols: The Next Aromatherapy* (Rochester, Vt.: Healing Arts Press, 2001).
24. Ernest Lucas, *Science and the New Age Challenge* (Leicester: Apollos, 1996).

and (c) about one-third of any treatment is attributable to the placebo effect.[25]

Like lawyers, skeptics are committed to analysis of evidence; therefore, they believe that open and balanced inquiry into therapies is to be encouraged. The National Council Against Health Fraud operates an informative Web site about fraudulent healers.[26] However, skeptics (like anyone else) can have entrenched prejudices, and this manifests itself in their blanket dismissals of complementary therapies. Ross Clifford has illustrated how nineteenth-century zoologists had an entrenched prejudice about the existence of the Australian platypus, because the creature's anatomy did not "fit" with the prevailing scientific paradigm. All evidence was treated as a hoax.[27] That kind of prejudicial mind-set often prevails when skeptics dismiss the evidence for the resurrection of Jesus.

The current evidence for the efficacy of aromatherapy warrants a middle position between the therapists and skeptics. Recent clinical tests show that there is some value in using aromatherapy to relieve agitation in patients with severe dementia.[28] Reduced anxiety and improvement of quality of life for

25. Stephen Barrett, "Aromatherapy: Making Dollars Out of Scents," retrieved 2 September 2002 from www.quackwatch.com/01QuackeryRelatedTopics/aroma.html. Robert Todd Carroll, "Aromatherapy," *The Skeptic's Dictionary,* retrieved 2 September 2002 from http://skepdic.com/aroma.html; Kurt A. Butler, *A Consumer's Guide to "Alternative Medicine"* (Buffalo, N.Y.: Prometheus, 1992); Stephen Barrett, *The Health Robbers* (Buffalo, N.Y.: Prometheus, 1993); Lynn McCutcheon, "What's That I Smell? The Claims of Aromatherapy," *Skeptical Inquirer,* May 1996, retrieved 2 September 2002 from http://www.csicop.org/si/9605/aroma.html; and Andy Barson, "Amateur Aromatherapy: The Case Against Aromatherapy," www.andybarson.btinternet.co.uk/against.htm (2 September 2002). Cf. Dónal O'Mathúa and Walt Larimore, *Alternative Medicine: The Christian Handbook* (Grand Rapids: Zondervan, 2001), 124–25. See the cautionary remarks about skeptical dogmatism in J. R. King, "Scientific Status of Aromatherapy," *Perspectives in Biology and Medicine* 37, no. 3 (1994): 409–15.
26. See National Council Against Health Fraud at www.ncahf.org/.
27. Ross Clifford, *Leading Lawyers' Case for the Resurrection* (Edmonton: Canadian Institute for Law, Theology, and Public Policy, 1996), 104–5.
28. D. J. Brooker, M. Snape, E. Johnson, D. Ward, and M. Payne, "Single Case Evaluation of the Effects of Aromatherapy and Massage on Disturbed Behaviour in Severe Dementia," *British Journal of Clinical Psychology* 36, no. 2 (May 1997): 287–96; J. Smallwood, R. Brown, F. Couter, E. Irvine, and C. Copland, "Aromatherapy and Behaviour Disturbances in Dementia: A Randomised Controlled Trial," *International Journal of Geriatric Psychiatry* 16, no. 10 (October 2001): 1010–13; C. Holmes, V. Hopkins, C. Hensford, V. MacLaughlin, D. Wilkinson, and H. Rosenvinge, "Lavender Oil as a Treatment for Agitated Behaviour in Severe Dementia: A Placebo Controlled Study," *International Journal of Geriatric Psychiatry* 17, no. 4 (April 2002): 305–8; and C. G. Ballard, J. T. O'Brien, K. Reichelt, and E. K. Perry, "Aromatherapy as a Safe and Effective Treatment for the Management of Agitation in Severe Dementia: The Results of a Double-blind, Placebo-controlled Trial with Melissa," *Journal of Clinical Psychiatry* 63, no. 7 (July 2002): 553–58.

cancer patients in palliative care has been measured through combining aromatherapy with massage.[29] Other studies indicate that aromatherapy affects brainwaves, reduces stress, and positively affects mood, EEG patterns of alertness, and math computations.[30] It also has some small benefits in pain control.[31] On the negative side, some people experience allergic reactions to certain oils.[32] Lastly, aromatherapy is recognized by the nursing profession's regulatory bodies in many countries, including the United States, the United Kingdom, and Australia.[33]

On the basis of the present evidence, one can render a tentative verdict. Both aromatherapists and skeptics are prone to making exaggerated statements. Essential oils cannot be viewed as a panacea for illnesses, though they do have some antiseptic properties. Similarly, the skeptics' blanket dismissal of aromatherapy is unwarranted. At best, the oils have a paramedical role to play in the wider context of treating patients, and aromatherapy can be incorporated into lifestyle routines. This position is the best one to adduce at present, but it is certainly open to modification in light of whatever relevant evidence arises in the future.

29. S. Wilkinson, J. Aldridge, I. Salmon, E. Cain, and B. Wilson, "An Evaluation of Aromatherapy Massage in Palliative Care," *Palliative Medicine* 13, no. 5 (September 1999): 409–17; and N. Hadfield, "The Role of Aromatherapy Massage in Reducing Anxiety in Patients with Malignant Brain Tumours," *International Journal of Palliative Nursing* 7, no. 6 (June 2001): 279–85.

30. N. Motomura, A. Sakurai, and Y. Yotsuya, "Reduction of Mental Stress with Lavender Odorant," *Perceptual and Motor Skills* 93, no. 3 (December 2001): 713–18; and M. A. Diego, N. A. Jones, T. Field, M. Hernandez-Reif, S. Schanberg, C. Kuhn, V. McAdam, R. Galamaga, and M. Galamaga, "Aromatherapy Positively Affects Mood, EEG Patterns of Alertness and Math Computations," *International Journal of Neuroscience* 96, no. 3–4 (December 1998): 217–24. Cf. Joachim Degel and Egon Peter Köster, "Odors: Implicit Memory and Performance Effects," *Chemical Senses* 24 (1999): 317–25.

31. M. Louis and S. D. Kowalski, "Use of Aromatherapy with Hospice Patients to Decrease Pain, Anxiety, and Depression and to Promote an Increased Sense of Well-Being," *American Journal of Hospice and Palliative Care* 19, no. 6 (November–December 2002): 381–86.

32. N. Bleasel, B. Tate, and M. Rademaker, "Allergic Contact Dermatitis Following Exposure to Essential Oils," *Australasian Journal of Dermatology* 43, no. 3 (August 2002): 211–13.

33. Jane Buckle, "The Role of Aromatherapy in Nursing Care," *Nursing Clinics of North America* 36, no. 1 (March 2001): 57–72; and idem, "Clinical Aromatherapy and AIDS," *Journal of the Association of Nurses in AIDS Care* 13, no. 3 (May–June 2002): 81–99.

AROMATHERAPY IN BIBLICAL AND THEOLOGICAL PERSPECTIVE

Can aromatherapy be used (like the altar to the Unknown God in Acts 17:23) as a missiological point of contact with non-Christians?[34] The answer to that question lies in Scripture and in theological reflection about pneumatology, creation, redemption, anointing, and healing.

Essential Oils in the Bible

The Scriptures abound with apologetic material about oils and essences. They are cited in a very positive way as toiletries (Ruth 3:3; 2 Samuel 12:20; Esther 2:12); for perfuming garments (Psalm 45:8); in lovemaking (Song of Songs 3:6; 4:6, 11; 5:1, 5, 13); to express hospitality toward guests (Luke 7:46); in food preparation (1 Kings 17:12, 14, 16); for lighting (Exodus 25:6; 27:20; Matthew 25:3); and for medicinal purposes (Isaiah 1:6; Luke 10:34). Oils were also traded as commodities (2 Kings 4:7; 2 Chronicles 2:10).

Acts of worship routinely included oil in the ceremonial offerings of praise (Exodus 25:6; 29:38–42; 30:22–38; Numbers 28:3–6); as tithes (Ezekiel 45:25); and the firstfruits offerings (Deuteronomy 18:4). Most food offerings were either mixed with oil or had it poured over them (Exodus 29:40; Leviticus 2:1; Numbers 28:5; Ezekiel 45:24). Oil was included in purification offerings for leprosy (Leviticus 14:10). The priests were anointed with oil (Exodus 29:7; Leviticus 8:12; 21:10). Likewise the tabernacle, the altar, and the utensils were consecrated for service in worship (Exodus 40:9–11). Jacob's stone and pillar were anointed (Genesis 28:18; 35:14), as was Elisha the prophet (1 Kings 19:16). Priests and prophets anointed the kings of Israel (1 Samuel 10:1; 16:3; 1 Kings 1:39; 2 Kings 9:6; 11:12). The spiritual significance of anointing with oil is that it was a symbol that the person was appointed and set apart for service (1 Samuel 10:9; Isaiah 61:1; Zechariah 4:11–14; Acts 10:38). Oils were also used as part of the healing ministry of the church (James 5:14).

Oils and essences are important in the life and ministry of Jesus. The magi's gifts to the Christ-child included myrrh and frankincense (Matthew 2:11). Jesus was anointed with expensive oils prior to his execution (Matthew 26:6–13;

---

34. On "the unknown god" and apologetics-missions see Dean Flemming, "Contextualizing the Gospel in Athens: Paul's Areopagus Address as a Paradigm for Missionary Communication," *Missiology* 30, no. 2 (April 2002): 199–214.

Mark 14:3–9; Luke 7:36–50; John 12:1–8), and oils were used in his burial (Matthew 26:12; Luke 23:56; John 19:40).

Finally, the Scriptures indicate that oil symbolizes joy (Psalm 45:8; Hebrews 1:9); signifies wisdom when carefully used (Proverbs 21:17, 20); is linked with fellowship and friendship (Psalm 133:1–2); and restored strength (Psalm 92:10). Anointing is specifically connected with the gospel (Isaiah 61:1–3; cf. Luke 4:18–21). Oil is also symbolic of the Holy Spirit (1 Samuel 16:13; cf. Isaiah 61:3).

Spirit and Creation

Scripture teaches that God is both transcendent and immanent. Ross Clifford and Philip Johnson clarify the meaning of these terms:

> By "transcendent" is meant that God is a being who is separate from the creation and is sovereign over it. By "immanent" is meant that God's being is present everywhere within the creation. Another way of using these terms is to think of transcendence as referring to ultimate things and immanence as referring to intimate things.[35]

In the West, we are being challenged by seekers in alternate spiritualities (New Age, Neo-Pagan, esoteric), who accept concepts of an immanent deity within the creation.[36] Some Christian apologists, upon encountering those concepts of immanence, often try to debunk them. This negative style of apologetic strengthens the boundary markers between Christians and non-Christians, and differentiates two mutually exclusive views of God. This has its place, but I am not persuaded it is the best stratagem for reaching non-Christians.

For apologetic and missiological purposes, the concept of immanence actually provides a positive starting point. We begin by discussing God's immanence—like the altar to the Unknown God—before we arrive at God as

---

35. Ross Clifford and Philip Johnson, *Jesus and the Gods of the New Age* (Oxford: Lion, 2001), 50.

36. Clifford and Johnson point out that New Age has both pantheist and panentheist views, the latter position allows for a personal God who develops in process with us. Clifford and Johnson challenge those New Age views but also urge Christian apologists to be alert to these nuances, because New Age has been simplistically equated with pantheism. Ibid, 104–12.

transcendent. This apologia builds on an understanding of God's Spirit in the creation. We tend to think of the Holy Spirit's work from a post-Pentecost standpoint, with the Spirit sealing us in Christ. Scripture certainly affirms that those who turn to Christ in repentance and faith have that intimate relationship with the Spirit (Romans 8:1–27).[37] However, B. B. Warfield reminds us that God's Spirit *(ruach)* is at work in the creation today and not just in the act of the original creation (Genesis 1:2). Warfield points out that God's Spirit is immanent in the creation "as the principle of the very existence and persistence of all things, and as the source and originating cause of all movement and order and life."[38] God's Spirit is responsible for giving, sustaining, and taking away the life of humankind and every living creature (Job 12:10; 27:3; Psalm 104:29–30; Genesis 2:7; 6:17).

R. C. Sproul notes that through the sphere of creation, God's Spirit sustains the non-Christian's life and breath:

> In the sense of creation (as distinguished from redemption), everybody participates in the Holy Spirit. Since the Holy Spirit is the source and power supply of life itself, no one can live completely apart from the Holy Spirit.[39]

So although Christians have a special relationship with God's Spirit, the Spirit is not working exclusively with or through us, but is also involved in the whole creation. Our view of God's immanence is not identical to that of the esoteric spiritual seeker, but it does constitute "common ground" from which meaningful witness can begin.

From the immanence of God's Spirit we naturally come to the Trinity. First, the creation shows in the ultimate sense that God the Father is sovereign over it. Second, we find that the creation belongs to Christ, because all things were made by, for, and through him (Colossians 1:16–17; John 1:3). Third, the Holy Spirit works to maintain and sustain the earth. All of God's handiwork was

---

37. See Edward Henry Bickersteth, *The Holy Spirit: His Person and Work* (Grand Rapids: Kregel, 1976); and Abraham Kuyper, *The Work of the Holy Spirit* (Grand Rapids: Eerdmans, 1979).
38. B. B. Warfield, "The Spirit of God in the Old Testament," in *Biblical and Theological Studies* (Philadelphia: Presbyterian and Reformed, 1968), 134.
39. R. C. Sproul, *The Mystery of the Holy Spirit* (Wheaton, Ill.: Tyndale House, 1990), 88. On the theological and missiological implications of pneumatology for understanding the world's religions, see Amos Yung, *Beyond the Impasse: Toward a Pneumatological Theology of Religions* (Grand Rapids: Baker, 2003).

originally good and none of the created objects are inherently evil. Evil was introduced through the moral actions of humanity in disobedience to God. Since the Fall, any created object can be used either for God's glory or for idolatry. Christ's atoning death for the sin of the world is not only about our forgiveness and salvation. The creation awaits our liberation (Romans 8:22ff.) and its renovation as envisaged in the new heaven and new earth (Isaiah 65:17–25; 2 Peter 3:13; Revelation 21). We are free in Christ to glorify God—even through using the created objects he originally blessed—without being straitjacketed by unwarranted taboos.

We must also recall how God's providential care is exercised toward all humanity (Matthew 5:45; Acts 14:17), such as in healing believers *and* unbelievers (2 Kings 5:1–14; Luke 17:12–17). It is inherent in God's nature to heal (Exodus 15:26). Sometimes, healing occurs miraculously; other times through the body's created capacities to repair and the physician's craft. In a wider sense, health and well being are embodied in the biblical material concerning diet, hygiene, fitness, rest, morality, and lifestyle.[40] Through each of these avenues, God blesses both the Christian and the non-Christian alike. Of course, in the deepest and most profound sense, a holistic healing of body, mind, and spirit is effected through the cross and resurrection of Jesus, and this is what aromatherapists must discover. It is the Spirit who exalts Jesus and empowers us to bring that "healing" to the nations.

FROM AROMATHERAPY TO JESUS

God has blessed the creation and that includes the oils that we can receive with thanksgiving (cf. 1 Timothy 4:4). Because the oils symbolize joy, wisdom, friendship, and restored strength, and are used in spiritual rituals like anointing, we have a rich vein of material with which to work. The act of anointing takes us to the threshold of both the gospel and encountering the Spirit. J. Barton Payne comments that "the ceremony of anointing by means of oil was the sacramental sign and seal of the coming of God's Spirit."[41] Wilf Hildebrandt concurs:

---

40. See S. I. McMillen, *None of These Diseases* (Old Tappan, N.J.: Revell, 1963); and Harold Taylor, *Sent to Heal* (Melbourne: Order of St. Luke, 1993).

41. J. Barton Payne, *The Theology of the Older Testament* (Grand Rapids: Zondervan, 1962), 175.

The externally flowing oil represented the internal reality of the Spirit's filling. The imagery of the oil and dew, therefore, indicates the work of the Spirit in bringing about unity and blessing in the community (Psalm 133). The anointed one is divinely enabled to fulfill royal and prophetic duties. In the anointing of the tabernacle furnishings, the oil marked out as sacred the dwelling place of God.[42]

The New Testament teaches that God anointed Jesus with the Holy Spirit to heal (Acts 10:38). That anointing of Jesus with the Spirit was a creative outpouring by the Father on the Son that inaugurated the incarnation. Jesus was uniquely anointed to fulfill what the Law, the Prophets, and the writings had foreshadowed (Luke 24:44). There were those who recognized this and brought to Jesus essential oils confirming his symbolic anointing (Matthew 2:11; 26:6–13; Mark 14:3–9; Luke 7:36–50; John 12:1–8). These gifts of oil were directly linked to Jesus' core mission: the Cross and the Resurrection. Through the cross and resurrection of Jesus we discover that God is not an impersonal energy but a personal being. The Resurrection confirms that Jesus is the Son of God (Romans 1:4). Lawyers have deftly argued that the direct and circumstantial evidences for the Resurrection are compelling.[43] The Resurrection validates that, on the cross, Jesus dealt with sin; therefore, divine forgiveness is available. It is after Jesus' resurrection and ascension that at Pentecost the Holy Spirit receives the church. So the Resurrection clinches for us the bestowal of the Spirit upon us, sealing us in Christ and empowering us to live according to Christ's teaching.[44] We then are "anointed" by the Spirit and become the tabernacle that God dwells in. That anointing operates for us only through our relationship to Jesus, who was uniquely anointed as the Son and Savior by God.[45]

This theology of anointing provides the basis on which creative outreach can be developed. An effective example is using aromatherapy as a point of contact in booth ministry. This has been successfully tested at the Mind-Body-

---

42. Wilf Hildebrandt, *An Old Testament Theology of the Spirit of God* (Peabody, Mass.: Hendrickson, 1995), 124.

43. John Warwick Montgomery, *History, Law and Christianity* (Edmonton: Canadian Institute for Law, Theology, and Public Policy, 2002).

44. See Ross Clifford and Philip Johnson, *Riding the Rollercoaster: How the Risen Christ Empowers Life* (Sydney: Strand, 1998).

45. My application of anointing theology is unrelated to televangelist Benny Hinn's eccentric views on anointing.

Spirit festival, with a booth where foot washing is performed using essential oils. As non-Christians have their feet cleaned and massaged, there is time for talking about spiritual matters. Seekers are shown through word and deed how the oils have spiritual significance, and that the key to it is unlocked in Jesus. As conversations unfold, a time for personal testimony, gospel proclamation, and prayer occurs.[46]

AROMATHERAPY AND OCCULTISM

Although very few Christian apologists have condemned aromatherapy, many utterly reject complementary healing. After reflecting on that literature, I see three possible objections to my contextual model emerge:

1. Because the principal architects of aromatherapy were committed to occult beliefs, and some use divinatory tools like astrology, the practice is spiritually contaminated.
2. Many aromatherapists claim they are using invisible energy forces, which must be devilish. Any Christian using aromatherapy is flirting with danger. First, exposure to spiritual deception is very high. Second, weaker and spiritually immature Christians may stumble in their faith if they see other Christians using something that has clear occult links.[47]
3. Aromatherapy involves extracting oils from plants, and many aromatherapists speak of activating the "universal life force" of the plant. This occult view of plants is also reflected in the views of many who advocate vegetarian, vegan, fruitarian, and macrobiotic diets.[48]

46. See Philip Johnson's essay, "Discipling New Age and Do-It-Yourself Seekers Through Booth Ministries," chapter 11 in this book.
47. These points sum up the basic stance taken in Neil T. Anderson and Michael Jacobson, *The Biblical Guide to Alternative Medicine* (Ventura, Calif.: Regal, 2003); John Ankerberg and John Weldon, *Can You Trust Your Doctor?* (Brentwood, Tenn.: Wolgemuth and Hyatt, 1991); Paul C. Reisser, Teri K. Reisser, and John Weldon, *New Age Medicine: A Christian Perspective on Holistic Health* (Downers Grove, Ill.: InterVarsity, 1987); Elliot Miller, "The Christian, Energetic Medicine, 'New Age Paranoia,'" *Christian Research Journal* 14, no. 3 (Winter 1992): 24–27; O'Mathúa and Larimore, *Alternative Medicine*; Samuel Pfeifer, *Healing at Any Price?* (Milton Keynes: Word, 1988); and David Sneed and Sharon Sneed, *The Hidden Agenda: A Critical View of Alternative Medical Therapies* (Nashville: Nelson, 1991).
48. A succinct profile on vegetarianism and the New Age is in J. Gordon Melton, Jerome Clark, and Aidan A. Kelly, *New Age Almanac* (Detroit: Visible Ink, 1991), 262–65. Vegetarians do not eat meat but do include animal products in their diet such as milk, eggs, and

Positive Observations

The Scriptures exhort us to test teachings (1 Thessalonians 5:21; 1 John 4:1–3; Acts 17:11) and to be discerning about false prophets, false Christs, and false doctrine (Deuteronomy 13:1–5; Matthew 7:15–23; 24:23–24; Galatians 1:6–9; Ephesians 4:11–16). Harold Brown has correctly stated that "faith makes a Christian, but doctrine creates the church."[49] So it is important to analyze through the Scriptures the unbiblical worldviews that aromatherapists espouse. Earlier, we documented some of the worldview concepts that many aromatherapists have embraced, and quite a few of those are incompatible with Scripture. What does not align with Scripture must be rejected. Clearly, we must safeguard against spiritual deception, and apologists are also quite right to warn about prohibited practices such as astrology.

Critical Crosscurrents

There are also issues that apologists must not overlook. First, aromatherapy is not ideologically static but has metamorphosed in several directions. Because not all practitioners are occultists, guilt-by-association arguments are unhelpful. If we reject aromatherapy because it has occult origins, we commit the genetic fallacy in logic. Robert Cook explains that this occurs "when something is judged not by the merits of its present form but by its origins."[50] By analogy, the planets were originally named after pagan deities. Times have changed and anyone referring to the planet Mars is unlikely to be a devotee of the ancient god of war.

Second, apologists need to recognize an Achilles' heel in rejecting aromatherapy on the grounds that some practitioners use divinatory tools prohibited in the Bible. Yes, the Bible condemns idolatrous forms of divination

---

honey. Vegans totally eschew consuming any animal products, and many (but not all) are inspired by a Hindu metaphysic. Fruitarians follow a diet based on uncooked fruit and nuts, whereas a macrobiotic diet emphasizes cereals and rice with a limited number of approved vegetables. On subtle forces and energies in plants as interpreted by an esoteric aromatherapist, see Davis, *Subtle Aromatherapy*, 51–58.

49. Harold O. J. Brown, *Heresies: The Image of Christ in the Mirror of Heresy and Orthodoxy from the Apostles to the Present* (Garden City, N.Y.: Doubleday, 1984), 21.

50. Robert Cook, "Alternative and Complementary Theologies: The Case of Cosmic Energy with Special Reference to Chi," *Studies in World Christianity* 6, no. 2 (2000): 184. It should be noted that, in citing Cook, I am not endorsing his commitment to process theology.

(Leviticus 19:26; Deuteronomy 18:9–14), but it also allows for other forms of divination, such as casting lots (Proverbs 16:33; Leviticus 16:7–10; Luke 1:9; Acts 1:26), using Urim and Thummim (1 Samuel 23:9–12), dream interpretation (Genesis 41:1–8; Daniel 2:1–11), firing arrows (2 Kings 13:14–19), and predetermined signs (Judges 6:36–40; 7:4–7; 1 Samuel 14:8–10).[51] My point is not to exonerate aromatherapists who use forbidden tools, but to highlight that apologists are vulnerable to fair critique on this topic.

Third, we must distinguish between the fallen idolatrous state of humanity and created objects. R. C. Sproul reminds us that there is a threefold process to idolatry: repression, suppression, and exchange.[52] Idolatry occurs whenever we turn away from the natural knowledge of God and substitute anything else in God's rightful place. The problem of idolatry is in the soul and not the created object. A New Ager in a spiritually darkened state does not give glory to God but attributes the oil's power to energy forces. Such an explanation may seem plausible to those sharing that worldview, but it does not change the fact that God made the oils with the properties they have. The underlying lesson is that phenomena can be interpreted according to various paradigms, but it does not logically follow that the phenomena is inherently evil.[53]

Fourth, as both Paul Hiebert and Robert Guelich have urged, we must not exaggerate the role and power of Satan, lest we unwittingly promote an unbiblical dualism.[54] Satan is not omnipotent, omniscient, or omnipresent. The biblical portrait is that Satan's role is principally that of a deceiver. The Bible indicates that he has limited powers and there are examples of false powers exercised (Exodus 7:10–12). Demons are shown to endow those they control with paranormal abilities (Mark 5:3–4; Acts 16:16–19).[55] It is also the case that Christ by cross and resurrection has in his triumph over sin and death disarmed the principalities and powers (Colossians 2:15; cf. 2 Peter 2:4; Jude 6).

---

51. Cf. D. E. Aune, "Divination," in *The International Standard Bible Encyclopedia,* ed. G. W. Bromiley, rev. ed. (Grand Rapids: Eerdmans, 1979), 1:971–74.

52. R. C. Sproul, *If There Is a God, Why Are There Atheists?* (Minneapolis: Bethany, 1978), 56–80.

53. Cf. Robina Coker, *Alternative Medicine: Helpful or Harmful?* (Crowborough: Monarch, 1995), 109–12.

54. Paul G. Hiebert, "Spiritual Warfare and Worldview," *Evangelical Review of Theology* 24, no. 3 (2000): 240–56; and Robert A. Guelich, "Spiritual Warfare: Jesus, Paul and Peretti," *Pneuma: The Journal of the Society for Pentecostal Studies* 13, no. 1 (spring 1991): 33–64.

55. On demonology start with John Warwick Montgomery, ed., *Demon Possession* (Minneapolis: Bethany, 1976).

Fifth, there are two proof texts (Matthew 24:24–26; 2 Thessalonians 2:9–12) favored by apologists to allege that Satan heals people through complementary remedies. In the Olivet discourse (Matthew 24), Jesus foretold of false Christs who would show great signs and wonders. Paul Barnett has shown that within the period from A.D. 40 to 70, various sign prophets arose in Judea, hoping to imitate the great salvific signs of God's deliverance of the nation of Israel (parting the river Jordan and making Jerusalem's walls tumble).[56] The signs were not about Satanic healing. In the Thessalonian epistle, the text is specifically focused on the Man of Lawlessness's signs and wonders and does not correlate to healings performed by other people or movements.[57] If one is going to prove that Satan heals (and no Bible passage explicitly confirms this), it certainly cannot be supported from these twin passages. An unresolved question is why healings among non-Christians must necessarily be explained as having an infernal source. Space precludes following this fascinating trajectory, but Western apologists should consider how Christians in Two-Thirds World contexts understand that God heals everyone and how they see God at work even in what we designate as complementary remedies.[58]

Sixth, spiritual deception is ever present and no Christian can claim invulnerability to deception and idolatry (1 John 5:21). Deception is the seat of Satan's power, more so than in any manifestations or phenomena (2 Corinthians 11:14). Discernment through the Scriptures allows us to detect the idolatry of non-Christian beliefs. Aromatherapists who propagate unbiblical spiritualities are deceived, but their deception does not equate to the oils being taboo. There is extensive scriptural justification for reframing the use of oils in a Christian context, and to demonize the oils means we "curse" something God made for us to enjoy.

Seventh, although the metaphysical beliefs of many vegetarians have been linked to occultism, Theosophy, and New Age, this is not a valid reason for making the use of plants off-limits for Christians. The biblical view is that one

56. Paul Barnett, "The Jewish Sign Prophets: A.D. 40–70 Their Intentions and Origin," *New Testament Studies* 27, no. 4 (1981): 679–97.
57. See F. F. Bruce, *1 and 2 Thessalonians* (Waco, Tex.: Word, 1982), 173–88.
58. See Harriet Hill, "Witchcraft and the Gospel: Insights from Africa," *Missiology* 34, no. 3 (July 1996): 319–44; and Eric Ram, ed., *Transforming Health: Christian Approaches to Healing and Wholeness* (Monrovia, Calif.: MARC, 1995), 289–334. Cf. Alan Crook, *A Christian's Guide to Homeopathy* (London: Winter Press, 1996). Philip Johnson, "Energy Healing: A Christian Theological Appraisal," retrieved 2 September 2002 from http://members.ozemail.com.au/~ptcsyd/JohnsonPage/energyheal.htm.

is free before Christ to choose any diet as long as it is ethical (cf. Acts 10:9–16; Colossians 2:16).

We should also recall that, in early Christian monasticism, "medical botany" or "herbalism" was used for healing people. Similarly, the twelfth century Catholic abbess Hildegard of Bingen (1098–1179) was an expert in herbal lore and medicine. During the Protestant Reformation, medical botany was taught at the Calvinist University of Basle.[59] Several Lutheran university lecturers in medicine, such as Caspar Bartholin, Leonard Fuchs, and Christian Torkelsen Morsing, were keen advocates of medical botany.[60] Morsing affirmed that all plants were created due to God's providential care for humanity, and Bartholin asserted, "The patient is not cured by words, but by herbs."[61] Similarly, Protestant physicians in England, such as William Bullein, John Gerarde, John Ray, and Nehemiah Grew, all published major texts on medical botany and herbal medicine.[62]

Lastly, all too often, innovative efforts in apologetics and missions are criticized or curtailed by the "weaker brethren" argument. Paul guided the Corinthians through the issue of food offered to idols, and how weaker believers might be affected. However, this was not a debate about evangelistic technique. John Warwick Montgomery has bitingly said, "Evangelicals reveal their ingrownness in regularly choosing the interests of their hypothetically weaker brethren over the Great Commission—the need for maximum witnessing contact with the unbelieving world."[63] Our twin priorities are the worship of God and the proclamation of the gospel. Aromatherapy offers a marvelous opportunity for Christians, especially women, to do both things for Christ in today's marketplace.

STUDY QUESTIONS

1. Are there other avenues where you believe that aromatherapy could be used as a point of contact for Christian missions?

---

59. See Ole Peter Grell, "Caspar Bartholin and the Education of the Pious Physician," in *Medicine and the Reformation,* ed. Ole Peter Grell and Andrew Cunningham (New York: Routledge, 1993), 85.
60. Ibid, 83, 86, and 93.
61. Ibid, 95.
62. A. W. Sloan, *English Medicine in the Seventeenth Century* (Durham: Durham Academic Press, 1996), 70–72. Cf. Douglas Guthrie, *A History of Medicine,* rev. ed. (London: Nelson, 1958), 131–33.
63. John Warwick Montgomery, *The Shaping of America* (Minneapolis: Bethany, 1976), 176.

2. Is it feasible for the model presented in this chapter to be transferred and used in bridge building for missions with other healing modalities? Which complementary remedies do you believe would be amenable to this?

3. Do you see any ramifications about the role of God's Spirit in the creation for missions with new religious movements?

4. Examine the following Bible verses: Colossians 2:15; 2 Peter 2:4; and Jude 6. What do you believe these passages are saying about fallen angels?

WHERE DO WE GO FROM HERE?

Transforming Evangelical Responses to New Religions

JOHN W. MOREHEAD II

In response to the growth of the new religions, evangelicals have utilized a variety of differing approaches. In this chapter, I will briefly survey these approaches and focus on the most common method, which involves doctrinal comparison and refutation of heresy. Although this method has been helpful to the church in defining and defending her theological boundaries, it has proven largely unsuccessful when applied outside the church as an evangelistic methodology. This is because the method is dramatically different from evangelical missions strategy to world religions, where success might be defined by the degree to which the gospel is conveyed and understood by receptors. By adopting a speaker-oriented apologetic rather than a respondent-oriented evangelistic model, typical evangelical approaches to new religions do not conform on balance to biblical examples for interreligious evangelistic encounters.

We will then explore how evangelical responses to new religions might be transformed in more promising directions through a holistic model that interacts with a variety of disciplines, most notably missiology, which will enable evangelicals to benefit from a cross-cultural missions perspective.

EVANGELICALS, NEW RELIGIONS, AND COUNTER-CULT MINISTRY

In response to the presence and growth of new religions in the United States, a segment of the evangelical community arose that came to be known as the "counter-cult" community. The late Walter Martin, author of *The Kingdom of the Cults,* is regarded as the granddaddy of this counter-cult movement that over time has become a virtual cottage industry.[1] Through his books, lectures, and national radio program, Martin helped establish what would eventually become the major evangelical model for responding to new religions. It will be helpful for us to consider this model in relation to the broader scope of counter-cult apologetics.

Philip Johnson, with the Presbyterian Theological Centre in Sydney, Australia, has categorized the various evangelical apologetic responses to new religions.[2] He identified six basic models that he named heresy–rationalist apologetics; end-times prophecy and conspiracy; spiritual warfare; former member testimonies; cultural apologetics; and behavioralist apologetics. Let us briefly examine the basic thrust of each of these, and then note the strengths and weaknesses of each. Given the prominence of the heresy–rationalist model, we will review this approach last.

End-Times Prophecy and Conspiracy

This model views the rise of new religions in general, and certain movements in particular, from an eschatological perspective, wherein the new religions are understood as a fulfillment of end-times prophecy.[3] Many times this eschatological model is combined with various conspiracy theories that see the rise and alleged influence of a given group or movement providing the

---

1. Tim Stafford, "The Kingdom of the Cult Watchers," *Christianity Today* 7 October 1991, 18–22. Keith Edward Tolbert and Eric Pement, *1996 Directory of Cult Research Organizations* (Trenton N.J.: American Religions Center, 1996), the last year this publication was produced included 443 evangelical counter-cult organizations.
2. Philip Johnson, "The Aquarian Age and Apologetics," *Lutheran Theological Journal* 34, no. 2 (December 1997): 51–60. Johnson expands on this classification system and critique of the counter-cult model in "Apologetics, Mission and New Religious Movements: A Holistic Approach" (pt. 3), *Sacred Tribes: Journal of Christian Mission to New Religious Movements,* retrieved 3 January 2003 from www.sacredtribes.com/issue1/apolog3.htm. Johnson's classification system is an artificial construct to assist in the analysis and comparison of various evangelical apologetic approaches.
3. Examples of this approach include Dave Hunt, *The Cult Explosion* (Irvine, Calif.: Harvest House, 1980); Constancy Cumbey, *The Hidden Dangers of the Rainbow: The New Age Movement and Our Coming Age of Barbarism* (Shreveport, La.: Huntington House, 1983); Dave Hunt, *Peace, Prosperity and the Coming Holocaust: The New Age Movement in Prophecy* (Eugene, Ore.: Harvest House, 1983); Texe Marrs, *Dark Secrets of the New Age: Satan's Plan for a One World Religion* (Westchester, Ill.: Crossway Books, 1987); and Dave Hunt, *Global Peace and the Rise of Antichrist* (Eugene, Ore.: Harvest House, 1990).

context out of which a one-world government will be established and an antichrist will assume power.

Two strengths of this model are its appeal to the apologetic value of predictive prophecy in the Bible, and its strong emphasis on the dangers of spiritual deception. Yet this model also has serious weaknesses. First, the eschatological hermeneutic employed by advocates of this model is employed without consideration of a broader spectrum of eschatological views in the history of the church, including the present.[4] As an aside, greater familiarity with the broader spectrum of eschatology might provide a helpful corrective for the evangelical fascination with suggesting dates for the time of the end, and the unfortunate track record of identifying various political and religious figures as the Antichrist.[5] The second drawback to this model is its uncritical acceptance of various conspiracy theories,[6] which often involve poor research and illogical argumentation. Although the problems associated with eschatological speculation and conspiracy theories do not necessarily invalidate this model in totality, these drawbacks should give us pause for reflection. Given this model's assumption of biblical authority and a certain eschatological framework, advocates of this approach might consider that it lends itself better to a confirmation of the Christian faith in some sense rather than as a model that communicates the gospel to adherents of non-Christian religions, who do not share evangelical theological preconceptions.

Spiritual Warfare

The subject of spiritual warfare is of great interest in the evangelical world.[7] One need only consider the best-selling novels of Frank Peretti for confirmation of this phenomenon.[8] The spiritual warfare model emphasizes Satanic

---

4. Thomas Ice and Kenneth L. Gentry Jr., *The Great Tribulation: Past or Future?* (Grand Rapids: Kregel, 1999).
5. Gary DeMar, *Last Days Madness: Obsession of the Modern Church* (Atlanta: American Vision, 1997).
6. Paul Coughlin, *Secrets, Plots and Hidden Agendas* (Downers Grove, Ill.: InterVarsity, 1999).
7. C. Peter Wagner, *Confronting the Powers* (Ventura, Calif.: Regal, 1996); George Otis Jr., *The Twilight Labyrinth: Why Does Spiritual Darkness Linger Where It Does?* (Grand Rapids: Chosen Books, 1997); Keith Bailey, *Strange Gods: Responding to the Rise of Spirit Worship in America* (Camp Hill, Pa.: Christian Publications, 1998); and Bob Larson, *Larson's Book of Spiritual Warfare* (Nashville: Nelson, 1999).
8. Frank E. Peretti, *This Present Darkness* (Westchester, Ill.: Crossway Books, 1986); and idem, *Piercing the Darkness* (Westchester, Ill.: Crossway Books, 1989).

and demonic deception in the rise and teachings of new religions and advocates various tools such as "spiritual mapping" in identifying Satanic strongholds, specialized warfare prayer, and sometimes even exorcism, as the needed
remedies.

Strengths of this approach include its emphasis upon the supernatural, the
need for prayer, and a reminder to Christians that evangelistic activities involve some form of spiritual warfare. This reminder is important because
missiologist Paul Hiebert has identified what he calls "the Flaw of the Excluded
Middle," a tendency among Western missionaries, under the influence of Enlightenment rationalism, to adopt a two-tiered view of reality that excludes
the interaction of the "religious" realm (including miraculous elements) from
mundane concerns.[9] This adoption of a nonbiblical worldview that
marginalizes or excludes the supernatural is corrected by the spiritual warfare
model's emphasis upon the impact of the supernatural in the natural world,
especially with regard to deception.

Despite these strengths, however, this model has serious weaknesses. One
major concern is that the spiritual warfare advocated by this model does not
reflect a biblical worldview. It overstates the influence of the demonic and
often resembles a form of cosmic dualism.[10] This deficiency notwithstanding,
a number of evangelicals have read Peretti's popular works of Christian fiction and used them as practical handbooks for instruction on spiritual warfare issues. An unfortunate result of the application of the spiritual warfare
model to adherents of new religions has been either the retreat of Christians
into their prayer closets to pray away demonic strongholds, or the demonization
of individuals, which curses the darkness but puts little emphasis upon proclaiming the light of the gospel or social involvement in combating evil. We
dare not neglect a response to new religions that incorporates a biblically informed approach to spiritual warfare (Ephesians 6:10–18), but we must exercise a more responsible use of it.[11]

---

9. Paul G. Hiebert, *Anthropological Reflections on Missiological Issues* (Grand Rapids: Baker,
1994), 189–201.
10. Ibid., 203–15. See also Paul G. Hiebert, "Spiritual Warfare and Worldviews," *Direction* 29,
no. 2 (fall 2000): 114–24, retrieved 3 January 2003 from http://www.directionjournal.org/
article/?1052.
11. Lausanne Committee for World Evangelization, *Deliver Us from Evil Consultation* (August
2000); cited at www.gospelcom.net/lcwe/dufe/Papers/dufeeng.htm (29 April 2003).

Former Member Testimonies

The third evangelical response to new religions that Johnson categorized is the personal testimonies model. In this approach, former members of new religions who have converted to Christian faith present the stories of their involvement in alternative spiritualities and their subsequent conversion.[12]

On the positive side, many individuals have been encouraged by the use of testimonies. We might explore how the incorporation of testimonies into a missions strategy might provide the missionary with another tool to touch the human heart in communicating the gospel.

Despite this positive consideration, however, the use of the former member testimony as the primary element of a paradigm for reaching adherents of new religions is cast into doubt by the tendency of former members to reflect in a largely negative fashion about their experiences in new religions. Without dismissing the validity of former member testimonies, it should be noted that, through exposure to other tales of negative "cult" experiences, individuals over time might unconsciously skew their understanding of their involvement with a new religion in a manner that may not accurately reflect upon the totality of their experiences.

In addition, several high-profile testimonies have been called into question.[13] Entire ministries have been built upon fraudulent testimonies of alleged former Satanists, Wiccans, and new religionists and have been all too readily accepted by an often less than discerning evangelical public. We might also remember that former member testimonies are a two-edged sword. For every testimony of a former non-Christian who converts to Christianity, we can find similar testimonies of former Christians who have converted to new religions, and also to atheism. Given the strength as well as the drawbacks of this approach, it seems best suited as a form of inspirational literature in confirming the faith of Christians. As such, it does not lend itself well to serving as the major component of an evangelistic model.

---

12. Mike Warnke, *The Satan Seller* (Plainfield, N.J.: Logos International, 1972); Edmond C. Gruss, *We Left Jehovah's Witnesses: A Non-Prophet Organization* (Phillipsburg, N.J.: Presbyterian and Reformed, 1976); Latayne Colvette Scott, *The Mormon Mirage* (Grand Rapids: Zondervan, 1979); Johanna Michaelsen, *The Beautiful Side of Evil* (Eugene, Ore.: Harvest House, 1982); and Rebecca Brown, *He Came to Set the Captives Free* (Chino, Calif.: Chick Publications, 1986).

13. Mike Hertenstein and Jon Trott, *Selling Satan: The Evangelical Media and the Mike Warnke Scandal* (Chicago: Cornerstone Press, 1993).

Cultural Apologetics

This apologetic approach refers to the model of cultural engagement developed by evangelist Francis Schaeffer and the L'Abri Fellowship, and its continuing use in the work of Os Guinness and Vishal Mangalwadi.[14] The basic thrust of this model is an acknowledgment of the cultural crisis that has arisen with the downfall of modernity in the West coupled with the influence of Eastern mysticism, and an evangelical response that involves a presentation of the meaninglessness of life in the absence of Christian presuppositions about the world.

A major drawback to this model is that it asks non-Christians to adopt Western Christian concerns for rationalism and logical consistency, and to cast their own worldview presuppositions aside while "trying on" the Christian worldview by means of comparison. Adherents of non-Christian worldviews are unlikely to be persuaded of the need to abandon their conceptions of reality, even if momentarily, and to adopt Christian presuppositions, especially with an eye toward critique of their own worldview. Rather than presenting a series of questions to the seeker to be addressed within a Christian framework of understanding, more fruitful methodologies might be receptor-oriented and begin with the adherent of an alternative spirituality and their frame of reference. Once the Christian is ministering from this perspective, the gospel can be communicated in culturally meaningful ways through points of contact with the Christian worldview.[15]

We might also consider that although worldview rationality and consistency are concerns of Western Christian theology and apologetics, oftentimes these concerns are not as widely held outside of our immediate cultural and spiritual context. While not denying the need for criteria of truth and the validity of apologetics,[16] Harold Netland reminds us that, even in our own camp, "Christian leaders in the non-Western world are becoming increasingly critical of theology as it has been conducted in the West."[17] Netland encourages

---

14. Os Guinness, *The Dust of Death: The Sixties Counterculture and How It Changed America Forever* (Wheaton, Ill.: Crossway Books, 1994); and Vishal Mangalwadi, *When the New Age Gets Old: Looking for a Greater Spirituality* (Downers Grove, Ill.: InterVarsity, 1992).
15. John G. Stackhouse Jr., *Humble Apologetics* (Oxford: Oxford University Press, 2002), 142–44.
16. Harold Netland, *Encountering Religious Pluralism: The Challenge to Christian Faith and Mission* (Downers Grove, Ill.: InterVarsity, 2001), 181–211, 247–83.
17. Harold Netland, "Toward Contextualized Apologetics," *Missiology* 16, no. 3 (July 1988): 289–90.

evangelicals to develop culturally appropriate apologetic strategies that will be effective in non-Western contexts. We might also consider the cultural appropriateness of our apologetic and missions strategies in the context of new religions.

Behavioralist Apologetics

A significant number of individuals in counter-cult ministry utilize a behavioralist apologetic approach. This model adopts a version of mind control (formerly called *brainwashing* but now also referred to variously as *thought reform* or *coercive persuasion*) as an explanation for conversion to new religions.[18]

The brainwashing hypothesis was put forward in the 1950s by Edward Hunter[19] and was picked up later in that decade by British psychiatrist William Sargent.[20] Robert Jay Lifton refuted Hunter and Sargent's thesis, but he put forward his own ideas about mind control that were adopted after the Patty Hearst trial in the late 1970s by a grassroots network of parents and former members of new religions, which eventually became the secular anticult movement.[21] This framework for understanding conversion and retention of members in new religions was eventually adopted by many evangelicals in the counter-cult community.[22] The main thrust of the current mind-control paradigm as understood by evangelicals is that certain new religions use intensified forms of traditional methods of persuasion, as well as nontraditional forms involving elements such as sleep deprivation, modification of diet, and worldview indoctrination, with the end result being a diminished capacity on

18. Expositions of mind control that have influenced evangelicals include Robert Jay Lifton, *Thought Reform and the Psychology of Totalism* (Chapel Hill, N.C.: University of North Carolina Press, 1989); Steven Hassan, *Combating Cult Mind Control* (Rochester, Vt.: Park Street Press, 1990); and Margaret Thaler Singer with Janja Lalich, *Cults in Our Midst: The Hidden Menace in Our Everyday Lives* (San Francisco: Jossey-Bass Publishers, 1995).
19. Edward Hunter, *Brainwashing in Red China* (New York: Vanguard Press, 1951).
20. William Sargant, *The Battle for the Mind: How Evangelists, Psychiatrists, Politicians, and Medicine Men Can Change Your Beliefs and Behavior* (Garden City, N.Y.: Doubleday, 1957).
21. J. Gordon Melton, "Brainwashing and the Cults: The Rise and Fall of a Theory." An Introduction to the forthcoming book *The Brainwashing Controversy: An Anthology of Essential Documents*, ed. J. Gordon Melton and Massimo Introvigne, retrieved 3 January 2003 from www.cesnur.org/testi/melton.htm.
22. Examples of evangelicals who accept the mind-control paradigm and have written books touching on the topic include Ronald M. Enroth, *Youth, Brainwashing and the Extremist Cults* (Grand Rapids: Zondervan, 1977); and Paul R. Martin, *Cult Proofing Your Kids* (Grand Rapids: Zondervan, 1993).

the part of an individual to make an informed choice as to membership or continued membership in a new religion. The remedy for this situation is to provide voluntary exit counseling to counter the effects of mind control, followed by a presentation of the gospel.

The mind-control issue has been the subject of much debate in evangelical circles. It is not my intention in this chapter to prove or disprove the existence of mind control, but its apparent assumption of a materialist anthropology, as well as its reductionism in explaining all religious experience, including Christian conversion, as a response to psychological and possibly physiological manipulation, may provide reasons for reassessing the widespread acceptance of this model among evangelicals. Given the disagreement in the evangelical community over the very existence of mind control, and the ability of Christian missions to successfully evangelize adherents of various religious movements throughout history without reference to the theory, the behavioralist apologetic seems inadequate as an effective model for responding to new religions in general.[23]

Heresy–Rationalist Apologetics

By far, the heresy–rationalist apologetic has been the dominant model used by the counter-cult community for responding to new religions. This approach was exemplified in Walter Martin's ministry, which was influential in spawning numerous "cult apologetics" organizations. This model begins with Protestant biblical orthodoxy on doctrines such as the nature of God, Christology, and soteriology, and then compares the orthodox understanding of these doctrines with the beliefs of various new religions. In this comparison, the heretical nature of the doctrine of new religions is noted, and a biblical refutation is offered. This refutation of heresy is often accompanied by an examination of the logical consistency of the new religions with an emphasis placed upon the rational consistency of the Christian worldview by way of contrast.

There are important strengths in this model. Christian apologists recognize the Bible's frequent warnings about false prophets and false teaching (Mat-

---

23. For evangelical critiques of mind control see Alan W. Gomes, *Unmasking the Cults* (Grand Rapids: Zondervan, 1995), 50–80; and Bob Passantino and Gretchen Passantino, "Critiquing Cult Mind-Control Model," *Kingdom of the Cults,* ed. Walter Martin, rev. ed. (Minneapolis: Bethany House, 1997), 49–78. An introduction to the mind-control debate from a secular perspective can be found in David G. Bromley and James T. Richardson, eds., *The Brainwashing/Deprogramming Controversy* (Greenwich, Conn.: JAI Press, 1993).

thew 7:15; 2 Peter 2:1). In our age of radical religious pluralism and competing truth claims, many times presented in the guise of Christianity, the church
needs to guard itself against false teaching, and to help Christians discern between truth and error. Christians need to follow the biblical admonition to
provide reasons for their faith with "gentleness and respect" (1 Peter 3:15).
The defense of the gospel and doctrinal orthodoxy has been an important
apologetic and theological task for the church that must continue.[24] In consideration of the positive benefits of the heresy–rationalist apologetic, we should
also remember that a number of individuals have found this method helpful
as they made their exit from new religions and into Christianity.

However, like the previous models we have examined, the heresy–rationalist
apologetic has its drawbacks. Given the widespread use of this model among
most, but not all, of counter-cult community, these limitations are worthy of
consideration and reflection. First, the model appears to be built upon biblical
texts that emphasize the need for guarding biblical orthodoxy but does not
also consider other passages that demonstrate examples of evangelism and
dialogue in interreligious contexts. The result is an imbalance of apologetics
over evangelism, producing a methodology that is largely polemical rather
than evangelistic in nature. In addition to the biblical texts warning of false
prophets and false teaching that are often appealed to by counter-cult
apologists,[25] we might also consider biblical examples of engagement with non-
Christian religionists such as Jesus' dialogue with the Samaritan woman (John
4:4–42), Paul and Barnabas's encounter with pagans at Lystra (Acts 14:8–18),
and the classic missions text demonstrating Paul's apologetic contextualization
of the gospel for sophisticated pagans at Athens (Acts 17:16–34).[26] Given the
very different perspectives and methodologies inferred from the biblical data
by the counter-cult community and missiologists, an evangelical reassessment
of the biblical texts that inform the encounter with new religions seems in
order.

A second drawback is that, although the heresy–rationalist model confirms
the faith of the Christian and so is valuable to identify orthodoxy and heresy

---

24. F. F. Bruce, *The Defense of the Gospel in the New Testament* (Grand Rapids: Eerdmans, 1977).

25. For example, Matthew 7:15; Acts 20:26–32; 2 Peter 2:1–3; 1 John 4:1–3.

26. See Stephen Rost's essay, "Paul's Areopagus Speech in Acts 17," chapter 5 in this book. Cf.
J. Daryl Charles, "Engaging the (Neo) Pagan Mind: Paul's Encounter with Athenian Culture
as a Model for Cultural Apologetics (Acts 17:16–34)," *Trinity Journal* 16NS (1995): 47–62;
and Dean Flemming, "Contextualizing the Gospel in Athens: Paul's Areopagus Address as a
Paradigm for Missionary Communication," *Missiology* 30, no. 2 (April 2001): 199–214.

in the church, it does little to communicate the gospel to adherents of new religions. Though many Christians have come to understand their faith more clearly in comparison with contemporary heresies by the use of this model, its speaker-centered evangelical orientation does not effectively communicate the gospel to adherents of new religions in terms that they can understand. Given the strengths of the heresy–rationalist model, it has demonstrated its effectiveness in speaking to the evangelical need for worldview delineation and preservation, rather than serving primarily as an evangelistic model.

THE MARGINALIZATION OF THE COUNTER-CULT MOVEMENT

Much good has been done in segments of the counter-cult community. Nevertheless, in the opinion of several observers, the overall response by the counter-cult to the new religions could be greatly improved.[27] Perceptions of the new religions as merely fringe phenomena resulted in a marginalization of the counter-cult community that responded to them. In effect, the counter-cult response to what was perceived as the religious fringe relegated the counter-cult to the fringes of the evangelical subculture. As far back as 1985, Gordon Melton commented on this situation:

> Unfortunately, the development of ministries to what are perceived as marginal religious groups has tended to marginalize the ministries as well, and has delayed the recognition and acceptance by both mainline and evangelical denominations of the need for missions strategy toward Eastern-metaphysical and occult religion in the West.
>
> Small, poorly funded, marginalized counter-cult ministries have had and can hope but to have minimal overall impact upon the continued growth and spread of the alternative faiths. In the face of this significant cultural phenomena, the small ministries must be content with occasional and individual converts and divert a high percentage

---

27. Philip Johnson, "The Aquarian Age and Apologetics," *Lutheran Theological Journal* 34, no. 2 (December 1997): 51–60; Gordon R. Lewis, "Our Mission Responsibility to New Religious Movements," *International Journal of Frontier Missions* 15, no. 3 (1998): 115–23; Everett Shropshire and John Morehead, "Hidden in Plain Sight: The Mission Challenge of New Religions Movements," *International Journal of Frontier Missions* 15, no. 3 (1998): 141–46; and J. Gordon Melton, "Emerging Religious Movements in North America," *Missiology* 28, no. 1 (January 2000): 85–98.

of their time away from ministry to fund-raising and survival. Churches assign such ministries a low priority when judged by the enormity of other perceived world missions needs.[28]

Some may simply dismiss Melton's characterization of the counter-cult as marginalized, but others have shared this perception. Writing in a special issue of the *International Journal of Frontier Missions* on new religions, Bryce Pettit shared his concerns about evangelical responses to new religions in the North American context:[29]

Christian responses to the burgeoning growth of [new religious movements] have been weak and ineffective. Most counter-cult ministries are absorbed with fund raising simply to remain active. Except for a few older and more visible organizations . . . , counter-cult groups have remained small and concentrated within the United States. Resources in languages other than English have been scarce, and are usually translations of older English works. In some areas this is beginning to change, but the need to go beyond the more highly visible groups such as the LDS church to indigenous groups who have never been analyzed is growing rapidly. Denominational responses to [new religious movements] have generally been apathetic.[30]

Despite the global nature of new religions on the mission fields of the world, the American counter-cult community that responds to new religions hovers on the fringes of evangelicalism. Much of the work of the counter-cult movement is unknown in the broader evangelical world—and when it is known, much of the time it is not viewed positively. Only a very small segment of the

28. Ronald Enroth and J. Gordon Melton, *Why Cults Succeed Where the Church Fails* (Elgin: Brethren Press, 1985), 130–31.
29. In Europe the response to new religions by evangelicals is somewhat different. There a number of Christian ministries blend theological critique with a missions-based paradigm. These sorts of ministries seek to engage in a dialogical witness with adherents in the marketplace—such as in New Spirituality festivals, at ashrams and at temples. Some of the best known examples are the Dialog Center International (Denmark), IKON (Denmark), In the Master's Light (Denmark), the Evangelical Centre for the Study of Worldview Questions (Germany), Emmaus (Norway), and Brommadialogen (Sweden). Thanks to Philip Johnson and Ole Skjerbaek Madsen for suggestions on this clarification.
30. Bryce A. Pettit, "New Religious Movements and Missions: An Historical Overview," *International Journal of Frontier Missions* 15, no. 3 (July–September 1998): 130.

evangelical church supports the work of the counter-cult, and as a result, ministries responding to the new religions come and go, and most of those that have been fortunate enough to be in existence for an extended period of time find themselves in a constant struggle for continued financial survival.

WORLD RELIGIONS AND NEW RELIGIONS: CONTRASTING METHODOLOGIES OF MISSIONS VERSUS REFUTATION

Undoubtedly there are many factors that contribute to the marginalization of the counter-cult movement. The evangelical subculture is itself marginalized in a religiously pluralized culture, and the influence of postmodernism on evangelicalism has lessened the emphasis on rationality and doctrinal acumen, two important emphases of the counter-cult movement. Another factor in the marginalization of the counter-cult is the common perceptions of its work as negative and confrontational. Thus the counter-cult may be unknowingly contributing to its own marginalization, at least in part due to its self-identity wherein the refutation of heresy is the *primary* reason for existence, rather than a more balanced approach that incorporates an important apologetic element, with evangelism as the primary concern.

Commenting on the counter-cult tendency to focus on apologetic refutation rather than evangelism, Gordon Melton observed that

> The counter-cult approach originated as an evangelism effort, but with that proving unfruitful, counter-cult spokespersons have now redefined their work as apologists and limited their public activity to boundary maintenance for the evangelical community.[31]

A survey of counter-cult activity reveals that Melton's observation is largely accurate, although the redefinition of the majority of counter-cult ministry from evangelism to apologetics of which he speaks should probably be understood as having taken place unconsciously. The counter-cult community does engage in evangelistic activity, but in general their primary emphasis is theological boundary maintenance, and the evangelistic emphasis often involves heavy apologetic content, drawing upon the heresy–rationalist model.

Readers familiar with the history of missions may already have noted the radically different approaches evangelicals have taken to world religions as com-

---

31. Melton, "Emerging Religious Movements in North America," 93–94.

pared to new religions. When ministering among Buddhists, Muslims, or tribal peoples, for example, evangelical missionaries endeavor to understand the culture in which they will minister, noting the language, customs, and worldview. Having completed this important study, the missionaries then pursue an incarnational ministry in the culture they seek to reach, and frame the gospel in an appropriate context so that non-Christian religionists can understand it. While missionaries in this context will be careful to identify and confront those elements of the non-Christian worldview and doctrine that are in conflict with the gospel, they also take care to identify those areas that are not in conflict. Missionaries among the world religions do not *major* on heresy refutation or worldview annihilation. Instead, they work to understand world religions within the cultural framework in which they are embedded and to present a holistic response that is missiologically oriented and communicates effectively.[32]

By contrast, counter-cult methods, operating from a more defensive and reactionary posture, particularly in relation to Bible-based new religions, tends to view new religions primarily as heretical systems in need of refutation. Broader elements of a new religion's culture, worldview, and epistemology are rarely considered. Ruth Tucker comments on this contrast:

> In cross-cultural evangelism overseas, missionaries are admonished not to ridicule other religious beliefs or practices. When a missionary visits a sacred shrine where shoes are to be left at the door, it would be unconscionable to defy the custom. Yet, these "cross-cultural" courtesies are often blatantly ignored when they pertain to situations within our own culture. We often ridicule or mock the unorthodox religious beliefs of people in our own communities, because *cultists* do not deserve respect.[33]

Perhaps it will be helpful to consider a specific example of the use of the heresy–rationalist apologetic in order to better understand its evangelistic shortcomings in contrast with cross-cultural missions.

---

32. This is not always the case with evangelical missions to world religions. H. L. Richard has outlined five evangelical approaches to Hindus that closely parallel evangelical responses to new religions. H. L. Richard, "Evangelical Approaches to Hindus," *Missiology* 29, no. 3 (2001): 307–16. He argues that the prevalent emphasis by evangelicals upon worldview confrontation has resulted in little evangelistic success among Hindu peoples.

33. Ruth A. Tucker, *Another Gospel: Cults, Alternative Religions and the New Age Movement* (Grand Rapids: Zondervan, 1989), 11–12 (emphasis in original).

In their encounters with Latter-day Saints (LDS), evangelicals typically engage them in a discussion of various doctrines such as the nature of God. The evangelicals argue for the existence of one eternal God, whereas the Latter-day Saints argue for the potential of human beings to progress to deification. Both sides may argue their positions based on biblical texts. This dialogue is essentially a hermeneutical battle, with the evangelicals attempting to point out the heretical nature of LDS teaching. With the utilization of this methodology, however, evangelicals rarely move beyond the refutation of heresy, and the conceptualization of Mormonism as primarily a heretical system prevents evangelicals from considering other key factors, such as LDS epistemology and anthropology. In the LDS epistemological framework, personal feelings are primary, rather than fidelity to Protestant biblical orthodoxy.[34] And LDS anthropology conceives of humanity as the same kind of being as God; thus, for evangelicals to question the LDS concept of God threatens the Mormons' very conception of themselves as human beings.[35]

Considerations of heresy and an appropriate apologetic response are important in addressing Latter-day Saints in certain contexts. However, more often than not, the end result of an emphasis upon these facets in evangelistic dialogue is that evangelicals defend biblical orthodoxy while Latter-day Saints become personally offended in the process of defending their "restored" faith. Through this apologetic encounter, the Latter-day Saints never have an opportunity to hear the gospel presented in a culturally meaningful way.

We acknowledge the continuing validity of preserving truth versus error, and the use of apologetics in the evangelical encounter with new religions, but in our contrast of cross-cultural missions methodology with the heresy–rationalist approach, it would seem that the counter-cult model's emphasis upon defending orthodoxy makes it better suited to an internal monologue within the church—supporting an important function in defining and maintaining theological boundaries—rather than an evangelistic methodology.

---

34. Dennis B. Neuenschwander, "Knowing What You Believe, Believing What You Know," *The Ensign*, September 2002, 20–25.
35. For a helpful discussion of these points see John L. Bracht, "Mormonism: The Search for a Personal God" (master's thesis, University of Sydney, 1988). See also his essay "The Americanization of Adam," in *Cargo Cults and Millenarian Movements: Transoceanic Comparisons of New Religious Movements*, ed. G. W. Trompf (Berlin: Mouton de Gruyter, 1990), 97–141.

CHARTING A WAY FORWARD

Despite the necessary function of theological boundary maintenance that the heresy–rationalist model facilitates, the use of this model as the dominant approach of the counter-cult community has been largely unsuccessful when applied evangelistically to adherents of new religions. Success is defined as the ability of a model to conform to the balance of biblical passages that exemplify not only the defense of the gospel, but also the communication of the gospel in terms the respondent can understand. The biblical example of receptor-oriented communication is confirmed by communication theory as practically demonstrated and applied in missiology. The heresy–rationalist model's failure to conform to the biblical model for cross-cultural communication of the gospel necessitates that we chart a new way forward for success in evangelistic persuasion.

The apostle Paul described his evangelistic ministry not only as proclamation, but also as a form of persuading men and women of the truthfulness of the gospel (2 Corinthians 5:11). In the fourth century b.c., Aristotle described a process of effective persuasion that involved three elements.[36] He defined the elements of persuasion as the *logos*—the argument used by the speaker; the *ethos*—the character of the speaker; and the *pathos*—the disposition created in the hearer by the speaker.[37] As we consider charting a new way forward in response to new religions, we will follow Aristotle's threefold division as basic headings, beginning with the second of Aristotle's elements, the character of the speaker.

The Character of the Evangelical Speaker

Representation of the New Religions

The character of evangelicals is many times called into question in their representation of the new religions. Evangelicals have not always been as careful or charitable as they should be in understanding or representing the views

---

36. Aristotle, *On Rhethoric: A Theory of Civil Discourse,* trans. George A. Kennedy (New York: Oxford University Press, 1991).
37. Christopher Carey, "Rhetorical Means of Persuasion," in *Persuasion: Greek Rhetoric in Action,* ed. Ian Worthington (London: Routledge, 1994), 26–45; and Wayne N. Thompson, *The Process of Persuasion: Principles and Readings* (New York: Harper and Row, 1975).

of various religious movements. Two examples will illustrate this. First, concerns have been raised about popular treatments of New Age spirituality. Irving Hexham and Karla Poewe have discussed the frequent reductionism of the New Age worldview in popular evangelical counter-cult treatments.[38] This formulaic reductionism tends to portray New Age spirituality as essentially monism, pantheism, and relativism, coming primarily from the influence of Advaita Vedanta Hinduism. Yet other important and perhaps more widely held notions—such as panentheism, and the influences of Western esotericism, hermeticism, and neo-Gnosticism—are rarely considered. In our second example, concern has been expressed about evangelicals and their understanding and representation of, and response to, the diverse and complex beliefs of the Church of Jesus Christ of Latter-day Saints. Carl Mosser and Paul Owen ignited a firestorm of controversy in the counter-cult community when they raised concerns about the evangelical awareness of LDS minimalist or neo-orthodox theology, as well as the quality of evangelical responses to LDS scholarship and apologetic arguments.[39] Douglas Cowan, a secular critic, has been even more scathing in his critique of the counter-cult in general.[40]

If understanding indeed precedes criticism, then evangelicals would do well to exercise more care in their understanding and representation of the new religions. Too often it seems that evangelicals criticize before really understanding the objects of their criticism. A more careful understanding and representation of the diversity and complexity of new religions would involve a review of primary sources, interaction with the best of evangelical and nonevangelical scholarship, and peer review of the results of research and conclusions.

Humility and Empathy

In addition to more careful representation of the new religions, evangelicals might also reassess their humility in ministry and their empathy for those in

---

38. Irving Hexham and Karla Poewe, *New Religions as Global Cultures* (Boulder, Colo.: Westview, 1997), 4–6. Cf. Irving Hexham, "The Evangelical Response to the New Age," in *Perspectives on the New Age*, ed. James R. Lewis and J. Gordon Melton (Albany: State University of New York Press, 1992).

39. Carl Mosser and Paul Owen, "Mormon Scholarship, Apologetics and Evangelical Neglect: Losing the Battle and Not Knowing It?" *Trinity Journal* 19 n.s. (Fall 1998): 179–205.

40. Douglas E. Cowan, "Bearing False Witness: Propaganda, Reality Maintenance and Christian Anticult Apologetics" (Ph.D. thesis, University of Calgary, 1999). Cowan modified his thesis and released it in the book *Bearing False Witness: An Introduction to the Christian Countercult* (Westport, Conn.: Greenwood Publishing Group, 2003).

new religions. Given the frequently confrontational and uncharitable nature of the relationship between evangelicals and adherents of the new religions, we might ask ourselves whether in our zeal for truth we have been caught up in a crusade against "destructive cults" or whether we genuinely love adherents of new religions and seek to communicate Christ to them. This reminder of the need for humility is important, because as missionary statesman David Hesselgrave tells us, we must "remember that although missionaries have been commanded by Christ to preach the gospel, they cannot command a hearing. *They must win a hearing by demonstrating that they are people of integrity, credibility, and goodwill.*"[41]

Further, Christopher Partridge has noted the changing religio-cultural landscape of the West and the resulting missiological implications for the church. He concluded that, "generally speaking, when communicating the Christian faith in the West, confrontational evangelism, rationalist apologetics, and dogmatically expressed exclusivist theologies are inappropriate. Rather, what needs to be appreciated is the value of genuine friendship, humility regarding one's knowledge of another's worldview, and a palpable desire to understand."[42]

Self-Identity

The counter-cult community might also consider reassessing its self-identity. As previously noted, the counter-cult community defines itself primarily in a negative way, largely in terms of refuting doctrinal error. But this self-identity is inadequate. Gordon Lewis, a major figure in the counter-cult community makes the following observation:

> The connotation of "countercult" is too negative to represent missionary's loving outreach to unreached people in need of the good news of God's grace. It is not enough for evangelical leaders primarily to react against non-Christian religious worldviews, epistemologies and ethics. We need to present a better way. Missions to Muslims would not call themselves CounterMuslims. This plays into the hands of those

---

41. David J. Hesselgrave, *Communicating Christ Cross-Culturally,* 2d ed. (Grand Rapids: Zondervan, 1991), 146–47 (emphasis in original).
42. Christopher Partridge, "The Disenchantment and Re-enchantment of the West: The Religio-Cultural Context of Contemporary Western Christianity," *Evangelical Quarterly* 74, no. 3 (2002): 251.

who dismiss any, even well-reasoned refutation of their views, as anti-Mormon, anti-Muslim, etc.[43]

Lewis goes on to describe a new and more promising self-identity for the counter-cult community:

> Evangelical ministers to [new religious movements] will remain alive and well insofar as they change their primary identity from mere counter cult agents to missionaries—frontier type missionaries to unreached people in alternative religions and cults.[44]

Counter-cult ministries must work with other segments of evangelicalism to rethink their collective identity and purpose. Rather than a defensive and reactionary identity, this new identity must be positive and thought of in terms of frontier missionary activity.

The Perceptions of Our Hearers

Another of Aristotle's elements of effective persuasion is the disposition created by the speaker in the hearer. In this regard, evangelicals committed to reaching adherents of new religions might consider the language used to describe these groups in writing and presentations (and sometimes in dialogue with their adherents), and the attendant perceptions that are created in the minds of the hearers they seek to reach. Counter-cult literature frequently uses the term *cult* to refer to the new religions. No matter how carefully such terms are defined theologically, the fact remains that adherents of new religions consider such terminology pejorative. Unfortunately, the characterization of new religions does not stop with pejorative language but many times also carries over into the general tenor of many (but not all) evangelical treatments of new religions. James Sire writes:

> So many Christian books on alternative religions are often so bitter, even nasty in tone. Cult leaders and followers alike are held up to ridicule as stupid, perverted, demonic, satanic, beneath contempt. Some

43. Gordon R. Lewis, *International Journal of Frontier Missions* 15, no. 3 (July–September 1998): 116.
44. Ibid., 118.

Christian writers seem to be at a fever pitch when they draft their books, articles and tracts.

A siege mentality is at work. Those who hold cultic ideas are seen as the enemy, the great threat to humanity, to Christians, even, some seem to suggest, to God himself. Like Satan they are "like a roaring lion, seeking some one to devour"(1 Peter 5:8). So in response anything goes: innuendo, name-calling, backhanded remarks, assumption of the worst motives on the part of the cult believers. And thus the Christian dehumanizes the enemy and shoots him like a dog.[45]

If our primary goal is not merely to apply a label for the Christian community, but also to persuasively communicate the gospel to the new religions, then we must consider how our terminology and tone are perceived by those we hope to persuade on behalf of Christ.

The Message Proclaimed

Aristotle's final element of effective persuasion is the message. It is in this area that the counter-cult community has devoted most of its energies in the form of the heresy–rationalist apologetic. Yet we have seen that this model, while providing an important definitional and defensive function for theological boundary maintenance, has not translated well into an evangelistic methodology in reaching new religions. If a successful methodology is defined in terms of how much truth is not only defended, but also proclaimed and understood by the receptor, then we must explore the creation of a new framework for not only understanding, but also evangelizing new religions. Here missiology can provide an excellent example for evangelicals in developing an interdisciplinary approach to new religions. Michael Pocock informs us that "missiology is not simply *informed* by other scientific disciplines. It is by definition inclusive of the sciences. It is a discipline itself wherein theology; missionary experience; and the methods and insights of anthropology, sociology, psychology, communications, linguistics, demography, geography, and statistics are brought together for understanding and advancing the missionary enterprise."[46]

45. James W. Sire, *Scripture Twisting* (Downers Grove, Ill.: InterVarsity, 1980), 18.
46. Michael Pocock, "Introduction: An Appeal for Balance," *Missiology and the Social Sciences* (Pasadena, Calif.: William Carey Library, 1996), 10.

Gailyn Van Rheenen also discusses the interdisciplinary nature of missiology with the illustration of a spiral of strands united together from various disciplines. He calls this spiral the "missional helix":

> The missional helix is a spiral because the missionary returns time and time again to reflect theologically, culturally, historically, and strategically in order to develop ministry models appropriate to the local context. Theology, social understandings, history of missions, and strategy all work together and interpenetrate each other.[47]

In response to the growing challenge of new religions, a holistic and multidisciplinary model is needed. This model will incorporate the strengths of the apologetic models noted above, including an emphasis upon apologetics and the need to contrast heresy with orthodoxy. But this new model must also interact not only with theology and apologetics, but also with cultural anthropology,[48] sociology,[49] communication theory, phenomenology, religious studies, patristic studies,[50] and other disciplines that rest upon the foundation of missiology. Missiology can be highly instructive in transforming evangelical responses to new religions. Consider three promising examples.

First, we might consider reframing our understanding of new religions as distinct religious or spiritual cultures rather than as heretical systems or cults. While not neglecting the heretical doctrine of some of the new religious movements, more positive results might be seen on the mission field if we rethink our long-held assumptions. The notion that new religions constitute spiritual cultures or unreached people groups is not new. In June 1980, the Lausanne

---

47. Gailyn Van Rheenen, "From Theology to Practice: The Helix Metaphor," Monthly Missiological Reflection #25. Retrieved 9 January 2003, from www.missiology.org/MMR/mmr25.htm.
48. "In missions we must study the Scriptures *and also* the sociocultural context of the people we serve, so that we can communicate the gospel to them in ways they understand." Paul G. Hiebert, *Anthropological Reflections on Missiological Issues* (Grand Rapids: Baker, 1994), 10.
49. While the missions community struggles with the possibility that missiology has embraced sociology uncritically (Edward Rommen and Gary Corwin, eds., *Missiology and the Social Sciences: Contributions, Cautions and Conclusions,* [Pasadena, Calif.: William Carey Library, 1996]), the counter-cult community has gone to the other extreme in largely ignoring or rejecting the discipline uncritically.
50. Fr. Brendan Pelphrey, "Using the Church Fathers in Response to Contemporary Heresy" (unpub. paper delivered at the annual conference of Evangelical Ministries to New Religions at Biola University, 25 January 2003).

Committee for World Evangelization sponsored the "Consultation on World Evangelization" in Pattaya, Thailand.[51] The purpose was to develop strategies for reaching unreached people groups. One of those groups was called "Mystics and Cultists," now referred to as new religious movements. The consultation formally recognized new religious movements as unreached people groups. In addition, Irving Hexham and Karla Poewe have put forward the idea that new religions should be understood as global cultures.[52] This conceptual framework will allow us to understand new religions in greater depth and to appreciate those aspects that make them increasingly attractive to growing numbers of people. By conceptualizing new religions as cultures or people groups, we can then understand the important cultural, social, theological, and apologetic considerations necessary to reach them. We can understand not only their heretical doctrine as it relates to our own, but also other important concerns, such as how their worldview allows them to interpret the world, and the foundational mythology that undergirds the group.[53] Reconceptualizing new religions, beyond heresy and more along the lines of spiritual cultures, will bring the evangelical response to new religions more in line with evangelical missionary responses to world religions in cross-cultural contexts.

Second, missiology will help in the process of presenting the gospel for the cultures of new religions in terms they can understand. In the heresy–rationalist model, the message presented to the new religions has been speaker-oriented, focusing on the apologists' cultural matrix and theological concerns, often to the neglect of the target culture of the new religionist. Missiology informs us that effective communication of the gospel is receptor-oriented and takes into account the cultural perspective of those hearing the gospel message. If we neglect this important consideration, we end up in a process of monologue where no genuine communication is taking place, and where the evangelical speaker assumes the message is being understood and rejected. After reflecting on New Testament examples of interreligious dialogue, David Hesselgrave concludes that "it is apparent that our Lord and Paul understood the religious

---

51. Lausanne Committee for World Evangelization, *Thailand Report on New Religious Movements: Report of the Consultation on World Evangelization Mini-Consultation on Reaching Mystics and Cultists* (1980), retrieved 26 September 2002 from www.gospelcom.net/lcwe/LOP/lop11.htm.
52. See Irving Hexham and Karla Poewe-Hexham's essay, "New Religions as Global Cultures," chapter 4 in this book. Cf. Irving Hexham and Karla Poewe, *New Religions as Global Cultures* (Boulder, Colo.: Westview Press, 1997).
53. Ibid., 97–98.

systems of their respondents and adapted to them. For altogether too long, evangelical missionary communication has been monological because of lack of this understanding."[54]

The process of communicating the gospel in receptor-oriented fashion is known as *contextualization*. Contextualization has been defined by David Hesselgrave and Edward Rommen as "the attempt to communicate the message of the person, works, Word, and will of God in a way that is faithful to God's revelation, especially as put forth in the teachings of Holy Scripture, and that is meaningful to respondents in their respective cultural and existential contexts."[55] It is beyond question that contextualization is a biblical concept. The Scriptures provide examples of it in the ministry of our Lord Jesus and the apostles (1 Corinthians 9:20–22).[56] Out of fear of compromising the gospel, some counter-cultists have raised concerns about contextualization as applied to new religions. We should be cautious and recognize that the church has approached contextualization in a variety of ways, including what might be understood as an uncritical emphasis upon the cultural context without consideration of the supracultural truths of the gospel. This approach can indeed lead to syncretism. But though this represents one extreme in contextualization, some conservative evangelicals have tended to adopt another extreme in the form of a "gospel over context" position. This approach is so concerned with protecting sound doctrine that it tends to view any effort at communicating the gospel in culturally relevant ways as compromise.

But in contextualizing the gospel we need not utilize such polarizing extremes. Hesselgrave and Rommen note that models of contextualization comprise a spectrum from orthodox to liberal, and they endorse a form they refer to as "apostolic contextualization."[57] Although we must be careful to avoid the dangers of compromise and syncretism in proclaiming the gospel, missionaries working among new religions will seek to practice a form of contextualization that is "true to the complete authority and unadulterated message of the Bible on the one hand, and . . . related to the cultural, linguistic, and

---

54. David J. Hesselgrave, ed., "Dialogue with the Non-Christian Religions," in *Theology and Mission* (Grand Rapids: Baker, 1978), 237.
55. David J. Hesselgrave and Edward Rommen, *Contextualization: Meanings, Methods and Models* (Pasadena, Calif.: William Carey Library, 2000), 200.
56. See chapter 1 in this book, "The Incarnational Ministry of Jesus: An Alternative to Traditional Apologetic Approaches."
57. Hesselgrave and Rommen, *Contextualization: Meanings, Methods, and Models*, 148–49.

religious background of the respondents on the other."[58] In rethinking the contextualization issue, counter-cultists might also consider that noted apologist Norman Geisler has acknowledged the need to contextualize the Christian message by adjusting to the worldview of respondents.[59]

Missiology can provide us with promising tools that may prove helpful in evangelizing adherents of new religions. In addition to providing us with a new conceptual framework and the means to communicate the gospel in culturally meaningful ways, missiological literature contains tools that can be of assistance to those in ministry to new religions. Two examples will illustrate this. First, Geert Hofstede examined leadership concepts in differing cultures and identified four dimensions of cultural variability important in understanding intercultural communication.[60] Fuller Seminary's School of World Missions adapted and applied Hofstede's cultural-distance dimensions in missions contexts.[61] An exploration of this concept might be helpful in application to new religions as missionaries and apologists gauge the cultural distance between their worldviews and the new religions. The insights gleaned from this tool might prove helpful in understanding the degree and manner in which the gospel must be contextualized for the respondent and may help inform the level of apologetic content as well. Understanding cultural distance will provide important background information for formulating appropriate evangelistic strategies in differing contexts.

In our second example of promising missiological tools, James Engel put forward a model of the spiritual decision-making process now known as the "Engel Scale."[62] This scale runs the spectrum for the respondent from a minus eight (only an awareness of a Supreme Being but no knowledge of the gospel) to a post-conversion number of plus one (representing a mature disciple involved in stewardship and evangelism). The Engel Scale might prove helpful for missionaries working among new religions because it reminds Western

---

58. Ibid., xi.

59. Norman L. Geisler, "Some Philosophical Perspectives on Missionary Dialogue," in *Theology and Mission*, ed. David J. Hesselgrave, 243.

60. Geert Hofstede, *Culture's Consequences—International Differences in World Related Values*, abridged ed. (Beverly Hills, Calif.: Sage Publications, 1984).

61. Robert J. Clinton, "Crosscultural Use of Leadership Concepts," in *The Word Among Us: Contextualizing Theology for Mission Today*, ed. Dean S. Gilliland (Dallas: Word, 1989), 187–90.

62. James F. Engel and H. Wilbert Norton, *What's Gone Wrong with the Harvest? A Communication Strategy for the Church and World Evangelization* (Grand Rapids: Zondervan, 1975).

evangelicals who tend to be more program- and results-oriented that evangelism might be more profitably thought of as a process. With a process-oriented perspective, evangelicals might be more willing to invest in long-term relational evangelistic strategies rather than one-time, event-, or program-oriented approaches. In addition, the Engel Scale reminds us that individuals encompass a broad spectrum in their spiritual decision making, and this insight might help us transition from source-centered communication, whereby the gospel is communicated to new religionists primarily from the frame of reference and concerns of the evangelical source, to a receptor-oriented or "other-centered" approach. The use of the Engel Scale in this context would work well with contextualization of the gospel.

We should note that the missiological ideas discussed in this chapter are not merely theoretical. Some promising field-tested approaches have already been done involving a reconceptualization of new religions from the perspective of cross-cultural missions, wherein evangelical practitioners have developed contextualized missions models for sharing the gospel with new religionists. Many have been discussed in this volume, whereas other approaches, such as Anne Harper's approach to the Iglesia ni Cristo in the Philippines, are being used as well.[63] Additional research and experimentation done with this approach to new religions likely will lead to the development of additional contextualized missions strategies that may result in greater evangelistic fruitfulness.

CONCLUSION

The ideas shared in this chapter have not been well received in all quarters of the evangelical counter-cult community. Some have mistakenly assumed that we are calling for the abandonment of apologetics to new religions. This is not the case. New religious movements have gained a cross-cultural sophistication that has outpaced evangelical churches, and the church must develop both an academically rigorous apologetic *and* a culturally relevant evangelistic response. In our call for consideration of a new interdisciplinary model for responding to new religions, we are suggesting a blending of *both* missions and apologetics, with missions serving as the foundation of the model out of which apologetics springs.

---

63. Anne Harper, "The Iglesia ni Cristo and Evangelical Christianity," *Journal of Asian Mission* 3, no. 1 (2000): 101–19.

But here an important reminder is in order for Enlightenment influenced, rationalist oriented evangelicals. As we have seen, given the changing cultural landscape of the West, apologetics will have to be appropriately contextualized in order to be effective. As Partridge has noted: "The presentation of abstract theological constructs, the communication of systems of belief, and the refutation of other plausibility structures in the style of modernist apologetics, the methodology behind which was developed in a passing culture of disenchantment, simply lacks persuasive force."[64]

Our present situation demands that evangelicals be willing to step outside their comfort zones in order to be creative and daring in formulating strategies for the future. During the 1980s, Melton put forward exactly this challenge, and it remains valid in the twenty-first century.

> Leaders of the counter-cult ministries, and sympathetic evangelical and mainline church leaders, must pool their collective resources and develop a new strategy which will engage the whole church in mission and ministry to non-Christian religions in the West. It will be painful to abandon present counter-cult approaches. Yet only with a more comprehensive model, one which can mobilize the entire Christian community, can such ministries hope to achieve either a measurable impact on those currently affiliated with alternative religions, or have a voice in determining the coming necessary changes in public policy.[65]

STUDY QUESTIONS

1. Summarize in your own words the "heresy–rationalist" model for responding to new religions. Why do you think this model has been so popular among evangelicals?

2. Describe a contrast between evangelical methodologies in addressing world religions, and then compare that with new religions. What are the differences?

3. Why might the interdisciplinary nature of missiology be helpful to evangelicals in responding to new religions?

---

64. Partridge, "Disenchantment and Re-Enchantment of the West," 252. See also David Wilkinson, "The Art of Apologetics in the Twenty-first Century," *Anvil* 19, no. 1 (2002): 5–17.

65. Enroth and Melton, *Why Cults Succeed Where the Church Fails*, 131.

4. What does it mean to contextualize the gospel? How might this be help-ful in presenting the gospel to adherents of new religions?
5. How might evangelicals move beyond program- and event-based evan-gelistic methods to long-term incarnational and relationship-based evangelistic strategies to new religions?

RECOMMENDED READING LIST

Barker, Eileen. *New Religious Movements: A Practical Introduction.* London: Her Majesty's Stationary Office, 1989.

Bosch, David J. *Transforming Mission.* Maryknoll, N.Y.: Orbis, 1991.

Carson, D. A. *The Gagging of God.* Grand Rapids: Zondervan, 1996.

Chryssides, George D. *Exploring New Religions.* London: Cassell, 1999.

Clifford, Ross, and Philip Johnson. *Jesus and the Gods of the New Age: Communicating Christ in Today's Spiritual Supermarket.* Oxford: Lion, 2001.

Conn, Harvie M. *Eternal Word and Changing Worlds: Theology, Anthropology, and Mission in Trialogue.* Grand Rapids: Zondervan, 1984.

Corduan, Winfried. *Handmaid to Theology: An Essay in Philosophical Prolegomena.* Grand Rapids: Baker, 1981.

———. *A Tapestry of Faiths: The Common Threads Between Christianity and World Religions.* Downers Grove, Ill.: InterVarsity, 2002.

Cowan, Douglas E. *Bearing False Witness? An Introduction to the Christian Countercult.* Westport, Conn.: Praeger, 2003.

Dawson, Lorne L. *Comprehending Cults: The Sociology of New Religious Movements.* Toronto: Oxford University Press Canada, 1998.

Drane, John. *What Is the New Age Still Saying to the Church?* London: Marshall Pickering, 1999.

Drane, John, Ross Clifford, and Philip Johnson, *Beyond Prediction: The Tarot and Your Spirituality.* Oxford: Lion, 2001.

———. *Cultural Change and Biblical Faith.* Carlisle, England: Paternoster, 2000.

Gnanakan, Ken. *Kingdom Concerns: A Theology of Mission Today.* Leicester, England: Inter-Varsity, 1993.

Hesselgrave, David J., ed. *Dynamic Religious Movements*. Grand Rapids: Baker, 1978.

Hesselgrave, David J. *Communicating Christ Cross-Culturally*. 2d ed. Grand Rapids: Zondervan, 1991.

———. *Scripture and Strategy: The Use of the Bible in Postmodern Church and Mission*. Pasadena, Calif.: William Carey Library, 1994.

Hesselgrave, David J., and Edward Rommen. *Contextualization: Meanings, Methods and Models*. Pasadena, Calif.: William Carey Library, 2000.

Hexham, Irving. *Concise Dictionary of Religion*. Vancouver, B.C.: Regent College Press, 1998.

———. *Pocket Dictionary of New Religious Movements*. Downers Grove, Ill.: InterVarsity, 2002.

Hexham, Irving, and Karla Poewe. *New Religions as Global Cultures*. Boulder, Colo.: Westview, 1997.

———. *Understanding Cults and New Religions*. Vancouver, B.C.: Regent College Press, 1997.

Hiebert, Paul G. *Anthropological Reflections on Missiological Issues*. Grand Rapids: Baker, 1994.

Hiebert, Paul G., and Eloise Hiebert Meneses. *Incarnational Ministry: Planting Churches in Band, Tribal, Peasant, and Urban Societies*. Grand Rapids: Baker, 1995.

Hutton, Ronald. *The Triumph of the Moon*. Oxford: Oxford University Press, 1999.

Igleheart, Glenn A. *Church Members and Nontraditional Religious Groups*. Nashville: Broadman and Holman, 1985.

Jenkins, Philip. *Mystics and Messiahs: Cults and New Religions in American History*. New York: Oxford University Press, 2000.

Kaiser, Walter C., Jr. *Mission in the Old Testament: Israel as a Light to the Nations*. Grand Rapids: Baker, 2000.

Kraemer, Hendrik. *Why Christianity of All Religions?* Translated by Hubert Hoskins. Philadelphia: Westminster, 1962.

Kraft, Charles H. *Christianity in Culture*. Maryknoll, N.Y.: Orbis, 1979.

McDermott, Gerald R. *Can Evangelicals Learn from World Religions?* Downers Grove, Ill.: InterVarsity, 2000.

Muck, Terry C. *Those Other Religions in Your Neighborhood*. Grand Rapids: Zondervan, 1992.

Netland, Harold A. *Dissonant Voices: Religious Pluralism and the Question of Truth*. Grand Rapids: Eerdmans, 1991.

———. *Encountering Religious Pluralism: The Challenge to Christian Faith and Mission.* Downers Grove, Ill.: InterVarsity, 2001.

Newbigin, Lesslie. *The Gospel in a Pluralist Society.* Grand Rapids: Eerdmans, 1989.

———. *Foolishness to the Greeks: The Gospel and Western Culture.* Grand Rapids: Eerdmans, 1986.

Ostling, Richard, and Joan Ostling. *Mormon America: The Power and the Promise.* San Francisco: HarperSanFrancisco, 1999.

Perry, Edmund. *The Gospel in Dispute: The Relation of Christian Faith to Other Religions.* New York: Doubleday, 1956.

Phillips, Timothy, and Dennis L. Okholm, eds. *Christian Apologetics in the Postmodern World.* Downers Grove, Ill.: InterVarsity, 1995.

Redford, J. A. C. *Welcome All Wonders: A Composer's Journey.* Grand Rapids: Baker, 1997.

Richard, H. L. *Following Jesus in the Hindu Context: The Intriguing Implications of N. V. Tilak's Life and Thought.* Pasadena, Calif.: William Carey Library, 1998.

Robinson, Martin. *To Win the West.* Crowborough, England: Monarch, 1996.

Rommen, Edward, and Gary Corwin, eds. *Missiology and the Social Sciences: Contributions, Cautions and Conclusions.* Pasadena, Calif.: William Carey Library, 1996.

Rommen, Edward, and Harold Netland, eds. *Christianity and the Religions: A Biblical Theology of World Religions.* Pasadena, Calif.: William Carey Library, 1995.

Saliba, John A. *Understanding New Religious Movements.* Grand Rapids: Eerdmans, 1995.

Stackhouse, John G., Jr. *Humble Apologetics: Defending the Faith Today.* New York: Oxford University Press, 2002.

Terry, John Mark, Ebbie Smith, and Justice Anderson, eds. *Missiology: An Introduction to the Foundations, History, and Strategies of World Missions.* Nashville: Broadman and Holman, 1998.

Van Rheenen, Gailyn. *Communicating Christ in Animistic Contexts.* Pasadena, Calif.: William Carey Library, 1991.

———. *Missions: Biblical Foundations and Contemporary Strategies.* Grand Rapids: Zondervan, 1996.

Wilson, Bryan, and Jamie Cresswell, eds. *New Religious Movements: Challenge and Response.* London: Routledge, 1999.

Yong, Amos. *Beyond the Impasse: Toward a Pneumatological Theology of Religions.* Grand Rapids: Baker, 2003.

York, Michael. *The Emerging Network: A Sociology of the New Age and Neo-Pagan Movements.* Lanham, Md.: Rowman and Littlefield, 1955.

SCRIPTURE INDEX

SUBJECT INDEX

A

Aagaard, Johannes, 20–21, 195
Ad Gentes, 69n. 35
Adams, Marilyn McCord, 132
Aeschylus, 126–27
African Independent Church, 98,
    108–10
Age of Reason, The (Paine), 100
Albanese, Catherine, 263
Allen, Charlotte, 213
alternative medicine. *See*
    complementary medicine;
    aromatherapy
Althaus, Paul, 69
ama-Nazarite movement, 109–10
American Academy of Religion, 81n. 93
Andrew, John J., 180
anointing, 14, 271–73
"anonymous Christian," 123–24
anthropology, biblical, 121–23
Antipater, 133
apologetics, 113; applied, 133n. 68;
    behavioralist approach, 285–86;
    Christadelphian, 182–84; cultural
    284–85; definition of, 25n. 1; end-
    times model, 280–81; former
    member testimonies model, 283;
    heresy-rationalist model, 114, 161–
    62, 286–88; historical-legal

approach, 193–94; incarnational,
    202–5; mythic approach, 217;
    Pauline, 118–36; pure, 133n. 68;
    spiritual warfare model, 281–82;
    traditional approach, 25, 26, 31, 40
Apostolic Advocate, 178
applied "biblical theology", 150–52
Aquinas. *See* Thomas Aquinas
Aratus, 122
archetypes, 202–4
Are the Dead Extinct? debate, 182
Areopagus approach, 113–36
Aristotle, 49, 115, 134n. 77, 135, 147,
    293
Aromatherapy: appeal of, 261–62;
    biblical-theological perspective on,
    268–73; definition of, 262; and
    esoteric spirituality, 262–65;
    ideological metamorphosis of, 274;
    and occultism, 273–77; scientific
    claims and medical status, 265–67.
    See also complementary medicine
Arya Samaj, 104
asceticism, 256
Ashton, Michael, 175
Askari, Hasan, 144
Athanasius, 25n. 2
Athenadorus, 133
Athens: agora, 115n. 10; philosophical

Epicureanism, 116–17, 121, 124–25, 127, 257n. 60
Epicurus, 115, 116, 120, 121, 257
Epimenides the Cretan, 122
Essence of Christianity (Feuerbach), 100–101
Ethiopian Independent Church. *See* African Independent Church
ethnic groups, 163, 163n. 9
ethos, 49, 293; and humility and empathy, 294–95; and representation of new religious movements, 293–94; and self-identity, 295–96
Eumenides (Aeschylus), 126–27
evangelism, 141–42, 188
exclusivism, 78–79
"extraction" evangelism, 188

F
Fee, Gordon, 118n. 22
feminism, 263
Fernando, Ajith, 138, 143
Feuerbach, Ludwig, 99, 100–101
Finney, John, 50–51
Flaherty, Gloria, 98
Flaw of the Excluded Middle, 282
Fletcher, Richard, 225
Foucault, Michel, 79
Fragments (Heraclitus), 85
Frameworks (Walrath), 118
Francis of Assisi, 53–55
Franciscans, 53, 55
Franke, August Hermann, 75n. 75
"Free Life" controversy. *See* "Clean Flesh" controversy
Freemasonry, 213
Freke, Timothy, 222
Freud, Sigmund, 101, 215
Fuchs, Leonard, 277
Fuller, Robert, 234

G
Gaffin, Richard, 199

Gandy, 222
Gardner, Gerald, 99, 213
Gattefossé, Rene-Maurice, 263
Gawain, Shakti, 232
Geisler, Norman, 301
Geivett, Douglas, 125
George, Timothy, 150
Gerarde, John, 277
Gilliland, Dean S., 45
Gilmore, Peter, 251
global culture, 91–94, 299; and globality, 92
God: aseity of, 119n. 29; cosmological argument for, 134, 134n. 77; immanence of, 74, 121, 269–70; transcendence of, 121, 269. *See also* Holy Spirit; Trinity
Goethe, Johann Wolfgang von, 72, 111
Gomes, Alan, 128
Gospel and Our Culture Network, 79n. 84
Great Century of Protestant missions, 63
Great Commission, 69n. 37, 113, 162–63
Gregory, 94
Grew, Nehemiah, 277
Griffen, Walter Burley, 231
Gripper, Ali, 233
Groothuis, Douglas R., 197nn. 17, 21
Grudem, Wayne, 26
Guelich, Robert, 275
Guinness, Os, 284

H
Habermas, Gary, 125
Hackett, Rosalind, 98
Hall, Edward T., 37
Hallam, Steven, 222
Hamilton, Malcolm, 237–38
Hanegraaff, Wouter, 235n. 33
Hanna, Mark, 130, 133n. 68
Hannerz, Ulf, 93–94
Hare Krishna Movement. *See*

International Society for Krishna
Consciousness.
Harper, Anne, 302
Harry Potter, 212
Harvey, Graham, 215
Hatch, Nathan, 177–78
Hay, Louise, 232
healing, 271, 276
Heelas, Paul, 196, 235n. 33
Heraclitus, 85, 120–21
Hesselgrave, David, 14, 129, 130–31,
    295, 299–300
Hexham, Irving, 26, 91, 196–97, 197n.
    18, 294, 299; empirical research in
    Africa, 93
Hick, John, 83–84, 84n. 100, 137
Hiebert, Paul, 26, 45, 68nn. 33, 34; 71,
    275, 282
Hildebrandt, Wilf, 271–72
Hildegard of Bingen, 277
Hinduism, 103, 104–5, 263–64
history of religion, 64, 72–73, 78–81;
    missiology and, 77–78; method,
    73–75
Hofstede, Geert, 301
Holy Spirit, 32–34, 135, 269–70
Holyoake, George Jacob, 100
Horne, Fiona, 214, 215, 221
How to Know God (Chopra), 199–200
Hume, Lynne, 212
Hunter, Edward, 285
Hunter, G. G., 49
Husserl, Edward, 73
Hutton, Ronald, 213

I
idolatry, 123, 275
incarnation, 14, 18, 26n. 3, 28, 29, 45
Incarnation of the Word, The
    (Athanasius), 25n. 2
incarnational ministry, 14, 18, 25–41,
    143; definition of, 26; traditional
    apologetics and, 40; in Acts, 27,
    31–35; framework of, 27; modeled,

27–32; personal involvement in,
    35–40
industrialism, 96
Innocent IV, 55
Insight curriculum, 151
interfaith dialogue. *See* interreligious
    dialogue
International Churches of Christ, 189n. 43
International Missionary Conference
    (1938), 80
International Society for Krishna
    Consciousness, 105
interreligious dialogue, 65–66, 67n. 29;
    biblical dialogue and, 152–55
Isis Unveiled (Blavatsky), 99, 103
Islam, 52–59, 94, 129

J
Jehovah's Witnesses, 102, 176; and
    rhetorical speech, 186
Jesus, incarnational ministry of, 28–31
Jesus the Man (Thiering), 221
Johnson, Philip, 114, 195, 238–42, 269,
    280
Jolly, Peter, 224
Jung, Carl, 99, 200, 203, 214, 217
Justin Martyr, 25–26n. 2

K
Kahler, Martin, 71
Kaptchuk, Ted, 265
Kaufman, Gordon, 77
Kemp, Daren, 238
Key to the Science of Theology (Pratt),
    102–3
*Key to the Understanding of the
    Scriptures* (Mansfield), 182
Kingdom of the Cults, The (Martin),
    128, 161, 279–80
Kistemaker, Simon, 119, 122–23
Kraemer, Hendrik, 80, 137, 148;
    "golden rule" of missionary
    communication, 142–43
Kruithof, Wim, 239